DEFCON-2

Selected books on the Cold War by Norman Polmar

*Aircraft Carriers: A History of Carrier Aviation
and Its Influence on World Events*

Atomic Submarines

Chronology of the Cold War at Sea, 1945–1991, with Eric Wertheim,
Andrew Bahjat, and Bruce Watson

*Cold War Submarines: U.S. and Soviet Submarine Design
and Construction* with Kenneth J. Moore

Guide to the Soviet Navy

Merchants of Treason with Thomas B. Allen

The Ships and Aircraft of the U.S. Fleet

Soviet Naval Power

Spy Book: The Random House Encyclopedia of Espionage
with Thomas B. Allen

Spyplane: U-2 History Declassified

Strategic Air Command with Tim Laur

Strategic Weapons: An Introduction

Selected books on the military by John D. Gresham

Submarine with Tom Clancy

Fighter Wing with Tom Clancy

Special Forces with Tom Clancy

Seapower with Ian Westwell

DEFCON-2

Standing on the Brink of Nuclear War during the Cuban Missile Crisis

Norman Polmar
John D. Gresham

Foreword by Tom Clancy

WILEY

John Wiley & Sons, Inc.

Published by John Wiley & Sons, Inc., Hoboken, New Jersey
Published simultaneously in Canada

For general information about our other products and services, please contact our Customer Care Department within the United States at (800) 762-2974, outside the United States at (317) 572-3993 or fax (317) 572-4002.

Wiley also publishes its books in a variety of electronic formats. Some content that appears in print may not be available in electronic books. For more information about Wiley products, visit our web site at www.wiley.com.

Library of Congress Cataloging-in-Publication Data:

Polmar, Norman.
    Defcon-2 : Standing on the brink of nuclear war during the Cuban missile crisis / Norman Polmar, John D. Gresham; foreword by Tom Clancy.
      p.   cm.
    Includes bibliographical references (p. 359) and index.
    ISBN-13 978-0-471-67022-3 (cloth)
    ISBN-10 0-471-67022-7 (cloth)
    1. Cuban Missile Crisis, 1962. I. Gresham, John. II. Title.
    E841.P65 2006
    973.922—dc22

                                               2005013196

Printed in the United States of America
10 9 8 7 6 5 4 3 2 1

Dedicated to
the Memory of Paul H. Nitze
(1907–2004)

In a career spanning nine presidencies, Paul Nitze has made enormous contributions to the freedom and security of his country. Paul Nitze exemplifies the powers of mind, commitment, and character needed to fulfill America's world responsibilities. He was present at the creation of the strategy that has kept us at peace for forty years. His deep understanding of the issues of war and peace, his discharge of high public assignments, and his advice to those in authority have been invaluable to our national well-being. He remains the most rigorous, demanding, and independent of analysts and the wisest of counselors.

Medal of Freedom Citation
Awarded by President Ronald Reagan
November 7, 1985

CONTENTS

FOREWORD
by Tom Clancy

Like most Americans who came of age in the second half of the twentieth century, my life and times were defined by the undeclared conflict
known as the Cold War. Lasting some forty-five years, that confrontation
held deadly consequences for mankind if it had ever gone "hot." For
most of those years, sanity and reason ruled the actions of both the United
States and the Soviet Union. Direct confrontation was considered unthinkable due to the ever-growing nuclear arsenals of the two nations.

During that period, there were conflicts supported by the superpowers—Korea, Vietnam, the Middle East, and Afghanistan, among others.
But the United States and the Soviet Union were careful to avoid a direct
confrontation.

The most dangerous exception came in 1962, with the Cuban Missile Crisis. I was in Loyola High School in Towson, Maryland, and I
remember as if it were yesterday the uncertainty and terror of that time.
The reason was obvious: the specter of nuclear war hung over the nation.
We talked about it in school and after classes with friends. Our mothers
bought "extra food" at the stores, and dads brought home extra flash-
lights, portable radios, and lots of batteries. And there was talk, if things
really got bad, of the family taking a road trip to get farther away from
Baltimore.

The Cuban Missile Crisis was the only time that the United States
and the Soviet Union came close to using nuclear weapons against each
other. While the actual balance of nuclear terror was unknown to most of
the citizens of the two countries, the implications were clear—both
countries could be destroyed, with millions of dead and many of the survivors mutilated.

We had good reason to be concerned. For most of the four decades
since the crisis, the popular notion has been that the world was saved by
sane, intelligent, and rational leaders, in direct communication, seeking
an amicable solution. However, the massive declassification efforts of

both sides since the end of the Cold War, the publication of several memoirs, and the candid recollections of many participants—who will now tell their stories—reveal that on several occasions in the fall of 1962 those leaders came very close to stumbling into nuclear Armageddon.

The origins of the Cuban crisis were in fact the final act of a march to confrontation that began in January 1961 with the inauguration of President John F. Kennedy. For Kennedy, the missile crisis was the unexpected result of an eighteen-month struggle to destroy the socialist regime of Fidel Castro, who had taken power from the despotic Fulgencio Batista in 1959. Castro soon became a major irritation to American government and business, as he nationalized U.S. holdings and threatened to export socialist revolution to South America. Such actions were unacceptable to the Kennedy administration. After the humiliating failure to overthrow Castro with the Bay of Pigs invasion in April 1961, the president entrusted his brother, Attorney General Robert Kennedy, to lead the effort to covertly overthrow Castro. But Castro proved to be a wily and tough opponent.

Nikita Khrushchev came to the Cuban Missile Crisis by another path, trying to resolve a number of Soviet problems in a single, bold stroke. Those included preserving the Castro regime in the face of American efforts to overthrow it, while at the same time trying to redress the Soviet inferiority in strategic nuclear weapons that could strike the American homeland. These seemingly divergent goals were to be accomplished by Operation Anadyr: the massive deployment of missiles and troops to Cuba in the summer and fall of 1962. There was just one problem: Khrushchev had lied about the Anadyr deployment to Kennedy, having assured the U.S. government that no "offensive" weapons were being sent to Cuba.

The relationship between Kennedy and Khrushchev had never been good. The vast differences in their ages, backgrounds, life experiences, and worldviews made a genuine rapprochement impossible, and this was exacerbated by the times they lived in. The pair met only once, a stormy 1961 summit meeting held in Vienna. So bad was the outcome that Kennedy remarked afterward, "It's going to be a cold winter." He was correct. The year that followed was filled with tension over Berlin and the growing nuclear arms race between the superpowers.

The stage was thus set for the players to act their parts, bringing the world to the "brink" of nuclear war. The intermediate steps, Kennedy's challenging speech, moving U.S. military forces to the DEFCON-3 level of readiness, and the commander-in-chief of the Strategic Air Command moving U.S. nuclear bombers and land-based missiles to DEFCON-2—

the highest state of readiness short of war—all seemed to lead to a nuclear finale.

Nuclear weapons on both sides were "cocked and ready." The leaders in Washington and Moscow were often confused, tired, and frustrated. Poor intelligence and unbelievable delays in communications compounded the problems. And Castro, seeking to preserve his bastion of socialism in the Western Hemisphere, was willing to see the world go to nuclear war rather than capitulate.

Fortunately, the leaders of the two superpowers were always concerned about the direction that their actions were leading. Kennedy, with surprising restraint in view of the United States' strategic superiority, held strong to his demands that the offensive weapons be removed from Cuba. Finally, Khrushchev "blinked."

In my novels I have written about superpower confrontations. The reality of the confrontation in October 1962 was more bizarre and more frightening than anything I have written. Probably the best popular account of the confrontation of 1962 that we will ever have has now been written by my longtime friends and peers, Norman Polmar and John D. Gresham. In *DEFCON-2* they have employed their extensive experience—Norman as an analyst and a historian, John as a researcher and a writer, as he has been previously to me—to provide this account.

Readers will find accounts in *DEFCON-2* that will surprise and shock them as the authors describe the several ways in which the world moved toward nuclear conflict. While the threat of nuclear conflict between the United States and what remains of the Soviet Union has now virtually disappeared, the events of that crisis shaped the remainder of the Cold War and, to a significant extent, the world that we live in today.

PREFACE

Scores of books have been written about the Cuban Missile Crisis of 1962. Whether authored by Americans, Cubans, or Russians, these books tend to concentrate on the political aspects of the crisis, rather than on operational issues. So much so, that many readers worldwide could be excused for believing that the crisis was an exercise conducted by a few American politicians sitting through thirteen days of meetings inside the West Wing of the White House. Indeed, those accounts published during the first three decades after the crisis could not accurately address the size and nature of the Soviet incursion into Cuba or the fact that nuclear warheads were actually landed on the island.

Most of those books provided only passing comment and relatively little information on the military aspects of the crisis. Indeed, not until the publication of *Operation Anadyr* by Generals Anatoli I. Gribkov and William Y. Smith in 1994 was the basic organization of the Soviet forces in Cuba known publicly. In fact, the Cuban Missile Crisis was a vast enterprise, lasting for months, with hundreds of thousands of participants from dozens of nations.

This inability to effectively address the military aspects of the crisis was ironic because it occurred as the direct result of contemporary Soviet and U.S. military technologies, forces, and actions. In this volume we seek to fully describe the military aspects of the crisis and to place them in the proper context, given the political environment and decision-making processes in *both* Moscow and Washington, D.C.

Another area of the Cuban Missile Crisis that has been improperly presented is the story of how the American intelligence community managed to pierce the Soviet veil of secrecy to expose what was known as Operation Anadyr. Despite restrictions on photoreconnaissance flights brought on by concerns of Kennedy administration officials about the consequences of a possible shoot down, dedicated pilots, sailors, analysts, and technicians all strove together to pry open the secrets of the Soviet deployment to Cuba. In the post-9/11 world, with the U.S. intelligence community being universally assailed, the courage, professionalism, and passion of American intelligence personnel during the crisis reached a peak that needs to be a model for the future.

Events in Havana—the third capital in the "axis of crisis"—are also described but, as will be seen, had little impact on the crisis. Rather, Fidel Castro was the pawn in the "game" that the Soviet leadership hoped to elevate to a most powerful piece—at least temporarily, the queen of the board—while the American leaders sought to "take" that pawn, by destroying the ruling Castro regime.

As the events of October 1962 unfolded, *on several occasions* the protagonists came close to the use of nuclear weapons, and not just ballistic missiles launched from Cuba against the United States. In fact, the closest both sides came to atomic weapons releases was from nuclear-armed torpedoes nearly launched by Soviet submarines, and nuclear air-to-air missiles almost fired by American fighters over the Arctic. Neither of the men with their "fingers on the button," President John F. Kennedy and Premier Nikita S. Khrushchev, wanted nuclear war in the fall of 1962. Nevertheless, nuclear war is what very nearly happened.

In both nations, however, there were some political and military leaders who thought that perhaps this was the time for a superpower "showdown." In the United States, that attitude was reflected in the knowledge that the United States had overwhelming strategic nuclear superiority over the Soviet Union, and that the imbalance of strategic weapons might never again be as favorable as it was at that time. Ironically, some in the Soviet Union believed—with somewhat similar logic—that the placement of a few dozen strategic missiles in Cuba—that is, nuclear weapons that could reach the United States—gave the Soviet Union a temporary nuclear advantage over the United States, which would soon be dissipated because of the massive U.S. Minuteman and Polaris strategic missile programs.

Both Kennedy and Khrushchev knew that they could keep their hardliners in check and their fingers off the triggers that could ignite a nuclear conflagration. Despite the notions of novelists, screenwriters, and even a few historians, there were no "rogue elephants"—generals plotting coups—in either the United States or the Soviet Union. Nor is there any evidence that any officer of either side attempted to initiate a preemptive missile launch or aircraft strike that could have ignited a nuclear war.

What, of course, neither man could control were the "small" details and events that occur when history is being made. A lost U-2 spyplane over the North Pole, a dehydrated and exhausted Soviet submarine captain, the bartender at a Washington, D.C., watering hole, and the reliability of Western Union messenger boys were just a few of the many details that determined the eventual course of the Cuban Missile Crisis. That war did not come in 1962 was decided by the slimmest of margins. Just how slim is only now becoming evident.

The aggregate of the events, the situations, and the assembly of nuclear weapons in the fall of 1962 contributed to the most dangerous moment of the forty-five-year Cold War. At no other time did U.S. military forces go to Defense Condition Two—DEFCON-2. At no other time were U.S. and Soviet *nuclear forces* "cocked and ready," as the novelist Tom Clancy has observed.

This book attempts to put the men, the events, and the weapons of those perilous days of October 1962 in perspective and to detail how close the world came to nuclear war—and how two national leaders, Kennedy and Khrushchev, men from very different cultures and backgrounds, came to the "brink" and then stepped back. That mankind and our planet are not ash and cinders is the lasting benefit of their actions.

ACKNOWLEDGMENTS

The authors are in the debt of many individuals and organizations for their assistance in writing this book and helping with the accompanying Discovery Channel film *DEFCON-2*, including Brian J. Kelly and William Howard of Henninger Productions for producing the film. Rarely have authors had more professional and understanding people to work with.

This project began as a joint effort with novelist Tom Clancy. However, other commitments forced Tom to withdraw from the project, but he kindly provided the foreword for this book, along with the introduction and the closing for the film *DEFCON-2*.

Many individuals allowed us to interview them, in the United States, Russia, and Cuba. Those whom we can publicly acknowledge are:

Thomas A. Brooks, a U.S. naval intelligence officer par excellence.

Charles Brown, a naval aviator on board the USS *Forrestal* in the Mediterranean at the time of the crisis.

Dino Brugioni, a senior U.S. photo analyst at the National Photographic Interpretation Center.

Mikhail Burnov, a technical officer of an SS-4 missile regiment in Cuba.

Keith K. Compton, the deputy chief of staff for operations of the U.S. Strategic Air Command during the crisis.

Aleksey Dubivko, the commander of the submarine *B-36* in the Caribbean area.

Michael Davis, the U.S. Air Force photo interpreter who first sighted the Soviet ballistic missiles in Cuba.

William Ecker, who led the U.S. Navy's low-level reconnaissance flights over Cuba.

Edward (Whitey) Feightner, a naval aviator who was on the carrier division staff aboard the USS *Enterprise* in October 1962.

Aleksandr Feklisov (alias Alexander Fomin), the KGB *Rezident* in Washington in 1962.

Anatoli N. Glinkin, the director of the research center, Institute of Latin American Studies, Russian Academy of Sciences.

Anatoli Gribkov, the Soviet General Staff representative to the forces in Cuba.

Georgi Kostev, a naval historian and an author.

Igor Kurenov, a junior political officer with Soviet ground troops in Cuba.

M. G. Kuzevanov, the commander of a Sopka anti-ship missile unit in Cuba.

Eugene Miasnikov, a Russian political scientist specializing in nuclear weapons issues.

Gerald E. Miller, the former Deputy Director of the U.S. Joint Strategic Target Planning Staff.

Paul H. Nitze, a member of the ExComm.

Nikolai Shumkov, the commanding officer of the submarine *B-130* in the Caribbean area.

William Y. Smith, a U.S. Army general officer and an aide to U.S. Joint Chiefs of Staff Chairman General Maxwell Taylor in 1962.

Ralph Tindal, an officer in the U.S. destroyer *Leary* on the quarantine line during the crisis.

Several other interviewees asked that they not be identified publicly. To them, a special thank you. Material for this book was also drawn from earlier interviews by one of the authors with:

Ray S. Cline, the former Deputy Director of Central Intelligence.

Thomas S. Gates, the Secretary of Defense, who established the Joint Strategic Target Planning Staff.

George H. Miller, the U.S. Navy's premier nuclear strategist.

Elmo R. Zumwalt, an aide to Mr. Nitze in 1962 and the U.S. Chief of Naval Operations from 1970 to 1974.

Others who contributed their talents and skills to this project include Dr. Sergei Khrushchev, a historian and the biographer of his father; Dr. George Sviatov, a political scientist and a former naval officer; Dr. David A. Rosenberg, a leading analyst of U.S. nuclear policy; Michael Markowitz, for his insightful comments on the time and culture of the crisis; and our artist Laura Newsome. Our agent, Mel Berger of the William Morris Agency, and our editor, Stephen Power of John Wiley & Sons, also deserve our thanks for their patience, persistence, and support in making *DEFCON-2* everything that it could be. Also of great assistance have been the staffs of the John F. Kennedy and Lyndon B. Johnson presidential libraries, the Air Force Historical Research Agency, the Army Library

(Pentagon), the Naval Historical Center, the Naval Historical Foundation, and the Naval Institute, particularly Ms. Dawn Stitzel. Aviation writer Peter B. Mersky kindly made several photos from his collection available to this project.

The authors also had access to documents from the Archives of the Communist Party of the Soviet Union and the Presidential Archives in Moscow, as well as the Cold War International History project in Washington, D.C. In addition, one of the authors attended conferences on the missile crisis held in Moscow, Washington, and at Offutt Air Force Base.

To all of these people, the authors are most grateful.

GLOSSARY

AFB	Air Force Base
ASW	Anti-Submarine Warfare
CEP	Circular Error Probability
CIA	Central Intelligence Agency (U.S.)
COG	Continuity of Government
DCI	Director of Central Intelligence (U.S.)
DEFCON	Defense Condition (levels 1 through 5)
DCI	Director of Central Intelligence
ExComm	Executive Committee (established October 22, 1962, under NSC Action Memorandum No. 196; previously referred to as "the group" and the "war council" of the National Security Council)
FKR	Frontal rocket (missile)
GRU	Military intelligence (Soviet)
ICBM	Intercontinental Ballistic Missile (range of approx. 3,450 to 9,200 statute miles)
Il	Soviet designation for aircraft designed by the Ilyushin bureau (followed by a number, such as the Il-28)
IRBM	Intermediate-Range Ballistic Missile (range of approx. 1,725 to 3,450 statute miles)
JCS	Joint Chiefs of Staff (U.S.)
JTF	Joint Task Force
KGB	Committee for State Security (Soviet)
KT	Kiloton—explosive force equivalent of 1,000 tons of TNT
MT	Megaton—explosive force equivalent of 1,000,000 tons of TNT
MiG	Soviet designation for aircraft designed by the Mikoyan-Gurevich bureau (followed by a number, such as MiG-21)
MRBM	Medium-Range Ballistic Missile (range of approx. 690 to 1,725 statute miles)
Mya	Soviet designation for aircraft designed by the Myasischev bureau (followed by a number, such as Mya-4)
NIE	National Intelligence Estimate (U.S.)
NPIC	National Photographic Interpretation Center (U.S.)
NSA	National Security Agency (U.S.)
NSC	National Security Council (U.S.)
OAS	Organization of American States
(Ret.)	Retired

SA	U.S.-NATO designation for Soviet Surface-to-Air missile (followed by a number, such as SA-2)
SAC	Strategic Air Command (U.S.)
SAM	Surface-to-Air Missile (generic)
SIOP	Single Integrated Operational Plan (U.S.)
SOSUS	Sound Surveillance System (U.S.)
SRF	Strategic Rocket Forces (Soviet)
SNIE	Special National Intelligence Estimate (U.S.)
SS	U.S.-NATO designation for Soviet Surface-to-Surface missile (followed by a number, such as SS-4)
TF	Task Force
Tu	Soviet designation for aircraft designed by the Tupolev bureau (followed by a number, such as Tu-20)
UN	United Nations
USA	U.S. Army
USAF	U.S. Air Force
USMC	U.S. Marine Corps
USN	U.S. Navy

TECHNICAL NOTES

Missiles

The Soviet Union in 1962 shipped two types of ballistic missiles to Cuba. Both types were capable of striking the continental United States with nuclear warheads. Although only one type of missile actually reached Cuba, U.S. government officials were concerned about both types after the first type and preparations for the second were identified in Cuba by U-2 photographic reconnaissance aircraft.

The missiles that reached Cuba had the Soviet designation R-12 and were given the U.S.-NATO designation SS-4 Sandal. The letters *SS* indicated a Surface-to-Surface missile, and all SS-series weapons were given a NATO code name beginning with the letter *S*.

In the fall of 1962 U.S. intelligence agencies credited the SS-4 with a maximum range of 1,020 statute miles (1,670 kilometers). This estimate was based on data from limited telemetry intercepts during Soviet missile flight testing, information from Soviet defectors, and material provided by Colonel Oleg Penkovsky, a military intelligence (GRU) officer who spied for Britain and the United States in 1961–1962. In reality, the maximum range of the SS-4 was 1,300 statute miles (2,080 kilometers), based on Soviet data available in support of the Intermediate-range Nuclear Forces (INF) agreement, signed in 1987. Thus, U.S. estimates were off by 22 percent.

Soviet R-14 missiles (NATO SS-5 Skean) were en route to Cuba when U.S. spyplanes discovered the SS-4 missiles and preparations for the SS-5. At the time, the U.S. intelligence community estimated that the SS-5 had a maximum range of 2,200 statute miles (3,600 kilometers). The actual range was 2,800 statute miles (4,500 kilometers). The difference between U.S. intelligence estimates and reality was again 22 percent.

Aircraft

The U.S. Department of Defense established the current scheme of military aircraft designations that became effective on October 1, 1962, just three weeks prior to the public announcement of the Cuban crisis. All U.S. Navy aircraft designations were changed at that time, as were those of several U.S. Air Force aircraft.

In this volume we cover events prior to the changeover, for consistency, so the pre-October 1 designations are used throughout. The major Navy aircraft mentioned in the text and their designations are listed in the table below.

Major Navy Aircraft

Name	Pre-1962	1962
Crusader*	F8U-1P	RF-8A
Neptune	P2V	P-2
Orion	P3V	P-3
Phantom II†	F4H	F-4
Skyhawk	A4D	A-4
Skyraider	AD	A-1
Tracker	S2F	S-2
Marlin	P5M	P-5

*Reconnaissance variant.

†U.S. Air Force designation was F-110.

ExComm Recordings

Most of the Executive Committee of the National Security Council (ExComm) meetings were held at the White House and were recorded by President Kennedy. In addition, many of his phone calls and personal meetings in the Oval Office were taped. The tapes are now available to the public at the John F. Kennedy Presidential Library in Boston, Massachusetts. The authors have listened to those tapes and in this volume have sourced the ExComm tapes to the published versions in Ernest R. May and Philip D. Zelikow, *The Kennedy Tapes: Inside the White House during the Cuban Missile Crisis* (1997), along with the expanded and updated multivolume set *The Presidential Recordings: John F. Kennedy, Volumes 1–3: The Great Crises* (2002), also edited by May and Zelikow, along with Timothy Naftali.

DEFCON-2

1

Most Dangerous Moments

By the spring of 1962 the United States had embarked on a concerted campaign of overt and covert political, economic, psychological, and clandestine operations to weaken the Castro regime. A covert destabilization operations program was under way, including attempts to assassinate Castro. Military contingency plans for air attacks and invasion of Cuba had been drawn up, and a series of military exercises training for possible execution of those plans was taking place.

It was thus not unreasonable for Cuban and Soviet leaders to be concerned in 1962 over intensified U.S. hostile action against Cuba, including the possibility of an invasion.

Raymond L. Garthoff
Reflections on the Cuban Missile Crisis[1]

At 10:30 A.M. Washington time on Wednesday, October 24, 1962, the U.S. Strategic Air Command (SAC) moved to Defense Condition Two (DEFCON-2)—the highest state of military readiness short of war. This was the first and only time during the Cold War that the U.S. armed forces reached such a level.

U.S. intercontinental ballistic missiles carrying nuclear warheads were readied for launching. Several hundred manned bombers armed with nuclear weapons on forty-three airfields in the United States and on a number of bases in other countries were prepared to launch within fifteen minutes. Other SAC bombers—some sixty of them—were already airborne, carrying nuclear weapons and flying predetermined patterns, ready to turn toward targets in the Soviet Union at a moment's notice. Relays of tanker aircraft refueled them in flight until the bomber crews reached the limits of their endurance after twenty-four hours and were replaced by other bombers. At sea, two U.S. Polaris submarines, each armed with six-teen nuclear-tipped ballistic missiles, steamed in the North Atlantic. Two

U.S. submarines carrying Regulus cruise missiles that could strike Siberia with nuclear weapons stood ready in the North Pacific.

Preparations for war were not restricted to the U.S. armed forces. At North Atlantic Treaty Organization (NATO) bases in Europe, fighters and bombers were also being loaded with nuclear weapons while troops from Norway to Greece were placed on alert. In Britain and Italy, joint teams readied Thor and Jupiter ballistic missiles for attacks on targets in the western USSR.

Officials in the Soviet Union readied a smaller number of intercontinental missiles, as well as scores of Medium- and Intermediate-Range Ballistic Missiles, the latter to strike Western European cities. Soviet Tu-20 Bear and Mya-4 Bison long-range bombers were loaded with nuclear bombs and prepared to fly to Arctic bases for refueling before heading across the polar wastes toward American cities.

As these and other U.S. and Soviet nuclear forces stood at their highest states of alert, incidents (such as a U.S. spyplane overflying Soviet territory), or miscalculations (such as Soviet surface-to-air missiles being fired at a U.S. reconnaissance aircraft) very nearly set off a chain of events that might have plunged the world into nuclear war.

It is difficult to determine precisely when the Cold War began. The United States and the Soviet Union were allies during World War II. Both fought against Nazi Germany from 1941 to 1945, and the USSR briefly joined the war against Japan in the summer of 1945. From virtually the time that German forces ceased fighting in early May 1945, however, U.S.-Soviet relations cooled, and by the time of the Berlin blockade in 1948, they had grown very cold indeed.

As America celebrated the end of the war in Europe, the Soviet Union consolidated its position in Eastern Europe. Previously agreed-upon zones of control in occupied Germany led to a forty-five-year division of East and West Germany. Austria, Bulgaria, Czechoslovakia, Hungary, Poland, and Romania fell under Soviet control. Soviet-supported insurrection followed in Turkey and Greece, threatening both countries with communist regimes. Soviet troops in northern Iran, occupied jointly by British and Soviet forces during the war, initially refused to withdraw.

Winston Churchill, the British prime minister during most of World War II, described the situation at the time. "From Stettin in the Baltic to Trieste in the Adriatic, an Iron Curtain has descended across the continent [of Europe]," he declared on March 16, 1946. His speech at Westminster College in Fulton, Missouri, aptly described the closure of Eastern Europe and the Soviet Union. Some historians mark his speech, made with President Harry S. Truman in attendance, as the beginning of the Cold War.

At the same time, more ominous aspects of the U.S.-Soviet relationship were being revealed. During the war, U.S. Army radio intercept stations had recorded Soviet government communications between the United States and Moscow. The messages were encrypted and could not be understood at the time; however, starting in 1943, some portions of the messages were deciphered.[2] Slowly, the messages revealed the existence of a massive Soviet espionage ring within the United States. Soviet intelligence services were garnering, among other things, secrets of the U.S. atomic bomb program. As these revelations were coming to light, in June 1948, the Soviet Union blockaded Western access to Berlin, the former capital of Germany, which had also been divided into sectors controlled by the West and by the Soviet Union. Red Army troops halted normal road and train traffic, causing the Allies to initiate a massive airlift to provide West Berlin with food, medicine, and coal.

Tensions ran high during the Berlin crisis, with U.S., British, and French troops preparing to hold West Berlin against a Soviet assault and to use troops to force access through Soviet-held East Germany to reach the city. In response to the Berlin Crisis, the United States dispatched sixty B-29 Superfortress bombers to Great Britain. However, they were not nuclear-capable aircraft.[3] Still, the Western allies saw them as a U.S. commitment. (Some of the B-29s that could carry nuclear weapons were deployed to Britain in mid-1949.)

The Cold War between the West—primarily, the United States—and the Soviet Union had escalated to nuclear intimidation. It escalated again in August 1949 when the Soviet Union detonated its first atomic bomb. Because at the time the full scope of Soviet espionage against the U.S. atomic bomb program in World War II was not known, Western experts were surprised at the speed with which the Soviets had developed the bomb.[4] There had already been one such shock in August 1947 when the Soviets displayed their own copy of the four-engined B-29, the Tupolev Tu-4 (NATO code-named Bull).[5] With the USSR now possessing both the atomic bomb and a long-range bomber capable of delivering it to targets in Europe and the Far East, the strategic nuclear arms race was on between the Soviets and the Americans.

In response to the Soviet Union entering the nuclear age, President Truman approved acceleration of U.S. development of fusion, or hydrogen, bombs. The United States exploded the first nuclear fusion, or thermo-nuclear, *device*—the precursor of the hydrogen bomb—on November 1, 1952; the Soviets dramatically followed this achievement nine months later with their first thermonuclear detonation.

During the 1950s, the arms race became more obvious to Americans as government buildings were surveyed to determine which were "suit-able" for use as atomic bomb shelters. Suitable structures were stocked with rations and bottled water, although few people could survive the radioactive fallout that would follow a nuclear exchange. American schoolchildren were taught to "duck and cover" when they saw the flash of a nuclear detonation. They were told to duck behind a wall so that they might have some protection from the nuclear flash and blast, and to find cover under a desk or a table to avoid shattering glass and falling debris. Some families prepared basements with beds, battery lighting, food, and drink for use as bomb shelters; others purchased prefabricated shelters and buried them in their backyards for promised protection from radioactive fallout, as well as from blast damage.

Throughout the country, at noon, air raid sirens were tested and radio stations went off momentarily to test a nationwide alerting system. (In the event of a Soviet attack, the radio stations would go off the air so that they would not become homing beacons for Soviet bombers.)

Massive command and communications facilities—so-called secure undisclosed locations—were dug beneath mountains to house military command staffs and for the president, cabinet members, and Congress. The facilities included presidential or national command bunkers beneath mountains at Mount Weather in Virginia and Raven Rock on the Maryland-Pennsylvania border, as well as a congressional bunker beneath the Green-brier Resort in West Virginia.[6] Specially modified aircraft were kept ready at Andrews Air Force Base near Washington, D.C., to serve as air-borne command posts for the president, while two Navy ships were con-figured to serve as presidential command ships afloat.[7]

In the Soviet Union, similar underground shelters were constructed for the military commands and for the Communist Party and national leadership. The shelters in the Soviet Union soon became increasingly complex and extensive, as the Soviet Union adopted a nuclear war-fighting strategy, rather than the deterrent strategy of the United States.

Both the United States and the USSR initiated new aircraft and long-range missile programs to deliver thermonuclear weapons to the other's homeland. The United States had an overwhelming advantage over the Soviet Union in the deployment of these weapons. First, the United States was a major maritime power, with a force of large aircraft carriers that could carry nuclear strike aircraft to launch positions at sea from which they could attack the Soviet Union. Second, U.S. allies—many of them members of the North Atlantic Treaty Organization—would permit U.S. nuclear bombers and, subsequently, missiles to be based on their territory, from which they could strike the USSR.[8] Even the bombers operating from the United States could take advantage of tanker aircraft based overseas, and those bases themselves were often used on a temporary basis by the forward rotation of American bombers.

Soviet bombers and missiles launched from the USSR could reach European NATO countries, as well as U.S. allies in the Far East (South Korea, Japan, and Taiwan). But to reach U.S. targets, the only route for the relatively few Soviet strategic bombers was to refuel at Arctic bases and then fly across the polar region. It was a long flight, probably twelve or more hours, with a high level of exposure to defensive fighters and missiles. Those aircraft would not be able to return to the USSR because of the distances involved, and any that survived attacks by U.S. and Canadian air defenses would undoubtedly come down at sea with loss of the aircraft and crews. (At the same time, U.S. planning provided for manned bombers to return to the United States or to forward bases to rearm, refuel, and carry out additional attacks. This was believed to be possible, in part, because of a large force of U.S. tanker aircraft that could refuel the bombers in flight.)

In the 1950s, the Soviet Union revealed a new series of jet-propelled bombers that caused American politicians and Air Force leaders to call for a U.S. response of more advanced bombers. Similarly, the Soviet missile and space achievements of the late 1950s sparked calls in the United States for ballistic missile defenses and for increased missile production. Nevertheless, the arms race favored the United States during this midcentury period since the United States had more locations and larger numbers of aircraft and could base them closer to the Soviet Union. Even when the Soviet Navy put to sea the world's first submarine-launched ballistic missiles, they suffered from limited range. Furthermore, the first Soviet nuclear-propelled missile submarines had major technical problems.

The few Soviet allies outside of Eastern Europe—China, North Korea, and later several Arab states—offered no advantages with respect to basing strategic weapons that could strike the United States. In the early 1960s, however, a new Soviet ally appeared on the scene: Cuba, under the regime of Fidel Castro. The western portion of Cuba was approximately ninety miles from the continental United States.

Castro, who took control of Cuba on New Year's Day 1959, initially sought cordial relations with the United States. The situation rapidly deteriorated as supporters of the ousted Cuban dictator Fulgencio Batista, operating mainly from Florida, sought to discredit and overthrow Castro. The new Cuban leader soon turned from the United States and in time accepted political and material support from the USSR. After the abortive effort by anti-Castro forces to invade Cuba at the Bay of Pigs in April 1961, the USSR provided substantial amounts of military aid to Cuba. In the aftermath of the Bay of Pigs fiasco, the U.S. Central Intelligence Agency (CIA) stepped up clandestine operations against Cuba (Operation Mongoose), and the U.S. armed forces began planning an assault on the island to depose Castro, with a tentative invasion date—for planning purposes only—of October 1962.

Nikita Khrushchev, the head of the Communist Party of the USSR and the premier of the Soviet government, believed that it was his duty to protect the fledgling communist regime in the Western Hemisphere—the first overseas ally of the Soviet Union. Khrushchev came to the conclusion that the best way to deter U.S. aggression against Cuba was to base *strategic* missiles on the island that could strike American cities. A deployment of Medium-Range Ballistic Missiles to Cuba would also help to compensate for the limited number of Soviet Intercontinental Ballistic Missiles (ICBMs) and long-range bombers. One of the Cold War's greatest secrets in the late 1950s and early 1960s was that the United States had vastly more bombers and ICBMs than did the Soviet Union. Khrushchev knew this and was desperate to find a way to close the Soviet shortfall in strategic weapons that could strike the United States.

Khrushchev's plan was formulated at a Bulgarian resort on the Black Sea in May 1962. During the next five months, in a remarkable and highly secretive operation—code-named Anadyr—the Soviet Union moved more than 40,000 troops and their equipment, 60 ballistic missiles that could strike the United States, tactical nuclear missiles, and 158 nuclear warheads to Cuba.

The United States learned of this deployment, which sparked the Cuban Missile Crisis. Intensive meetings involving President Kennedy and his closest advisors followed as they, like their counterparts in Moscow, sought to resolve the crisis without conflict. As the situation worsened, on Saturday evening, October 27, Secretary of Defense Robert S. McNamara sat in his fourth-floor, E-ring office of the Pentagon, preparing for still another meeting of Kennedy's senior advisors.[9] McNamara later recalled that it was a beautiful fall evening with a sliver of the moon rising in the east. McNamara wondered if he would ever see another Sat-

President Kennedy's closest confidant and advisor was Attorney General Robert Kennedy, his brother. The men were close as brothers and as government executives.

urday night. It was not, however, despite the dread of McNamara and many others, the most dangerous moment of the Cold War.

Despite the fears of millions on both sides, that night passed without any real danger of an exchange of strategic weapons by either side. Both the United States and the Soviet Union had invested vast sums in the command and control systems for their strategic nuclear forces, and these held up well throughout the crisis. The same, however, could not be said of the numerous tactical nuclear weapons deployed by both sides during the crisis.

Both sides had seeded their military forces with a variety of weapons systems armed with so-called tactical nuclear weapons. *Tactical*, to most people, means "small," which generally was the case for this class of arms in the early 1960s. Also modest were the requirements for their use, with release authority for tactical nuclear weapons frequently being delegated to fairly junior officers (lieutenants, captains, and so on), particularly in the U.S. military.

Ironically, it was the near use of these smaller weapons that almost turned the Cuban Missile Crisis into World War III. Earlier the same day, an American U-2 spyplane on an Arctic atmospheric sampling mission became lost and accidentally overflew Soviet territory in Siberia. In response, the Soviet air defense forces launched MiG fighters to intercept the reconnaissance aircraft, which was finally headed back to base in

Alaska. To help escort the U-2 home, the Alaskan Air Command launched a pair of its own interceptors: F-102s armed with Falcon AAMs that had tactical nuclear warheads. Fortunately, the Soviets recalled their MiGs before the F-102s could get into range, and the U-2 made a successful landing in Alaska. However, while the governments of the United States and the Soviet Union had been looking at the crisis in Cuba, nuclear war had almost broken out over the Bering Strait.

Another tactical nuclear "bump" encounter occurred the same day in the Caribbean, when a Soviet submarine, *B-59*, attempted to escape from an American Anti-Submarine Warfare (ASW) task group conducting a "hold down" procedure. U.S. destroyers dropped small explosive charges to force the Soviet submarine to run down its batteries and surface. Fearing that the next explosion might be a full-size depth charge meant to sink them, the submarine's captain ordered a nuclear-tipped torpedo armed and prepared for launch. For a few tense minutes, it looked like he might launch the weapon at American ships overhead, but he calmed down and decided to surface instead.

This was the closest anyone had ever come to using nuclear weapons in anger, and a nuclear attack on American warships on the high seas would have predictably escalated to full-scale war. While the world was watching with deadly interest the fate of the sixty strategic missiles on or headed to Cuba that day, the real danger of a nuclear exchange had been the so-called tactical nuclear weapons on the edges of the crisis. This was just one of the many facts about the Cuban Missile Crisis that was either classified and withheld from the public or not even known by both sides. Only in the last two decades have the real facts of the Caribbean crisis of 1962 begun to come out, totally changing the story that many of us thought we knew, because we had lived through it. What these facts tell us now is that we were closer to nuclear war than *anyone* knew at the time.

2

Imbalance of Terror

[C]ruisers like ours no longer play a decisive role. Nor do bombers.
Now it's submarines that rule the sea, and missiles that rule the air—
missiles that can strike their targets from great distances.

Nikita Khrushchev
Khrushchev Remembers[1]

O ne of the oddities of the Cold War was that both the United States
and the Soviet Union based their basic military doctrine around the
same goal: never again! In 1941, both nations had suffered the worst preemptive attacks in their history as nations and had paid a terrible price
for prewar negligence and inattention. For the Soviet Union, the event
was the opening of Operation Barbarossa on June 22, 1941, the massive
German invasion of the USSR. Despite repeated warnings by a variety of
intelligence and political sources, Soviet Premier Josef Stalin refused to
put his armed forces on alert and suffered one of the worst defeats in the
history of warfare. On the first day alone, more than twelve hundred
Soviet aircraft were destroyed on the ground, and some Nazi armored
columns penetrated almost a hundred miles on a front running from the
Baltic Sea to the Black Sea.[2]

The Soviet Union eventually recovered and in 1945 led the defeat of
Nazi Germany into Berlin. The cost, however, had been unimaginable.
Officially, the Soviet Union suffered more than 8.6 million military dead,
though with civilian losses this figure may have been well over 29 million. By any measure, these were the highest casualties in history, between 15 percent and 20 percent of the total population of the USSR.[3]
Added to the other millions of dead from the Russo-Japanese War, World
War I (1914–1917), the Russian Civil War, and Stalin's "Great Terror" in
the 1930s, it was amazing that the Soviet Union survived the first half of
the twentieth century. Nobody was more aware of this than Josef Stalin,

who began the Cold War in the late 1940s to build a buffer around the USSR to ensure that the Soviet homeland would never again suffer invasions of the kind that had become all-too-common since the time of Frederick the Great.

Stalin spent the remaining years of his life in a paranoid struggle to maintain the secrecy of the USSR, rebuild its devastated industrial base, build a credible nuclear deterrence force of atomic weapons and bombers, and conduct a conventional arms race with the rest of the world. Stalin had always craved a "balanced" military that would be as powerful as any in the world. This would include a world-class navy, with aircraft carriers, battleships, cruisers, destroyers, and the world's largest fleet of submarines.[4] The expenditures of money and manpower required for this unrealistic rush to military power kept the Soviet Union impoverished for a decade following the Second World War and were terminated only by Stalin's death on March 5, 1953.

While it took several years of purges and Kremlin intrigue, the leadership of the Soviet Union fell on a former peasant farmer who had risen through the Moscow political machine to become Stalin's primary military observer in World War II: Nikita Sergeyevich Khrushchev. Though officially carrying only the title of Chairman of the Communist Party of the Soviet Union, by 1955 Khrushchev was the de facto leader of the USSR.[5]

Khrushchev inherited a Soviet Union that was a study in extreme contrasts. Geographically the largest nation on the planet, it was among the poorest per capita. While the USSR had atomic weapons and one of the largest armies in the world, it was still vulnerable to attack from every point of the compass, thanks to America's global system of air bases and allies. Resource-rich, the Soviet Union was industrially backward and on the verge of economic collapse when Khrushchev took power.

Amazingly, Khrushchev proved to be a political grandmaster, able to denounce the excesses of Stalin and put down a coup, while at the same time turning the Soviet economy around and transforming its military. Scrapping Stalin's massive conventional military buildup, Khrushchev personally remade the Soviet military into a force based upon nuclear weapons and guided missiles to protect the USSR. By doing this, he was able to demobilize almost a third of the Red Army and provide both manpower and money to build the technical and industrial base that would make the USSR a true superpower. In just five astonishing years, he took the Soviet Union to the top of the geopolitical world, leading the world in space exploration and political influence. To the Western world, he

Bombastic and a braggart, Nikita Khrushchev still sought to overturn Stalin's "cult of the individual," release political prisoners, and improve the lot of the Soviet citizen. But he misjudged both the efficacy of his commander in Cuba and American reaction to Operation Anadyr.

became the personal embodiment of everything represented by the threat of Communism.[6]

For all this apparent success, Khrushchev had significant challenges to overcome in his early years in power. While projecting a public image of military strength, he had to conceal his nation's real weaknesses from the inquisitive eyes of the Western intelligence services. As Stalin's personal commissar during the Moscow, Stalingrad, and Kursk campaigns, he had seen every horror that war could bring and was totally committed to a "never again" strategy of national defense for the Soviet Union. Khrushchev's plan for accomplishing this was to build up a force of long-range ballistic missiles armed with thermonuclear warheads, so that any potential foe would be deterred from ever again attacking the USSR. And the probable enemy nation that he feared most was the United States of America.

The United States had suffered its own preemptive strike by an enemy when a Japanese carrier force attacked the U.S. Pacific Fleet at Pearl Harbor, Hawaii, on the morning of December 7, 1941. Like the USSR, the United States had strategic warning of Japan's intentions and failed to ensure that its military forces were ready when the blow fell. Although America's losses at Pearl Harbor were a fraction of those of the Soviet Union the previous June, they were heavy enough to stun the United States out of its previous isolationist stance and into becoming an unstoppable engine of modern war.[7] Unlike the Soviet Union's, the U.S. population actually grew during World War II, and the American economy, sluggish from the Great Depression, became the largest and most productive in the world. By the time of the signing of the Japanese surrender in

August 1945, the United States had become the most powerful, wealthy, and productive nation in the history of the world.

America entered the postwar world confident in its security, having developed and deployed both the atomic bomb and long-range bombers in time to use them against Japan. The demonstrated destructive power of atomic bombs was thought to be enough to keep the peace after World War II, and the United States demobilized the majority of its military forces. However, by the late 1940s, it was clear that Stalin was moving to gain control in the nations surrounding the Soviet Union, and in 1948, the crisis in Berlin made the Cold War a hard fact. The shocking revelation of the first Soviet atomic bomb being detonated in 1949 and the surprise outbreak of the Korean War in June 1950 shook the notion that the world was ready for universal peace, and America began to rearm to fight a potential atomic war with the USSR.

Just six weeks before the death of Josef Stalin, Dwight David Eisenhower was inaugurated as the thirty-third President of the United States on January 20, 1953. The Supreme Allied Commander in Europe during World War II and the first commander of the North Atlantic Treaty Organization (NATO), "Ike," as the gentle general was known, had a reputation and respect unseen for a military politician since Ulysses S. Grant. Elected in a landslide over the popular Adlai Stevenson in November 1952, Eisenhower was in many ways faced with the same kinds of military challenges that his Soviet counterpart, Khrushchev, confronted.

The American military he inherited from President Harry S. Truman was little changed from the forces he had commanded in Europe during World War II and faced threats that made a major defense-transformation effort vital. Badly stung by the preemptive strike on Pearl Harbor, Eisenhower made the detection and deterrence of any such attack on America during his watch a personal obsession. As it did with Khrushchev, "never again" became a battle cry, albeit one quietly ringing deep within his impressive mind.[8]

President Eisenhower spent his eight years in the White House as intelligently and efficiently as any chief executive in America's history. Instead of recklessly throwing money at every weapons systems he could build, Ike used his intelligence services to tell him exactly what to build, based upon the probable threats the United States would face. When information on Soviet nuclear weapons was lacking, he authorized the CIA to build the famous U-2 spyplane to covertly overfly the Soviet Union and determine exactly what threats the United States faced. By Ike's carefully balancing the needs of the military with a sound monetary and

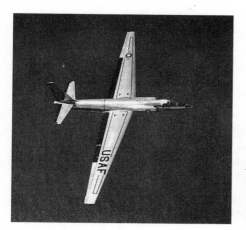

A U-2 spyplane flown by the U.S. Air Force. The CIA, subsequently joined by the Air Force, operated these aircraft worldwide to reveal otherwise hidden secrets. They were responsible for the first detection of Soviet strategic weapons in Cuba.

economic policy, the United States knew unprecedented prosperity in the 1950s. Overseas, Eisenhower used the armed forces and the CIA to keep threats to this prosperity and security away from American shores, keeping communism at bay and increasing U.S. influence around the world.[9]

All these successes came at a cost. Almost all of the Eisenhower-era CIA operations were covert and the facts behind them classified until long after his retirement. Later known as the "hidden hand" strategy, the "Eisenhower Doctrine" was to manipulate events with covert action and to support military and diplomatic action with superior intelligence information. This meant that few people outside his administration had access to the facts of his covert actions and operations, leading to something of a political and public relations vacuum with his political opponents and the American public.[10]

When faced with the aggressive public image of Khrushchev and the Soviet Union in the late-1950s, Eisenhower remained mute on the true state of Soviet military strength versus that of the United States. He did so to protect America's key strategic intelligence sources—like the U-2 reconnaissance flights—which were judged too valuable and sensitive for public disclosure. The result, however, was a series of perceived American technological "gaps" in thermonuclear weapons, long-range bombers, and strategic missile developments. In fact, throughout the 1950s, U.S. strength in both conventional and strategic military forces grew steadily in size, power, and capability.[11]

By the late 1950s, the United States was in a de facto arms race with the Soviet Union, to be the first to deploy long-range ballistic missiles armed with thermonuclear warheads. The holy grail of this race was the

Intercontinental Ballistic Missile (ICBM), which would be capable of striking targets on the other side of the world from bases in a nation's home territory. With a flight time of thirty minutes and a range of more than 6,000 miles, American and Soviet ICBMs could hold each other's national population as hostages. This meant, at least theoretically, that a small force of ICBMs might be used to deter military action by another nation, even one on the other side of the earth. This fit perfectly within Khrushchev's vision for the Soviet military, and ICBM development and deployment became his personal obsession in the late 1950s.[12] Unable to control political and public pressure over the so-called missile gap without revealing his covert intelligence-gathering activities to the world, Eisenhower chose to accelerate American guided missile development in reply. It was the beginning of the road to the Cuban Missile Crisis of 1962.

The Nuclear Balance

The Soviet Union initially led the world in the development of long-range strategic missiles in the Cold War era. The Soviets built on German technology, which had produced the world's first ballistic missile, the V-2, in 1944. A Soviet team led by Sergei P. Korolev then began extending the range and accuracy of the German missile.[13]

Early Soviet ballistic missiles carried high-explosive payloads, but the development of an atomic bomb, first tested in 1949, promised more potent ballistic missiles. In 1956, the first Soviet missile to carry a nuclear warhead, a 300-kiloton weapon, became operational. The R-5M (NATO SS-3 Shyster), with a maximum range of 745 miles, brought most of Western Europe under the threat of Soviet missile attack.

More ominous, on August 3, 1957, a Soviet R-7 ICBM (NATO SS-6 Sapwood) rocketed several thousand miles from its launchpad to impact in Soviet Siberia.[14] In guarded words, the Soviet news agency TASS announced that a "super-long distance intercontinental multistage ballistic rocket flew at an . . . unprecedented altitude . . . and landed in the target area." Not for another sixteen months would an American ICBM—the Atlas—be flight tested to its full range.

Barely two months after the first Soviet long-range ICBM test, an SS-6 missile booster carried *Sputnik 1*, earth's first artificial satellite, into orbit. This satellite weighed 184 pounds, compared to just 18 pounds for the first U.S. satellite, the *Explorer 1*, which would not be placed into orbit for another three months. On November 3, 1957, a month after *Sputnik 1*, the Soviets launched another satellite, placing the then-phenomenal pay-

The SS-6 Sapwood was the first operational Soviet intercontinental ballistic missile. This photo shows an SS-6 being prepared for launch at the massive Soviet space/missile complex at Tyuratam. At the time of the missile crisis, there were two SS-6 ICBMs at Tyuratam and four located at Pletesk.

load of 1,121 pounds into earth orbit. A live dog named Layka was on board *Sputnik 2*. Layka was instrumented to relay biological data to earth about the animal's reactions to weightlessness, radiation, and other environmental changes. The satellite *Sputnik 3*, launched into orbit in May 1958 and weighing 2,926 pounds, was a feat of orbital weight lifting that the United States did not match until 1964.

By 1962, however, the U.S. strategic missile program had overtaken that of the Soviet Union. Spurred on in large part by the early Soviet achievements, President Eisenhower had accelerated the U.S. missile program. At the same time, the USSR was experiencing problems with its ICBM development, as well as with production. Soviet attempts to put ballistic missiles to sea in submarines—despite an initial lead over the United States—similarly suffered problems.

Indeed, by late 1962, the balance of strategic weapons was heavily weighed against the Soviet Union; the following table shows long-range weapons that could strike the United States and Soviet homelands.

Even such simplistic comparisons belied the American advantages in strategic weapons. The U.S. B-47 and B-58 medium bombers could strike the Soviet Union from bases in Britain, French Morocco, Spain, Labrador, and Canada. However, the Soviet Union's 1,350 medium-range jet bombers—mostly Tu-16 Badgers and the new Tu-22 Blinders—could not reach targets in the United States; they were intended for attacks against Western European and Asian targets.

U.S. and Soviet Strategic Weapons
(Late 1962)

United States	Soviet Union

Homeland-Based Missiles

142 Atlas ICBMs	6 SS-6 Sapwood (R-7) ICBMs
62 Titan I ICBMs	Approximately 20 SS-7 Saddler (R-16) ICBMs

Overseas-Based Missiles

60 Thor IRBMs in Britain	None*
30 Jupiter IRBMs in Italy	

Submarines

32 Polaris A-2 SLBMs in two nuclear-propelled submarines[†]	None[‡]
6 Regulus cruise missiles in two diesel submarines	

Bombers

639 B-52 bombers	Approximately 100 Tu-20 Bear and Mya-4 Bison bombers
880 B-47 bombers	
76 B-58 bombers	

Tactical Aircraft

220 nuclear strike aircraft on five deployed aircraft carriers[§]	6 Il-28 Beagle bombers in Cuba[‖]

* This does not include the thirty-six SS-4 Sandal (R-12) MRBMs that were operational for a short period in Cuba during the crisis.
† Available Navy records indicate that only two Polaris submarines (each with sixteen Polaris A-2 missiles) were on station in late October 1962, the *Ethan Allen* and the *Sam Houston.* However, it seems likely that one or two earlier submarines were also on station, each with sixteen Polaris A-1 missiles. No Soviet missile submarines were in the Western Atlantic during the crisis.
‡ The Soviet Navy did in fact have a number of nuclear-powered ballistic missile submarines, though none were operational through much of 1961 and 1962 due to reactor problems. This included eight Hotel-class (Project 658) ballistic missile submarines, each with three SS-N-4 Sark (R-13) missiles, though none were considered deployable during the crisis.
§ USS *Oriskany, Bon Homme Richard,* and *Kitty Hawk* in the Western Pacific; and *Forrestal* and *Franklin D. Roosevelt* in the Mediterranean.
‖ Some of these may have been operational for a short period during the crisis. Each was armed with a single nuclear gravity bomb.

Another aspect of the U.S.-Soviet strategic weapons balance, which would have a significant impact on the forthcoming superpower confrontation, were the short-range "strategic missiles," the Intermediate-Range Ballistic Missiles (IRBMs), with ranges of up to 3,450 statute miles; and the Medium-Range Ballistic Missiles (MRBMs), with ranges of up to 1,725 statute miles. Both the United States and the Soviet Union had produced these weapons, albeit for different purposes. The U.S. missiles—sixty Thor IRBMs in Britain and thirty Jupiter IRBMs in Italy—were targeted against Soviet territory. The Jupiters were actually under NATO command, an attempt to counter the French claim that NATO nations must develop their own nuclear weapons if they were to have an authentic role in world affairs. In both Britain and Italy, the U.S. missiles were under two-nation—known as "dual key"—control, but control of their nuclear warheads was wholly vested in American officers.

In contrast, the Soviet Intermediate- and Medium-Range Ballistic Missiles, most of them located in the western USSR, were aimed at targets in Western Europe. Thus, there was an asymmetry in these missile deployments: all U.S. strategic weapons could reach Soviet territory, but very few Soviet bombers and missiles could reach the United States. This was the factual imbalance of nuclear power at the time of the Cuban Missile Crisis in 1962.

Deploying Strategic Missiles

Nikita Khrushchev was a major proponent of strategic missiles. So much so, that in the late 1950s he had reduced Soviet conventional military forces and accelerated the development of ballistic missiles. In December 1959, he had established the Strategic Rocket Forces (*Raketnyye Voyska Strategicheskogo Naznacheniya*) as a separate military service, the equal of—and, in some aspects, superior to—the Soviet ground, naval, air, and air defense services. High priority was given to the development of ICBMs and lesser-range ballistic missiles for the Strategic Rocket Forces, the latter for striking targets in Western Europe, as well as in China and Japan. In 1962, there was a belt of several hundred SS-4 MRBMs and SS-5 IRBMs based in western Russia to hold Western Europe at risk. But by 1962, the quality and quantity of U.S. strategic missiles, as well as of U.S. strategic bombers, were overwhelmingly superior to those of the Soviet Union.

One reason was that the first generation of Soviet ICBMs, the SS-6s, required a huge and expensive launch complex that was unable to be

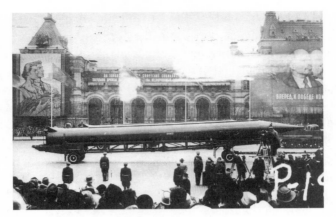

A Soviet R-12 missile (NATO SS-4 Sandal) on parade in Red Square, Moscow. Such parades provided Western diplomats and journalists with close views of new Soviet weapons.

hardened against nuclear attack. The SS-6 also used a mix of Liquid Oxygen (LOX) and kerosene, which meant that it took many hours to prepare for launch and could not stay on alert very long due to the "boil off" of the LOX. This meant that just one operational SS-6 launch installation with only four launchers was ever built (at Pletesk in northern Russia), along with the two test pads at the Tyuratam test center. The second generation of Soviet ICBMs was able to use so-called storable liquid fuels—in the case of the R-16 (NATO named SS-7 Saddler), a combination of kerosene and red fuming nitric acid. While difficult to handle and highly corrosive, these fuels allowed the SS-7s to be smaller and based in somewhat more survivable "coffin" launchers. Eventually, the SS-7 would be based in hardened silos, although that would be several years after the Cuban Missile Crisis.

Deployment of the SS-7 was delayed because testing of the new ICBM had gone disastrously wrong on October 23, 1960, when a prototype missile exploded on the launchpad at Tyuratam, killing eighty-two technicians and military personnel. Among the dead was Artillery Marshal Mitrofan Nedelin, the Commander of the Soviet Strategic Rocket Forces. The damage to the launch complex, along with the loss of skilled personnel, meant that SS-7 testing and deployment were delayed by more than a year, just when Khrushchev needed them most: 1961 and 1962. When the SS-7s finally began to be deployed in 1961, they were few in number and lacked any protection against nuclear attack.[15] By the time of the Berlin Crisis in the summer of 1961, Khrushchev had perhaps a dozen ICBMs that could hit the U.S. homeland, with none of them in launchers that had any chance of surviving an enemy nuclear first strike.[16]

There were other Soviet efforts to develop strategic missiles to strike the United States, the most promising of which was a new class of nuclear submarines armed with short-range ballistic missiles.[17] These were developed in parallel with the ICBMs; the idea behind the nuclear-powered Project 658 (NATO Hotel-class) ballistic missile submarines was that they would covertly sneak up on the American coast. Then, when ordered, they would quickly surface and launch their three R-13s (NATO SS-N-4 Sark) at coastal cities and military bases. While noisy and tactically clumsy compared with the American Polaris ballistic missile submarines, the Project 658 submarines would give the Soviet Union a means of striking at the U.S. homeland.[18] But on July 4, 1961, the first Hotel-class boat, the *K-19*, suffered a catastrophic reactor cooling loop leak, killing seven of the crew members and causing every nuclear submarine in the Soviet Navy to be taken into port for inspections and modifications. Not until 1963 were the first of the Hotels ready for regular patrols. For Khrushchev, these twin disasters meant that he was to go into the most critical period of the Cold War with just a handful of nuclear weapons to threaten the United States with.

By comparison, the United States was more successful in deploying its first generation of ICBMs, despite a number of test failures. The Atlas and Titan I ICBMs were, like the SS-6, fueled with kerosene and LOX, but designed for more rapid fueling and erection that their Soviet equivalents. By mid-1962, more than two hundred American ICBMs were deployed at sites in the United States, the majority of which were based in hardened "coffin" launchers or underground silos. This meant that even if a Soviet first strike were made against them, most of the U.S. ICBM force would survive to make a killing retaliatory attack.[19] More significantly, on the heels of this first wave of American ICBMs was a second generation, equipped with storable solid or liquid fuels that allowed the missiles to stand alert indefinitely and be launched in just minutes from a launch order. At the time of the Cuban Missile Crisis, these new ICBMs were rapidly coming into service, with the first solid-fueled Minuteman I squadron scheduled to become operational before the end of 1962. These ICBMs were relatively cheap, easy to operate and maintain, and more operationally reliable than any missile systems previously deployed.[20]

Given Soviet difficulties with deploying the SS-7 and other follow-on ICBM designs, it was unlikely that the USSR would have parity in this class of missiles before the end of the 1960s.

While the U.S. Air Force was bringing the Atlas and Titan I ICBMs into service, the U.S. Navy was rapidly deploying the new Polaris ballistic missile system aboard the *George Washington* and *Ethan Allen* classes of nuclear ballistic missile submarines (SSBNs). Unlike the Soviets, who had modified existing liquid-fueled designs to create their first Submarine-Launched Ballistic Missiles (SLBMs); the U.S. Navy went a different direction. Betting that it could develop a number of new technologies all at once—solid rocket propellants, compact thermonuclear warheads, inertial guidance systems, and so on—the U.S. Navy leapfrogged the Soviet Navy's first SSBNs and SLBMs by a wide margin. When the USS *George Washington* went out on her first deterrence patrol in late 1960, she actually beat the Soviet *K-19* into service by several months and generations of technology.

Quieter than the Soviet Hotel-class boats and armed with sixteen solid-fuel Polaris A-1 SLBMs, each with a range of more than 1,200 miles and a 1.2 MT W47 warhead, the American SSBN force rapidly became the most survivable and deadly weapons system in history. By 1962, a half-dozen of the new boats were either in service or on trials, with another thirty-five contracted or under construction.[21] As if this were not bad enough news for the Soviets, there were improved models of the Polaris missile on the way, which could be fitted into the existing SSBNs. These included the new Polaris A-3, with a range of 2,500 miles, which allowed greater standoff from the Soviet coastline when launching and deeper penetration of the target countries.[22] That in 1958 America began installing sixty Thor and forty-five Jupiter IRBMs in Great Britain, Italy, and Turkey just made the U.S. threat all the more menacing to the Soviet Union.

All of this meant that as Khrushchev began to deal with the crisis situations that developed between the Soviet Union and the United States in 1961 and 1962, he had no credible strategic nuclear deterrent force. Thus, the Soviets had no means to significantly threaten American citizens, territory, or interests outside of Europe and the Far East. By comparison, when the American ICBM, IRBM, and SLBM force was added to the sixteen hundred strategic bombers of the Strategic Air Command, the Americans had an overwhelming strategic nuclear superiority. Worse yet, the Americans knew of the Soviet weakness and were beginning to use it against the interests of the USSR.[23]

By the end of 1961, American defense leaders were openly announcing that the United States had nuclear supremacy over the Soviet Union, a fact that made a favorable resolution of the fall Berlin Crisis for the USSR all but impossible. Worse, there was a genuine fear within the Soviet central leadership that American "hawks" in the U.S. military and the Kennedy administration might be considering a first-strike attack against the Soviet Union, to eliminate the threat of communism once and for all. Within the Soviet government by early 1962, there was a view that unless Khrushchev could find a way to get more Soviet nuclear weapons within range of the American homeland, there might be no future at all for their nation.

3

The Cuban Decision:
Coming to America

*Fidel appeared deep in thought. Then . . . he said firmly that he thought
it was an especially interesting idea [to bring nuclear weapons to Cuba]
because it would serve the interests of world socialism and oppressed
peoples in their confrontation with insolent American imperialism, which
was trying to dictate its will throughout the world.*

Sergei N. Khrushchev
Nikita Khrushchev[1]

The year following the June 1961 summit meeting in Vienna between
Chairman Khrushchev, President Kennedy, and their staffs was a
tumultuous one, so much so, that it would have been almost impossible
to imagine the next six months could be even more tense and dangerous.
The spring of 1961 had been the high-water mark of Khrushchev's power
and prestige, with the Soviet Union launching the cosmonaut Yuri Gagarin
into orbit on April 12 for the first manned mission into space. This had
been followed by Khrushchev's domination of the Vienna summit with
President Kennedy, where he had laid down his demands for the resolution of the Berlin problem. By the summer of 1961, Khrushchev was the
"boogeyman" in the minds of Westerners.

Nikita Khrushchev had reached the top of the Soviet political and government structure shortly after the death of Josef Stalin. Khrushchev would
hold that position for more than a decade, until he was forcibly retired in
October 1964. For more than a decade, he won political "victories" over
the West, doing so from a position of extreme military and geographic
disadvantage. His ability to bluff and bluster marked him as one of the
twentieth century's most effective national leaders—and politicians.

In 1956, while the rest of the world was watching Great Britain,
France, and Israel invade Egypt and occupy the Suez Canal, Khrushchev

Khrushchev and Kennedy met once, at a summit conference in Vienna in 1961. At best, the meeting was inconclusive, as each leader came away with misjudgments about his "opponent" and made no real effort to follow up the personal contact. That lack of understanding contributed to the missile crisis the following year.

brutally crushed the budding democratic movement in Hungary and solidified his position at home and abroad as a Communist "iron man." Khrushchev had gambled that the United States and its allies would be so busy sorting out the Suez Crisis that they would ignore the brutal suppression of a small Eastern European democracy movement. Just to hedge the bet, Khrushchev then threatened to use nuclear weapons against NATO if it tried to respond to the Soviet invasion of Hungary. He bet right, despite not having a credible way to reach Western Europe at the time with nuclear-armed missiles or bombers.[2]

Chairman Khrushchev handled the Soviet Union's inferiority in strategic nuclear weapons in a similar fashion. Shortly after the launch of *Sputnik 1* in 1957, he made a statement that he had a factory producing ballistic missiles "like sausages."[3] While this was patently untrue, the rest of the world publicly had no way to repudiate his claims. Only a handful of American intelligence, military, and political leaders knew the truth, that most of Khrushchev's nuclear deterrence was based upon the charisma of the Soviet Party Chairman himself. Thus, by the end of 1961 when senior U.S. officials announced that Soviet strategic nuclear forces were actually inferior to those of the United States, Khrushchev had very little in the way of political or military capital to support his efforts to promote and protect the interests of the USSR.

The truth was that Khrushchev really did not need many weapons that could strike the United States to make his missile force credible. In 1962, as few as one hundred deliverable thermonuclear warheads would have been enough to hold most large American population centers and key military facilities "at risk." Having bought some time by deterring the American "hawks," Khrushchev might then be able to get his SS-7 force built up, get the Hotel-class SSBNs back into service, and begin deployment of the follow-on ICBMs that were already on the Soviet drawing boards. Then the Soviet Union might have enough strength to protect Cuba and the Warsaw Pact nations, to negotiate arms limitations treaties that would halt what was already a massively expensive arms race, and to pump more money into a Soviet economy still sputtering despite his best efforts. The key to this path forward was to find a way to quickly get fifty to sixty more Soviet ballistic missiles into range of the American homeland by the end of 1962.[4]

The Decision

On May 14, 1962, Khrushchev arrived in Sofia, Bulgaria. Troubled by the strategic imbalance, he gave speeches in Bulgaria's capital that included calling NATO missile bases around the Soviet Union a threat to peace. After meetings with the Bulgarian leadership, on May 17 he traveled to the Black Sea resort of Varna for a brief holiday. During his quiet strolls along the beach, the problems facing the Soviet Union, Cuba, and Berlin, along with the weak Soviet ICBM force, were at the top of his concerns.[5]

Fidel Castro's revolution had taken over Cuba on New Year's Day 1959, and had subsequently turned the island nation into a socialist state just ninety miles from the coast of the United States. Furthermore, Castro's key lieutenant, Ernesto "Che" Guevara, was attempting to export revolution to several South American states. In response, the United States sought to destroy the Castro regime. The American government had sponsored the failed anti-Castro landings at the Bay of Pigs in April 1961 and, subsequently, had initiated Operation Mongoose, a massive CIA effort to bring down the Castro regime through acts of sabotage, terrorism, and assassination.

In response to the American aggression, the Soviet Union became a major supplier of arms and finance to Castro. As more real and perceived threats to Cuba from the United States emerged in the fall of 1961, Castro had asked for more sophisticated weapons, including the Soviet V-75 Dvina (NATO SA-2 Guideline), an advanced surface-to-air missile. An SA-2 had brought down the U-2 spyplane flown by Francis Gary Powers on May Day in 1960. Khrushchev had hesitated to approve the SA-2s for a variety of reasons, and difficulties in Soviet-Cuban relations began to emerge. However, in April 1962, Khrushchev approved the transfer to Cuba of about 180 SA-2 missiles (previously earmarked for Egypt), as well as coastal-defense missiles, all to be operated by Soviet personnel.

Castro's 1963 visit to the Soviet Union: from left, Marshal N. I. Krylov, commander of the Strategic Rocket Forces; Nikita Khrushchev; Marshal Rodion Ya. Malinovsky, the Minister of Defense; and Fidel Castro. The man wearing glasses behind Krylov is Soviet ambassador to Cuba Aleksandr Alekseyev.

A motorized rifle regiment of some 2,500 troops was also scheduled for deployment to the island to provide security for the missile installations. This would be the first time that Soviet ground combat troops were sent beyond the borders of Warsaw Pact states.[6]

In late April 1962, before those troops and weapons had been dispatched, Khrushchev is reported to have raised the question of also sending ballistic missiles to Cuba during a private, informal discussion with Anastas Mikoyan, an old-line politician who traveled extensively throughout the world to develop trade relations for the USSR. Mikoyan, who had been to Cuba and had met with Castro, opposed the missile proposal, predicting that the Cuban leader would reject such weapons out of fear of the U.S. reaction.

Still, Khrushchev was increasingly troubled by American threats to the Castro regime:

> The fate of Cuba and the maintenance of Soviet prestige in that part of the world preoccupied me. . . . While I was on an official visit to Bulgaria, for instance, one thought kept hammering away at my brain: what will happen if we lose Cuba? I knew it would be a terrible blow to Marxism-Leninism. It would gravely diminish our stature throughout the world, but especially in Latin America. If Cuba fell, other Latin American countries would reject us, claiming that for all our might the Soviet Union hadn't been able to do anything for Cuba except to make empty protests to the United Nations.[7]

April 1962 also saw Khrushchev troubled by domestic economic problems and, on April 25, the United States resumed atmospheric testing of thermonuclear weapons with an airdrop by a B-52 near Christmas Island in the Pacific. More tests followed, and, for the first time, a nuclear-armed Polaris missile was launched from a submarine in early May.[8] This resumption of nuclear testing and the first Jupiter missiles being installed

A Soviet SA-2 Guideline missile poised on a launcher. The SA-2 was the world's most effective surface-to-air missile when first deployed in the Soviet Union in 1957–1958, and it soon proliferated to a number of allied countries.

in Turkey also distressed Khrushchev. Thinking back to this period, Khrushchev later wrote that "it was high time America learned what it feels like to have her own land and her own people threatened."[9]

Thus, while vacationing in Varna in May 1962, Khrushchev decided to send strategic missiles to Cuba. They would threaten the United States, serving as a deterrent to future American aggression against Cuba. Furthermore, strategic missiles that were based so close to the United States would help to compensate for the shortfalls in Soviet ICBM and submarine missile deployments. Moreover, this would provide retribution for the American encirclement of the USSR with nuclear weapons, of which the Jupiter missile emplacement in Turkey was only the most recent link. Finally, a successful foreign adventure would distract Soviet politicians and citizens from the domestic difficulties.[10]

Khrushchev's idea was unprecedented. Cuba was almost 8,000 miles from the Soviet Union. Heretofore, Soviet combat troops had not previously left the Eurasian landmass, although military advisors had been dispatched in large numbers to Egypt, Iraq, and Syria, only a few hundred miles from Soviet borders. Nuclear weapons had never been sent beyond Soviet borders, except for the clandestine movement and deployment of twelve R-15 (SS-3 Shyster) missiles with nuclear warheads to East Germany in 1959—Operation Atom.[11]

Khrushchev and Nikolai A. Buglanin, the Chairman of the Council of Ministers, decided to place nuclear missiles in East Germany in 1955, seven years before the decision to place nuclear weapons in Cuba. It had taken four years to deploy the dozen nuclear missiles to a nation connected by land transportation to the Soviet Union. Now Khrushchev was proposing to move and deploy sixty much larger nuclear missiles and a ground battle group some 8,000 miles and separated from the Soviet Union by an ocean. It was an audacious strategy to get back into the nuclear arms race. If it were successful, the problems with Cuba, Berlin, and the ICBM race might be solved all at once.

As Khrushchev walked the grounds of the resort at Varna in May 1962, he kept his thoughts to himself. En route back to Moscow on May 20, he shared his thoughts with Andrei Gromyko, the Soviet minister of foreign affairs, who had been a member of the official delegation visiting Bulgaria. After listening carefully to Khrushchev, Gromyko gave his support to the idea, believing that the United States would not risk nuclear war over such a Soviet move.

The members of the Presidium, the senior officials of the Soviet government, met Khrushchev when he arrived at the Moscow airport, and, together, they traveled to the Kremlin. There Khrushchev revealed his proposal to his colleagues. He explained, "We have to act in a way that will preserve our country, not allow war to break out and not allow Cuba to be crushed by U.S. forces. . . . We have to make Cuba a torch, a magnet attracting all the destitute peoples of Latin America, who are waging a struggle against exploitation by American monopolies. The blazing flame of socialism in Cuba will speed up the process of their struggle for independence."[12]

The following day, May 21, there was a routine meeting of the Defense Council in the Kremlin. The purpose of the session was to update Khrushchev on military developments while he was away from the capital. Khrushchev chaired the council, which included several senior political and military officials, among them Marshal of the Soviet Union Rodion Ya. Malinovsky, whom Khrushchev had personally appointed to the position of Minister of Defense.[13] Among the other officials present were the Presidium members Leonid Brezhnev and Aleksei Kosygin (who together would succeed Khrushchev) and Marshal Andrei Grechko (who would succeed Malinovsky).

Khrushchev took this opportunity to again share his ideas on Cuba. It was made clear at the meeting that Khrushchev's principal purpose in sending missiles to Cuba was to defend the island nation from American attack. He asked Malinovsky how long it would take for the Soviet armed forces to seize a hypothetical island ninety miles off the Soviet coast in the face of desperate resistance.

"Three to five days," Malinovsky replied. "No more than a week."[14]

Thus Cuba was shown to be vulnerable to an American assault. A year earlier, in April 1961, the invasion of Cuba at the Bay of Pigs had failed because of the lack of direct U.S. military participation. Such a constraint could not be guaranteed in the future. Khrushchev contended that the only way to ensure the survival of that socialist state was to place nuclear missiles in Cuba that could threaten the United States. In the strictest secrecy, planning began at the Ministry of Defense that same day. Three days later, on May 24, a select group of General Staff officers made a presentation centered on a memorandum from Malinovsky that outlined the forces to be sent to Cuba. The seven-page memorandum began: "In accordance with your instructions the Ministry of Defense proposes: To deploy on the island of Cuba a Group of Soviet Forces comprising all branches of the Armed Forces, under a single integrated staff of the Group of Forces headed by a Commander-in-Chief of Soviet Forces in Cuba."[15]

The remainder of the memorandum listed in detail the forces to be sent to Cuba: ballistic missiles, ground combat forces, aviation and naval units, even the support units—including "one field bakery factory." The total strength initially proposed for the Cuban command was about forty-four thousand military personnel and thirteen hundred civilians. The memorandum called for using the staff of the 44th Missile Army at Vinnitsa to form the staff for the Group of Soviet Forces in Cuba. Such group structures were formed to direct large combat forces drawn from several services and arms in forward areas. During the Cold War, there was a similar command structure for the massive Soviet military force in East Germany.

Following discussion of the memorandum, all members of the Presidium except Anastas Mikoyan endorsed Khrushchev's plan. A typed endorsement was prepared. All full (voting) members of the Presidium signed it and indicated that they were "for" the plan. Mikoyan, however, simply signed the document, acknowledging that he had read it and did not oppose the plan. (The candidate, nonvoting members of the Presidium were asked only to sign the document.)

Khrushchev's son Sergei, working with senior military officers while at the Chelomi missile design bureau in this period, later wrote, "Most of the people I talked to supported the plan. I didn't hear any objections. Perhaps those who disagreed with Father didn't want to talk to me, but in all likelihood there were no such people."[16]

The plan was given a code name on the day of presentation: Operation Anadyr. Anadyr was the name of a gulf, a river, and a town in north-

Although some Operation Anadyr troops embarked with cold-weather clothing as part of the cover story, in Cuba, the soldiers wore casual clothes—sport shirts and slacks—as they marched on parade.

eastern Siberia. The marshals hoped that anyone coming across the code name would assume that it referred to an exercise in the Arctic. To further this ruse, winter clothing and equipment would be issued to some of the troops being shipped to Cuba. Finally, when the Soviet troops and the technical personnel arrived in Cuba, they would be flagged as "agricultural advisors" and would wear local civilian sports shirts whenever in public places. Early in the planning, the General Staff proposed sending two types of missiles to Cuba: the SS-4 Sandal, an MRBM with a range of 1,300 miles; and the SS-5 Skean, an IRBM with a range of 2,800 miles.[17] Launched from Cuba, those weapons could strike all population and industrial centers of the continental United States.[18] Sergei Khrushchev recalled, "After taking into account what was available at the time, it was proposed that no fewer than half a hundred missiles be installed on the island. The number kept changing. Some missiles on the way to the Army were diverted, but most of the missiles were removed from launch positions. It was decided to carry out the operation without delay, without waiting for factories to fill orders; there was no time to lose."[19]

The younger Khrushchev observed that the Soviet missile force facing Western Europe would have to be reduced to send the missiles to Cuba. The reduction "didn't please everyone. Some thought that we were concerned with Cuba's security at the expense of our own." The final plan called for sending twenty-four SS-4 launchers and sixteen SS-5 launchers, with three missiles for every two launchers; forty launchers and sixty nuclear-tipped missiles altogether. During discussions among the few military and political leaders who had access to the highly classified planning for Operation Anadyr, there were proposals to send more of the longer-range SS-5 missiles. However, additional SS-5 weapons were not available, as the system had only gone into service the previous

U.S. intelligence underestimated the ranges of the Soviet SS-4 and the SS-5 ballistic missiles by just over 20 percent. This diagram shows the actual ranges of the two missiles: the SS-4 missiles, ready for launch during the crisis, could target much of the United States, including the main cities of the eastern and central United States. The SS-5, not operational, could have targeted all of the country, as well as most of Canada, all of Central America, and major portions of South America.

year. Reportedly, Khrushchev planned eventually to replace the SS-4 missiles with the SS-5s when production permitted.[20]

The Soviet planners were concerned with the security and the method for transporting nuclear warheads. While the missiles would be sent to Cuba by merchant ship, some officials believed that their nuclear warheads—which were much more secret—would be vulnerable to capture if sent by ship. The Soviets considered sending the warheads to Cuba by submarine or by aircraft. Perhaps each submarine could take several warheads, but when they were operating submerged, the craft were slower than merchant ships. Two types of Soviet aircraft could fly directly from the Soviet Union to Cuba: the Tu-20 Bear strategic bomber and its derivative Tu-114 commercial airliner, the world's largest at the time.[21] These aircraft were powered by four turboprop engines and were the world's fastest propeller-driven bomber and transport. The bomber could be rigged to carry several nuclear warheads; the passenger aircraft, without cargo fittings or large doors, would require modifications to carry up to ten warheads.[22] But mass flights to Cuba and the withdrawal of the Tu-114s from commercial service would give rise to speculation by Western intelligence as to what they were carrying. In the event, the decision was made to send the nuclear warheads and their KGB security teams by special merchant ships.

As planning for Anadyr moved forward, seeking permission from the Cubans became an issue. Khrushchev was convinced that Castro would welcome Soviet missiles in Cuba as a means of deterring American aggression.[23] Anastas Mikoyan, who was probably the most traveled member of the Presidium and who had met Castro, did not share Khrushchev's view. According to his son, Mikoyan predicted that the Cuban leader would reject the missiles out of fear of U.S. reaction to them.[24]

Sharaf Rashidov, the first secretary of the Communist Party Central Committee of Uzbekistan, was named to head the Soviet delegation to Cuba. "[I]t was thought that representatives of our border republics would be better at finding a common language with the leaders of peoples fighting for liberation," speculated Sergei Khrushchev.[25] Marshal of the Soviet Union Sergei S. Biryuzov, recently appointed to command the Strategic Rocket Forces, headed the military segment of the delegation. Also a longtime associate of Nikita Khrushchev, Biryuzov had commanded the National Air Defense Forces until April 1962. Accompanying him to Cuba were Lieutenant General Sergei F. Ushakov, the deputy head of the air staff of the Air Forces, and Major General Pyotr V. Ageyev of the operations directorate of the General Staff. The military men would travel in civilian clothes with false identities and fake passports, the oft-used procedure for Soviet officers traveling abroad.

Aleksandr I. Alekseyev, a KGB intelligence officer and an accomplished journalist who met Fidel Castro shortly before he took power in Cuba, was also in the delegation. His reports—the classified ones—had helped to shape the Kremlin's views of Castro and his revolution. Now serving as the KGB *Rezident* at the Soviet Embassy in Havana, Alekseyev continued his close contacts with Castro and his brother Raúl, as well as with Che Guevara. Alekseyev had been called back to Moscow in late April 1962 and was told that he would be the new Soviet ambassador to Havana. He returned to Cuba with the Biryuzov party.

In late May, the party's Tu-114 airliner left the Soviet Union and flew around the North Cape, down the Norwegian Sea, and across the Atlantic directly to Cuba, a distance of almost 8,000 miles. In transit, the officials and the military officers carried no documents related to Anadyr in the event that the aircraft was forced to land en route. Upon arrival in Cuba, they were not to communicate with Moscow by radio in the event that Soviet codes had been compromised.

The Soviet delegation met with the Castro brothers on May 29, immediately after their arrival in Havana. Fidel Castro's initial reaction to the proposal was positive. On the second day of meetings, he accepted the Soviet proposal without qualification. His only request was that acceptance of Soviet missiles must be articulated in such a way as not to offend the Cuban people by implying that they could not defend themselves.[26] Raúl Castro, Fidel's brother and the Cuban minister of defense, was appointed to negotiate the details in Moscow. Marshal Biryuzov and his colleagues made a cursory inspection of potential missile sites, and the delegation quickly departed for the Soviet Union. Biryuzov's survey led to him to advise Khrushchev that offensive missiles could be hidden from U.S. spyplanes and satellite cameras in the forests of Cuba.

When the delegation returned to Moscow, the members found Khrushchev fully engaged with a domestic problem that would have a direct impact on events in Cuba. On June 1, 1962, Khrushchev announced an increase in retail food prices in a nationwide television broadcast. There were immediate protests in several cities and rioting in Novocherkassk, in southern Russia. By what has been described as a "tragic coincidence," work norms at the city's locomotive plant had been increased in February 1962, which led to a decline in the workers' earnings, in some cases as much as 30 percent.[27] On the morning of June 1, the workers in the foundry shop went on strike. The ranks of strikers continued to grow until, by the end of the day, some three thousand men and women had left their jobs.

The situation in Novocherkassk quickly got out of hand, and troops of the Ministry of Internal Affairs (MVD) were unable to quell the disturbances. At that point, Khrushchev ordered the Soviet Army to take action, and General Issa A. Pliyev, the Commander of the North Caucasus Military District, took charge. Upon arriving on the scene, Pliyev ordered, "No force or weapons should be employed in carrying out the operation."

The MVD troops did fire some shots, initially over strikers' heads, but some MVD troops panicked and fired into the crowds, killing five protesters. Hundreds of protesters were arrested, and a hundred were tried, of whom seven were found guilty and executed. Many protesters and a number of soldiers were injured. The incident was so traumatic for the Soviet regime that never again, from 1962 until the collapse of the Soviet Union in 1991, did the government dare to raise basic food prices beyond the simple promise of "bread for a kopek."

Subsequently, Minister of Defense Malinovsky proposed that General Pliyev command the forces in Cuba despite his lackluster performance during the June protests. Khrushchev had met Pliyev during World War II and accepted him on Malinovsky's recommendation. Pliyev was a career cavalry officer whose service dated from World War I and the Russian Civil War; he had virtually no experience with modern warfare or weapons. Lieutenant General Anatoli Gribkov, a General Staff officer directly involved with all aspects of Operation Anadyr, would later write,

> That important personnel choice was an error, on several counts. Pliyev, an accomplished and much decorated cavalry officer who enjoyed great respect in the armed forces, lacked the gift of diplomacy needed in the complex circumstances in which he soon found himself. Part of the problem arose from the General Staff's error of assigning him a headquarters staff drawn from the rocket army that his immediate deputy had commanded. It would have been better had Pliyev been supported by senior officers from the joint staff of the North Caucasus Military District, which he led. These men had the experience required to manage a large organization made up . . . of units from all branches of the Soviet military.[28]

When Khrushchev could return to the business of missiles in Cuba, he wrote to Castro saying how pleased he was about the Cuban leader's reception to the proposal. Reportedly, Khrushchev "admitted to Castro that it was not only the wish to protect Cuba but also the attempt to improve the strategic position of the USSR that had motivated the Soviet proposal to deploy nuclear missiles on Cuba."[29]

Raúl Castro arrived in Moscow on July 2 and began meeting with Khrushchev and senior Soviet officials in the Kremlin on the following day. Alekseyev, just appointed the Soviet ambassador in Havana, served as translator. Castro and his Soviet hosts rapidly reached consensus on all points. On July 17, Raúl Castro departed the Soviet Union, carrying back to Havana a draft copy of the final agreement of the defense pact between Cuba and the Soviet Union. And in a decision that would have far-reaching effects, it was agreed to keep the agreement secret until the Anadyr deployment was completed in the fall of 1962.

Already, General Pliyev—carrying a passport in the name of Pavlov and traveling in civilian clothes—had departed Moscow on July 10 at the head of a team of officers to make preliminary surveys of missile sites, to mark locations for other military activities, and to identify unloading ports. Even Pliyev's flight to Cuba was disguised as the inauguration of a new Moscow–Havana air route via Conakry, Guinea. Two days later, two additional aircraft flew the same route to Havana, carrying sixty-seven staff officers, also in civilian clothes and carrying documents to identify them as agricultural and industrial specialists to help the new Cuban regime.

Planning for Operation Anadyr moved into high gear. The Red Army was coming to America.

4

Cuba: The American View

*To our sister republics south of our border, we offer a special pledge—
to convert our good words into good deeds—in a new alliance for
progress—to assist free men and free governments in casting off the
chains of poverty. But this peaceful revolution of hope cannot become
the prey of hostile powers. Let all our neighbors know that we shall
join with them to oppose aggression or subversion anywhere in the
Americas. And let every other power know that this Hemisphere intends
to remain the master of its own house.*

President John F. Kennedy
Inaugural Address, January 20, 1961

When John Fitzgerald Kennedy spoke of a pledge to South American countries just minutes after being sworn in as America's thirty-
fifth president, it is doubtful that he had any idea that the main crisis of
his presidency would take place on a Caribbean island just ninety miles
from Florida. In just a matter of weeks, Cuba and its revolutionary leader
Fidel Castro would become his preeminent concern and presidential
obsession.[1]

No foreign leader in history has been more of an irritant to American
presidents than has Fidel Castro. Beginning with President Eisenhower
and continuing to the present day, American chief executives have endured the antagonistic rhetoric of the charismatic former lawyer and
baseball player. For while the man, whose full name is Fidel Alejandro
Castro Ruz, may look like a caricature of a left-wing Latin-American
dictator, that very image may be the secret to his longevity.[2] Since Castro's rise in the late 1950s, one American president after another has consistently underestimated Castro's ability to reach across borders, politics,
and time to become a center of the world's attention. His seemingly
unlimited ability to create international mischief belies a more dangerous
potential to control dialogue and generally influence global events to a

35

degree far out of proportion to the feeble powers of the island nation that he has controlled since 1959.

John F. Kennedy came to the White House with a desire to directly confront forces that he saw threatening American interests and ideals. In that sense, he was continuing the prevailing policies of his predecessor. However, unlike President Eisenhower, who preferred to conduct U.S. foreign policy behind a veil of discretion, the new president felt the need to be more public in his approach to overseas challenges. Part of this approach was derived from his relative youth, compared to the older and more experienced Eisenhower. There was also a sense of manifest destiny around the Kennedy White House—the feeling that people born in the twentieth century were finally taking control and were going to show the world a better way. The first few months of the Kennedy administration would prove that even "the best and the brightest" of a generation could still fall into the traps of history.[3]

The roots of U.S. policy toward South America in the 1960s date back to just after the American Revolution, when a new nation was stretching its arms and wondering just how much of the New World it would control. While American families had originally come to the New World for a variety of reasons—such as religious freedom—many came in search of a chance to develop land holdings and business interests. Such opportunity had been the basic motivation of all the European powers that had sent their conquistadors and colonists to exploit the vast wealth of the Americas. The United States was the first sovereign nation to emerge in the Western Hemisphere. On December 2, 1823, President James Monroe gave his annual message to Congress, which spelled out for the first time an implied sphere of influence of North and South America. While the so-called Monroe Doctrine was actually a warning to the European powers to take a "hands off" attitude toward the Americas, it was a short step to a tacit claim of hemispheric hegemony by the United States.[4]

Although many nineteenth-century Americans thought about expanding south into Mexico and possibly even Latin America, the U.S. government limited its conquests to the acquisition of the disputed southwestern territories that eventually made up the so-called sun belt of states from Texas to California. While leaders of the various slave-owning states may have cast a longing eye on Cuba and Puerto Rico prior to the Civil War, most of the U.S. expansionist efforts remained rooted in North America. The westward expansion of the United States continued until it reached the Pacific Coast in the late 1800s.[5] Until then, U.S. interests in the Caribbean and Latin America were mostly economic, concerned with the acquisition of raw materials and foodstuffs.

Those interests changed with the publication of a book and the digging of a ditch. Captain Alfred Thayer Mahan's classic *The Influence of Sea Power upon History 1660–1783*, published in 1890, set off a wave of expansionist thought in the United States. Mahan's book stimulated the expansion of the U.S. Navy from a coastal defense force into a seagoing fleet with an overseas reach in just a few years. Both the fleet and President Monroe's 1823 doctrine were given a test in 1898 during a brief and one-sided anti-colonial war with Spain, which concluded with spectacular results.[6] Suddenly, the United States found itself in possession of territories that had no physical connection to the North American continent. From the Philippines to the Caribbean Sea, America had become a global empire in just a matter of weeks, and it quickly moved to build the tools to protect the new acquisitions.[7]

By the early 1900s, President Theodore Roosevelt had fundamentally changed the course of U.S. policy toward Latin America. Roosevelt saw a need to have a fleet capable of ranging across both the Pacific Ocean and the waters of the Eastern and Gulf Coasts of the United States. He embraced the centuries-long dream of a path through Central America and seized the opportunity to build the Panama Canal. Such a pathway between the oceans would allow a fleet to move rapidly from one theater to another, minimizing the costs of building and maintaining two such fleets. The canal was the supreme engineering achievement of the age, allowing easy movement of warships and commercial shipping between the Pacific and the Atlantic Oceans without the need for the long and dangerous voyage around South America.

However, the "big ditch" across Central America was not created without costs, both human and political. Along with the toll of human lives to disease and accidents, the American effort to build the canal was based upon a covert political sham. To provide a secure environment for the new canal, the United States stage-managed a separatist revolution against Colombia, creating the new "state" of Panama. Roosevelt promptly signed a ninety-nine-year lease and basing treaty with the Panamanian government, ensuring guaranteed access and military bases in the new country. It was an imperial landgrab on a grand scale, clearly in the best interests of the United States and its future allies. Nevertheless, America's Panamanian adventure left a bad taste in the mouths of many Latin American nationalists, who began to resent heavy-handed *Yanqi* neocolonial policies.[8]

The next five decades followed the trend established by Roosevelt's treatment of Colombia in building the canal. Any time that U.S. commercial or political interests were threatened, Navy warships and Marines quickly intervened. Costa Rica, Nicaragua, Guatemala, Mexico, Santo Domingo, and Haiti all felt the tread of American boots during the first half of the twentieth century. These interventions often supported right-wing dictatorships, suppressing any movement toward national rebellions or populist movements. Although this policy resulted in a stable regional environment for U.S. business and commerce, an intense anti-American resentment grew among both urban intellectuals and impoverished rural peasants.[9]

Throughout this period, Cuba remained in an odd sort of stasis. Although technically a sovereign nation following the Spanish-American War in 1898, Cuba had a permanent U.S. military presence in the form of the Guantánamo Bay naval base. In addition, Havana, Trinidad, and other Cuban ports became important assets during World War II, as Allied warships and aircraft hunted down German U-boats trying to sink tankers and other merchant ships in the Caribbean and the Gulf of Mexico.

All the while, Cuba became a resort playground for American tourists who came south to temporarily escape the morals and the climate of the United States. American business saw the opportunity that such an open society offered, and companies such as ITT and AT&T invested heavily in Cuban ventures. Another group that expanded its interests to the island was American organized crime, which built hotels and casinos, catering to the vices that many Americans could not find at home. All of these factors combined to create a strong sense of victimization among the Cuban people, who had spent the previous four centuries as a colonial possession under Spanish rule. However, the 1950s would change the status quo of the Caribbean basin forever.

Rogue Elephant: The CIA in the 1950s

When President Eisenhower was inaugurated in January 1953, he brought with him a new approach to national security policy. Following the creation of the CIA in 1947, he was the first U.S. president to have an established and unified intelligence apparatus to support America's foreign and military policy.[10] Eisenhower was uniquely qualified to employ the CIA's emerging capabilities because of his World War II experience as Supreme Allied Commander in Europe and, after the war, as the first Commander-in-Chief Europe in NATO. Heading the CIA for "Ike" was Allen Dulles, a wealthy and well-connected lawyer who had run the Bern, Switzerland, branch of the Office of Strategic Services (OSS) in World War II.[11] Taking his marching orders from Eisenhower, Dulles sought to make the CIA into an agency that could not only collect and analyze intelligence, but could also act as a covert operations force to discreetly implement American foreign policy.[12]

In the late 1940s, CIA field operations had been limited to political actions such as influencing elections in France, Italy, and Greece. In the 1950s, as the Eisenhower administration began to build up military forces to deter potential Soviet aggression, the job of protecting American interests in the peripheral regions of the world fell to the CIA. In particular, the CIA began to keep an eye on any country showing signs of socialist or communist leanings. In the event of such a turn, the CIA was prepared to support opposition elements that would overthrow the offending government or leaders. This had the benefit of also protecting Western business interests from nationalization or takeovers by governments unhappy with capitalist exploitation, real or perceived.

The first such operation occurred in Iran during 1953, when a Leftist government under Mohammed Mossadegh overthrew Shah Mohammed Reza Pahlavi. What made this change so dangerous for American (and British) interests was that the flow of petroleum from the northern Persian Gulf oilfields was cut off. Also, Mossadegh's government was showing pro-Soviet leanings. To spy out and hopefully reverse the outcome in Iran, the CIA dispatched Kermit Roosevelt—the grandson of President Theodore Roosevelt—to Tehran. Seeing that Mossadegh's government was weak, Roosevelt set up Operation Ajax, which incited the Iranian military under General Fazollah Zahedi to revolt against Mossadegh. Using only a few hundred thousand dollars in cash to bankroll the effort, Roosevelt was able to overthrow Mossadegh, restore the Shah back to power, and obtain a series of long-term contracts for American and British oil companies.[13]

One year later, the CIA struck closer to home in Guatemala with Operation PBSuccess. The target was a socialist government under Jacobo Arbenz, the former defense minister, who had begun the nationalization of a number of American-owned business concerns. When a shipment of 2,000 tons of Soviet-bloc arms arrived from Czechoslovakia, the CIA had its justification for another covert action. The plan for PBSuccess involved a small army under Colonel Castillo Armas to march on the capital, with CIA-piloted aircraft supporting the drive. When PBSuccess bogged down, Dulles rushed additional funds and resources south to try

Political map of Cuba—the largest island in the Caribbean.

40

and finish the job. Assisted by a campaign of "black" propaganda broadcasts, the CIA managed to literally scare Arbenz out of power and to restore the property of the American companies.[14]

While Ajax and PBSuccess were seen as great victories within the CIA, both operations had long-term negative effects—known as "blowback," in the jargon of intelligence professionals—on the countries they involved.[15] The Shah was deposed in 1979 when his economic plans failed to create a viable middle class in Iran, and his suppression of Shiite fundamentalism led to a religious revolution. PBSuccess was in some ways even more damaging, since it perpetuated the stereotype of the "Ugly American" in Latin America. Throughout the region, the impression that the United States was more interested in protecting American business interests than in promoting democracy became a rallying theme for nationalist movements, which would learn from the failures of Arbenz and Mossadegh. Neither Ajax nor PBSuccess remained secret for long, and revolutionary leaders around the world were taking notes and deriving their own lessons from what had happened in Iran and Guatemala.[16]

Meanwhile, Allen Dulles and the CIA continued to move from one apparent success to another. By 1956, they had created the U-2 spyplane to photograph the secrets of the Soviet Union and other countries of the communist world. Four years later, the CIA would launch the first photographic reconnaissance satellites into orbit. Within the Eisenhower administration, the CIA seemed to be an agency that could do no wrong. In Latin America, though, the agency was seen as a rogue elephant, trampling over everything that did not meet the approval of the *Yanqi* government in Washington.

Viva Fidel!

One of the Latin American revolutionary movements that began to pick up steam in the 1950s was a response to the Cuban dictatorship of Fulgencio Batista. Having led a military coup against the elected government in 1952, ex-sergeant Batista established himself as dictator and began a campaign of racial apartheid and financial corruption that became a stain across the Caribbean basin.[17] One of his early opponents was the young lawyer Fidel Castro, who tried—unsuccessfully—to have Batista's government declared illegal in court. Castro then organized 160 students and professional workers to attack a Batista barracks and fortress, which also failed. Jailed for the attack and then released due to public pressure, Castro left Cuba for Mexico to regroup and to rebuild his forces.[18]

Castro's new band of eighty men—called the *July 26* movement after the day of their failed attack in Cuba—returned to Cuba in 1956 on a boat named *Grandma*. For two years, the *July 26* force fought out of the Sierra Maestra Mountains until there were only twelve survivors of the original band. Among them would be the men who would change the course of history in Cuba and parts of Latin America. The dozen included Fidel's brother Raúl, an avowed Marxist, and an Argentine doctor named Ernesto "Che" Guevara, a Maoist supporter. Despite early losses, new recruits helped the *July 26* movement grow so that by 1958, Castro was able to lead his men out of the mountains to march toward Havana. Along the way, Castro spread his message of racial, social, and economic equality in charismatic speeches that thrilled audiences wherever he spoke.

By 1958, Batista was losing support even from his patrons in the United States, which had cut off his arms supply. The Cuban Catholic Church openly appealed for him to resign and accept exile, and he barely survived several assassination attempts. By the summer, the government forces were in full retreat, and the Castro-led rebels began to move into the major cities. On January 1, 1959, Batista fled to the Dominican Republic, and Castro led his *July 26* movement into the capital city of Havana. Six weeks later, Castro was declared prime minister and recognized as the head of a new Cuban government.[19]

As soon as he had consolidated power, Castro began to transform every element of Cuban society. He instituted a public health-care system, along with free education for all citizens. All private land holdings over a thousand acres were seized and broken up, while most industrial plants were nationalized without significant equity payments to the former owners. It was this last action that provoked the American government, which was deluged by protests from U.S. companies ranging from sugar suppliers and oil companies to the telecommunications and hospitality industries.

Nearly as troubling was a rapid series of visits and contacts in 1960 between the communist bloc and Castro's new government. Finally, Castro began a systematic liquidation of his political rivals and former Batista supporters, sending them into exile or to jail, if they managed to avoid outright execution. Despite promises of elections once the revolution had been completed, none was held. Nevertheless, Castro and his revolutionaries became the darlings of liberal elites around the world, with Che Guevara becoming a virtual sex symbol.

Initial U.S. government responses to Castro and his revolution were lukewarm at best. Castro's visit to the United States in April 1959 left U.S policy makers with nothing but questions about Castro's politics and intentions. Consensus was quickly reached within the U.S. government that Castro was a dangerous socialist with communist supporters among his closest advisors. In fact, Castro was using every technique of mass media and communications to build an image of his revolution being under attack by the *Yanqi* forces of America. That theme was reinforced when a shipment of Belgian arms on the French cargo ship *La Coubre* exploded in Havana Harbor on March 4, 1960, destroying the ship and killing more than a hundred Cubans. Castro angrily compared the explosion to the sinking of the U.S. battleship *Maine* in Havana in 1898, using the *La Coubre* disaster as a pretext for opening full relations and trade with the Soviet Union as a response to U.S. hostility.[20]

The new relationship with the Soviet Union included not only economic and financial aid but also a promise of weapons and military training to rebuild the weakened Cuban arsenal. The U.S. weapons embargo, dating back to the Batista era, had never been rescinded, and President Eisenhower had added additional economic pressure in the form of petroleum and sugar quota restrictions. Soviet-bloc small arms, artillery, armored vehicles, and trucks were being delivered to Cuba by the end of 1960. By that time, the CIA was already planning to deal with Castro and his revolution.

While some U.S. government officials may not have known what to think or do about Fidel Castro, there was no such confusion at CIA headquarters. Intelligence officers under Richard Bissell, the Deputy Director of Plans at the CIA, saw the job of removing Castro and his revolutionary regime as falling into what was called the "Guatemala Model," recalling Operation PBSuccess five years earlier. However, Bissell had already added some touches that made PBSuccess look puny by comparison. He had inquired whether an assassination of Castro was possible as part of a larger plan to destroy the revolutionary regime. By March 1960, President Eisenhower had approved a general draft program to remove Castro and restore a pro-American government in Cuba.[21] In addition, the Joint Chiefs of Staff had their own thoughts on the elimination of Castro, in the form of an active disinformation program known as Operation Northwoods. Northwoods would have consisted of a series of "Reichstag Fire" style incidents and blamed them on Castro to provide justification for military action against Cuba.[22]

Throughout the spring, Bissell's staff fanned out across the United States and the Caribbean basin to begin putting together the equipment and the personnel needed for the effort.[23] A small ground force of expatriate Cubans, most of them exiles driven out by Castro's regime, began to train at a secret CIA base in Guatemala. Even the American Mafia, driven out of its Cuban hotel and casino properties by Castro, offered to help by assassinating Castro prior to the planned assault. What originally had been modeled on small, compact operations like Ajax and PBSuccess was rapidly becoming a major military campaign. Security breaches began to develop, and throughout the region people began to take notice of the training program known as Operation Zapata. The American media were even aware of the planned assault; the *New York Times* ran a story on the Guatemalan training camp in November 1960.

Operational security for Zapata was breaking down, and intelligence reports began to come into the CIA that the opportunity to use covert action against Castro might be coming to a close. In October 1960, the National Security Agency (NSA) began to intercept radio traffic revealing an increasing flow of Soviet arms and training personnel into Cuba.[24] Early indications that Cuban pilots were being trained to fly the new MiG jet fighters that were expected the following spring were even more worrying.[25] Operation Zapata was based on the premise that Castro's dozen or so 1940s vintage combat aircraft, left over from the Batista regime, could be easily knocked out by CIA-controlled attack planes before the invasion force landed. State-of-the-art MiGs would make it impossible for the CIA's elderly B-26 Invader bombers (borrowed from the Alabama Air National Guard) to obtain air supremacy discreetly. This set the time limit for executing the invasion.[26]

The U.S. political landscape shifted when Senator John F. Kennedy defeated Vice President Richard M. Nixon for the presidency in November 1960. Nixon had been an early supporter of the Zapata plan but would now exit the scene before it could be executed. Allen Dulles and Richard Bissell briefed the incoming president shortly after the election about Zapata and other ongoing CIA projects (the U-2 and satellite reconnaissance programs, among others). Kennedy approved continued training and planning for the invasion, and it now fell upon his incoming administration to approve the execution of Operation Zapata.[27]

January 19, 1961, the day before John Kennedy's inauguration, was a key date on the road to what became the Bay of Pigs fiasco. The outgoing Eisenhower administration briefed the incoming Kennedy national security team on Zapata. That same day, in one of his final official acts,

A woman of the Cuban militia stands guard over the U.S. Embassy in Havana during the crisis. Initially, the Castro and the Eisenhower regimes attempted to have normal relations, but they soon soured.

President Eisenhower broke diplomatic relations with the Cuban government, reinforcing the limited economic embargo of the Castro regime that had begun the previous summer.[28]

As soon as the Kennedy national security staffers began to look at the Zapata plan, they became concerned about the size and the scope of the operation. There were doubts over "credible deniability," as well as over the possibility of collateral casualties in the planned invasion area, the southern Cuban port of Trinidad. This began a series of last-minute changes to the basic plan, which would make a bad idea even worse when the force of expatriate Cubans hit the beach. The site of the invasion was moved west to the Bahia de Cochinos (Bay of Pigs), a marshy area near an airfield. The number of air strikes supporting the invasion was cut back, and a deception program of "black" propaganda was added to try to frighten Castro into running, much as Arbenz had done in Guatemala in 1955.

An air of unreality developed among the senior leaders handling Zapata, who actually expected the Cuban people to rise up and overthrow the regime that had restored their civil rights, public utilities, health-care system, and schools. In reality, Bissell and his deputies never had a true idea of the level of support the Castro regime had among the Cuban population, who generally loved the dynamic and charismatic leader.

Operation Zapata was doomed before it started, and it resulted in the worst disaster in CIA history.[29] Most modern historians agree that Zapata was destined to fail because of the false assumption that the landing of fifteen hundred anti-Castro fighters would incite a popular uprising. Beyond that fact, the actual execution of the operation was the stuff of a bad horror film. The reduced preinvasion air strikes failed to destroy the Cuban Air Force on the ground, which then responded by sinking the invasion's principal supply ship and shooting down a number of the CIA's aging B-26 bombers. The Cuban military's vigorous response was enhanced by the bizarre coincidence that the Bay of Pigs was one of Castro's favorite fishing spots, the topography of which he knew intimately.[30] By the time the invasion attempt ended, more than a hundred of the Cuban expatriates had been killed and almost twelve hundred survivors taken prisoner (they would remain hostages until December 1962, when they were ransomed for $53 million in medicine, food, and agricultural equipment). This would be the last overt attempt by Cuban expatriates to restore "democracy" to their homeland. But it was only the beginning of the American effort to overthrow Fidel Castro and his revolution.

Blowback: The Cuba Project

Even before the end of Operation Zapata on April 19, the CIA cover story had fallen apart in a most public way. When one of the CIA's B-26s landed at a Florida airfield, with its crew trying to pass itself off as a defecting Cuban Air Force crew, the press rapidly saw though the deception.[31] With the cover plan for Zapata falling apart and the disaster at the Bay of Pigs available for the entire world's press to cover, President Kennedy made the wise decision to take public responsibility for the failed invasion. Amazingly, the new president found that his own public support soared; apparently, the American people preferred a leader who had tried, failed, and taken responsibility for his actions over someone who refused to acknowledge the deed. Privately, the anger of the president and his brother, Attorney General Robert Kennedy, knew no bounds. A number of senior CIA officials, including Allen Dulles and Richard Bissell, were quietly retired over the next year. The agency itself was reorganized, and a new DCI, John A. McCone, took over in November 1961.[32]

Within days of the Bay of Pigs disaster, a remarkable series of four memos was generated in the offices of National Security Advisor McGeorge Bundy. Written by Walter W. Rostow, one of Bundy's senior policy staffers,[33] the memos laid out in detail the foreign policy challenges

The nation's intelligence leaders
pose with the president: from left,
Allen Dulles, Richard M. Bissell Jr.,
the president, and John McCone.

facing the Kennedy administration following the Bay of Pigs disaster,
and they proposed courses of action. In particular, the section labeled
"Steps to Isolate and Weaken Castro Regime" became a blueprint for the
upcoming covert action program. Sent to the president, the attorney general, the national security advisor, Secretary of State Dean Rusk, Secretary of Defense Robert S. McNamara, Allen Dulles, and the presidential
advisor Richard Goodwin, the memos were a vision, a road map, and a
warning about future actions related to Cuba. One chilling prophecy fore-
saw "The Threat of an Offensive Base" as one of the potential threats
represented by Castro's Cuba. In the spring of 1961, the Kennedy administration's goals were far simpler: get Castro. While the administration's
attentions turned publicly to the space race, the summit meeting with
Nikita Khrushchev (June 1961), and the Berlin crises (August and October 1961), Castro and Cuba remained at the top of President Kennedy's
personal agenda.

Much of John F. Kennedy's personal attention must be seen in the
context of the Kennedy family values, which demanded winning at any
price and retribution against anyone seen as getting the better of a family
member. In many ways, the Bay of Pigs was the first defeat suffered by
the Kennedy family political machine, which had never lost an election
of real importance. Now there was a challenge from a self-made communist dictator on an insignificant island just off the American mainland.[34] It thus was no surprise that almost as soon as the decision was
made to undertake a new covert action program against Castro, the president appointed his brother Robert to head the endeavor. That effort—
known as the Cuba Project within the administration and as Operation
Mongoose at the CIA—would become Attorney General Robert Kennedy's personal obsession for the remainder of his brother's presidency.[35]

The Cuba Project was a multidepartmental effort, led by an executive committee (known as "the Special Group—Augmented" or SGA) composed of senior officials from the CIA, the Department of Defense, and the Department of State.

The SGA brought in a counterinsurgency expert, Air Force Brigadier General Edwin Lansdale, to plan operations against Cuba.[36] Lansdale laid out a vast array of possible actions and initiatives against Castro and his government, some of which actually were carried out. Some of the more unorthodox ideas were to poison Castro's daily milkshake or cause his hair and beard to fall out to ruin his masculine image. One plot almost succeeded when one of Castro's former mistresses, Marita Lorenz, after being trained by the CIA, managed to return to Cuba and gain access to him but could not go through with the assassination. CIA-backed Cuban expatriates, recruited, trained, and run out of a facility on the south campus of the University of Miami, conducted hit-and-run raids on oil refineries, factories, and sugarcane fields in Cuba. Unfortunately, none of these covert operations had any significant effect on the Castro regime.[37]

What the Special Group never understood was that Castro had genuine support from the Cuban people, both middle and lower class. Continuing attacks, which clearly were originating from the United States and its regional allies, only hardened the resolve of the Cuban people. This became obvious in late 1961, although Operation Mongoose was allowed to continue actively until just before the missile crisis of 1962. With the apparent failure of Operation Mongoose in mind, President Kennedy and his advisors decided to look beyond covert action and cross into the threshold of active military intervention: a military invasion of Castro's Cuba.

The American military has drafted hypothetical war plans as far back as the late 1800s. They are normally kept in locked file cabinets and rarely see the light of day. Some, like Plans Orange and Rainbow from the late 1930s, have become historical curiosities, providing a look at the thinking and intentions of the U.S. military before the Japanese attacks on Pearl Harbor and the Philippines in December 1941.[38]

By the early 1960s, war plans had taken on a more realistic flavor. They provided an operational road map for conducting a campaign against selected countries. In the case of Cuba, the document was known as Operations Plan (OPLAN) 312 and reflected a general approach for a "forced entry" assault (military jargon for "invasion") against the island nation. In early 1962, Admiral Robert L. Dennison, commander in chief of the U.S. Atlantic Command, tasked his staff with updating OPLAN 312 and preparing several quick-reaction scenarios for invading Cuba and eliminating the Castro regime. One key requirement for the new versions of the Cuban OPLAN was that each had to be capable of execution on extremely short notice from the White House. Over several months, representatives of the military services, the CIA, and other departments met at Dennison's headquarters in Norfolk, Virginia, to hammer out the details of the new OPLANs.

The two revised OPLANs—numbered 314 and 316—initially were developed to be executed with a warning time of only four and two days, respectively, for the participating U.S. units. Either OPLAN would have been one of the largest American military ventures since World War II. Each OPLAN projected pairs of Marine amphibious and Army airborne divisions assaulting Cuba, followed by additional heavy Army formations. The invading forces would be transported by an array of amphibious shipping, along with every transport aircraft that the services could muster. Massive air strikes were to precede the landings, with a sustained air campaign from airfields throughout the southeastern United States. All told, roughly 100,000 American troops plus hundreds of ships, combat aircraft, and transport planes would be tasked with defeating the roughly 275,000 soldiers and militia that Castro could assemble.[39]

Neither version of the OPLAN was particularly subtle or "surgical." It was clearly understood within the U.S. government that execution of either OPLAN would result in large American casualties, the destruction of the Cuban armed forces, and massive Cuban civilian casualties. Obviously, the elimination of Castro and his government was a key objective of any invasion, although the costs of doing so would probably be high. Interestingly, neither plan seems to have considered the possibility of Soviet intervention of any kind.

Both documents were highly classified, with specific sections designated Top Secret. However, the Navy and the Marines needed to practice the complex landing operations that were core to OPLANs 314 and 316, which they did openly on the Caribbean Island of Vieques during the summer of 1962. The hypothetical enemy of these war games was a notional regime called "Ortsac," which is Castro spelled backward. Thus, the existence of the invasion plans was not unknown to either the Cubans or their Soviet comrades. Several times in 1961 and early 1962, Castro issued invasion alerts based upon warnings from Soviet intelligence and his own extensive network of agents in the United States. Although none of these alerts actually had to repel a *Yanqi* invasion, they did raise tensions and concerns in both Havana and Moscow. The leaders in both capitals would have been even more nervous if they had known the one critical detail associated with OPLANs 314 and 316: the target execution date was October 1962.

5

Operation Anadyr

Every ship carried thick folders prepared by Defense Ministry staffers who had assembled background information on a number of countries with which the Soviet Union had good relations. Buried in these packets, so that not even the compilers would know the real focus of Operation ANADYR, were the study materials on Cuba.

Lieutenant General A. I. Gribkov
Operation Anadyr[1]

O ne of the most remarkable military achievements of the entire Cold War was Operation Anadyr—the Soviet movement of strategic missiles and protective air and ground forces almost 8,000 miles from the Soviet Union to Cuba. Earlier, Great Britain, Japan, and the United States had, on numerous occasions, transported tens of thousands of troops and their weapons across oceans and seas. But they were traditional sea powers with large navies and merchant fleets. In 1962, the Soviet Union had neither a major surface fleet nor a large merchant marine. Indeed, in 1962, the Soviet Navy did not possess a single ocean-going amphibious or landing ship. Furthermore, beyond military advisors, the Soviets had never sent troops great distances by sea.

Under these severe limitations, the Soviet armed forces began the massive undertaking of moving troops and weapons from Soviet ports to Cuba. While Khrushchev realized that he could not hide these shipments of arms to Cuba from the prying eyes of the U.S. intelligence services and other NATO nations, the Kremlin leadership believed that it could keep the precise contents of those shipments secret. Indeed, even after the weapons and the troops arrived in Cuba, the Soviets made special efforts to keep their numbers and identification secret from the Cubans, as well as from Americans.[2]

Group of Soviet Forces in Cuba – October 1962
(Final Planned Table of Organization)

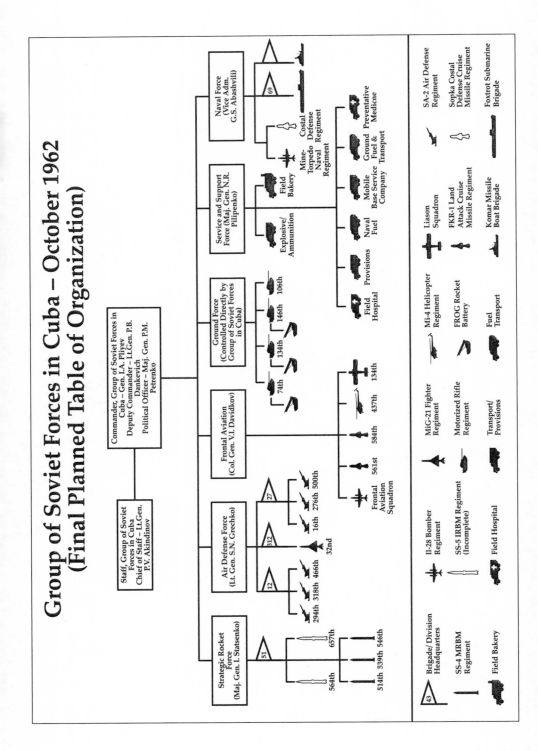

Starting at the Presidium offices in the Kremlin and the Ministry of Defense building on nearby Kalinin Prospekt in Moscow, secrecy and *maskirovka* (strategic deception) became the watchwords for every participant in Operation Anadyr. Written documents related to the operation were kept to a minimum, often consisting only of handwritten copies distributed to a short list of people. No messages were sent by telephone or radio; rather, couriers carried sealed orders to military units and to the embarkation ports.

As military units arrived at the ports, many of these ports were already sealed and closed to Western shipping and visitors, with all troops restricted to their temporary bivouacs and to the dock areas. No letters, telephone calls, or telegrams were allowed. As embarkation times approached, the troops turned in their Communist Party or Komsomol (Communist Youth League) cards, as well as their military service books, which were indispensable documents to the Soviet serviceman. Although some troops were issued Arctic gear to help the Anadyr cover story, the ships also carried tropical civilian clothes for everyone. The former action gave rise to officially circulated "rumors" that the troops were participating in a major northern exercise (i.e., near Anadyr) or in an exercise in transporting troops long distances by ship.

Ships carrying troops, as opposed to those transporting conventional weapons and equipment, were assigned detachments from the KGB's Third Directorate, the state security organization responsible for military counterintelligence and for ensuring the "ideological fitness" of troops. KGB officers were to suppress rumors and any discussion of the troops' objective, at least until their officers revealed it to them. In addition, two of the cargo ships, the *Alexandrovsk* and the *Indigirka*, the ships carrying nuclear warheads to Cuba, carried KGB security detachments. Those were also the only ships fitted with demolition charges that could scuttle the ships if they were about to be boarded by foreigners. The scuttling instructions stressed that the charges were to be set only after all of the ships' crews had gotten overboard and into lifeboats and rafts.[3]

Ships carrying troops on board were provided with heavy machine guns, which their crews kept concealed. The machine guns were to be used in the event of air attack or if foreign personnel attempted to board the ships. No foreigners, not even port pilots, were allowed on board. The Soviets took unconventional steps to keep people off their boats. When merchant ships departing from Black Sea ports passed through the Dardanelles, they lowered bottles of vodka over the sides to bribe Turkish pilots to stand off.

As the military units moved toward embarkation ports, and Soviet- and Eastern-bloc merchant ships steamed toward the same ports, the Soviet high command was continuing to adjust the composition of the forces being sent to Cuba. The massive air-ground-naval force being sent to Cuba was intended to protect the strategic missiles, as well as the island itself, from a massive American invasion force.

Air Defense and Air Forces

The first weapons being shipped to Cuba in Operation Anadyr were the SA-2 surface-to-air missiles that had been promised to Castro before the May decision to send strategic missiles.[4] The 12th and 27th Antiaircraft Divisions of the National Air Defense Forces were to sail for Cuba.[5] Each division had four regiments with a total of 72 SA-2 missile launchers, plus missiles (4 per launcher); there were just over 2,000 air-defense troops in each division. The 144 launchers and 576 missiles destined for Cuba would be deployed (by battalion) in 24 firing batteries or launch sites of 6 launchers each.

At the time, the SA-2 was the most capable surface-to-air missile in the world. The first SA-2 missiles (NATO Guideline) had been installed in 1957–1958 around Baku, Moscow, and Leningrad.[6] Launch sites were rapidly established to defend other industrial centers (with SA-2 deployment in the Soviet Union peaking at about 4,800 launchers by 1968). The SA-2 was a two-stage, command (radar) guided missile. It carried a 419-pound high-explosive warhead to altitudes above 90,000 feet, sufficient to engage American U-2 spyplanes.

The proposed twenty-four SA-2 missile sites would ring Cuba with an impregnable defense against high-flying U.S. reconnaissance aircraft, while also providing a potent defense against attacking bombers. To deter low-flying aircraft, the Soviets had already transferred hundreds of 14.7-mm and 57-mm anti-aircraft guns to the Cubans. (The Soviet motorized rifle regiments also had anti-aircraft guns.)

The earlier Soviet plan to provide air defense for Cuba with SA-2 missiles was reinforced in the April plan with the 32nd Fighter Aviation Regiment of forty MiG-21 F-13 fighters (NATO Fishbed C), arguably the world's most advanced air-defense fighter.[7] The MiG-21 was a Mach 2 fighter, normally armed with a pair of infrared homing R-13 air-to-air missiles (NATO code-named AA-2 Atoll) and an NR-30 30-mm cannon.[8] Along with fairly advanced avionics for the period—air-intercept radar, autopilot, radar warning receiver, and so on—the MiG-21 could also carry

A Soviet MiG-21 (NATO Fishbed). This aircraft with Yugoslav markings shows the sleek lines of this high-performance fighter. The Soviets introduced MiG-21s into Cuba to help provide air defense for Operation Anadyr forces.

unguided rocket pods and small bombs for air-to-ground missions. Aviation writer William Green observed, "The success of the MiG-21 is indisputable. It has been criticized on the score of armament, avionics, poor engine response, and short radius of action, but it is universally praised on the score of handling ease, performance, servicing and maintenance simplicity, and ability to operate from relatively poor surfaces and short runways."[9]

Although the MiG-21s were intended primarily for the air-defense role, all fighter pilots were ordered to train for operations with ground and naval forces. Under Soviet procedures, in the air-defense role the MiG-21s would be closely tied to the integrated radar/control system being established in Cuba, which was a derivative of the massive Soviet homeland air-defense system. (The Soviets previously had provided some sixty older MiG-15, -17, and -19 fighters and trainers to the Cuban armed forces; the first arrived in mid-1961. The Cuban pilots had been trained in Czechoslovakia. Only Soviet pilots would fly the MiG-21s.)

The Soviets also provided additional aircraft to defend Cuba and to provide logistics support for the ground forces. There was a squadron of seventeen Il-28 light bombers (NATO Beagle) provided for offshore patrol and to attack amphibious ships approaching Cuba. The Il-28 was a straight-wing, twin-turbojet, subsonic aircraft, already outdated.[10] Still, the aircraft could be useful against lightly defended amphibious ships. The maximum payload of the Il-28 was four 1,100-pound bombs or an anti-ship torpedo. However, the aircraft could be modified to provide an enlarged weapon bay to carry a nuclear bomb.

A regiment of thirty-three Mi-4 helicopters (NATO Hound) was also en route to Cuba to provide logistical support for Soviet forces there.

The Soviet Il-28 light bomber (NATO Beagle) was outdated in 1962 but still became part of the controversy over offensive weapons. Unknown to U.S. authorities, some of the Beagles sent to Cuba were nuclear capable.

A squadron of eleven Li-2, An-2, and An-24 light aircraft for intra-island transport and liaison duties was also on its way. The Mi-4 was one of the most powerful single-rotor helicopters of its time; it could lift more than a dozen armed troops. The fixed-wing light planes were vital for General Pliyev and his staff because Moscow's ban on the use of radio for communication among the Soviet commands in Cuba meant that messages and reports needed to be delivered by air, motorcycle, or car. All of the aircraft for use in Operation Anadyr were crated and sent to Cuba in merchant ships.

Soviet Ground Forces

When the decision was made to base SA-2 missiles in Cuba in April 1962, Khrushchev and his military advisors decided to send a rifle regiment to Cuba to provide minimal defense of those weapons, which would be manned by Soviet air-defense troops. These rifle units were known as motorized rifle regiments within the Ground Forces (the proper name of the Soviet Army).[11]

In 1962, the Soviet Ground Forces were in the midst of a major reorganization. A significant feature of the changes was the introduction of a nuclear capability at the division level with the Luna tactical unguided missile (NATO FROG).[12] This missile had a range of almost twenty miles, carrying a 2-kiloton nuclear warhead. The reorganization also included troop reductions, improvement of support services, and the introduction of new conventional weapons and equipment.

Plans for the Cuban buildup in May 1962 were revised to include sending four motorized rifle regiments to Cuba—the 74th, 106th, 134th, and 146th.[13] The principal components of the regiments were three rifle battalions and a tank battalion. The regiments also had anti-tank, anti-

Among the nuclear-capable weapons introduced into Cuba was the FROG-5 battlefield rocket, mounted on a PT-76 amphibious tank chassis. Here a technician checks a training missile (note the bulbous nose section).

aircraft, mortar, engineer, reconnaissance, chemical defense, signal, and support components, making them more self-sufficient than were Western infantry regiments. Each Soviet regiment had almost twenty-five hundred officers and enlisted men. The tank battalions in the regiments that were sent to Cuba had thirty-one of either the new T-55 tanks or the older, battle-tested T-34-85s, the former mounting a 100-mm cannon, while the latter had 85-mm guns. Each regiment could also muster six 122-mm towed howitzers, ten self-propelled 100-mm guns, and nine 120-mm mortars. All of the rifle troops rode in armored personnel carriers.

Most of the troops carried the new Kalashnikov AKM assault rifle. This weapon entered service in 1961, replacing the similar but heavier AK-47. The AKM was a 7.62-mm weapon, characterized by a high rate of fire and simplicity of maintenance. The AKM was far superior to the new M14 rifle being issued to elite U.S. forces, the airborne and Marine units that would be in the vanguard of an assault against Cuba. The U.S. weapon, firing a .30-caliber long round, had a propensity to jam and was difficult to maintain. The rifle comparison was typical of the small arms and crew-served weapons of the two armed forces. In general, the Soviets were seeking major advances in their weapons, while the U.S. military tended to improve upon World War II designs and technologies. The four motorized rifle regiments were formidable combat units.

As these forces were being prepared for dispatch to Cuba, Khrushchev asked Marshal Rodion Malinovsky whether tactical nuclear weapons could be flown to Cuba.[14] The strategic missiles being prepared for shipment could not be operational before mid-October, and tactical nuclear weapons could be used to help defend the island from U.S. amphibious landings before the larger weapons were ready.

Soviet FKR-1 missiles (NATO SSC-2a Salish) on parade. This frontal rocket—*Frontoviye Krilatiye Raketi*—was a long-range battlefield missile capable of delivering a nuclear warhead. These and other nuclear weapons would undoubtedly have been used to resist a U.S. invasion of Cuba.

In his September 6 response to Khrushchev, Marshal Malinovsky reported that both the Luna missile (NATO FROG) and the R-11 missile (NATO SS-1a Scud) could be transported by plane, but he recommended against doing so. The two cargo planes that could carry the nuclear weapons, the An-8 and An-12, would have to make refueling stops en route to Cuba, which would increase their vulnerability.[15] In view of Khrushchev's concerns, however, Malinovsky recommended that Il-28 Beagle light bombers fitted for nuclear weapons be shipped to Cuba along with a brigade of Scud missiles and two or three batteries of Luna missiles. A Scud brigade had eighteen missiles and was manned by 1,221 troops; each Luna battery had two launchers with four missiles and was manned by 102 troops.[16] Both types of missile carried nuclear warheads.

Khrushchev annotated the report himself on the following day, September 7. He approved the dispatch of the six nuclear-capable Il-28s and a Luna battalion with three missile batteries (i.e., six launchers and twelve missiles). One battery would be attached to three of the rifle regiments, the 74th, the 134th, and the 146th. The Scud brigade was not approved for the Cuban force.

Six Il-28 light bombers modified to carry nuclear weapons and six 407N atomic bombs, each with a yield of 12 kilotons, were added to the Frontal Aviation squadron already being sent to Cuba.[17] By comparison, the U.S. atomic bombs dropped on Hiroshima and Nagasaki in August 1945 were just under 20 kilotons each. The U.S. bombs had each devastated a major city. The other Il-28s being sent to Cuba could not carry nuclear weapons.

Also included in the tactical nuclear weapons being sent to Cuba were the Air Forces' 561st and 584th Regiments armed with the FKR-1 tactical cruise missiles (NATO SSC-2a Salish).[18] Each regiment had eight launchers and forty nuclear missiles. The FKR-1 missile, a scaled-down version of the MiG-15 turbojet fighter, had a range nearing ninety miles and carried a warhead of 12 kilotons. In addition, these missiles were to be employed to defeat possible U.S. invasion forces, with the regiment in the eastern area also to be prepared to strike the U.S. naval base at Guantánamo Bay.[19]

Naval Forces

Operation Anadyr was, in the Soviet tradition, a combined arms operation with components of all services being easily integrated into the command structure. The Navy provided a coastal defense regiment with six Sopka cruise missiles (NATO SSC-2b Samlet). The Sopka missiles had a horizontal range of fifteen to twenty-five miles and could carry a nuclear warhead, although none was reported to have been sent to Cuba. Like the Luna missiles, the launchers for the Sopka missiles were mobile.

Early planning for Operation Anadyr had provided for a large naval contingent, with surface ships and submarines to be based in Cuban ports. The submarines were to operate off the U.S. Atlantic coast, while surface warships and submarines would prevent U.S. ships from approaching Cuba to carry out landings. They would also be prepared to carry out a sea blockade of the U.S. base at Guantánamo Bay. Four diesel-electric ballistic missile submarines of Project 629 (NATO Golf) would each be armed with three short-range nuclear R-13 (NATO SS-N-4 Sark) nuclear ballistic missiles. There would also be four Project 641 (NATO Foxtrot) diesel-electric submarines, armed with torpedoes (each boat would have one with a nuclear warhead).

The surface force would consist of two *Sverdlov*-class gun cruisers, two guided missile destroyers, and two gun destroyers, complemented by a dozen of the new missile boats (NATO Komar). The small craft would each have two anti-ship missiles, weapons against which U.S. warships had no effective defense at that time.

Ashore, the Soviet Navy would establish an aviation mine-torpedo regiment with thirty-three Il-28 Beagle light bombers, and, of course, there would be the Sopka missile regiment. To protect ships at anchor, the Soviet Navy planned to send four nuclear mines to Cuba. The mines were to be planted offshore in order to stop American submarines from attacking the Soviet ships at anchor. The USSR was the only nation to develop nuclear mines during the Cold War.[20]

To support the submarine and the surface forces, the Soviet Navy would send to Cuba two submarine tenders, two tankers, two cargo ships, and a repair ship. The main fleet base would be in the Havana area and in the ports west of Havana—Mariel, Cabañas, and Bahia Honda. Finally, a detachment of the missile boats was to be based at Banes, on the eastern end of Cuba. The total naval personnel needed to man those ships, submarines, aircraft, and missile units would be approximately six thousand men.

But as preparations proceeded, the decision was made not to send the naval forces to Cuba because officials feared that they would be too provocative to the American leadership. Instead, a brigade of four Project 641 (NATO Foxtrot) diesel-electric torpedo submarines and the Komar missile craft would be dispatched to Cuba, the latter as deck cargo on merchant ships. The issue of sending some of the few available Soviet nuclear-propelled submarines to Cuba, the first of which had gone to sea on trials in July 1958, was debated long and hard within the Soviet Navy and the Ministry of Defense. Ultimately, they were rejected in favor of the slower, more-vulnerable diesel submarines because of the few "nukes" available and the major technical "teething" problems with the new nuclear craft. However, each of the Foxtrots was provided with one nuclear-armed torpedo, in addition to the normal loadout of conventional, high-explosive torpedoes.[21]

Strategic Missiles and Warheads

Of all the missiles being sent to Cuba, the most threatening were the ballistic missiles that could reach the United States. The organization operating these missiles in the Soviet Union was the 43rd Missile Division of the Strategic Rocket Forces. At one point, it was proposed to send only the longer-range SS-5 missiles to Cuba, but the limited Soviet missile inventory led to dispatching both types. Khrushchev planned eventually to replace the shorter-range weapons with SS-5s when they became available. For Anadyr, the Strategic Rocket Forces created an entirely new headquarters unit, the 51st Rocket Division, with personnel drawn from the 43rd.[22]

The USSR was producing 2-megaton warheads for the SS-4 missile and 2.3-megaton warheads for the SS-5 missile. But, according to Sergei

Khrushchev, the Soviets did not send the recently tested 2-megaton warheads. Since they were just entering production, sending them would have caused delays in shipping the weapons to Cuba.[23]

The strategic and tactical missile warheads, 6 atomic bombs, and 4 nuclear naval mines added up to at least 162 nuclear warheads that needed to be transported to Cuba. Air and submarine transport were ruled out because they were impractical. The Soviets did not want to send an armada of naval ships to carry the nuclear weapons because it would have focused too much attention on the operation. Consequently, they decided to send the warheads by merchant ships, which would appear to be standard ships en route to Cuba. The two Soviet ships selected to transport the warheads were the *Alexandrovsk* and the *Indigirka*. Both were relatively large (for the Soviet merchant marine) and new; the *Alexandrovsk*, built in Finland, had been delivered in 1959, and the *Indigirka*, built in Holland, was delivered in 1957. They could carry 10,826 and 7,500 tons of cargo, respectively.[24] The two "atomic ships" were indistinguishable from other Soviet merchant ships steaming toward Cuba.

The men, weapons, munitions, equipment, and provisions destined for Cuba were loaded on ships in nine Soviet ports: Kronshtadt, Liepaya, and Baltiysk in the Baltic area; Murmansk and Severomorsk in the Arctic; and Feodosia, Nikolayev, Poti, and Sevastopol on the Black Sea. The first ship to depart a Soviet port with a cargo related to the decision to deploy nuclear missiles to Cuba was the *Maria Ulyanova*, a small passenger ship that departed Murmansk in mid-July and arrived safely in the Cuban port of Cabañas on July 26.[25]

Neither the commanders of the embarked troops nor the captains of the ships knew their destination when they left port. On board all Cuba-bound ships, the troop commander or, if no troops were embarked, the ship's captain would receive a sealed envelope immediately before sailing. Only when the ship was at a specified position in midocean—and in the presence of the senior KGB officer, if a security detachment was on board—could he open the envelope that revealed the ship's destination. In some instances there were two sealed envelopes, one directing the ship to the Strait of Gibraltar or the North Cape and the second to be opened when the ship was in the Atlantic, ordering the ship to Cuba. While en route to Cuba, the ships were to make no radio transmissions, but that order was soon modified because the Ministry of Defense became concerned about the location and status of some ships. Accordingly, ship captains were instructed to send daily position reports to the Ministry of Merchant Marine. That information was then collated and passed to the Ministry of Defense. The same data were also being collected and analyzed by the

U.S. National Security Agency (NSA), which was tasked with monitoring overseas electronic and communications traffic.

But knowledge of the massive arms shipments to Cuba—which began before the decision to send strategic missiles to Cuba—soon became evident in Soviet ports. As Sergei Khrushchev recalled, "[Y]ou can't hide an eel in a sack. Despite these measures, all of Odessa knew that ships were being secretly fitted out for Cuba. It was discussed at the local flea market and provided gossip for women peddlers around the port. Even the reserved Balts couldn't keep the secret. But they tried not to spread the information around too much, saying, "Let them go to Cuba if they have to."[26]

There is no evidence that Western intelligence detected the massive Soviet shipment of missiles, troops, and equipment to Cuba as a result of these rumors. As large numbers of Soviet merchant ships steamed through the Danish Straits and the Dardanelles, none seemed to be headed toward European ports. Consequently, NATO air forces and navies turned their attention to these ships.

The voyage of up to twenty days was hell for the troops; crammed below steel decks with the hot sun beating down, they sweated in temperatures well above 100 degrees F. They could come topside for brief periods only at night, when they would not be seen by prying eyes in NATO ships and aircraft. There were normally two meals served each day. As the ships entered the tropics, the lack of adequate refrigeration in some ships caused food to spoil. Neither berthing nor toilet facilities were adequate in the ships carrying troops.

Operation Anadyr took place during the Atlantic and the Caribbean tropical storm season, which produced weather conditions that helped to mask the deployment. But it did not help the troops. They were seasick in relatively calm weather conditions. When some ships encountered storms, the conditions below deck became unimaginable. One sergeant died during the voyage, and his body was committed to the deep.

The initial contingent of Soviet officers, now wearing Cuban military uniforms, met the first ships as they reached Cuban ports and impressed upon the arriving officers, who were dressed in civilian clothes, the need for continued secrecy. Ships with Anadyr cargoes were unloaded at night. Weapons and equipment that could not immediately be dispersed from ports were temporarily stored in sheds and warehouses. Cuban military trucks were used to move the Soviet troops and weapons until Soviet cargo ships arrived with trucks and personnel carriers.

An average of two merchant ships per day carrying Anadyr cargoes arrived in Cuban ports during the latter half of July—a total of thirty

A U.S. Navy P5M-2 Marlin flying boat takes a close look at a Soviet merchant ship during the crisis. The U.S. Navy operated these aircraft until 1967, with some of them seeing extensive service in the Vietnam conflict.

ships. There were fifty-five merchant ship arrivals in August, sixty-six in September, and about forty in the first half of October—a total of almost two hundred shiploads carried by eighty-five ships in just three months: certainly, an impressive mark for a nation lacking a major merchant fleet.[27] In addition, Soviet and mostly chartered neutral merchant ships carried some arms for Cuban troops, in addition to oil, building materials, and other cargoes bound for Cuba.

The Soviet units moved to uninhabited areas to establish their camps and missile batteries. While roads near the ports were generally good, the Soviet vehicles were soon moving over remote roads and trails to reach their objectives. It was a challenge for the Soviet troops to move missile trailers, some about 90 feet long, through small towns and villages. Telephone poles had to be cut down in some places, with sheds and fences destroyed to permit the vehicles to pass. The main problem was the bridges. The heavy military vehicles could not cross the numerous light bridges in the Cuban countryside. Soviet engineer units sometimes laid temporary bridges over the larger crossings. At other locations, using their experience from World War II, the troops moved tons of gravel into the stream with bulldozers and hand shovels and then poured cement over the gravel. The water passed through the gravel, while the heavy vehicles were able to move over the temporary cement bridges.[28]

To maintain secrecy, Cuban troops were used to block incoming roads and to clear the streets for the nocturnal Soviet truck convoys. In areas of western Cuba where Soviet units were setting up camp, the local Cuban population was moved out, sometimes straight onto flights to the United States—and debriefing at an émigré center located at Opa-Locka.[29] But despite these efforts and the Soviets wearing civilian shirts and slacks, and attempting not to speak in Russian, it soon was obvious to every Cuban that the Red Army had arrived. The accompanying table shows the planned deployment of the main Soviet units in Cuba.

Planned Disposition of the Group of Soviet Forces in Cuba

Weapons	Quantity	Location
Launchers + Missiles		
R-12/SS-4 Sandal MRBM	16 + 24	Near Cristobal
R-12/SS-4 Sandal MRBM	8 + 12	Near Sagua la Grande
R-14/SS-5 Skean IRBM	8 + 12	Near Guanajay (not completed)
R-14/SS-5 Skean IRBM	8 + 12	Near Remedios (not completed)
Aircraft		
MiG-21 Fishbed	40	Santa Clara
Il-28 Beagle bombers	33*	San Julián Asiento
Il-28 Beagle bombers	23†	Holguin
Motorized Rifle Regiments		
74th MR Regiment		Near Artemisa (with Luna missiles)
106th MR Regiment		Near Holguin
134th MR Regiment		Near Managua (with Luna missiles)
146th MR Regiment		Near Santa Clara (with Luna missiles)

*Naval aircraft; not assembled.
†Air Forces aircraft; only about seven assembled.

Maps of the remote areas were marginal at best. Except for tests of their communications equipment, the Soviet troops observed complete radio silence, complicating their movement and the linkup of units, which had often been divided among several ships during the trip to Cuba.[30] General Gribkov observed, "Their success was a tribute to the discipline and fortitude and to the enthusiasm with which they took up the cause of the Cuban Revolution as their own."[31]

The first missile sites to be established and manned were the twenty-four SA-2 surface-to-air missile batteries, with their associated air search, target acquisition, and missile guidance radars. The 12th Air Defense Division provided SAM coverage west of Havana, while the 27th Air Defense Division covered the remainder of the island to the east. The SA-2 sites were followed by the FKR-1, Luna, and Sopka cruise missiles, which were spread across the island for defense against a U.S. assault. General Pliyev's headquarters were established near Managua, south of

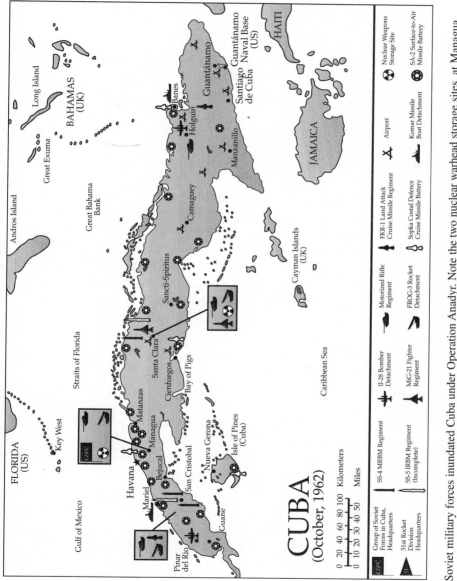

CUBA
(October, 1962)

Soviet military forces inundated Cuba under Operation Anadyr. Note the two nuclear warhead storage sites, at Managua and Santa Clara. Although the construction of nuclear storage bunkers was carefully photographed by U.S. reconnaissance aircraft and watched by the U.S. intelligence community, they were not used during the missile crisis.

Havana, in western Cuba. Nearby were the headquarters of the 51st Rocket Division and the command center for the air defense commander, as well as the 134th Motorized Rifle Regiment with an attached battery of Luna rockets. The Soviets established their central nuclear warhead depot at Bejucal, twelve miles southwest of Havana. The depot was planned as the repository for most of the nuclear warheads on the island. A second nuclear depot was begun at Santa Clara in the central area. The 74th Motorized Rifle Regiment, with a battery of Lunas, and the 561st FKR Regiment were deployed farther west, near Artemisa; the 146th Motorized Rifle Regiment with another battery of Lunas was near Santa Clara; and the 106th Motorized Rifle Regiment was in eastern Cuba, near Holguin. The regiment at Holguin and the 584th FKR Regiment, established to the east of the town, would prevent any ground excursion by U.S. troops from the naval base at Guantánamo. The four battalions of Sopka anti-ship cruise missiles were emplaced just east of Havana, southeast of Cienfuegos, northeast of Banes, and on Cape Buenavista on the Isla del Piños (Isle of Pines).

The SS-4 missile sites were established in western and central Cuba; the planned SS-5 missile sites were to be in the same general areas. These locations were designed to cover the maximum number of cities and other important targets in the United States. Two of the SS-4 regiments (the 539th and the 547th) and one regiment of SS-5s (the 564th) were emplaced near San Cristobal in western Cuba. The remaining two missile regiments (the 514th with SS-4s and the 657th with SS-5s) were set up in central Cuba near Santa Clara. All of the strategic missile regiments would be heavily defended, surrounded by SA-2 SAM sites.

In mid-September, the merchant ships *Omsk* and *Poltava* arrived in Cuba. They were recently built ships, with large cargo holds and 60-ton-capacity derricks. The two ships transported the thirty-six SS-4 missiles, their launchers, and support equipment. The *Poltava* also carried concrete pads for the SS-4 launchers in the event that ground conditions were unsuitable for the missiles. After the missiles had been loaded into their holds, trucks and agricultural machinery were placed on the open decks to make the ships appear to be carrying "innocent" cargoes. The two ships made their transit to Cuba without incident. The *Omsk* went to Casilda, and the *Poltava* went to Mariel.[32] The only missing components for those missiles were the nuclear warheads.

A little more than two weeks after the arrival of the *Omsk* and the *Poltava* in Cuba, the cargo ship *Indigirka* arrived on October 4 at the port of Mariel, approximately forty miles west of Havana on the island's northern coast. Nineteen days earlier, on September 15, she had departed Severo-

A closeup of an MRBM site photographed by a low-level reconnaissance aircraft. The photo shows a pair of missile shelter tents, three missile transporters, a missile erector, and a firing table/launchpad. All of this equipment was unique to the SS-4 MRBM system, making identification and status of the launch site possible for NPIC analysts.

morsk, the site of the Northern Fleet headquarters.[33] Severomorsk was a closed military port a few miles north of the city of Murmansk, on the Kola inlet, which flows into the Barents Sea.[34] The warheads had been loaded into the ship with the greatest secrecy possible. Never before had nuclear warheads been sent by sea outside of the borders of the Soviet Union. Until 1962, other than nuclear weapons in warships, the only weapons sent outside of Soviet territory had been deployed in East Germany.

With a special detachment of heavily armed KGB troops embarked, the *Indigirka* reportedly carried ninety nuclear warheads to Cuba—more nuclear warheads than had ever before been concentrated in so small a space by any nation. The cargo consisted of thirty-six 1-megaton warheads for SS-4 (R-12) ballistic missiles, thirty-six 14-kiloton warheads for FKR-1 cruise missiles, twelve 2-kiloton warheads for FROG (Luna) tactical ballistic missiles, and six 12-kiloton nuclear gravity bombs for Il-28 Beagle bombers.

At the same time that the *Indigirka* was unloading her nuclear warheads in the port of Mariel, the cargo ship *Alexandrovsk* departed

The Soviet merchant ship *Poltava* (shown here) and her sister ship *Omsk* were used to transport the SS-4 ballistic missiles to Cuba. These relatively new ships had large cargo holds and 60-ton-capacity derricks, making them ideal for the task. At the time, the Soviet Union was in the process of building a modern merchant fleet.

Severomorsk for Cuba, carrying twenty-four additional nuclear warheads for the SS-5 ballistic missiles and forty-four for FKR-1 cruise missiles.[35] She arrived on October 23 at the port of La Isabela, on the north central coast of Cuba. More merchant ships were en route to Cuba, among them the *Poltava*, carrying the twenty-four SS-5 ballistic missiles. By the third week of October, there were 41,900 Soviet troops and advisors in Cuba. Other merchant ships carried aircraft and other weapons, as well as an additional 3,300 troops and military technicians.

The Soviet troops in Cuba labored day and night to establish their bivouacs, set up tents, build privies, run telephone lines, and position their weapons. The officers and the men of the missile regiments set up their launchers, laid power and control cables, started up generators, and checked out their missiles, in addition to preparing their own camps. The goal Moscow laid down was to have the strategic missiles, as well as the island's defenses, all operational by late October. Then, shortly after the American congressional elections in early November 1962, Khrushchev would speak at the United Nations and reveal the establishment of the Soviet bastion in Cuba and the invulnerability of the first socialist state in the Western Hemisphere. And when he did, with the Soviet force fully established in Cuba, there would be sixty nuclear warheads for the strategic missiles, ninety-two warheads for the tactical missiles, six nuclear bombs for the Il-28 bombers, and four nuclear sea mines.

6

Surveillance and Discovery

I think I know what you guys think they are, and if I think they are the same thing and we are both right, we are sitting on the biggest story of our time.

Arthur C. Lundahl
Director, National Photographic Interpretation Center
October 15, 1962[1]

When Nikita Khrushchev made the decision to initiate Operation Anadyr, he did so with the assumption that Soviet armed forces could deliver an expeditionary missile and ground force to Cuba with discretion and stealth. A believer in the time-proven Soviet doctrine of *maskirovka*, Khrushchev was betting his political future, and possibly the survival of the Soviet Union and Cuba, on a cloak of secrecy fabricated from lies and deceptions.[2] Unfortunately for Khrushchev and the Soviet leadership, they were sailing Operation Anadyr into an intelligence-gathering network that they did not fully understand or properly respect.[3]

The Soviet attempt at *maskirovka* was in reality a duel between the Soviets and the American intelligence community. Although the CIA may have blundered in its efforts to kill Fidel Castro and destroy his revolution, the same cannot be said of the agency's ability to discover the intent of Operation Anadyr.[4]

American Eyes and Ears

Americans old enough to remember President Dwight D. Eisenhower recall his soft-spoken and fatherly image, along with the eight years of peace and prosperity of his administration. Some recall the construction of the Interstate Highway System, which today bears his name. However, one could make a case that Eisenhower's greatest achievement was a covert one: national technical intelligence collection. When he entered the White House in January 1953, Eisenhower saw that the communist world was a black hole to American military intelligence. Concerned that such uncertainty was an open invitation to a nuclear Pearl Harbor, he chartered the Office of Defense Management's Science Committee. Composed of scientists, industrialists, and other leaders, the committee was to outline possible responses to the twin threats of strategic nuclear weapons and surprise.[5]

One of the working groups, the Technical Capabilities Panel headed by Dr. James R. Killian, then the president of MIT, was assigned to address the issue of strategic warning and reconnaissance. Composed of fifty of America's finest minds, including Edwin Land, the inventor of the Polaroid instant camera, the working group wrote a report titled *Meeting the Threat of Surprise Attack*. The conclusions of the top-secret study were personally briefed to the president in his office by Killian and Land in February 1955. Key among their conclusions was, "We recommend adoption of a vigorous program for the extensive use, in many military procedures, of the most advanced knowledge in science and technology." In that one sentence was the original seed of America's present-day national technical intelligence systems.[6]

At the same time that Killian and Land were delivering their report, the U.S. Air Force was evaluating proposals from the Martin, Bell, and Fairchild corporations for a new, high-altitude reconnaissance aircraft. After the evaluation, the Air Force issued contracts to Martin and Bell for prototype aircraft. There should have been a fourth bidder, but Lockheed's legendary "Skunk Works" was not invited to participate.[7]

Led by its chief engineer and designer Clarence L. (Kelly) Johnson, the Skunk Works engineers had designed their own spyplane, known internally by the designation CL-282. This radical design, typical of the thoroughbred planes that were the hallmark of Kelly Johnson's fertile mind, became the famed U-2 spyplane. Little more than a jet engine mated to a glider, the U-2 promised an operating range of more than 3,000 miles and an altitude of over 70,000 feet. The latter was previously unimaginable for an operational aircraft. However, no one in the U.S. Air Force was interested. Rather, the Air Force sought a multiengined reconnaissance aircraft.[8]

The CIA, on the other hand, was interested.[9] By the mid-1950s, the U-2 program was being supported by Allen Dulles, Richard Bissell, and President Eisenhower as the way to see behind the Iron Curtain. Eisenhower made the decision to let the CIA procure the Lockheed design and operate it. On July 4, 1956, CIA pilots began flying the U-2 on spy missions over the Soviet Union. During the next four years, two dozen missions were flown over the Soviet Union, along with scores of missions over China, the Middle East, and other "denied territory."[10] The U-2 was so successful that the Air Force scrapped its contracts with Bell and Fairchild and procured its own force of the Lockheed aircraft.

The U-2 was just part of a wide-ranging technical intelligence–collection effort by the United States, which covered the spectrum from high-altitude photography to underwater surveillance systems. Even the time-honored work of human spies, such as classic "black bag" jobs, took on a technical flavor as the various intelligence agencies sought to pry open the curtains of secrecy surrounding the communist world.[11]

While the CIA U-2s were enabling Eisenhower and his advisors to more accurately evaluate the Soviet strategic weapons programs, the armed services and the National Security Agency were running a program of covert eavesdropping on Soviet communications and radar signals around the world.[12] Based at ground stations, on aircraft, aboard ships, and, eventually, in earth-orbiting satellites, the elements of this wide-ranging network provided exactly the kind of early warning that Land and Killian had recommended in their 1954 report.

By the summer of 1962, the United States had a wide selection of platforms, sensors, and services available to monitor the Anadyr deployment and try to penetrate the Soviet *maskirovka*. The first opportunity probably came in June and July, as elements of the five Soviet ballistic missile regiments began to pack up and make ready for rail movement to their embarkation ports. During this period, the CIA launched four successful Corona-series reconnaissance satellites from Vandenberg Air Force Base in California.[13] Corona was perhaps the most highly classified program of its day, having been developed as an eventual replacement for the U-2 spyplane.[14]

Launched on Thor rocket boosters, Corona satellites carried Keyhole-series camera packages to record the scenery a hundred miles below.[15] After flying a preprogrammed mission with timers turning the camera on and off to conserve film, the satellite would eject a film capsule known as a "bucket" to carry the prized images back to earth. To ensure that buckets did not fall into unwanted hands following reentry, the capsules were snatched in midair over the Pacific Ocean by specially configured C-119 and C-130 transport aircraft flying out of Hawaii.[16] The film would then be flown back to the CIA's National Photographic Interpretation Center (NPIC) in Washington, D.C., for processing, analysis, and interpretation.

While the image quality and the resolution of the Corona-series photographs never matched those collected by the U-2, the satellite-based system was discreet, reliable, and relatively unobtrusive to the Soviet Union and other countries.[17] Furthermore, Corona allowed the CIA to photograph vast tracts of the USSR, China, and other parts of the world not previously mapped.[18] Flying missions every few weeks, Corona was able to monitor changes and new developments in Soviet weapon deployments.[19]

There were some drawbacks to the Corona program and its film-based Keyhole camera system. The 10- to 25-foot resolution of Corona imagery could not match the 6-inch resolution of the U-2 cameras in clear, calm atmospheric conditions. There was also the inevitable problem that a fair percentage of the photos from a Corona mission would be obscured by cloud cover. Other limitations included having to expend a complete Corona satellite every time a particular target needed to be photographed, and the inevitable delays of a film-based camera system. Erecting a new booster-satellite "stack," launching, imaging, recovery, processing, analysis, and interpreting the results from a Corona mission might take a week to ten days. Unlike the U-2, however, Corona satellites were not vulnerable to Soviet surface-to-air missiles.[20] While Corona was good enough to count Soviet strategic missile sites being built in the Soviet Union, it hardly matched the pace of the fast-breaking crisis situations that were common during the Cold War.[21] It is unlikely that the four Corona missions flown in the early summer of 1962 caused U.S. photo analysts to take particular note of anything related to Anadyr.[22] The early 1960s were a busy time for the Soviet Strategic Rocket Forces (SRF), and occasional repositioning of units was not unusual. What the missions probably did do was to cue U.S. intelligence personnel to be on alert for where the five missile regiments reappeared and perhaps to make sure that they did reappear in the SRF order of battle in a reasonable time frame. The nature of intelligence gathering is that subtle trends, rather than sudden revelations, tend to reveal new developments. Four additional Corona missions were to be flown before the end of the missile crisis, and they supported the overall intelligence effort, especially with regard to monitoring the loading of ships and cargo in the Soviet Union.[23]

While the approximately fifty thousand Soviet military personnel being sent to Cuba could easily be disguised as tourists and so-called agricultural advisors, their equipment and weapons were another matter. Operation Anadyr depended heavily upon the Soviet merchant fleet to move the tens of thousands of tons of cargo needed to arm, equip, and supply the force being sent to Cuba. This meant that some eighty-five Soviet-bloc merchant ships were all moving toward Cuba and having to transit through waterways observed by nations of the NATO alliance. Every one of those ships would have to run a series of acoustic, electronic, and airborne gauntlets, giving America and its allies a number of "looks" at each ship.

The main source of hard information during these early phases of the Anadyr deployment was probably the National Security Agency (NSA). Created in 1952 to monitor foreign communications, the NSA, with headquarters at Fort George Meade, Maryland—midway between Washington, D.C., and Baltimore—has always been one of America's most secretive agencies and is several times larger than the CIA in terms of budget and personnel.[24] The NSA has two seemingly simple, though functionally complex, missions: the first is to listen for radio signals, which can be monitored or recorded for later decoding, translation, and analysis; the second NSA mission in 1962 was to use its worldwide network of receivers to obtain bearings on Soviet radio transmitters, so that positioning reports could be created on ships and military units of interest.

While the Soviet *maskirovka* plan called for ships en route to Cuba not to discuss the details of their cargoes and schedules in radio transmissions, a surprising amount of information could still be derived from their radioed daily position and local weather reports. The vast majority of the shipping being sent to Cuba in 1962 did not carry "offensive" cargo—that is, nuclear weapons that could strike the U.S. mainland— and the ships' masters were made aware of or bound by the full coverage of the *maskirovka* plan. Therefore, some of the ships assigned to Anadyr occasionally transmitted messages "in the clear," using Morse code or radiotelephone.

The NSA had made major contributions to tracking arms shipments to Cuba from the Soviet bloc even before the start of Anadyr. As far back as mid-1960, the NSA intercepted radio communications about arms shipments related to Czechoslovakia and other Warsaw Pact nations. In early 1961, the NSA obtained evidence of tanks being delivered to Cuba in the Soviet merchant ship *Nikolay Burdyenko*. Such weapons were an important part of the Cuban force that defeated Brigade 2506 at the Bay of Pigs a few weeks later. The NSA collection efforts against Cuba rapidly grew into a worldwide effort when the NSA was able to monitor the status of Cuban MiG fighter pilots training in Czechoslovakia, as well as early indications of ground control radar installations in Cuba.[25] The NSA's collection efforts would be critical, as they provided the first (and sometimes best) evidence of Soviet and Cuban intentions during the growing crisis in the Caribbean.

Once the arms-carrying ships were under way for Cuba, even more intelligence "assets" monitored them. As the ships transited through the Kattegat and Skagerrak, the Strait of Gibraltar, or the so-called Greenland-Iceland-United Kingdom "gaps," Western intelligence agencies got close looks at the ships of the Anadyr fleet. By 1962, each of those "choke points" had been wired for sound, by placing acoustic sensors, called the Sound Surveillance System (SOSUS), on the seabed.[26] Although primarily designed to track Soviet submarines as they headed out into the deep ocean basins, the system had some capability for tracking surface ships.

As the ships of the Anadyr deployment reached international waters, a new and more obvious threat to the secrecy of the operation appeared overhead: NATO maritime patrol aircraft. From bases across Europe and North Africa, multiengined aircraft, primarily the Lockheed P2V Neptune and the new Lockheed P3V Orion, fanned out over the seas to get a close look at who and what the Soviets were sending to Cuba. Carrying radar, electronic intelligence-gathering equipment, and cameras, the patrol aircraft were capable of searching large areas of ocean. They brought back a continuous stream of information about the Anadyr deployment, including the first photos of the merchant ships. This allowed analysts at the U.S. Office of Naval Intelligence in Suitland, Maryland, and other intelligence agencies to begin studying the ships and their cargoes. Some of the U.S. ships and aircraft that came close to Soviet merchant ships, while observing and photographing them, also used devices to measure possible radioactive emissions from the ships in an effort to determine whether nuclear weapons were on board. No confirmed emissions were detected.

More productive was one of the more arcane sciences in the intelligence business known as "cratology," the technique of figuring out what is being transported inside of crates and other forms of packaging.[27] For example, by knowing which kind of crate a disassembled MiG-21 fighter was transported in, a skilled photo analyst could track the movement of such aircraft to their delivery points. Cratology became especially useful when large, high-volume objects like aircraft, vehicles, and missiles were stowed as deck cargo. Particularly evident were the crated Komar-class missile patrol boats carried as deck cargo on a freighter in September.

A Soviet merchant ship carries "boxed" Project 183 (NATO Komar) missile craft to Cuba. Similar Soviet-built craft would sink the Israeli destroyer *Eilat* steaming off the coast of Egypt in 1967.

The character of the maritime surveillance began to take on a more North American flavor as the Anadyr fleet approached the Caribbean. Canadian and American forces performed much of the daily reconnaissance of the merchant ships in the western Atlantic. As the first of the ships approached their destinations on the northern coast of Cuba, U.S. land-based surveillance aircraft were constantly overhead while the ships were in international waters.

When the ships reached their Cuban destinations and unloaded the cargo and the passengers, another type of intelligence gathering began to come into play: human intelligence or spies, called "Humint." Spy reports of Soviet activity on Cuba came from several sources. Despite the stringent security efforts by Castro's intelligence agencies, a small network of CIA agents was still able to forward reports from inside Cuba. Foreign intelligence agencies, notwithstanding the stated policies of their parent governments toward Cuba, were also willing to share what their operatives observed. In addition, some diplomats, reporters, and businessmen from Latin America and Europe were willing to forward eyewitness reports and personal photographs to assist the CIA. Finally, Castro's continued policy of allowing political opponents and their families to immigrate overseas contributed to U.S. intelligence. Those arriving in the United States were funneled though a centralized processing facility in Opa-Locka, south of Miami, Florida. Every one of the refugees was interviewed, and those with relevant information were written up in a series of contact reports, which were forwarded to Washington for further analysis.[28]

Finally, the crown jewels of the American surveillance effort of Cuba were brought into play: the Lockheed U-2 spyplanes, which had been overflying the island since late 1960, just prior to the Bay of Pigs invasion. These missions were flown by a small group of CIA pilots known as "Detachment G," operating from Edwards Air Force Base (AFB) in the high desert of southern California. Missions to Cuba were flown using in-flight refueling from tankers based at Edwards or at Laughlin AFB in Texas. The U-2 flew monthly missions over Cuba and supplied a regular stream of photographs to Art Lundahl's photo analysts to assess the strength and capabilities of the Cuban military.[29] Under clear-sky conditions, the U-2's "B" camera could photograph identifiable objects as small as 6 inches from an altitude of fourteen miles. The fourteen months of overflights between the Bay of Pigs and the beginning of the Anadyr deployment had given NPIC a good base of comparative imagery for use in the coming crisis.[30]

Telltales: Early Indications

By June 1962, more than forty Soviet-bloc merchant ships were unloading at or were on their way to Cuban ports, and the *maskirovka* effort had held, although the prying eyes of the United States and its allies followed the deployment closely. By the Soviets' keeping troops below decks during the day, there was little chance of the NATO maritime patrol aircraft seeing the large number of personnel en route to Cuba. However, the sudden increase in the numbers of ships headed for Cuba had already alerted the U.S. intelligence agencies.

By early June, the NSA was picking up indications that something clandestine was going on in Cuba regarding the sudden surge in Soviet-bloc ship arrivals. The large number of Cuba-bound ships caused Secretary of Defense Robert McNamara on July 16 to order the U.S. Navy and the NSA to increase their scrutiny of Cuba. This included moving the intelligence-collection ship *Oxford* toward the Cuban coast to more closely and continuously monitor electronic signals from the island.[31] At the same time, the NSA and the U.S. Air Force began tasking more airborne electronic and communications intelligence–collection aircraft, such as those from the 55th Strategic Reconnaissance Wing at Offutt AFB near Omaha, Nebraska. Almost immediately, these electronic "ferrets" began to detect an increase in the tempo of training for the Cuban Air Force, including the first indications of new air defense radars.[32] Finally, the NSA reported on June 24 that as many as five small passenger ships were on their way to Cuba, with more than thirty-three hundred people on board.[33]

By the end of July 1962, indications at the CIA pointed to some sort of large-scale deployment of military personnel and equipment to Cuba, although exactly what weapons and personnel were involved was unclear. DCI John McCone was concerned enough to increase the U-2 missions over Cuba, the first of which was flown on August 5 and was known as Mission 3086.[34] The mission was too early to see much new base construction and weapons deliveries. However, at that point the Soviet *maskirovka* plan and the Caribbean weather took control. Soviet planners of the Anadyr deployment had counted on the hurricane season to provide some cover for the operation. The hope had been that bad weather would keep the prying eyes of the U-2s away from the missile bases that were being built below.

The next U-2 overflight of Cuba (Mission 3088) was scheduled for August 8 but was not flown until August 29, a three-week delay because of bad weather. When the U-2 film was processed, the photos were a bombshell in Washington. Along the coast were a number of emplacements for the Sopka coastal defense cruise missiles.[35] More important, eight sites for SA-2 Guideline Surface-to-Air Missiles (SAMs) were photographed in western Cuba, clearly being tied to the radar reports of the previous month by the NSA. Suddenly, the situation in Cuba took on a new and more dangerous character. Two days later, DCI Director John McCone reported the Soviet SAM sites to President Kennedy.[36]

The SA-2s raised a question and posed a threat to the United States. The question was, what had the SAMs been emplaced to protect? Thus far, nothing of note could be seen in the areas near the SAM sites, which were not yet operational. Nevertheless, no one protects empty space; there clearly was going to be a need to watch specific areas of Cuba more closely, meaning more frequent overflights by the U-2s. However, less than two years earlier, an SA-2 battery near Sverdlovsk in the Soviet Union had shot down a CIA U-2. That shoot down had wrecked a budding rapprochement between President Eisenhower and Chairman Khrushchev and had severely embarrassed the United States. Now, the one weapon known to be able to shoot down U-2s was in Cuba, threatening the ability of the United States to monitor what was happening on the island. When the CIA flew another U-2 overflight on September 5 (Mission 3089), its photos showed three additional SA-2 sites and what appeared to be MiG-21 Fishbed fighters; the top officials of the Kennedy administration began to worry.[37] There was genuine concern in Washington about possible repercussions if one of the CIA U-2s were shot down over Cuba.

At the same time, McCone began to make known his suspicions that the most likely explanation for the radar, the SAMs, and the MiGs was that the Soviet Union was readying Cuba to become a base for Soviet

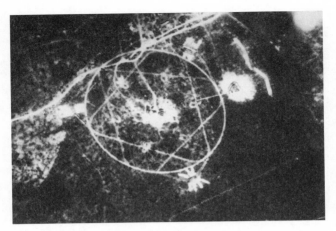

The star-shaped deployment of Soviet V-75 Dvina (NATO SA-2 Guideline) surface-to-air missiles was a strong indication to U.S. intelligence analysts that the Soviets had "something" important to protect in Cuba.

ballistic missiles. Longtime CIA analysts from the Board of National Estimates, headed by Sherman Kent, felt that McCone was out of his league to make such a judgment. Both Secretary of State Rusk and Secretary of Defense McNamara disagreed with McCone's assessment of emerging events.[38] They continued their disagreement during a National Security Council meeting with the president on August 23, but Kennedy nevertheless ordered the first studies of contingencies if offensive weapons were introduced into Cuba.

Meanwhile, the Soviet military buildup in Cuba took a public turn when Republican Senator Kenneth B. Keating from New York announced in the Senate on August 31 "that there are Soviet rocket installations in Cuba." While he declined to reveal his sources, Keating urged President Kennedy to take "immediate action."[39] This public declaration set off a storm of debate over the weapons buildup that would continue on September 10 when Keating announced that "six missile bases" were on the island.[40]

While the public portion of the emerging crisis began to grow, the debate within Kennedy's own administration continued to simmer.[41] On September 3, Deputy National Security Advisor Walt Rostow delivered an assessment that the buildup did not pose a threat to American security.[42] However, on September 4—the day before the September 5 U-2

Director of Central Intelligence John McCone "got it right" from the start, believing that the Soviets intended to place nuclear weapons in Cuba, despite CIA and other government officials arguing otherwise.

overflight (Mission 3089)—the president, McNamara, and Rusk met again to discuss Cuba. That same day, Attorney General Robert Kennedy had one of his occasional informal meetings with Soviet Ambassador Anatoly Dobrynin, who assured the president's brother that the weapons sent to Cuba were purely defensive, and that offensive weapons—such as ballistic missiles—would not be introduced. What neither man knew is that they both had just become pawns of Soviet *maskirovka*. Dobrynin had been intentionally denied knowledge of the Anadyr deployment and had been told by the Kremlin that the Soviet Union had no intentions of introducing offensive nuclear weapons into Cuba or the Western Hemisphere.

The next day, the attorney general also met with Georgi Bolshakov, a Soviet back-channel contact, and received the same assurances. Nevertheless, Robert Kennedy had more than a few doubts that his Soviet friends were being completely truthful. Part of his suspicions had to do with his close working relationship with the one man in the administration who seemed to have a clear opinion on the Cuban arms buildup: Director of Central Intelligence McCone. And while McCone was out of town getting married in early September, Robert Kennedy continued to act as the voice of concern over Cuba.[43]

Although the men underneath him might disagree over what the Soviet buildup in Cuba meant, John F. Kennedy had to make a decision on what American policy would be in the days ahead. Taking the assurance of the Soviets and his own senior advisors into consideration, President Kennedy issued a tough public statement on September 4, that included the following passage: "There is no evidence of any organized combat force in Cuba from any Soviet bloc country; of military bases provided to Russia; of a violation of the 1884 treaty relating to Guantá-namo; of the presence of offensive ground-to-ground missiles; or of other significant offensive capability either in Cuban hands or under Soviet direction and guidance. Were it to be otherwise, the gravest issues would arise."[44]

Spooks versus State and the NSA

A serious policy debate erupted on September 10, when Dean Rusk, Robert McNamara, McGeorge Bundy, and Deputy Director of Central Intelligence General Marshall S. Carter met to discuss the potential vulnerability of the U-2s overflying Cuba.[45] Ostensibly, the meeting was to review a CIA proposal to run two long overflights that would cover the entire island, but it rapidly became a policy meeting on further U-2 missions over Cuba. Secretary Rusk, in particular, strongly objected to further overflights inside of the SAM engagement envelopes.[46] Much of his argument was based on the fact that the day before, a CIA U-2 flown by a Taiwanese pilot of the Republic of China Air Force had been shot down while on a mission over China.[47] This was the second U-2 aircraft to fall to the SA-2 in a little more than two years, and it represented a grave threat to the continued use of the U-2 over territory defended by Soviet-built SAMs.[48] Rusk was clearly interested in avoiding another embarrassing incident at a time of increasing tensions with Cuba and the Soviet Union.

The increasing vulnerability of the U-2 was hardly news to the CIA, which had projected the need for a replacement aircraft within two years of the first overflights of the Soviet Union in 1956. By 1958, two "black" CIA reconnaissance programs emerged, one of which was the Corona satellite program, which was operational in August 1960. The other was a manned aircraft that could deliver the same kind of high-resolution photos as the U-2 and survive in a heavy air-defense environment. The contract for the new aircraft—code name Oxcart—was awarded to Kelly Johnson's Skunk Works in 1960; the aircraft was originally designated the A-12.[49] The A-12 was the direct predecessor of the SR-71 Blackbird (which would enter Air Force service in 1966).[50]

With nothing but risks and poor options available, but still needing to try and discern what was happening on Cuba, Bundy and General Carter reached a compromise: four more U-2 missions would be authorized, the flight paths of which would provide only limited overflights of the island itself and would completely avoid areas near the known SAM

A CIA map showing the location of Surface-to-Air Missile (SAM) sites in Cuba. Note how their firing arcs overlap to provide mutual protection and almost complete coverage of the island, the largest in the Caribbean.

sites. Now weather again interfered, masking Operation Anadyr for two more critical weeks. The U-2s flew again on September 26 (Mission 3093), on September 29 (Mission 3095), on October 5 (Mission 3098), and on October 7 (Mission 3100). None of the five flights found signs of offensive weapons, although they did locate additional SAM sites being built and a huge influx of Soviet personnel and equipment. John McCone, back from his honeymoon, continued to rail at the restrictions over the use of the U-2, over objections from Rusk and Bundy.

Meanwhile, the Cubans were already harassing U.S. Navy aircraft flying in international air space between the island nation and Florida. On August 30, an unarmed S2F Tracker anti-submarine aircraft twelve miles north of Cuba was fired upon by a Cuban patrol boat. Then on September 8, two S2Fs were overtaken by a Cuban-piloted MiG-17, which made simulated gunnery firing runs on the U.S. planes. This incident took place forty-five miles southwest of Key West and was within the U.S. air-defense zone. The MiG was detected by radar in Key West, and two Navy F4D Skyray turbojet fighters scrambled to provide protection for the S2Fs. At their appearance, the MiG-17 streaked away.[51]

On September 11, the Soviet government responded to Kennedy's September 4 warning with its own shrill message, filled with bellicose words and platitudes. It included the key phrase: "But at a moment when the United States is taking measures to mobilize its armed forces and is preparing for aggression against Cuba and other peace-loving states, the Soviet Government would like to draw attention to the fact that one cannot now attack Cuba and expect that the aggressor will be free from punishment for this attack. If this attack is made, this will be the beginning of the unleashing of war."[52]

Four days later, on September 15, the specially configured cargo ship *Poltava* docked at Mariel and began to unload the first of the SS-4 ballistic missiles destined for installation in Cuba. Mariel was one of the areas where National Security Advisor Bundy and Secretary of State Rusk were preventing the CIA U-2s from overflying for five critical weeks in September and October. That same day, the freighter *Indigirka* left Murmansk in the Soviet Union loaded with the 1-megaton nuclear warheads for the SS-4 missiles.[53]

On September 11, the same day as the Soviet warning about the consequences of a possible U.S. attack on Cuba, the director of the NSA, Lieutenant General Gordon A. Blake, established a new code word for reporting information that dealt specifically with Soviet nuclear weapons in Cuba.[54] The use of the code word, "Funnel," was to call attention if evidence was detected of offensive weapons on the island.[55] Finally, on September 19, the NSA reported the indications of radar emissions from "Spoon Rest" radar, the first definitive signs of activity from the SA-2 SAM sites.[56]

One of the most controversial events of the missile crisis occurred on September 19 when the U.S. Intelligence Board approved the release of the CIA's Special National Intelligence Estimate (SNIE) 85-3-62, titled *The Military Buildup in Cuba*.[57] Sherman Kent's Board of Estimates, normally a reliable and highly accurate organization, had created SNIE 85-3-62 to explain the broad features of the Soviet deployment to Cuba for senior Kennedy administration officials. However, a lack of *any* overhead photographic coverage of western Cuba since late August meant that SNIE 85-3-62 was a flawed document before it even reached the desks of the men it was designed to inform.[58] Kent's analysts were honest to a fault, and since they had no firm evidence of the strategic missile deployment, SNIE 85-3-62 made no assumption that offensive weapons had yet been introduced into Cuba. Furthermore, the document did not project the Soviet Union deploying them anytime in the near future, a fact that would heighten the shock a month later when ballistic missiles *were* discovered. SNIE 85-3-62 represented one of the worst intelligence policy failures of the Cold War, a fact made more damning because the Kennedy administration had denied the CIA permission to *look* in western Cuba with the U-2s since late August.

While much of the U.S. government may have been in denial about the possibilities of Soviet offensive weapons in Cuba, there were American officials working on contingencies, "just in case." On September 27, General Curtis LeMay, the Air Force Chief of Staff, approved a coordinated attack plan for Cuba from the Tactical Air Command (TAC) at Langley AFB. The plan, which was designed to fit within the existing OPLAN 314 and 316 framework, was to be ready for execution on October 20. During the following week, other elements of the Department of Defense began to update their standing contingency plans for Cuba as well.

In the last week of September, more senior U.S. officials were converted to John McCone's theory that Cuba was being transformed into a Soviet base for offensive weapons. On September 28, a U.S. Navy patrol plane photographed the Soviet freighter *Kasimov* carrying ten large crates as deck cargo. A "cratology" analysis indicated that they were the kind used to transport Il-28 jet bombers, which *were* capable of delivering nuclear bombs. Suddenly, the harassment of the two Navy S2F Trackers on September 8 began to look like an attempt to deny the United States the opportunity to observe maritime traffic in international waters. For the first time, a nuclear-capable weapons system with the range to strike the United States mainland had been observed headed to Cuba.

By October 1, the Joint Chiefs of Staff were given a briefing covering all of the intelligence that had been collected in the previous few weeks. Analysts at the Strategic Air Command at Offutt AFB and the Defense Intelligence Agency (DIA) at Bolling Air Force Base in Washington, D.C., had noted that some of the SAM sites in Cuba were arranged in a specific pattern similar to those observed protecting ballistic missile sites in the western Soviet Union. What made the argument more persuasive was that two such areas in the Pinar del Rio province of western Cuba had no other significant military installations. Furthermore, overseas sources and émigré intelligence reports from Opa-Locka indicated that local residents of the two areas were being evacuated and

The Soviet merchant ship *Kasimov*, completed earlier in the year, en route to Cuba with a deck cargo of crated Il-28 Beagle fuselages, photographed by a U.S. Navy aircraft on September 28, 1962. The crates are lashed on top of the ship's unusually long, 98-foot No. 3 cargo hold.

that heavy security had been established. There were also unconfirmed reports from Cuban sources of ballistic missiles being delivered in mid-September, although the exact model and characteristics were unknown.[59]

On October 5, John McCone met with McGeorge Bundy to go over a variety of topics. Once again, he hammered Bundy with concerns about the Soviet weapons deployments in Cuba. McCone finally suggested that more active measures needed to be taken, and that the president should schedule regular meetings on the Caribbean situation. Then, on October 9, came the turning point in the CIA's fight to restart the U-2 overflights of Cuba, when the Special Group—Augmented (which oversaw the Cuba Project/Operation Mongoose) met to discuss efforts to oust Fidel Castro from power.

One of the main topics discussed was the recommendation of the Committee of Overhead Reconnaissance (COMOR) to overfly western Cuba, which was now suspected of being a location for Soviet ballistic missile bases. The text of the recommendation was ominous; it included the following comments on the discovery of new SAM sites and possible Soviet ballistic missiles: "The absence of [U-2] coverage of the western end since August 29, coupled with the rate of construction we have observed, means that there may well be many more sites now being built of which we are unaware. Ground observers have in several recent instances reported sightings of what they believe to be the SS-4 (SHY-STER) MRBM in Cuba. These reports must be confirmed or denied by photo coverage."[60]

While the COMOR recommendation had confused the NATO designation of the SS-4 Sandal medium-range ballistic missile with that of the SS-3 Shyster, the meaning was clear: new reconnaissance photos were needed from western Cuba. The area around San Cristobal was of particular interest, as it was ringed by one of the formations of SAM sites that had caught the eyes of SAC and DIA analysts. If the Soviets were moving ballistic missiles into Cuba, this was where they seemed to be planning to put them. The SGA discussion apparently turned quite animated, with various suggestions about what platforms might be used to obtain the photos of San Cristobal most efficiently. Use of CIA U-2s, Air Force RF-101 Voodoos, and new unmanned Model 147 drones were all discussed, along with whether the reconnaissance of Cuba should be made public.

The main discussion centered on *who* should be flying the reconnaissance missions if the U-2s were to do the job. The September 8 shoot down over China still troubled Rusk and Bundy. They were concerned that the loss of a CIA U-2 over Cuba and the possible capture of an agency pilot would likely cause a firestorm of public controversy worldwide and would weaken the Kennedy administration's position vis-à-vis Castro. One suggestion that generated consensus within the SGA was the idea of letting the Air Force fly U-2 missions over Cuba, drawing pilots from the 4080th Strategic Reconnaissance Wing (SRW) of the Strategic Air Command, which also flew the U-2. The problem was that the U.S. Air Force's older U-2B and U-2C model aircraft had less powerful engines and a 5,000-foot lower ceiling than the U-2F models operated by the CIA. The altitude difference was seen as a significant survival factor against the SA-2s and eventually led to a consensus within the SGA.

President Kennedy finally approved the proposed overflight of western Cuba, with SAC taking charge of the overflights.[61] The moratorium on overflights of Cuba was ended, but the battle over who would fly them and how the information from the missions would be processed was not. Although John F. Kennedy did not realize it yet, he had just saved his presidency. Despite having consistently made the wrong assumptions about Soviet intentions in Cuba during the previous two months, "the best and the brightest" of Kennedy's administration were about to be given one final chance to deal with the looming offensive weapons threat in Cuba.

A delay of the U-2 flights of just another week would have allowed the SS-4 missiles to become operational. As it was, the same men who had denied McCone and the CIA permission to overfly Cuba during the most critical phase of the Soviet buildup would spend the next four decades proclaiming an "intelligence failure" by the CIA. Those self-serving opinions failed to place the blame where it rightfully belonged: on McGeorge Bundy, Dean Rusk, and John F. Kennedy. While an intelligence failure occurred in the late summer of 1962, it was *not* a failure of the intelligence community. The men and women of the CIA, NSA,

NPIC, and other agencies had done everything asked of them and more. In the final analysis, the failure was one of intelligence collection policy and of officials more concerned about not risking doing something wrong, rather than doing what was necessary to be sure and secure.

Two days after Kennedy's decision to resume U-2 flights, U.S. Air Force and CIA officials met to resolve how the 4080th SRW would take charge of the Cuban overflight program. There was concern about the limited performance of the Air Force U-2s and the ability of SAC pilots to fly into denied territory. Still, the decision was made to turn over control of the operation the next day, October 12. SAC's commander-in-chief, General Thomas Power,[62] and the CIA's General Carter would work out the details of the transition.[63] For General Power, the chance for SAC to finally control an overflight program with the U-2 was a dream fulfilled. Since the start of U-2 operations in 1956, Power and Curtis LeMay (his predecessor at SAC) had tried to gain control of the overflight operations and the flow of intelligence data derived from the missions.

President Eisenhower had given the CIA control of the program specifically to keep the intelligence analysis-and-assessment process free of a "SAC bias," which had dominated much of U.S. strategic planning during the 1950s. General Carter knew this and was prepared to do battle with SAC to maintain the integrity and objectivity of the intelligence collection-and-analysis process. General Power's first request was an expected one: the transfer of two CIA U-2F aircraft to the 4080th and transition training for a small cadre of SAC pilots. When faced with the argu- ment that it was not reasonable to expect the 4080th U-2 pilots to be ready with only three days of training, Power replied, "We can do it! We'll qualify them. We'll fly the mission on Sunday [October 14]. I'm the judge of whether they're qualified or not."[64]

General Carter then made one final attempt to suggest that CIA pilots, all of whom had previous Air Force service, simply be reinstated into the military. When General Power refused to consider the idea, Carter agreed to the SAC transfer-and-transition plan, commenting, "I think it's a hell of a way to run a railroad." What Carter did insist upon, and got in return for the CIA's rapid cooperation, was a dual-control scheme for the product generated by the missions: the film. The U-2F was equipped with two camera systems: the high-resolution "B" camera system, which made use of an 18-by-18-inch format negative and provided the best-quality images, and a smaller horizon-to-horizon "tracking" camera, which used

2-inch-wide film that was useful for doing prestrike mission planning.[65] Carter reasoned that if SAC flew the missions, it could process and analyze the tracker camera film, which would provide needed intelligence for possible air strikes against Cuba. The CIA would retain control over the "B" camera film, since it would provide the best-quality pictures for senior officials to use in developing national policy.

Both SAC and the CIA would share copies of all film and analyses from the missions. General Power sealed the deal by promising that his chief of intelligence would personally deliver the "B" camera film to Andrews AFB in Maryland after each mission. With the agreement struck, both sides swung into action to get ready for Mission 3101, scheduled for Sunday, October 14, 1962.[66]

The quickest way to get SAC pilots qualified and the U-2F aircraft transferred from the CIA to the 4080th was to fly the Air Force pilots to Detachment G at Edwards Air Force Base. The SAC pilots could then fly missions directly from Edwards or could ferry aircraft back to the home of the 4080th at Laughlin Air Force Base in Texas. The first pilot to fly out to California was Major Richard Heyser, who had been flying U-2s since the beginning of the program six years earlier. Major Rudolf Anderson, another experienced 4080th U-2 pilot, joined him over the weekend of October 13–14.[67]

As the debate was held on how the U-2 overflights of Cuba would be conducted, the island's air defenses were being improved almost daily. On October 10, the National Security Agency reported that the Cuban air defense system appeared to have been completed: "They had just begun passing radar tracking from radar stations to higher headquarters and to defensive fighter bases using Soviet procedures. Their system, with Russians in advisory positions at every point, was ready for business."[68] The NSA evaluation was based on communication intercepts, many of which were being provided by the U.S. Navy spy ship *Oxford* steaming offshore, in international waters. There may also have been electronic and other covert missions being carried out by U.S. Navy submarines, which could operate freely inshore in Cuban territorial waters.

Sunday, October 14: Mission 3101

By the evening of October 13, preparations for U-2 Mission 3101 were complete.[69] At 8:30 P.M., Major Heyser was awakened, was fed a low-residue meal, conducted the standard preflight routine of breathing pure oxygen to purge his body of nitrogen, and suited up for the ride out to the North Base hangar at Edwards AFB.[70] Sometime around 2 A.M. (Pacific time), Heyser climbed into his U-2 and began his preflight checklist. All systems were functioning properly, and the weather forecast was perfect. As part of the buildup of intelligence assets for the growing crisis in the Caribbean, SAC had begun to move planes from the 55th Strategic Reconnaissance Wing from Offutt AFB into bases in the southeastern United States. Five of the wing's RB-47H Stratojet photoreconnaissance aircraft were sent to MacDill AFB near Tampa, Florida, to photograph shipping off Cuba and to evaluate the weather around the western end of the island. When the RB-47Hs reported "all clear," the authorization to fly Mission 3101 was given.

At 2:30 A.M. (Pacific time) on October 14, Major Heyser took off from Edwards AFB and headed toward Cuba on Mission 3101. Flying one of the U-2F aircraft acquired from the CIA, Heyser was to fly a single pass over the western end of Cuba, from south to north, with a recovery in Florida. No in-flight refueling was required.

At 7:31 A.M. Eastern time, Heyser turned north for his photo run over the island. The weather was clear, all of the camera systems functioned properly, and there were no indications of hostile emissions from the SAM radar below. After a twelve-minute photo run, he continued north and landed at McCoy AFB near Orlando, Florida. During his debriefing, Heyser characterized the mission as "a piece of cake—a milk run."[71]

The film canisters from the U-2 cameras were rapidly unloaded and packed into protective shipping containers. The film from the high-resolution "B" camera system was picked up by Air Force officers and flown to Andrews Air Force Base. At Andrews, about an hour was lost figuring out who had custodial responsibility for the highly classified film before representatives of the Naval Photographic Interpretation Center in southeast Washington arrived to pick up the eight cans. The Navy had high-speed film processors and would develop the film for the CIA/NPIC. Meanwhile, the film from the U-2's tracker camera was sent to the 554th Target Materials Squadron at Offutt AFB.

At the same time, the 4080th was moving its U-2 operations to McCoy Air Force Base so that if an increased tempo of overflights was necessary, they could be better supported. Major Anderson ferried a second U-2F to McCoy AFB from Detachment G at Edwards AFB that afternoon, and both aircraft and pilots were put on alert for another mission the following day. While they waited, Heyser and Anderson began to transition several other SAC U-2 pilots to the U-2F, so that there would be a chance for crews to rest between missions.[72]

Analysis and Interpretation

At Offutt AFB, the photo analysts of the 554th Target Materials Squadron pored over the 2-inch-wide tracker film from the Cuban overflight. Airman 1st Class Michael Davis was the squadron's expert on Soviet ballistic missiles. The twenty-three-year-old photo interpreter had inspected U-2 and satellite films of the Soviet Union for almost two years, searching for ICBM launch sites and other missile complexes. "I developed a trick in which I would seek out the more visible SA-2 missile sites," he explained. "The Soviets always deployed SA-2s batteries in a broad circle around their ballistic missile launchers. Once I identified a circle of SA-2s, I would bisect the circle and there, in the center, was the hidden ICBM site," he told the authors.[73]

On October 14, Davis had already worked a shift of about twelve hours, scrutinizing KH-4 satellite photos of the Soviet Union. Every part of his body ached after the shift, and his eyes were stinging when he went home about 11 P.M. Central time. Near midnight his boss, Major Calvin B. Olsen, telephoned him. "He wanted me back, immediately. Olsen told me to come in as I was 'in civies,' but I changed back into uniform," Davis recalled. In the squadron's "vault," he was shown the U-2 tracker film and was asked to look for indications of Soviet ballistic missiles.

About 1 A.M., after perhaps an hour of scanning the film, Davis found the pattern of SA-2 launchers that he was seeking. Then he identified the missiles and other equipment of an SS-4 Sandal MRBM system near San Cristobal. Major Olsen immediately informed his commanding officer, Lieutenant Colonel Eugene Tighe, and "at two o'clock I was walking into the general's conference room—BD-12—a room full of generals," recalled Davis.[74]

After Airman Davis briefed the officers in the conference room on his findings, General Power, the Commander-in-Chief Strategic Air Command, rose from his chair and came over to Davis. Pointing at Davis, the general said sharply, "Airman . . . if you ever say anything to anyone about this, it will be detrimental. . . ." Power stopped in mid-sentence. Tighe, Olsen, and others in the room were pale at the general's words, Davis remembered. Power was obviously concerned about the CIA-SAC agreement that made NPIC the agency responsible for photographic assessments that might affect national policy. But Power quickly passed the word of the Cuban missile find to Air Force Chief of Staff LeMay.

Meanwhile, Tighe called Davis aside and told him to "go home and be with your family." That order, also given to the other enlisted men and junior officers of the 554th Squadron, was construed as meaning that "we would soon be at war," reflected Davis. "I really thought that we would go in there [Cuba] the next day and get rid of them."[75]

The photo-interpretation process of the large-format film at NPIC in Washington would take a little more time, but Operation Anadyr's *maskirovka* effort had finally been cracked. The United States of America now officially knew that the Soviet Union was deploying offensive nuclear ballistic missiles in Cuba.

Processing the large-format "B" camera film took a good deal longer than did the tracker camera film. The developed film did not arrive at NPIC until the early morning of October 15. At the time, NPIC was located over a dilapidated Ford automotive dealership at Fifth and K Streets in Northwest Washington, which was a perfect cover for a covert intelligence facility. Physically squalid, NPIC was the finest photographic analysis center in the world, staffed with a unique team of experts covering a dizzying array of specialties. At the top of the team was Arthur Lundahl, a passionate, longtime believer in photoreconnaissance as an instrument of national security. Lundahl had founded NPIC as part of the original U-2 startup program in the mid-1950s, and in just seven years had managed to assemble a state-of-the-art facility with a talented team of professionals. That they were creating the science of national photo interpretation as they went along just made the achievement that much more impressive.[76]

The "B" camera film took most of the day shift to scan. Three two-man teams of photo interpreters leaned over light tables looking for anything new or unusual. None of the teams had been informed that they were to look for ballistic missiles, having been cued to look for additional coast defense cruise missile or SAM sites. Gene Lydon of the CIA and Jim Homes of the Air Force handled the two rolls of film taken over San Cristobal. The two men initially discovered a new SAM site, which had yet to receive its requisite SA-2 launchers, radar, and other equipment. Then Lydon and Homes spotted the same six canvas-covered objects on trailers that had attracted Airman Davis. They rapidly assessed that the equipment was "missile related." Within minutes, a team of experts on Soviet missile systems was gathered around the table, working quickly to figure out exactly what they were looking at.[77]

Arthur Lundahl was the founding director of the CIA's National Photographic Interpretation Center (NPIC). His foresight permitted the U.S. intelligence community to rapidly glean intelligence from the mass of U-2 photography taken over Cuba. Subsequently, NPIC expanded its efforts to interpret the "take" from the Corona spy satellites.

By the time NPIC Deputy Director Dino Brugioni arrived with another specialist, the analysts had measured the six trailers and the objects under canvas with precision optical tools and were calculating their probable size. They then pulled a notebook from a shelf and thumbed through pages filled with photographs and data about Soviet ballistic missiles. At the top and the bottom of each page was a series of code words detailing the source of the information on the sheet. *Talent*, for example, meant that the data came from information derived from overhead photography—U-2 or satellite photography. *Keyhole* told the analysts that Corona satellite data was responsible for the images at which they were looking. On many of the pages of this particular book was the code word *Ironbark*, which gave most of them no clue to its origin.[78] *Ironbark* referred to the material supplied by Colonel Oleg Penkovsky of Soviet Military Intelligence (GRU).

The "Ironbark" material, derived from Soviet manuals and technical documents, gave NPIC analysts an incredible amount of information to help them understand what was happening at San Cristobal. For example, they were able to identify the missiles not only by their dimensions but also from the various pieces of support equipment. In addition, NPIC personnel could tell the exact operational status of the missile regiment, from the detailed time line that was in the field manuals Penkovsky supplied. From the Mission 3101 photos, they could tell that the main components of the SS-4 missile regiment were just arriving at the site, but that the Soviets had yet to begin setting them up.[79]

Around 5 P.M., just as the day shift was about to catch carpools home, Art Lundahl decided what was to be done with the revelation on

A photo analyst at the National Photographic Interpretation Center reviews rolls of film from a U.S. reconnaissance aircraft after a mission over Cuba. The NPIC and the Navy and Air Force photo centers did a remarkable job of photo interpretation.

NPIC light tables. After looking over the material, he asked questions of each analyst, getting the best opinions on what each man had just seen. Realizing what would be needed for briefings in the morning, Lundahl ordered everyone from the day shift who had not left to call home and plan to stay overnight in the office. Then, around 5:30 A.M., Lundahl called the CIA's Deputy Director of Intelligence, Ray Cline, at his office. Cline, a man of superb intellect and longtime intelligence experience, spoke with Lundahl at length over the secure telephone line about what the NPIC analysts had found. Cline ordered him to have a complete briefing package at CIA headquarters at 7:30 A.M. the following day. Cline then phoned General Carter, who agreed to let him call McGeorge Bundy.

Cline informed Bundy by secure telephone early in the evening of October 15 that Mission 3101 had found hard evidence of Soviet SS-4 MRBMs in western Cuba. Bundy immediately ordered Cline to get the photos and a briefing team to the White House the following morning. Bundy also made another decision, one that would prove controversial to future second-guessers. He decided on his own authority not to immedi-

Oleg Penkovsky, a colonel in Soviet Military Intelligence (GRU), provided the United States with documents and information that revealed the weakness of the Soviet strategic arsenal. That intelligence helped President Kennedy to develop his position in the missile crisis. Penkovsky paid for his disloyalty to the Soviet Union with his life.

ately call President Kennedy, who had just returned from a weekend of campaigning for the upcoming midterm congressional elections. Bundy wanted Kennedy and his advisors to have one last night of sleep before the start of what he now knew could become the most serious crisis since World War II. Due to Bundy's decision, the official start of the Cuban Missile Crisis was now scheduled for Tuesday morning, October 16, 1962.[80]

7

ExComm

I now know how Tojo felt when he was planning Pearl Harbor.

Attorney General Robert F. Kennedy,
note to President Kennedy, October 16, 1962[1]

Tuesday, October 16, 1962, promised to be particularly pleasant for President John F. Kennedy. After weeks of strife over integrating colleges in the Deep South and days of hard campaigning for the upcoming midterm congressional elections, he was back in the White House. Despite a busy schedule, Kennedy found time for some fun with one of his favorite benefactors, Astronaut Walter M. (Wally) Schirra. One of the Original Seven, Schirra had just completed *Sigma-7*, an orbital mission that had almost doubled America's aggregate man-in-space time. The playful astronaut was bringing his family for the traditional postflight White House visit, of which political staffers had planned to take advantage. The space race with the Soviet Union was one area where the superpowers competed head-to-head, and *Sigma-7* had been an unqualified American success.[2]

Throughout the night of October 15–16, NPIC photo interpreters had worked to verify their initial assessment that SS-4 ballistic missiles were being installed at San Cristobal. The staff then produced materials for the inevitable rounds of briefings that would begin early the next morning. Fortunately, this was exactly the kind of situation that Art Lundahl had envisioned years earlier when he had first conceived the NPIC operation to support the U-2 spyplane. Realizing that crisis situations might become round-the-clock affairs, Lundahl had coined the term "HTAUTOMAT" to describe how he wanted the NPIC facility to operate. Lundahl envisioned a place, patterned after the twenty-four-hour Automat restaurants of New York City, that would be capable of generating specific intelligence products for decision makers at all hours. Now his team's task was to supply the tools for understanding and monitoring a crisis that could be weeks long.

Once the team had verified its earlier assessment, it had to decide how to best present its findings. This was a difficult problem because of the nature of the audience and the complexity of NPIC materials. Unlike members of the Eisenhower administration, most of the senior personnel of Kennedy's White House lacked a high-level understanding of intelligence matters. Eisenhower had personally participated in planning routes for the U-2 overflights of Cuba and had been known to take rolls of film from the Corona satellite missions and examine them on the floor of the Oval Office with a hand magnifying glass.[3,4] John Kennedy and his senior advisors had no such interest or skills. Teaching Kennedy and his staff to understand intelligence became Lundahl's personal challenge. In late 1960, Lundahl had met with President-elect Kennedy and begun to tutor him on the rudiments of intelligence analysis and photo-interpretation. In a little under two years, Lundahl had gained an insight into how the young president and his inner circle wanted to be shown intelligence data, and NPIC had developed a number of tools to maximize the impact of the photos presented to officials of the New Frontier. Lundahl's favorite presentation tool was the briefing board, his primary way of showing the latest and most important of the photos that were flooding into NPIC from U-2 flights and spy satellites. The briefing boards were large sheets of stiff poster board, about three feet by five feet in size. Each board focused on a single point or subject, with a few photos that had annotations and, where necessary, supporting maps and line drawings. Simplicity and clarity were key.

Late on October 15, Lundahl ordered his NPIC staff to produce several sets of the boards since there would be multiple teams of CIA briefers working at different locations around Washington the following day. Several sets were destined for the Pentagon, where the Joint Chiefs of Staff, as well as the military services, would receive their first look at the U-2 photos from Mission 3101. Another set was headed for the Department of State. The set of boards occupying most of Lundahl's attention, however, was the one destined for the White House, where he would personally make several presentations during the day. Starting with his trip over to CIA headquarters to brief Deputy Director of Intelligence Cline, Lundahl would then brief National Security Advisor Bundy, Robert Kennedy, and, eventually, the president's entire inner circle of advisors. It was a routine that NPIC would develop into a daily affair in the days and weeks ahead, although the actual briefing duty would be rotated among senior NPIC staff. While Lundahl often briefed critical presentations himself, he sometimes sent Dino Brugioni or others.

The NPIC staff was not alone in missing sleep that night. At CIA headquarters, the analysts of Sherman Kent's Board of Estimates were working hard to translate findings from the U-2 photos into a short memo. This memo was vital because few senior government officials were cleared to see "overhead" reconnaissance photographs from U-2s and Corona satellites. The Board of Estimates worked through the night to produce a document that would provide key mid- to senior-level officials with their first intelligence about the missiles in Cuba. The memo, titled *Probable Soviet MRBM Sites in Cuba*, was a study in brevity, running just a handful of pages, plus an annex.[5]

While *Probable Soviet MRBM Sites in Cuba* was somewhat conservative in its analysis of whether the missiles were SS-3 Shyster or SS-4 Sandal models, there was no question that Kent's group was intellectually honest in reversing its September 19 assessment in SNIE 85-3-62. Perhaps the most striking—and chilling—feature of the report was the map at the end of the annex section that showed the probable ranges of both the SS-3 and the SS-4 missiles from the San Cristobal base. At the edge of the SS-4 range envelope was the city most of them would be sitting in as they read the memo over coffee on the morning of October 16: Washington, D.C.

Point of View: American-Soviet Relations

America's reaction to the Soviet missile deployment to Cuba was driven to a great degree by events of the previous few years between the United States and the Soviet Union. The genesis of the increasing tensions was the May 1, 1960, shoot down of a CIA U-2 on what was planned as the twenty-fourth overflight of the Soviet Union. While the volatile reaction of Nikita Khrushchev may have been a shock to people in the United States, it was hardly so to President Eisenhower. When the U-2 went down and the pilot, Francis Gary Powers, was captured, Khrushchev's response was not so much vengeance toward Eisenhower as it was venting frustration over the Soviet inability to stop the aerial intrusions during the previous four years. Since July 1956, when the U-2s had begun their overflights of the Soviet Union, Khrushchev's emissaries had been protesting the covert missions regularly *but* privately to the U.S. government, to virtually no response.

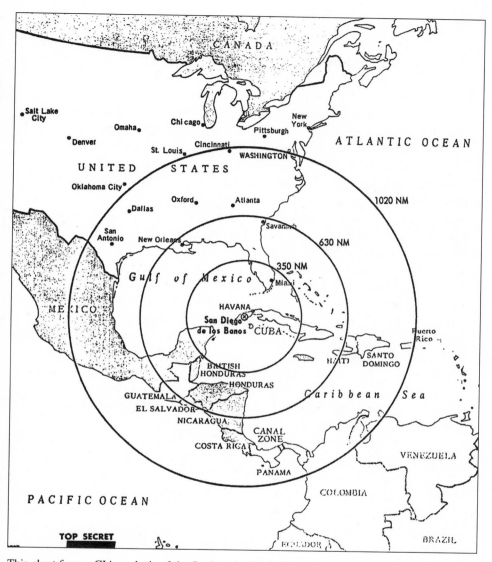

This chart from a CIA analysis of the Soviet missiles in Cuba, dated October 16, 1962, shows the estimated ranges of the Scud, SS-3, and SS-4 missiles. The range estimates for the medium- and intermediate-range ballistic missiles were significantly less than the actual ranges, which seems odd in view of the information provided by Colonel Oleg Penkovsky.

In May 1960, Khrushchev decided to make the Americans pay for his embarrassment over the U-2 flights. He wrecked the planned four-power summit conference in Paris later in 1960, the first of several Soviet actions that raised the level of concern among Americans that year. The pace of Soviet space launches, which were seen as a measure of the potential to deploy nuclear-armed intercontinental ballistic missiles, increased as 1960 progressed. The height of the Soviet grandstanding came that fall during the opening of the United Nations' annual session in New York City. Leading the Soviet delegation, Khrushchev actually banged his shoe on the table for emphasis. More provocative, however, was Khrushchev's trip to a squalid hotel in Harlem, where he publicly embraced Fidel Castro, creating the impression of a Soviet-Cuban alliance. In the minds of the American public, Khrushchev had become the living embodiment of the communist world. The meeting created an interesting image: the godless communist leader in an ill-fitting suit, embraced in a bear hug with a bearded Latino revolutionary wearing combat fatigues.

President Kennedy's inauguration in January 1961 did little to change the deteriorating superpower dynamic, which only grew more tense as a result of the failure of the CIA-sponsored attempt in April 1961 to invade Cuba at the Bay of Pigs. Publicly humiliated, the Kennedy administration spent its first months in office struggling from crisis to crisis. Just days before the CIA's failure at the Bay of Pigs, the Soviet Union launched the cosmonaut Major Yuri Gagarin on the first manned flight into space. Gagarin beat the American Alan Shepard into space by three weeks. Then Khrushchev roughed up Kennedy during a June summit meeting in Vienna, threatening the young president over the status of Berlin and East Germany.[6] Kennedy's response, "It's going to be a cold winter," was exactly how the coming world situation looked that spring.

The summer and fall of 1961 were dominated by the twin crises over Berlin, which included the erection of a barbed-wire barrier that quickly became the infamous Berlin Wall. Nevertheless, by the fall of 1961, the Kennedy administration saw real benefits to dispelling the myth of Soviet strategic nuclear superiority. Not only would such a move allow Kennedy to posture more aggressively against Khrushchev over Berlin, but it would also allow the president to hold back the unrestrained ambitions of military "hawks" like Generals Curtis LeMay and Thomas Power. For example, Power had ambitions of growing the American ICBM force to ten thousand Minuteman missiles, based upon earlier National Intelligence Estimates (NIEs) of a huge Soviet ICBM production and deployment program.

During the summer of 1961, Sherman Kent's Board of Estimates had developed and, on September 21, issued *Strength and Development of Soviet Long Range Ballistic Missiles Forces* (NIE 11-8/1-61). Based upon imagery from the twenty-three successful U-2 overflights of the Soviet Union and the Corona satellite missions flown since August 1960, NIE 11-8/1-61 was a revised intelligence estimate of Soviet ICBMs that reflected the true state of Soviet nuclear forces. It stated,

> The low present and near-term [Soviet] ICBM force level probably results from a Soviet decision to deploy only a small force of the cumbersome, first generation ICBMs, and to press the development of a smaller, second-generation system. . . . Soviet ICBM strength will probably not increase substantially until the new missile [SS-7] is ready for operational use, probably sometime in the latter half of 1962. After this point, we anticipate that the number of operational launchers will begin to increase significantly. On this basis, we estimate that the force level in mid-1963 will approximate 75–125 operational ICBM launchers.[7]

Thus, a year later (1962), the Soviet ICBM force would pale in comparison with even a "limited" U.S. Minuteman program, while Soviet submarine-launched missiles would also lag far behind the U.S. Polaris program.

Within weeks, Under Secretary of Defense Roswell Gilpatrick publicly revealed the broad details of NIE 11-8/1-61 in a speech, and Nikita Khrushchev's myth of Soviet strategic nuclear superiority began to crumble. American senior policy makers saw an apparent withdrawal of aggressive Soviet moves in Berlin that October and began to consider the possibility of a rapprochement with the Soviet Union. There were even early moves toward an atmospheric test ban treaty for nuclear weapons, a first step on the road to strategic arms control. Unfortunately, these ideas did not take into consideration the actual state of Soviet strategic thinking, which was being driven by the desire to catch up with the United States in the field of intercontinental ballistic missiles. The winter of 1961–1962 was very cold indeed.

American ignorance of Soviet thinking would be at the core of the rise in tensions over Cuba during the spring and summer of 1962. Part of the disconnect resulted from the lack of a regular dialogue between senior American and Soviet diplomats and government leaders. That Khrushchev and Kennedy had only one tense face-to-face meeting in 1961 did little to improve the flow of understanding and goodwill between the two countries. In particular, the September crisis in Berlin, which was re-solved by the use of unofficial "back-channel" communications between Kennedy and Khrushchev, actually did additional damage to relations between the two superpowers. Robert Kennedy, who was the primary conduit to the Soviet "back-channel" contacts, actually spent more time with Ambassador Dobrynin than did Secretary of State Rusk, who was becoming estranged from the U.S-Soviet dialogue. By the spring of 1962, when Khrushchev made the decision to send missiles to Cuba, senior U.S. government leaders had little insight into Soviet motivations and intentions and lacked the necessary intimacy with their Soviet counter-parts to effectively deal with the coming crisis in Cuba.

The Morning Briefings

At 6 A.M. on October 16, after a few hours at his home, Art Lundahl arrived at NPIC to pick up his briefing boards. Accompanied by a courier to carry the boards, Lundahl headed off on what would be one of the longest days of his life. The first briefings began in Ray Cline's office at CIA headquarters, then at 2430 E Street in Northwest Washington.[8] At approximately 7:30 A.M., Lundahl began his briefing for senior CIA officials. Thirty minutes later Cline, Lundahl, and the courier were on their way to the White House. After showing the photos to McGeorge Bundy, they waited while the national security advisor called the president to inform him that Soviet ballistic missiles had been sighted in Cuba.[9]

By 9 A.M., Lundahl was briefing Robert Kennedy on the missiles. The attorney general was deeply upset over the Soviets' deceit, especially in light of his recent back-channel conversation with Ambassador Anatoly Dobrynin and military intelligence Colonel Georgi Bolshakov. Despite the obvious danger shown in Lundahl's briefing photos, Kennedy still found a small bit of humor when he asked, "Will those goddamn things reach Oxford, Mississippi?" The attorney general was referring to the recent problems with racial segregation at the University of Mississippi, where he was attempting to get a young black student named James Meredith enrolled. Later in the crisis, Lundahl had his graphic artists add Oxford as a major city, along with Washington and New York, to the maps on the briefing boards.

Lundahl spent the next couple of hours briefing Secretary of the Treasury Douglas Dillon; Lieutenant General Marshall Carter, the Deputy Director of Central Intelligence; and Sydney Graybeal, the CIA's top ballistic missile analyst. Bundy was working to clear President Kennedy's calendar for a meeting of the president's top advisors while still

The ExComm—Executive Committee—meeting in the White House. President Kennedy sought the opinions and ideas of his closest advisors, but the ultimate decisions during the crisis were his alone to make.

keeping the appearance of a normal day at the White House. Deciding that Carter should represent the CIA at the meeting with the president, now scheduled for noon, Cline headed back to coordinate the increasing activities at CIA headquarters.

Already, Majors Heyser and Anderson of the 4080th SRW had flown two additional U-2 missions over Cuba (3102 and 3103), and film was being processed for analysis and interpretation at NPIC and SAC. The pilots had surveyed the entire island, and the resulting photos would require a major effort from the entire NPIC staff to be ready for presentations the following day. This process would become the routine for the next few months as the CIA attempted to keep up with the growing flow of intelligence from the Caribbean.

ExComm: The Players

By 11:45 A.M., the group invited to meet with the president was beginning to gather in the White House. When the men entered the Cabinet Room, they found the president playing with his five-year-old daughter, Caroline. Kennedy sent her back to the residence, and the meeting began at 11:50. The "Group," as they were initially known, would eventually be flagged as the "Executive Committee of the National Security Council," or ExComm.[10] While the actual size and makeup of ExComm would vary from day to day during the crisis, the working style and the dynamic in the Cabinet Room, where they usually met, did not. In fact, ExComm was a distilled version of how President Kennedy had staffed and run his administration since his arrival in Washington a year and a half earlier. ExComm also reflected Kennedy's personal style of leadership and management. Unlike President Truman, who preferred to make decisions on his own, or President Eisenhower's "board of directors" method of policy making, Kennedy preferred a more detached form of personal counsel.

In most matters involving important decisions, the young president liked to surround himself with a small group of intelligent and engaged people who, in his opinion, could offer the best range of ideas and concepts from which he could choose. That these individuals might not reflect his own preferences or ideals was of little consequence, and Kennedy actually seemed to have preferred a bit of tension between the participants. Tension was actually quite easy to achieve within ExComm because some members genuinely disliked others in the group. Despite popular notions that the Kennedy administration was some sort of modern-day political "Camelot" or band of brothers, it was anything but.

Kennedy's narrow margin of victory over Richard M. Nixon for the presidency in 1960 had taken every deal, promise, and pledge of patronage that his family's political machine and its money could make. As a result, his cabinet and administration had been built of an odd coalition of people, from the cold and mercurial Robert S. McNamara as Secretary of Defense to the pacifist Theodore Sorensen as his personal speechwriter. Now the key leaders in his diplomatic, national security, military, and intelligence agencies would be asked to put forth their personal opinions and ideas and form them into a single, unified policy response to Operation Anadyr.

The man who had called the first ExComm meeting, National Security Advisor McGeorge Bundy, had previously served as the dean of Arts and Sciences at Harvard University. Bright and forceful, Bundy had been the architect of the Kennedy administration's policies on the Soviet Union and Cuba. Robert McNamara had been the president of the Ford Motor Company prior to becoming Secretary of Defense. He was one of the few high-ranking American corporate executives to back John F. Kennedy in 1960. Detached and unemotional to the point of being cold, McNamara believed in systems analysis, centralized command, and absolute conformity to established norms. Undersecretary of Defense Roswell Gilpatrick, on the other hand, was a Wall Street lawyer, and Assistant Secretary of Defense Paul H. Nitze was one of the principal designers of the American strategy for containing communism.[11]

ExComm also included participants from the Department of State, headed by Secretary Dean Rusk. A native of Georgia and a Rhodes scholar, Rusk had held a number of State Department positions in the Truman administration. Under Secretary of State George Ball who, like Nitze, had been on the U.S. Strategic Bombing Survey following World War II, had practiced international law. Three regional specialists also joined Rusk:

President Kennedy's two senior cabinet advisors were Secretary of Defense Robert S. McNamara (left) and Secretary of State Dean Rusk. The president had complete confidence in these men.

Assistant Secretary for Latin American Affairs Edwin Martin, Deputy Under Secretary for Political-Military Affairs U. Alexis Johnson, and former U.S. ambassador to the Soviet Union Llewellyn (Tommy) Thompson, one of the few American diplomats who personally knew the Kremlin leaders.

Along with these obvious participants, a number of other Kennedy administration officials joined the October 16 ExComm meeting: Secretary of the Treasury C. Douglas Dillon was a sharp-minded Republican who had served as ambassador to France in the Eisenhower administration; the new Chairman of the Joint Chiefs of Staff, General Maxwell Taylor, was another personal favorite of President Kennedy; perhaps the oddest ExComm participant was Theodore (Ted) Sorensen, Kennedy's chief speechwriter and a conscientious objector to military service in World War II; and also present, though almost irrelevant to the proceedings of the missile crisis, was Vice President Lyndon B. Johnson, who was an ExComm participant more out of constitutional need than out of Kennedy's desire for his opinion.

By late 1962, Robert F. (Bobby) Kennedy had become his brother's most trusted and influential advisor. The keeper of the Kennedy family flame—following his father's, Ambassador Joseph Kennedy's, stroke—Bobby Kennedy was not only the attorney general, he was the de facto "prime minister" of the United States. Cool and thoughtful in his daily routine, but ruthless and brilliant when necessary, Bobby Kennedy was his brother's keeper and soul mate.

The center of attention for all these impressive men was President John F. Kennedy. The second-youngest man to ever serve as president—he had been one year older than Theodore Roosevelt, when "Teddy" entered the White House—Kennedy remains one of the most complex men to rise to the post of chief executive and perhaps one of the most enigmatic. Physically brave and mentally tough, Kennedy was reckless in his personal and political life. A man of diverse personal contrasts, Kennedy was a legendary womanizer who apparently adored his family. He cultivated many friendships with people from the docks of Boston to the top of the entertainment world. A natural scholar, a public speaker, and an author, Kennedy lacked something of an intellectual focus for is work and never kept meaningful personal notes or diaries. Ironically, he liked to doodle as he read and digested the many staff memos and policy papers that crossed his desk, often leaving the only real record of his thoughts in the badly proportioned cartoons and comments in the margins.

Kennedy was also seriously ill, having suffered from a variety of illnesses from gastric colitis to Addison's disease for much of his life. Sickly as a child, Kennedy spent most of his adult life in serious pain. Despite back surgery in the 1950s, Kennedy required regular medication and steroid treatments, details that were kept secret from the public until well after his death. In fact, despite the fabricated image of President Kennedy's youthful vigor and health, he was probably in worse overall health when taking office in 1961 than the wheelchair-bound Franklin D. Roosevelt when FDR was first inaugurated in 1933.

The late summer and fall of 1962 found President Kennedy in the best and the worst health of his presidency. On the plus side, his battery of illnesses was in remission, being controlled by a daily regime of drugs and other treatments. This was a vast improvement from just fifteen months earlier, when he had badly thrown out his back while in Canada, just prior to the Vienna summit with Khrushchev. That had perhaps been the low-water mark of his presidency, with his having been forced to sit upright for many hours over two days and being browbeaten by the Soviet leader. Kennedy had returned to the White House barely able to stand. It took weeks for the young president to be able to work sitting up, and Kennedy spent much of the rest of 1961 in severe pain.[12]

The president's health was being maintained only through an intense daily infusion of drugs and other medical treatments. Along with daily doses of anti-spasmodics to control colitis and antibiotics for a long-term urinary tract infection (probably chlamydia), there was a cocktail of hydrocortisone, testosterone, and salt tablets for his Addison's disease. Some days there might be antihistamines to deal with food allergies or point injections of anti-spasmodics and painkillers into his back.[13] There were also occasional injections by the well-known celebrity physician Dr. Max "Feelgood" Jacobson, of a mysterious mix of vitamins, amphetamines, and other drugs to increase the energy levels of patients.[14] At no time during the crisis was President Kennedy not in pain or not being medicated to deal with the discomfort.

The result of this multifaceted personality was a president who could share his daughter's pony with an astronaut's family in the morning and discuss nuclear conflict in the afternoon. President Kennedy could also be a man with a temper, although the events of the next few weeks would show him to be in total control of his emotions. In fact, more than one biographer has concluded that one positive effect of all of his medical problems was to give John F. Kennedy an iron will, along with an endurance for stress and physical fatigue that would serve him and the United States well in the difficult days ahead.[15] In fact, when other senior American and Soviet leaders were at the end of their emotional wits and physical endurance, the brothers Kennedy would still be sharp.

Other men would join and support ExComm meetings over the next few weeks. In addition to the daily briefing personnel from the CIA, military service chiefs, diplomats, and others would add their expertise to the Cabinet Room dialogue. All would do great service for their country and for the world as the Kennedy administration tried to find a way back from the brink.

October 16: The First Meetings

As soon as Caroline Kennedy had left and the Cabinet Room doors were locked, Art Lundahl set up his briefing boards for the final time on October 16. As he did so, President Kennedy pressed a concealed button to start an audio recording system. While other presidents had occasionally recorded White House conversations, Kennedy was the first to systematically do so. In the summer of 1962, he had ordered wiretaps on his personal phones, as well as microphones in the Oval Office and the Cabinet Room. While Kennedy's exact reasons for taping the meetings and the calls remain a mystery, one possibility is that following his presidency, he may have planned to use the tapes to help write his memoirs. This is supported by the fact that Kennedy had poor handwriting; he rarely took notes or wrote letters that might later jog his memory. Whatever the reasons, most of the ExComm meetings were recorded, and today those tapes provide a tantalizing window on what happened in the White House that October.[16]

Following an introduction from General Carter, Art Lundahl wearily explained what Mission 3101 had found the previous Sunday. Along with General Carter and Graybeal, Lundahl tried to describe to ExComm what was in the photos. Many of the questions came directly from President Kennedy, who was trying to understand exactly the numbers and the readiness of the Soviet ballistic missiles in Cuba. In particular, the status of the analysis of the Mission 3101 (October 14) film was clarified, as well as how long it would be until the films from the two October 15 missions could be analyzed. Ensuing conversations were almost surreal, as the ExComm participants calmly and coolly gave their opinions, expressed thoughts, and put out ideas for consideration.

The initial unreality of the meeting may have been based upon the revelation that the Soviet Union had decided to break out of the established norms of international behavior. The fact that Soviet representatives had openly lied about not placing offensive weapons in Cuba only made the shock more intense. There was also the question of the purpose of the SS-4 missile deployment. While NPIC was still assessing the actual number of missiles in Cuba, the targets that the SS-4s could hit gave politicians and warriors grave concern. Within the range arc of the SS-4s were many of the important bases for U.S. bombers and ground forces, as well as the government, including Washington, D.C. To many of the men looking at Lundahl's briefing boards that morning, the missile deployment looked like the opening moves of a preemptive strike—a nuclear Pearl Harbor but against the U.S. capital, not against an overseas military base as had occurred on December 7, 1941.

The discussions then began with General Taylor and Secretary McNamara giving their analysis of the military situation and clarifying for everyone in the room exactly what kinds of missiles were being discussed. Next, Secretary Rusk launched into a long oration about the nature of the international situation and possible response options. McNamara followed Rusk's comments to open the discussion of whether air strikes on the missile sites would be advisable. The group had a wide-ranging discussion that covered everything from the status of the U.S. Jupiter missiles in Turkey and the position of NATO to whether air strikes could take out all of the Soviet missiles without the need for a follow-up invasion.[17]

The meeting ended with plans to convene a further gathering that evening to discuss military options for destroying the missiles in Cuba and to authorize additional reconnaissance of Cuba. There was also an agreement for the participants to keep a low profile and to use different entrances to reduce the chance that the press would pick up signs of an emerging crisis. With that, the first meeting of ExComm came to an end.

Perhaps the most important outcome of the meeting was an agreement not to rule out *any* possible solution for resolving the crisis, including political and diplomatic. While the ExComm participants were clearly upset by the Soviet missile deployment to Cuba, they did not lose their tempers nor did they appear rattled.[18]

During the afternoon break, Robert Kennedy held a meeting of the Special Group—Augmented in his Justice Department office to discuss events in Cuba. At the Pentagon, CIA briefers were finishing their presentations, and the Joint Chiefs were advising Admiral Robert Dennison, the Commander-in-Chief Atlantic Command, on developments and possible courses of action.[19]

By 6:30 P.M., the ExComm members had reconvened in the White House, and General Carter presented additional details on the Soviet missiles. Secretary of State Rusk and Edwin Martin then weighed in on possible diplomatic options, though the discussion rapidly turned back to the question of military action. For the first time in the crisis, Secretary McNamara introduced the idea of a blockade of Cuba as an intermediate step to force the Soviets to the bargaining table. Although it was only a brief remark, the idea would soon begin to develop support from other ExComm members. McNamara also began to lay out the broad strokes of an air campaign designed to destroy the Soviet missiles.

In the middle of it all, Bundy gave John McCone, the Director of Central Intelligence, who was in California burying his son-in-law, the ultimate credit for having predicted that the Soviets would send ballistic missiles to Cuba.[20] With a bit of grudging respect, the rest of the ExComm members paid the absent McCone his due, then continued on with their discussions. As the meeting drew to a close, President Kennedy left, apparently favoring the air strike option over the other ideas presented. His exit allowed the remaining ExComm participants to discuss their ideas and vent opinions more freely. When the meeting finally broke up, various smaller meetings continued until 11 P.M. As October 16 drew to a close, most of the weary ExComm members finally headed home. Secretary McNamara, however, chose to sleep on his Pentagon office couch.

October 17: The Picture Focuses

ExComm got started early on October 17, meeting at 8:30 A.M., without the president, to consider the U.S. response to Operation Anadyr. Overnight, the intelligence picture had firmed up considerably, and John McCone, who had flown home the night before, presented the findings. NPIC had now positively identified a total of five ballistic missile sites and twenty-three SA-2 SAM sites and was looking for more in the films from the two missions flown on October 15. Six more U-2 missions were scheduled to be flown over Cuba on the 17th, with the results due two days later, on Friday, October 19. Immediately after the intelligence briefing, Taylor, McCone, Thompson, and Ball all stated their opposition to an air strike response to Anadyr and began to build a consensus toward something other than a direct military response.[21]

The meeting was a short one, and by 9:30 A.M., McCone was giving President Kennedy his morning intelligence briefing. It was during this briefing that Kennedy asked McCone to go to President Eisenhower's home at Gettysburg to update the former president on the Cuban situation. Despite their political differences, Kennedy had great respect and admiration for Eisenhower and would take counsel from the elder statesman during the crisis. Kennedy also received his first input from United Nations Ambassador Adlai Stevenson, who had also been briefed on the Soviet missiles in Cuba. In a note to Kennedy, Stevenson expressed his concerns that an attack against Cuba might likely lead to Soviet moves against Turkey or Berlin, and that the ultimate solution to the growing crisis would inevitably involve diplomacy and negotiation.

His morning's work done, President Kennedy left to keep another busy day's schedule of appointments and campaign appearances. Everyone on ExComm had agreed that it was best if the president kept his planned schedule to keep the press and the Soviets from deducing what the American government knew. Time was both a friend and an enemy for American leaders as they continued to try and figure out just what action to take against the Soviet Union. At the Pentagon, the Joint Chiefs of Staff were putting the finishing touches on listing targets in the first draft of an air strike plan—a set of target options—designed to destroy the Anadyr force in Cuba.[22]

The Joint Chiefs viewed the idea of a blockade only as a complement to air strikes. Part of the reason for this view was that, traditionally, international law categorized naval and air blockades as overt acts of war, something with a particular meaning for the military.

Most of the ExComm group met again on the afternoon of October 17, again without the president, who was now campaigning in Connecticut. The air strike-versus-blockade factions again argued their cases, this time with the added influence of former Secretary of State Dean Acheson. A forceful anti-communist, Acheson was in favor of immediate air strikes, and many at the meeting rallied around his views. The discussions continued well into the evening and resulted in five basic options being developed:

1. An ultimatum to Khrushchev, followed by an air strike
2. Limited air strikes without prior warning or negotiation
3. Political warning, followed by a naval blockade, with notification to key allies
4. Large-scale air strikes after limited political preparation
5. Proceed directly to an invasion, as laid out in OPLANs 314 and 316

Members of ExComm proceeded to write briefing papers overnight to present at the next meeting with President Kennedy, scheduled for late morning the following day. In general, the members from the intelligence and the defense agencies were in favor of immediate military action, while those from the State Department favored the blockade-and-negotiation route.

October 18: The Big Lie

Thursday, October 18, became the formative day for American policy during the Cuban Missile Crisis. News arrived from NPIC that the analysts had found something new and disturbing on the film from the two U-2 missions on October 15. When the group, including President Kennedy, met at 11 A.M., Art Lundahl showed them briefing boards with the first indications of equipment for SS-5 Intermediate-Range Ballistic Missiles (IRBMs). This meant that along with the SS-4 MRBMs, which could strike at the southeastern United States, the Soviets intended to install IRBMs, believed by U.S. experts to have the range to attack every city in the contiguous forty-eight states except Seattle. ExComm members were understandably upset. Suddenly, the Anadyr deployment looked like an attempt to gain a decisive edge over American strategic superiority by making a disarming first strike possible from Cuba.[23]

The meeting continued where the previous evening's gathering had left off, the discussion centering on American options to get the missiles out of Cuba. Again, Secretary Rusk launched into a long monologue on the dangers of leaving the Soviet missiles in place. Secretary McNamara, who had been leaning toward the air strike options the previous evening, began to make a case *against* air strikes as the number of apparent Soviet missiles increased, according to the U-2s and NPIC's efforts. There were also further conversations on the merits and liabilities of McNamara's blockade option. Concerns about the need to notify Khrushchev and Castro were presented, although the ExComm members generated no real consensus.[24] Also during the meeting came the first real discussion of a possible "swap" of the Soviet missiles in Cuba for the American Jupiters being installed in Turkey.

With the ExComm discussions seemingly going nowhere, President Kennedy is heard on the tape to say, "Is there anyone here who doesn't think that we ought to not do something about this?" The comment seemed to focus the ExComm members' attention, and slowly the discussion began to center on the merits of the blockade option. By that time, Robert Kennedy had joined the ranks of those who saw merit in the blockade idea, partly for the maneuvering room it would give both sides without going straight into a combat scenario. Once again, President Kennedy left to attend to other matters, and McNamara joined the discussion in support of a blockade, which he had been first to propose. By the time the meeting broke up a few minutes later, there was the beginning of a solid base of support for a blockade to show American resolve to the Soviets, while preserving options for both sides in the crisis.

Meanwhile, President Kennedy began to prepare for one of the more interesting confrontations of the missile crisis: a long-planned meeting with Soviet Foreign Minister Andrei Gromyko. There was nothing sinister about the meeting: it was one of a series of such encounters intended to help improve dialogue between the superpowers. Now the president planned to spring a possible trap on the Soviet foreign minister by having a set of the U-2 photographs on hand to show Gromyko in the event that he could be maneuvered into telling an overt lie to Kennedy's face.

The opportunity did not arise. When the meeting began at 5 P.M., Gromyko launched into a diatribe about American actions overseas, from Berlin to Cuba, leaving little room for direct questioning by Kennedy. Gromyko was a shrewd character, and he gave no indication that he knew about the missile deployment to Cuba during the discussion—unlike Ambassador Dobrynin, who had accompanied him to the meeting and had no knowledge of Anadyr. Even when President Kennedy asked him directly whether the Soviet Union understood what the American

President Kennedy met with Soviet Ambassador Anatoly Dobrynin (left) and Foreign Minister Andrei Gromyko at the White House on October 18. The meeting led the Soviets to believe that something was amiss with their Anadyr operation.

reaction would be if "offensive" weapons were found being shipped to or already installed in Cuba, Gromyko played dumb. Unsure of whether the Soviet foreign minister was ignorant or lying, Kennedy kept his photos hidden and allowed Gromyko to exit without Kennedy's learning anything of value from the meeting.[25]

Late that evening, the president dictated a memo on the day and conferred with his brother Robert, Bundy, Rusk, Thompson, and several other advisors. It was now clear to Kennedy that the Soviet Union was planning a fait accompli in Cuba and that not all elements of the Soviet government were being informed of the action. Although he wanted a solid consensus within ExComm, President Kennedy appears to have made up his mind on the blockade option sometime after his meeting with Gromyko. The problem was that forging agreement within the various factions of the ExComm membership was going to be difficult, and Kennedy had another set of campaign appearances scheduled for the weekend. On his brother's advice, Kennedy decided to make the political trip and to allow the other ExComm members to hammer out the policy option he desired. In his memo, he noted that he planned to announce the blockade on Sunday, October 21, after he returned from Chicago.[26]

8

Consensus and Notification

President Kennedy rather summed up the dilemma stating that action of a type contemplated would be opposed by the alliance—on the other hand, lack of action will create disunity, lack of confidence and disintegration of our several alliance and friendly relations with countries who have confidence in us.

Director of Central Intelligence John McCone,
memorandum for file regarding ExComm meeting
of October 18, 1962[1]

While President Kennedy may have made up his mind on the evening of October 18 about which course of action to take, the same cannot be said for everyone on ExComm. For that matter, within the relatively small group of Americans aware of the Soviet offensive missile deployment to Cuba, it is doubtful whether those favoring the blockade option were in the majority. Consensus would come only with several more days of debate, arm-twisting, and compromise within ExComm, the Kennedy administration, and the U.S. military. In addition, Kennedy and his advisors felt that any action against the Soviets in Cuba would require the notification, agreement, and involvement of allies and other regional powers. All would have to be sold on the idea that Operation Anadyr was a real and present danger to their national security and interests.

This wide-ranging program of consensus building and notification took almost a week to complete and was accomplished against the backdrop of the emerging military confrontation in the Caribbean. However, to U.S. leaders, the battle to win the hearts and minds of politicians, military leaders, and ordinary people around the globe was just as important a campaign as any being considered in the halls of the Pentagon or the Soviet Defense Ministry.

New Photos and Analysis: Friday, October 19

The four days following Airman Davis's discovery of the Soviet missiles on the U-2's tracker camera film from Mission 3101 had been fruitful for American intelligence analysts. Their progress in further understanding the Soviet deployment showed in the stream of reports and memos that arrived on the desks of U.S. policymakers throughout the day. Most important was an innocuous looking report called *Joint Evaluation of the Soviet Missile Threat in Cuba*, which was based on photography from the nine U-2 missions of October 14, 15, and 16. The Guided Missile and Aeronautics Intelligence Committee, the Joint Atomic Energy Intelligence Committee, and the National Photographic Interpretation Center collectively issued a new edition each day at about 4 P.M. (Eastern time), and the report became the most reliable evaluation of ground truth with regard to the Soviet missiles on Cuba.[2] Each edition listed the current state of construction and readiness of the Soviet coastal defense missiles, ballistic missiles, nuclear warhead storage sites, and SAM sites, along with a short overall summary.

Another vital document for Kennedy administration leaders that was published on a continuing basis during the crisis was Special National Intelligence Estimate (SNIE) 11-18-62, titled *Soviet Reactions to Certain U.S. Courses of Action on Cuba*. Produced by Sherman Kent's Board of Estimates at the CIA, this report provided a daily interpretation of various U.S. military, political, and diplomatic options and the probable USSR reactions to each. *Soviet Reactions to Certain U.S. Courses of Action on Cuba* was an "all source" document, meaning that it drew from every credible source (NPIC, NSA, State Department, etc.) to reach its conclusions.[3] Generally, the Board of Estimates did a good job on these "instant" analysis reports, and the information was thought-provoking.

Thus far, the U.S. intelligence agencies had done a good job of tracking the Anadyr deployment, although they were beginning to miss important details in the "noise" of the overall Soviet buildup on Cuba. For example, the total number of Soviet troops and technicians was consistently being underestimated. Both documents issued on October 19 had items of key importance that appear to have gone unnoticed by senior administration leaders. SNIE 11-18-62 brought up the question of possible Soviet reactions to U.S. attacks on their Red Army personnel in Cuba. Paragraph 11 raised the point: "On the other hand, the Soviets have no public treaty with Cuba, and have not acknowledged that Soviet bases are on the island. This situation provides them with a pretext for treating

US military action against Cuba as an affair that does not directly involve them, and thereby avoiding the risks of a strong response."

The only problem with this assessment was that Cuba and the Soviet Union *did* in fact have a secret agreement regarding Soviet bases on the island.[4] Thus, SNIE 11-18-62 was wrong, and the suggestion that attacks on Cuba-based Soviet units would not provoke a greater strategic response by the Soviet Union was also probably wrong.

Another tantalizing tidbit that most readers probably didn't notice was in the daily edition of the *Joint Evaluation of the Soviet Missile Threat in Cuba*, which noted, "Tactical Missiles . . . There are several refugee reports indicating the presence of tactical (FROG) missiles in Cuba, although there is no photographic confirmation thus far."

This was the first suggestion by the CIA that battlefield weapons with nuclear warheads *might* be part of the Soviet deployment to Cuba. There were, however, several shortcomings to the notice. The first, and most obvious, was that the report had not been confirmed by U-2 imagery. The second and perhaps most important omission was that the October 19 edition of *Soviet Reactions to Certain U.S. Courses of Action on Cuba* gave no indication of the possibility that tactical nuclear (battlefield) weapons might be part of Anadyr. Unless the reader knew that the FROG (Soviet Luna) missile was capable of carrying a tactical nuclear warhead, he would not necessarily make the connection.

This was not the first time since the beginning of the Soviet deployment to Cuba that the CIA had focused its attentions too closely on the SS-4 and the SS-5 strategic missiles and ignored the possibility that other nuclear weapons were being brought to the island. It appears that the October 19 notice of the FROG launchers and support equipment was the *only* detection of possible Soviet battlefield nuclear weapons during the entire crisis. That the use of smaller nuclear weapons might provide a pathway for escalation to a wider nuclear exchange was simply not considered. With the Cuban Missile Crisis now in full swing, the participants were developing a sort of group "tunnel vision," focusing only on the most obvious threats, not on those that might actually be the least controllable or potentially most dangerous.

Nevertheless, beginning with the U-2 film from Mission 3101 on October 14, NPIC analysts were able to progressively track the progress of the Soviets' ballistic missile site construction using a technique known as "comparative coverage." By looking at photography of the same area over time, intelligence such as unit readiness and effectiveness could be assessed with surprising accuracy. For example, the appearance of the first of the SS-4 ballistic missile sites on the Mission 3101 film was

On October 25, 1962, an F8U-1P Crusader on a low-level mission caught a rare view of an exposed FROG missile launcher, shown in the boxed area of the above photo. The FROG launcher shown below is depicted at roughly the same angle. (upper USN; lower DIA)

The famous latrine photo taken by a low-flying U.S. reconnaissance aircraft. It shows a "three-holer," with one hole occupied and one hole empty. The photo was used to illustrate a point during a briefing to President Kennedy.

noticed quickly because the earlier U-2 missions in August and September had seen only open farmland in the area where the missiles were being emplaced. The limitation of this system was that the initial readout of film from a particular mission took a full day, followed by another to get the intelligence briefed to ExComm and other key decision makers in the U.S. government.

The lack of experience in dealing with overhead photography and other intelligence products by Kennedy administration personnel did have an occasional humorous side during the crisis. Despite the personal tutoring of Art Lundahl, there were some technical terms and concepts that President Kennedy just could not seem to grasp. One of these was the use of the word *occupied*, indicating that a particular site or facility was staffed, equipped, and operational. One day during the crisis, a set of photos from a low-level F8U-1P mission came in showing one of the Soviet motorized rifle regiment's encampments. One particular shot showed a three-hole, open-air latrine with a single occupant probably trying to pull up his pants to react to the fast-moving aircraft directly overhead. Realizing the opportunity to teach a lesson and perhaps add some levity to the ExComm meetings, Lundahl had NPIC staff make up a briefing board showing the latrine as a "new three-position military site in Cuba." When the briefing board was produced, the president broke into a broad smile and was heard to say, "Why didn't I have this earlier? Now I understand the occupied/unoccupied problem perfectly!"[5]

Meeting with the Chiefs: Friday, October 19

October 19 had been planned as the beginning of a three-day political campaign swing through the Midwest by President Kennedy and was to start in Ohio that afternoon. Before the president left Washington, he had the first and only meeting of the crisis with the Joint Chiefs of Staff—the senior U.S. military officers. Earlier that morning General Taylor and the four service chiefs had met at the Pentagon, where NPIC personnel had briefed them on the latest photographs taken by the six U-2 flights flown on October 16 (Missions 3104, 3105, 3106, 3107, 3108, and 3109). These missions had covered the entire island, and the "take" from this single day would keep NPIC and SAC photo analysts busy for days. The 4080th Strategic Reconnaissance Wing at McCoy Air Force Base would fly an average of two U-2 missions a day for the next few days.

The news from NPIC that morning confirmed what had been reported at the ExComm meeting the previous day: the Soviets were also installing two regiments of SS-5 Skean (R-14) intermediate-range ballistic missiles in Cuba.[6] Credited by U.S. intelligence with a range of 2,200 miles, the SS-5 would be able to strike targets anywhere in the continental United States except in the extreme Pacific Northwest, around Seattle, Washington.[7,8] Unlike President Eisenhower, who had enjoyed generally good relations with his senior military officers, John Kennedy often seemed to be publicly at odds with the Joint Chiefs of Staff (JCS). Starting with the Bay of Pigs, when Kennedy had refused to provide U.S. air cover or naval support, there were stories that senior military professionals had suspected that the president was somehow "soft" when it came to making tough decisions. The reality was somewhat different. Like much of the public story of the Kennedy years, the supposed friction between the president and the U.S. military leadership was part truth and part myth.

Kennedy entered the presidency with only limited firsthand military experience and almost none in dealing with senior officers. Having lied about his health to get a reserve officer's commission in 1941, Kennedy spent his early days in a minor intelligence assignment.[9] Knowing it was a backwater job, Kennedy soon sought and found greater fulfillment and adventure in motor torpedo boats. Neither assignment provided him contact with senior officers and probably did much to set his views—or lack of them—on the qualities of the military leaders serving him when he became president.[10]

There is also some merit to the argument that the service chiefs were not always happy with, or trusting of, President Kennedy. Part of this situation clearly came from President Kennedy having commanded just a handful of men on a tiny PT boat, while the Joint Chiefs were some of the most skilled and revered commanders of World War II and the Korean War. Some of the service chiefs had commanded thousands of men in combat. Kennedy's relative youth, wealth, and intellectual background certainly reinforced their impression of the president as lacking the professionalism of his three predecessors.

In addition, there had been a great deal of displeasure over the president's decision to use federalized National Guard troops to enforce the admission of James Meredith at the segregated University of Mississippi. Kennedy had considered the military unresponsive to his orders, telling an aide after the Meredith affair, "They always give you their bullshit about their instant reaction and their split-second timing, but it never works out. No wonder it's so hard to win a war."[11]

Such private outbursts formed the core of the mythology about President Kennedy's relationship with his military chiefs following his assassination in 1963.[12] That such animosity has been depicted in a number of feature, television, and documentary films has only reinforced the myth. In fact, during the crisis, relations between the president and his military chiefs were generally professional and straightforward.

This is not to say that there were not moments of great tension and even anger between the civilian members of Kennedy's administration and his military commanders. But at no time did *any* military leader in the U.S. chain of command commit a rogue act or violate the rules of engagement set down by the civilian leadership. Even the most outspoken of U.S. military leaders like Air Force Generals LeMay and Power "stayed in their lanes," always acting within their standing orders and mandated responsibilities.[13]

Most likely, the tension and distrust between President Kennedy and his senior military leaders came more from their different upbringings and life experiences than from any disrespect toward each other as men. John Kennedy came to the White House from a world of privilege, glamour, and power. His top military leaders were all combat veterans of World War II, some having known the deprivation of the Great Depression prior to joining the military. With the exception of Maxwell Taylor, none would have been chosen by the president as a friend or an intimate. They were just too different from the president and his inner circle to ever have been comfortable around the West Wing of the Kennedy White House.

It was with this mutual disrespect that the Joint Chiefs prepared for their meeting with President Kennedy that Friday morning. The chairman of the Joint Chiefs of Staff—the senior U.S. military officer—was General Maxwell D. Taylor. He had been sworn in as chairman on October 1,

1962. Taylor had commanded the vaunted 82nd Airborne Division in 1943 and then the 101st Airborne Division, which he had led on a night jump into Normandy hours before the Allied D-Day invasion. Earlier in the war, General Eisenhower had sent Taylor on a secret mission into German-occupied Rome, causing Eisenhower to later write that the risks run by Taylor "were greater than I asked any other agent or emissary to undertake during the war—he carried weighty responsibilities and discharged them with unerring judgment and every minute was in imminent danger of discovery and death."[14]

Taylor retired after serving as Chief of Staff of the Army from 1955 to 1959. But after reading Taylor's controversial book *The Uncertain Trumpet*, President Kennedy had appointed him a White House aide and, subsequently, Chairman of the Joint Chiefs of Staff. Because of Taylor's perceived close ties to Kennedy and his having been recalled to active duty to serve as chairman, some senior officers felt restrained from being completely candid in his presence.

In addition to the chairman, there were four other four-star officers on the Joint Chiefs of Staff, representing their respective services.[15] General Earle Wheeler, the Army Chief of Staff, had a reputation as a brilliant staff officer and a Washington planner. Admiral George W. Anderson, the Chief of Naval Operations, was called "Straight Arrow" for his clean living and good looks. Widely admired in the fleet as "a sailor's sailor," Anderson had succeeded the incomparable Admiral Arliegh A. Burke after that man had criticized the administration's handling of the Bay of Pigs invasion.[16] Legendary Air Force Chief of Staff General Curtis LeMay was the best known, but also the most controversial, member of the group. His leadership and personal charisma had taken SAC from being a token force to the most powerful weapon of mass destruction in history. He was respected, feared, and despised—frequently all at the same time.[17] General David Shoup received the Medal of Honor for heroism in the bloody landing at Tarawa in 1943 but was known to be a bit uninformed and erratic in the world of 1962 Washington politics.[18] He could sit with the JCS when issues of concern to the Marine Corps were under discussion, but he was not a full member.

The five officers discussed the idea of a blockade in response to the Soviet move into Cuba, an action that the entire group opposed. They agreed to advise the president that a massive air strike was a superior option and that there should be no advance warning. While the service chiefs disagreed on the desirability of an invasion of Cuba following the air strikes, all felt a need for a more decisive action than simply stopping the further shipment of offensive weapons to Cuba. Their Pentagon meeting completed, the five men rode over to the White House for a 9:45 A.M. conference with the president and Secretary of Defense McNamara.

The gathering in the Cabinet Room was tense but respectful, as each military leader was given a chance to state his opinion and then discuss his concerns over the blockade option. General Taylor said little during the forty-five-minute meeting, allowing the service chiefs to reveal their personalities and inclinations to the president.

President Kennedy led the discussion, making clear his concern about possible Soviet retaliation against Berlin and NATO in the event of an American attack on Cuba. In turn, each officer expressed his concern about the shortcomings of a blockade and the necessity for greater force and action on the part of the U.S. government toward Cuba. Ironically, it was General LeMay who broke the serious tone of the discussion when he said, "You're in a pretty serious fix, Mister President."[19] Kennedy's reply of, "You're in it with me . . . personally," was followed by a light chuckle from the group. From that point, the discussion centered on just what form the blockade might take and how it might be implemented. In particular, Kennedy emphasized that the blockade was only a first action, which still allowed for the air strikes and an invasion, if needed.

The issue of defending and using the Guantánamo Bay naval facility was being discussed when the president had to leave the meeting to board a helicopter to catch Air Force One at Andrews Air Force Base for his flight to Ohio. Whether intentional or not, Kennedy left the Cabinet Room taping system on to record the voices of the Joint Chiefs, who were anything but pleased with the results of the meeting. General Shoup, in particular, became notably animated, telling LeMay, "You're screwed, screwed, screwed."

Clearly, the Joint Chiefs were unhappy with the blockade plan, although it was equally clear that the service chiefs would follow their orders and do their duty. While it might not have been the consensus that the president desired, the military was on board for whatever he chose to do. Exactly what that would be was still not completely decided in Kennedy's mind. Just before he left Washington, the president ordered McGeorge Bundy to revisit the air strike option and asked his brother Robert to get a final consensus from ExComm on which policy should be carried out. Kennedy also told the attorney general to call him back to Washington as soon as the group decided, so that the response could be carried out immediately. Security was becoming difficult, and the press was beginning to sniff out the story of what was happening in Cuba.

Weekend Discussions

While John Kennedy was on the campaign trail, members of ExComm continued to thrash out the question of air strike versus blockade. Meeting initially at the State Department and later at the While House, ExComm finally began to generate the solution that President Kennedy had demanded the previous day. Despite a split in the blockade faction about specifics, a plan emerged that Dean Rusk was now calling a "quarantine." The isolation of Cuba would be a first action, while preparations for air strikes and an invasion continued. This would give the Soviets time to consider their options. The quarantine would eliminate the shock and anger of a sudden, unannounced air strike. It would also demonstrate American willingness to consider peaceful alternatives, which would help the U.S. cause in the international community. Other options to the blockade would be presented when the president returned, but everyone in ExComm now agreed that immediate action was necessary and that McNamara's "quarantine" was an option with which they could live.

The leaders of the blockade group—Robert McNamara and Robert Kennedy—realized that they finally had a viable set of policy options to present and made the call to the president on Saturday morning, October 20, asking him to return from Chicago. At the time, the president was in his room at the Blackstone Hotel, preparing for a long day of campaigning for Mayor Richard Daley's political machine, which one just did not walk away from.[20] Realizing that the break in his schedule would be the subject of national attention, the president finally told his press secretary, Pierre Salinger, to announce to the media that the president had a cold and was cutting short his campaign tour to return to the White House. The action set off a wave of speculation in the press about what actually was happening, which meant that Kennedy had to act quickly before the press and the Soviet leadership figured it out.

By midafternoon, President Kennedy had returned to the White House, where he found more reasons to quickly make up his mind. The CIA was assessing that the first SS-4 MRBMs in Cuba were operational and that the Soviets were capable of launching up to eight missiles.[21] During Kennedy's flight home, Secretary of Defense McNamara had ordered what would eventually become a worldwide alert to American military forces in preparation for whatever decision Kennedy chose to make.

The president and ExComm were back in the Cabinet Room by 2:30 P.M., laying out the various options. The first was for air strikes, the favored alternative of General Taylor and McGeorge Bundy. The second, for a blockade with an ultimatum and possibly follow-up air strikes, was presented by Robert Kennedy, Douglas Dillon, Tommy Thompson, and John McCone. Dean Rusk favored a third option, a blockade to "freeze" the crisis so that negotiations might take place. The fourth alternative, with Robert Kennedy, Robert McNamara, Adlai Stevenson, and, apparently, Theodore Sorensen supporting it, was for a blockade as an opening for negotiations leading to a summit meeting to solve the crisis.[22]

Deciding that a blockade followed by some sort of negotiation presented the best options, President Kennedy accepted that path of action. Preparations for a possible invasion would continue, publicly this time, just in case the Soviets refused to withdraw their offensive weapons from Cuba. The plan was for the president to make an address to the nation on Monday evening, October 22. As the discussion continued, UN Ambassador Stevenson openly suggested that the Jupiter missiles being installed in Turkey might be "traded" for the Soviet missiles in Cuba. While many ExComm members considered the idea an invitation for appeasement, President Kennedy admired Stevenson's courage to put forth an unpopular and pragmatic idea. Finally, when General Taylor made one final push for air strikes, Kennedy replied, "I know you and your colleagues are unhappy with the decision, but I trust you will support me in this decision." While Taylor assured the president that the Joint Chiefs of Staff would stand behind him, the chairman was less sanguine when he returned to the Pentagon. He reported to his colleagues, "This was not one of our better days." General Wheeler is said to have replied, "I never thought I'd live to see the day when I would want to go to war."[23]

While the Joint Chiefs of Staff may not have been pleased, they all had a mission to accomplish and things to do. In fact, the Kennedy administration now had just two days to prepare to announce the blockade and to find a way to explain the action to the rest of the world. The presidential speechwriter Ted Sorensen was drafting a speech for the planned Monday evening address, which was proving particularly difficult for the pacifist scribe.[24]

Before finishing the day, John Kennedy made one more decision, this time of a personal nature. Calling his wife, Jacqueline, at their weekend home in Glen Ora, Virginia, Kennedy asked her to return to Washington with their two children. Though he would later offer the first lady the option of taking shelter with John Junior and Caroline in a nearby presidential bunker, John Kennedy wanted his family close during the coming days. Over the next few days, Jackie Kennedy offered her husband every counsel and help to alleviate the stress, which became almost unbearable. And, throughout the period, President Kennedy's thoughts were never far from his wife and children as he sat at his desk or in ExComm meetings. Sometimes, following NPIC briefings, Kennedy would keep the briefing boards for further study. When they were retrieved, some were covered with blue crayon drawings, a sign that Caroline had been playing in the office while he worked. "She always used blue," recalled Dino Brugioni, the senior NPIC photo analyst and sometime ExComm briefer.[25]

Decision Point: Sunday, October 21

Although the decision for the blockade had been made, President Kennedy wanted to take one final look at the air strike alternative, perhaps as much to know what he might have to do if the quarantine failed. This time, however, the president decided to talk with someone more focused on the potential air campaign against Cuba: General Walter C. Sweeney, the commander of the Air Force's Tactical Air Command, based at Langley Air Force Base, Virginia. Robert Kennedy, Secretary McNamara, General Taylor, and John McCone joined the president and Sweeney. Significantly, General LeMay was absent from the 11:30 A.M. meeting. The others might have believed that LeMay's presence would intimidate Sweeney. They need not have worried. Sweeney was a longtime fighter pilot who had no fear of his Chief of Staff at the Pentagon.[26]

Together, General Sweeney and McNamara laid out the air campaign for the group, including how the various Soviet missile sites (ballistic, cruise, SAM) would be "taken out" using rockets, cannon fire, bombs, and napalm. Then came a moment of clarity and honesty that sealed the deal on the blockade. When asked by President Kennedy whether air strikes would be successful in destroying all of the Soviet ballistic missiles in Cuba, Sweeney replied that there was probably no way to get all of the known missiles from the air alone. In addition, there would be the problem of missiles and other equipment that were not yet discovered. Robert Kennedy weighed in on the discussion, opposing air strikes because a surprise attack on Cuba would draw comparisons to the Japanese sneak attack on Pearl Harbor. McCone agreed with the attorney general, although he emphasized the need for the air strike option to be ready and available at any moment after 7 P.M. on Monday, October 22.

Following this meeting, President Kennedy met with an old friend, the British Ambassador David Ormsby-Gore. After outlining the coming blockade and considering possible Soviet actions against Berlin, the pair discussed the probable reasons for the Soviet deployment to Cuba. Ormsby-Gore promised to forward the news privately to British Prime

President Kennedy met with General Walter C. Sweeney, the head of the Tactical Air Command, on October 21, 1962, to hear firsthand about the expected effectiveness of a tactical air strike against the ballistic missile sites in Cuba. Kennedy, who had halted plans for U.S. tactical air support of the Bay of Pigs invasion a year earlier, approved planning for massive tactical air strikes against Cuba during the missile crisis of 1962.

Minister Harold Macmillan in London.[27] The president then had several additional meetings with various ExComm members, including a private session with DCI McCone. During this period, the decision was made to use the term *quarantine* in place of *blockade*.[28] The legal meanings of *blockade* and *quarantine* were stated to be the same, but Secretary of State Rusk preferred the latter term to avoid comparison with the Soviet-imposed Berlin Blockade of 1948–1949.[29] Furthermore, they could always change it.

Before the day was over, there was one final detail to be handled: the press. The Washington press corps of 1962 was an impressive and aggressive group and by the weekend of October 20–21 had rooted out the main details of the Soviet missiles in Cuba. Despite the best efforts of the Kennedy administration and the total isolation of Press Secretary Salinger from the ExComm meetings, several reporters had learned about the missiles in Cuba. On Sunday evening, after being informed that the *New York Times* was about to publish a detailed account of the crisis, Kennedy personally called the reporter James (Scotty) Reston to ask him to hold the story until after the speech on Monday night. Reston reluctantly agreed, and President Kennedy had bought himself one more day of secrecy.

Monday, October 22: A Hard Day

Although President Kennedy had committed to the blockade option the previous Saturday, there were still a number of things to be done prior to his national address, now scheduled for 7 P.M. Eastern time on Monday, October 22 (known as "P" Hour in the White House). The first was a call to President Eisenhower at his home in Gettysburg, telling him of the action that would begin the following day. Kennedy had asked McCone to keep the former chief executive informed on the Cuba situation, and the intelligence chief had called Eisenhower by phone the previous day.

Ambassador Stevenson's proposal of possibly trading U.S. Jupiter missiles in Turkey for the Soviet missiles in Cuba had angered some ExComm members, all of whom remembered with disgust Prime Minister Neville Chamberlain's appeasement of Hitler over Czechoslovakia at Munich in 1938. Talking with White House Chief of Staff Ken O'Donnell the previous Saturday evening, Stevenson had said, "I know that most of those fellows will probably consider me a coward for the rest of my life for what I said today, but perhaps we need a coward in the room when we are talking about nuclear war."[30]

Robert Kennedy questioned Stevenson's ability to stand up to the Soviets in the United Nations during the coming days and suggested that someone "tougher" represent the United States. President Kennedy had a somewhat different opinion of the old Democratic warhorse.[31] The president knew that Stevenson's bringing up the question of a trade with the Soviets had taken a great deal of personal courage, especially in light of the aggressive proposals of many ExComm members. Nevertheless, realizing that his brother's opinion was perhaps a moderate version of what others were thinking, the president probably discounted what Stevenson had suggested but pragmatically decided to preserve the option of a trade by taking a middle line on replacing his United Nations ambassador. Early on Sunday morning, President Kennedy met with John J. McCloy, his special assistant for disarmament matters, and suggested that McCloy, a firm-minded Republican, along with some of his staff, join the American UN mission to "support" Stevenson in the coming days. McCloy agreed to clear his schedule and move up to New York. Kennedy also had one of his closest advisors, Arthur Schlesinger Jr., draft Stevenson's UN speech that would announce the blockade on Tuesday, October 23.[32]

President Kennedy then met with Dean Rusk and other State Department officials to discuss how to handle the diplomatic fallout that the speech would generate and to lay out a strategy to help turn the power of world opinion into a force to help resolve the crisis.[33] The key to this effort would be a planned resolution on the Soviet missiles by the Organization of American States (OAS), often known as the "Latin American Branch Office of the State Department." Notwithstanding this cynical nickname, the agreement of the OAS to the blockade would be key to showing the world that the nations of the Western Hemisphere wanted the USSR and its weapons out of Cuba.

There was also a late-morning meeting to plan for possible Soviet responses against Berlin in the event that the Cuban situation got out of control.[34] During this meeting, the group had its first discussions of notifying key allies and using high-profile Americans to deliver the notification. While Prime Minister Macmillan of Britain had already been informed via Ormsby-Gore, the rest of NATO and the other allies would need to be told. It was no secret that French president Charles de Gaulle would be a particular problem, as relations between France and the United States were strained.

After the Berlin discussion ended, President Kennedy returned to the White House residence, had lunch with his wife, and went down to the Oval Office to sign a most interesting document: National Security Action Memorandum No. 196. It was the Presidential Finding that ordered the official establishment of ExComm, something that had been in existence for the previous five days.[35] This done, Kennedy moved on to a meeting with ExComm at 3 P.M.

The Cabinet Room was filled to capacity as a number of other senior administration officials had been invited to the session. In effect, this was a statement to everyone present that the blockade was the official policy of the United States, and that the president expected everyone present to support that position. DCI McCone then gave a further update on the ground situation on Cuba, emphasizing the readiness of the Soviet ballistic missiles, based on the latest NPIC analysis of U-2 photography.

One final meeting would occur before the president's speech that evening, one that would take President Kennedy to the brink of his own tolerance. The meeting involved informing the congressional leadership of the crisis and the quarantine. Kennedy had telephoned the senior leaders of the House of Representatives and the Senate the previous day and had been forced to use some unusual methods to pull them back from vacations and campaigning. Hale Boggs, the House majority whip, got the message on a fishing boat in the Gulf of Mexico when a bottle with a message to call the White House was dropped to him from an airplane.[36] Kennedy made arrangements for the Air Force to fly the congressional leaders to Washington for a briefing in the Cabinet Room.

At 5:30 P.M., twenty members of Congress and Vice President Johnson filed into the Cabinet Room.[37] Cline, Lundahl, McCone, McNamara, Rusk, and Tommy Thompson were there to brief the legislators and answer questions. What followed was a stormy and uncomfortable hour for the young president and his national security staff. Some of the worst comments came not from Republicans but from the leadership of Kennedy's own party.

When Senator Richard Russell (D-Georgia) heard about the delay in action following the U-2 mission of October 14, he quipped, "Well, why didn't you start [the air strikes] when you first got these notifications of all these missiles down there? It's been over seven days." Senator J. William Fulbright (D-Arkansas) said of the quarantine, "It won't be legal—I'm not making the arguments for legal. This is self-defense."

Strangely, perhaps the calmest and most thoughtful words came from Senator Everett Dirkson (R-Illinois), who wanted to know the details of the blockade, as well as the possible follow-up operations in the event that the Soviets refused to remove the missiles. In the end, the legislators agreed to back the president, although they clearly felt that the blockade was an inadequate and tardy response. This done, John F. Kennedy prepared to make the most important speech of his presidency.

The Speech

For several days, Theodore Sorensen had been struggling to compose two separate speeches for the evening of October 22. One for the air strike option, the other for the blockade option. In the end, he wrote only the blockade speech, unable to finish a speech announcing that the country was going to war. Earlier that day, Press Secretary Salinger had finally been briefed on the events of the previous week and had promptly announced to the press "a presidential address of national importance." He had also asked for time on all three major television networks—ABC, NBC, and CBS—as well as on the major radio networks. This done, the press secretary spent the rest of the day coordinating the arrival of the television and radio equipment to be set up in the Oval Office.

Just before delivering his speech, Kennedy authorized the U.S. armed forces to go to Defense Condition Three (DEFCON-3). At 6:55 P.M. he arrived in the Oval Office to sit down, do a quick sound check, and look over the text. His secretary, Evelyn Lincoln, tried to brush his hair but was waved away as the announcer came on to start the broadcast. Although the world did not know it, the president was wearing a corset

In one of the most dramatic addresses by a U.S. president, on October 22, President Kennedy told the world about the Soviet duplicity and the threat of nuclear missiles to the United States and the world.

to help him sit up straight because he had been experiencing severe back pain for several days. With the help of two pillows to keep him pinned into the chair, Kennedy began to speak.[38]

> Good evening my fellow citizens.
>
> This Government, as promised, has maintained the closest surveillance of the Soviet Military buildup on the island of Cuba. Within the past week, unmistakable evidence has established the fact that a series of offensive missile sites is now in preparation on that imprisoned island. The purpose of these bases can be none other than to provide a nuclear strike capability against the Western Hemisphere.

While he had been less than truthful about "the closest possible surveillance," President Kennedy continued to speak on the nature of the missile threat before getting to the meat of his announcement:

> Acting, therefore, in the defense of our own security and of the entire Western Hemisphere, and under the authority entrusted to me by the Constitution as endorsed by the resolution of the Congress, I have directed that the following initial steps be taken immediately:
>
> First: To halt this offensive buildup, a strict quarantine on all offensive military equipment under shipment to Cuba is being initiated. All ships of any kind bound for Cuba from whatever nation or port will, if found to contain cargoes of offensive weapons, be turned back. This quarantine will be extended, if needed, to other types of cargo and carriers. We are not at this time, however, denying the necessities of life as the Soviets attempted to do in their Berlin blockade of 1948.

Second: I have directed the continued and increased close surveillance of Cuba and its military buildup. The foreign ministers of the OAS, in their communiqué of October 6, rejected secrecy in such matters in this hemisphere. Should these offensive military preparations continue, thus increasing the threat to the hemisphere, further action will be justified. I have directed the Armed Forces to prepare for any eventualities; and I trust that in the interest of both the Cuban people and the Soviet technicians at the sites, the hazards to all concerned in continuing this threat will be recognized.

Third: It shall be the policy of this Nation to regard any nuclear missile launched from Cuba against any nation in the Western Hemisphere as an attack by the Soviet Union on the United States, requiring a full retaliatory response upon the Soviet Union.

After telling the world that he was reinforcing the Guantánamo base, calling for a meeting of the Organization of American States to support action against Cuba, and asking for an emergency meeting of the UN Security Council, the president aimed his last major point directly at Nikita Khrushchev:

I call upon Chairman Khrushchev to halt and eliminate this clandestine, reckless and provocative threat to world peace and to stable relations between our two nations. I call upon him further to abandon this course of world domination, and to join in an historic effort to end the perilous arms race and to transform the history of man. He has an opportunity now to move the world back from the abyss of destruction—by returning to his government's own words that it had no need to station missiles outside its own territory, and withdrawing these weapons from Cuba—by refraining from any action which will widen or deepen the present crisis—and then by participating in a search for peaceful and permanent solutions.

The president concluded,

Our goal is not the victory of might, but the vindication of right—not peace at the expense of freedom, but both peace and freedom, here in this hemisphere, and, we hope, around the world. God willing, that goal will be achieved.

Thank you and good night.[39]

The speech lasted until 7:17 P.M., and when the klieg lights went dark, Kennedy was heard to say, "Well, that's it unless the son of a bitch fouls it up," probably referring to Nikita Khrushchev.

President Kennedy had reason for concern. When he revealed the existence of the Soviet ballistic missiles in Cuba on October 22, he had "blindsided" Khrushchev and Castro. The Soviet plans to place strategic weapons in the Western Hemisphere had depended upon completing the task without discovery prior to all the ballistic missiles becoming operational in late October. Now, with the Anadyr deployment still in progress, the Soviet leader faced a situation he had not anticipated when he had conceived Operation Anadyr the previous spring.

The text of Kennedy's statement had been handed to Ambassador Dobrynin earlier in the evening and was now cabled to American embassies around the world. At U.S. military bases and on warships around the globe, the American armed forces went to their DEFCON-3 alert posture and waited for further orders. Reservists and National Guardsmen gathered at reserve centers and armories, getting equipment ready and sorting out their roles in the growing crisis. Now it was time to await the Soviet reaction and to start the quarantine of Cuba.[40]

In Cuba—the target of the U.S. military action—there was massive mobilization. The Cuban armed forces had been on some stage of alert since the time that President Eisenhower had broken off diplomatic relations in early 1961. At noon on October 22, it was confirmed in Cuba that President Kennedy would speak that evening. At 5:50 P.M. the Cuban leadership issued an alert, and at 5:35 the alarm was sounded throughout Cuba. By the next morning, there were an estimated 270,000 troops—regular and militia—in position to repel an invasion.[41]

9

Taking Action

Do nothing and live with the situation. It was pointed out clearly that Western Europe, Greece, Turkey, and other countries had lived under the Soviet MRBMs for years; therefore, why should the United States be so concerned.

Director of Central Intelligence John McCone
"Memorandum for Discussion Today," October 17, 1962[1]

President Kennedy's establishment of a blockade would not, of course, remove the missiles that were already in Cuba. Rather, the blockade would be coupled with demands to Chairman Khrushchev to remove the offensive missiles. And, in the event that those weapons were not removed, the Joint Chiefs of Staff were instructed to plan air strikes against the ballistic missiles, as well as against the Il-28 Beagle light bombers and MiG-21 Fishbed fighters. According to the historians Ernest R. May and Philip D. Zelikow, Kennedy chose a point midway between the "hawks," who wanted an immediate air strike against Cuba, and the "doves," who sought resolution through negotiation.[2] Furthermore, Kennedy demonstrated his flexibility by continuing to seek advice and counsel from all factions of his circle of advisors.

The rules for conducting a military blockade had been precisely spelled out in the Declaration of Paris at the close of the Crimean War in 1856 and at the subsequent Declaration of London in 1909. Significantly, under the accepted international rules, no nation had the right to declare a blockade unless it had the power to enforce it. During ExComm discussions, President Kennedy made it clear that his decisions would not be based on the Monroe Doctrine, which sought to exclude European countries from influencing events in the Americas. Nevertheless, later accounts of the missile crisis would often cite that doctrine as the basis for the quarantine. The reality was that the planned quarantine stood on very poor legal grounds, except that it was generally supported by those nations most affected by the missiles in Cuba. To make the quarantine "legal" would require an international consensus that did not exist when President Kennedy signed the order.

The initial decision was to establish the blockade line 800 statute miles from Cuba, a distance dictated by the estimated 740-mile combat radius of Il-28 bombers flying from Cuban air bases. Interestingly, the 1909 rules for a blockade stipulated that a blockade must not be extended beyond the coasts and the ports belonging to or occupied by an enemy.

Orders were given to Admiral Robert L. Dennison at Norfolk to prepare to establish the blockade.[3] The U.S. Atlantic Fleet in 1962 consisted of almost one-half of the U.S. Navy's nine hundred surface ships and submarines then in commission worldwide. Of these, a significant portion of the Atlantic Fleet was deployed to the Mediterranean; some ships and submarines were in the North Atlantic, while others were in overhaul at shipyards along the Atlantic coast. Still, Dennison had a considerable force available to carry out the ordered blockade of Cuba.

By mid-1962, the Atlantic Fleet had already been "engaged" in the Cuban situation for more than a year. During the abortive Bay of Pigs landing in April 1961, the U.S. Navy had two carrier task groups steaming in the area, ready to provide air support of the landings—which they were never called upon to give. In 1962, U.S. Navy aircraft, mainly flying out of Key West, Florida, were involved in several incidents with Cuban forces. Based on these incidents, on September 19, Admiral Dennison sent six F8U-2N Crusader fighters to Key West for air defense and escort duties. Three weeks later, as the political situation deteriorated, these fighters were reinforced by a squadron of Navy F4H Phantoms, the newest and most capable fighter aircraft in the West.

In early October, several U.S. warships were conducting routine operations in the Caribbean. Among them were the large guided missile cruiser *Canberra*, six destroyers, and one amphibious ship in the area of the U.S. base at Guantánamo. Naval aircraft were flying out of Key West, as well as from the large naval base at Roosevelt Roads, Puerto Rico, and the Guantánamo base.

In response to the growing tension in the region, on October 3, Admiral Dennison ordered an increase in the aerial surveillance of shipping in the western Atlantic, the Caribbean, and the Gulf of Mexico. He wanted a special focus on the approaches to Cuba; thus he directed maritime patrol aircraft to photograph shipping that entered and departed Cuba. A jet courier service from the naval air station at Norfolk, Virginia, to Washington was established to rush the photographs to the Chief of Naval Operations, Admiral George W. Anderson.

Also on October 3, Admiral Dennison took the initial steps to prepare his forces for a possible blockade of Cuba. He ordered the commander of Joint Task Force 122, the prospective blockade commander under Atlantic Fleet Operational Order 41-62, to ready all available naval forces to carry out a blockade. Although this operational order was not the one followed when the quarantine actually began, the advance planning expedited the establishment of the quarantine.

Three days later, on October 6, in his role as Commander-in-Chief U.S. Atlantic Command (CINCLANT), Admiral Dennison directed U.S. military forces in the Atlantic area to begin preparations to execute Operations Plans 312, 314, and 316. The objectives of those plans were the removal of the Castro regime and the securing of a new regime responsive to presumed Cuban national interests. Plan 312 was for air attacks, Plan 314 was for a large-scale invasion after eighteen days of preparation (including air strikes), and Plan 316 was a quick-reaction version of 314, with an airborne landing after five days of air strikes to be followed three days later by an amphibious assault.

An Atlantic Fleet landing exercise was under way at that time, Amphibious Training Landing Exercise (PHILBTRALEX) 3-62 in the area of Vieques, Puerto Rico, with a Navy amphibious squadron and a Marine battalion taking part in the exercise. To disguise the further buildup for an assault against Cuba, Admiral Dennison received approval from the Joint Chiefs of Staff to announce that his amphibious forces were being assembled for another major landing exercise named "Quick Kick," the Amphibious Brigade Landing Exercise (PHILBRIGLEX) 62, to be held during the period of October 15–20, rather than in November, as previously announced. The exercise was to land four thousand marines on Vieques Island and overthrow its imaginary tyrant "Ortsac"—Castro spelled backward. As part of these preparations for an actual assault against Cuba, in addition to Atlantic Fleet marines, a ten thousand–man marine brigade from the West Coast had embarked in amphibious ships and was steaming toward the Panama Canal and the Caribbean. The West Coast marines had been training specifically for a landing in Cuba. "We had been practicing and were prepared for a major amphibious assault," recalled Thomas A. Brooks, an intelligence officer with the amphibious forces. "We were studying maps and potential landing beaches, but we knew nothing of potential Soviet defenses."[4] Marines and Army paratroopers would be the vanguard of the invasion force. Thus, Atlantic

Command's air, ground, and naval forces prepared for an assault against Cuba, as well as for a blockade. Target folders—including details of targets, approach routes, and air defenses—were prepared for air strikes. But the folders contained little hard information on Soviet or Cuban military installations until the first low-level photo missions were flown on October 23.

By October 19—the eve of Kennedy's decision to impose the blockade—Admiral Dennison had assembled more than 350 combat aircraft on area airfields to support operations against Cuba.[5] Also at Key West were ten F8U-1P Crusader photo planes for Operation Blue Moon with Navy and Marine Corps aviators standing by to make low-level reconnaissance flights over Cuba; seven additional Crusader photo planes could be quickly made available if needed. These airfields were becoming crowded as more Navy, Marine, and Air Force tactical aircraft were brought within striking range of Cuba. Dennison sent unneeded aircraft off to other airfields, away from the southeastern United States. Also, Army and Marine Hawk anti-aircraft missile launchers were being flown and trucked to area bases (including Guantánamo) to provide defense against a possible Soviet-Cuban air strike.

In addition to his land-based aircraft, Admiral Dennison's forces initially included two large aircraft carriers, the *Independence* and the brand-new, nuclear-propelled *Enterprise*. The "Big E," commissioned in November 1961, was the world's largest—and most expensive—warship. The carriers each had two squadrons of fighter aircraft, along with four or five attack squadrons. Most of the attack squadrons flew the A4D Skyhawk, a small turbojet aircraft designed to carry a single nuclear bomb. However, the subsonic A4D also proved to be an effective conventional attack aircraft with a limited fighter capability. En route to the Caribbean, the *Enterprise* flew off her squadron of large A3J-1 Vigilante nuclear strike aircraft and landed aboard in its place a squadron of twenty Marine A4D Skyhawks to provide increased tactical strike and close air support capabilities.[6] The shift was carried out while the ship was under way, with cargo aircraft transferring the nonflying personnel and equipment between land bases and the carriers, demonstrating the flexibility of large aircraft carriers.[7] Each carrier also had a squadron of AD Skyraider piston-engine attack aircraft. The *Independence* kept several large, 35-ton A3D-2 Skywarrior attack aircraft on board during the crisis. Of course, the early deployment of carriers attracted far less attention and speculation from the press than did the massive recalls of Air Force and Army personnel to bases throughout the country.

The anti-submarine carrier *Essex* with submarine-hunting aircraft, both fixed-wing and helicopters, was also at sea. Anti-submarine warfare S2F Trackers could carry out both surface and undersea surveillance. These aircraft had a variety of sensors—radar, magnetic detectors, and expendable sonobuoys—and could carry acoustic homing torpedoes or nuclear depth bombs. The *Essex*'s HSS-1 Seabat helicopters, which used "dipping" active sonar to detect submarines, could also carry homing torpedoes or nuclear depth bombs.

The three carriers added approximately 200 aircraft to Admiral Dennison's air forces, placing well over 550 combat aircraft at his immediate command. These planes, however, included maritime patrol and anti-submarine aircraft. Even more Navy fighters and attack planes might have had to be assembled if the United States were to make a massive air strike against Cuba. Pentagon planners added continually to the target list, expanding it beyond the ballistic missiles, to include the MiG fighters, the Il-28 bombers, the large number of SA-2 missile sites, and the numerous Cuban-manned anti-aircraft guns, as well as air warning radar systems. Almost five hundred air strikes were deemed necessary to destroy those targets. Of course, with targets only ninety miles from Key West and slightly farther from other Florida bases, some land-based aircraft, as well as planes from the aircraft carriers, could have flown two and even three sorties in a single day.[8]

The "weapons of choice" for the attackers would be high-drag "Snakeye" bombs, which could be dropped from treetop level. Special fins pop open from the tails of these bombs to slow them, enabling the low-flying aircraft to escape their blast. The U.S. planes would also use napalm canisters and rockets and would strafe with their 20-mm cannon.

Target Options in Cuba

Option	Targets	Sorties Required
I	Ballistic missile and nuclear storage sites	52
II	Same as option I, plus MiG-21 and Il-28 aircraft	204
III	Same as option II, plus SAMs, cruise missiles, and other aircraft	194
IV	All military targets except tanks	474
V	All military targets as a prelude to possible invasion	2,000

On Sunday, October 21, when General Walter C. Sweeney, the commander of the Tactical Air Command, met with President Kennedy, he had told the president, "The best we can offer you is to destroy 90 percent of the known [ballistic] missiles."[9] In listening to details of the proposed air strikes, President Kennedy noted that the air attack plan was not for a "surgical" strike, but for a massive military commitment that could involve heavy casualties on all sides. Although Secretary of Defense McNamara had initially sought such a precision strike against the offensive missile sites, the Joint Chiefs countered that no action at all would be better than a surgical strike against the missiles that would leave the MiG-21 and the Il-28 aircraft unharmed.[10] As if to underscore the scale of the proposed U.S. military air attack on Cuba, one member of the Joint Chiefs reportedly suggested the use of tactical nuclear weapons.

The mass of amphibious ships that would be available to Admiral Dennison—forty-two ships from the Atlantic Fleet and twenty-two from the Pacific Fleet—could lift a landing force of some forty thousand marines, the equivalent of two assault divisions. The later (October 27) activation of twenty-four Air Force reserve troop carrier squadrons, plus the few active squadrons, would enable a paratroop drop by the assault units of the Army's 82nd and 101st Airborne Divisions in a single lift.[11]

At the ExComm meeting on Sunday afternoon, October 21, General Taylor said that an invasion of Cuba could be carried out seven days after the decision was made to invade the island. The airborne and amphibious landings would follow a series of intensive air strikes. Describing the assault, Taylor and McNamara said that twenty-five thousand men could be put ashore on the first day and that, including follow-up echelons, ninety thousand troops could be landed within an eleven-day period.[12] Cruisers and destroyers would steam close to the landing beaches to provide gunfire support, and carrier-based aircraft would also provide support to the amphibious landings, as required. There was no mention of employing tactical nuclear weapons to facilitate the landings.

Although Kennedy initially wanted to declare the blockade on Sunday, October 21, he was persuaded to wait another day to enable additional military preparations and to provide time for State Department officials to notify U.S. allies. Also on Sunday, the Joint Chiefs of Staff directed Admiral Dennison to make preparations for the evacuation of American dependents from the Guantánamo base and to reinforce that base on

Monday. Dennison was also to assume operational control of the Army and the Air Force units included under various assault plans, and to be prepared to furnish riot control forces to Latin American countries, if they were requested, should there be mass demonstrations in the wake of President Kennedy's speech.

In Washington, at 10 P.M. on Sunday, Secretary McNamara approved the procedures for the quarantine. Special communications procedures and channels were established to ensure the timely flow of information concerning the blockade to the Navy's "flag plot" on the fourth floor of the Pentagon, which would then speed information to the Chief of Naval Operations, the Joint Chiefs, the White House, and other affected agencies.

In Norfolk, Admiral Dennison ordered the evacuation of dependents of Navy and Marine Corps families from the sprawling Guantánamo base, which covered almost forty-five square miles of eastern Cuba. At 10 A.M. on Monday, October 22, word was spread around Guantánamo that there would be an immediate evacuation. Everyone on the base had known that it would eventually happen, and no one was surprised. Evacuees were told to pack one suitcase per person, to tie up pets in their yards, to leave keys to their houses on the dining room tables, and to stand in front of their houses ready to board buses. In a single day, the 2,820 dependents at Guantánamo were evacuated: the Navy transport *Upshur* embarked with 1,703, while another 727 were taken on board three other Navy ships. All were under way by 5 P.M., en route to the Norfolk-Little Creek area. Another 390 dependents were flown out on the 22nd.

Meanwhile, transport aircraft and amphibious ships were bringing additional marines into Guantánamo to bolster the base's defenses. There were soon three reinforced battalions at "Gitmo," totaling some five thousand marines, plus two naval construction battalions, the famed "Seabees"—sailors who could build and fight with equal skill.

Farther north and east, as U.S. warships were establishing the blockade line, U.S., Canadian, and other NATO maritime patrol aircraft were fanning out across the North Atlantic to more precisely locate and track Soviet merchant ships en route to Cuba. Beyond the U.S. Navy's use of land-based and seaplane patrol aircraft, as well as anti-submarine aircraft in that role, the Strategic Air Command contributed sixteen piston-engine KC-97 tankers and five photoreconnaissance variants of the B-47 Stratojet bomber to search out merchant ships bound for Cuba. RB-47H aircraft, flying from MacDill Air Force Base near Tampa, Florida, were to photograph shipping around Cuba and to evaluate the weather around the western end of the island in support of U-2 overflights.[13]

Thus, by Monday the 27th, much of the blockade force was steaming toward assigned stations. In the White House that afternoon, the question of Soviet nuclear weapons reaching Cuba was raised during an ExComm meeting. Secretary of State Rusk then asked whether the quarantine would extend to aircraft. President Kennedy responded "not yet" with regard to stopping aircraft, again expressing concern that the Soviets could retaliate in kind to the blockade by interfering with U.S. access to West Berlin if it was precipitously extended to stopping Soviet aircraft from reaching Cuba.[14]

(Unknown to U.S. military planners and naval commanders, the Soviet merchant ship *Indigirka*, which had already arrived in Cuban waters, carried 84 nuclear warheads for ballistic missiles, as well as for short-range tactical weapons, and 6 nuclear bombs for the Il-28 bombers.)

In Washington and elsewhere, U.S. military commanders voiced concerns over MiG-21 fighters and Il-28 bombers armed with conventional weapons, as well as for the Komar missile boats, attacking American warships. Admiral Anderson expressed the view that Soviet surface ships could not reach the area to escort merchant ships in less than ten days, and that Soviet submarines could not reach the area in less than ten to fourteen days.[15] In response to a question about Soviet submarines entering the area, Anderson responded that if they were detected, he would seek permission to attack them.[16]

On Monday evening, October 22, President Kennedy spoke to the world from the Oval Office; U.S. military forces around the world went to the DEFCON-3 alert posture, with the exception of U.S. Forces in Europe, which remained at DEFCON-4 because of its integration with NATO forces.[17] In the United States, twenty-two fighter aircraft were airborne over the southeastern part of the country in the event that the Cuban government's reaction to the speech was to mount an air attack against Florida.

Ironically, on the day of Kennedy's speech, the first U.S. Jupiter missile in Turkey was formally turned over to the Turkish Air Force for operation. Although the move was publicized in Turkey and was undoubtedly detected by Soviet intelligence, U.S. decision makers apparently were not aware of the event. Almost simultaneously, President Kennedy asked Assistant Secretary of Defense Paul Nitze to examine the possibility of withdrawing the Jupiter missiles from Italy and Turkey.

Confrontation at Sea

There was a day's delay between the president's speech and the establishment of the blockade to give the Soviets time to communicate with their ships. The blockade line, initially planned at 800 miles from Cuba to avoid possible interference from the Il-28 bombers, was soon moved closer to the island as implementation of the quarantine was further delayed to give the Soviets more time to consider the situation. The Navy formed a line of destroyers to intercept merchant ships steaming toward Cuba. At least one Russian-speaking officer was placed on each destroyer. The U.S. carrier task groups—with aircraft carriers, cruisers, and more destroyers—were positioned both to support the blockade and to assist in defending the Guantánamo base if it was attacked.

On Tuesday, October 23, ExComm discussed which Soviet ships were approaching the blockade line and which of those ships to stop. Secretary McNamara felt it "extremely important" that the first intercept be of a ship carrying missiles or other offensive weapons: "It would be an unfortunate incident if we hailed a ship that refused to stop; we then disable it and found it didn't have offensive weapons on it. That would be a poor way to start."[18]

Discussions also explored how Soviet ships would be forced to stop if they refused signals from the U.S. destroyers. The destroyers were to attempt to shoot out a resisting ship's rudder to disable the ship. There was also apprehension that the troop-carrying ships might be fitted with guns and would refuse a U.S. boarding party. (Indeed, some of the Soviet merchant ships were clandestinely armed.)

Perhaps of most concern to ExComm members were the Soviet submarines reported to be approaching the blockade. McNamara noted, "They sent a ship under high speed to fuel a submarine yesterday, which did fuel and was observed fueling. And the sub was obviously going to move into the Cuban area. There may well be others that we're not aware of."[19] Soviet submarines would be a constant worry to ExComm members.

Low-Level Reconnaissance

On the 23rd, the United States began low-level reconnaissance flights over Cuba. Six Navy F8U-1P Crusaders, led by Commander William Ecker flying from Key West, undertook the first flights of Operation Blue Moon. The Vought F8U Crusader was a high-performance, carrier-based fighter

Hi- & Low-level Photography

The above photo, taken by a U-2 on October 15, 1962, shows a Soviet SS-4 missile regiment being set up. The photo below, taken at low-level by an F8U-1P on October 23, 1962, shows the same area as indicated by the box. (upper CIA; lower USN)

A Navy F8U-1P Crusader photo plane with some of the aircraft's camera ports visible (beneath the national insignia). These carrier-based aircraft operated from airfields in Florida to provide the first low-level photos of the Soviet buildup in Cuba.

Commander William Ecker, the commanding officer of Navy Light Photographic Squadron 62, makes a point during a debriefing following a low-level flight over Cuba.

capable of speeds in excess of 1,100 mph. The "straight" normally carried four 20-millimeter cannons and four Sidewinder air-to-air missiles. The F8U-1P photo variant was unarmed, instead being fitted with five aerial cameras for high-speed, low-level photography. The cameras, except for a 16-millimeter movie camera, were produced by Chicago Aerial and were considered the best in the world for low-level, high-speed photography. And Commander Ecker, the commanding officer of Navy Light Photographic Squadron 62 (VFP-62), was considered a master of his trade.[20]

The Blue Moon reconnaissance missions would provide photos of much better quality and resolution than those from U-2 overflights and

A low-flying U.S. reconnaissance aircraft caught these Cuban troops racing to man their S-60 57-mm anti-aircraft guns. Although often fired upon, none of the low-flying U.S. Navy RF-8A Crusader or Air Force RF-101 Voodoo aircraft was hit.

Technicians check the camera of a Navy F8U-1P Crusader photo plane on a Florida airfield during the missile crisis. These were the only U.S. aircraft fitted with effective low-level, high-speed cameras when the crisis began.

were needed to provide intelligence for the planned air campaign and invasion. The low-level reconnaissance photography also provided much greater detail on the status of the ballistic missile launch sites: an issue critically important to members of ExComm.

As the VFP-62 pilots began their photo runs over Cuba, the planes flew at speeds of 400 mph and at altitudes of about 400 feet but apparently made their final runs at lower altitudes.[21] They encountered no enemy gunfire and flew too low to be engaged by the Soviet SA-2 missiles.[22] Colonel Anatoli Burnov, the technical officer of an SS-4 regiment overflown by the Navy photo planes, recalled that they were as low as 100 meters (328 feet) and that "we could see the pilot in his helmet."[23] Commander Ecker remembered, "I saw the missiles with camouflage netting . . . and all kinds of equipment. One, two, three seconds [Whistle], and you are out of there!"[24] Unlike the depiction in Kevin Costner's film *Thirteen Days,* none of the low-flying photo planes were hit by anti-aircraft fire, either on the flights made on the 23rd or on any of the subsequent low-level photo missions.[25]

A photo intelligence officer from Navy Light Photographic Squadron 62 looks at low-level photography taken by a Navy F8U-1P Crusader over Cuba a few hours earlier. The CIA/NPIC, Air Force, and Navy conducted photo interpretation at a remarkable speed.

Ecker's flight returned to Jacksonville, Florida, where the film canisters were quickly removed from the Crusaders and rushed to the photo lab. These pictures would be shared with SAC, NPIC, and all of the armed services with a role in the planned air campaign or invasion. Ecker was about to climb down from his F8U-1P when he was told to immediately fly up to Washington. Protesting that he had only his underwear beneath his flight suit, a commander on the tarmac handed him his own shirt, along with a carton of milk and a ham sandwich. Ecker took the food but not the proffered shirt.

After Ecker's plane was refueled, without his climbing down from the cockpit, he took off and streaked northward, landing at Andrews Air Force Base near the capital. The flight took fifty-eight minutes. Two Air Force helicopters were turning up at Andrews, and one of them immediately flew Ecker to the Pentagon. Met at the Pentagon helipad, he climbed into a "big black limousine" for the two-minute ride to the underground garage. Ecker was hurried to an elevator. Minutes later, he was greeted by Admiral Anderson and, together, they walked to the JCS conference room. There, Ecker was relieved of his .38-caliber pistol before being ushered into the Joint Chiefs of Staff meeting.

After being congratulated warmly by General Taylor for his successful flight, Ecker was told to brief the Joint Chiefs on his mission. He began by apologizing for being in his "sweaty flight gear" but was immediately interrupted by General Curtis LeMay, the Air Force chief of staff. "You've just been flying a combat mission?" asked LeMay. When Ecker nodded, LeMay declared, "Then you have a right to be sweaty." Ecker proceeded to give his views of the mission, the first of thirty low-level flights made by Navy and Marine Corps pilots in F8U-1P Crusaders

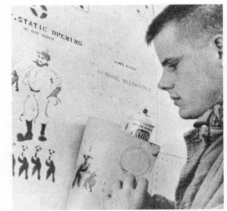

A sailor spray paints "mission marks" on a Navy F8U-1P Crusader reconnaissance aircraft to indicate photo missions over Castro's Cuba during the missile crisis. The "chicken" mission marks refer to a visit to the United Nations in New York City, where the Cuban delegation boiled chickens in their rooms.

from October 23 to October 28, "when Khrushchev said 'Uncle,'" Ecker quipped later. (Air Force RF-101s did not provide low-level photography until the 29th.)[26]

The quarantine went into effect in the early hours of Wednesday, October 24. Although U.S. electronic intercepts had detected an intensive exchange of coded radio messages between Moscow and ships steaming toward Cuba, the Soviet ships continued to approach the island. Robert Kennedy spoke with the president for a few moments before they went into the 10 A.M. ExComm meeting. President Kennedy said, "It looks really mean, doesn't it? But then, really there was no other choice. If they get this mean on this one in our part of the world, what will they do on the next?"

"I just don't think there was any choice," Robert replied, "and not only that, if you hadn't acted, you would have been impeached."

The president thought for a moment and said, "That's what I think— I would have been impeached."[27]

As the president and his brother spoke, the U.S. Strategic Air Command went to DEFCON-2, the highest state of the U.S. military alert short of war.

Up to the Line

ExComm members convened about 10 A.M. DCI McCone reported that two Soviet cargo ships, the *Yuriy Gagarin* and *Komiles*, were within a few miles of the quarantine line.[28] The *Yuriy Gagarin* carried a most-sensitive cargo—the commanding officer and the staff of an SS-5 (R-14) missile regiment, as well as fuel trucks, erectors, and cranes for the missiles. The expectation was that at least one of the ships would be stopped and boarded between 10:30 and 11 A.M. The *Komiles* was of particular interest to the Americans because the ship's No. 3 hold was unusually long—98 feet—suitable for carrying missiles or disassembled aircraft.[29] A Soviet submarine was tracking the *Komiles*. This report was soon changed to "a submarine relatively close to both of them . . . it should be 20 to 30 miles from the ships at the time of the intercept." And, said McNamara, "this is a very dangerous situation."[30]

A short time later, the ExComm members received word that the twenty Soviet merchant ships closest to the quarantine line had stopped dead in the water or had reversed course, away from Cuba. "So no ships will be stopped or intercepted," announced the president.

But other Soviet ships were continuing toward Cuba. And there were several that had earlier passed the barrier of destroyers and were already nearing Cuban ports. These included the *Alexandrovsk*, with at least twenty-four nuclear warheads on board for the SS-5 missiles, which had not yet arrived in Cuba. Concerned that the U.S. Navy might board and capture the ship, Khrushchev ordered that the *Alexandrovsk* make for a Cuban port with all haste. The *Alexandrovsk* did so, dropping anchor at the small port of La Isabela on October 23. The historians Aleksandr Fursenko and Timothy Naftali noted that having the *Alexandrovsk* proceed to Cuba "signaled Khrushchev's thinking about the future of Anadyr. Should the Soviet Union continue with its plan of deploying a complete strategic rocket division to Cuba? The Kremlin decided that it had to proceed."[31]

Among the cargo ships that were still outside of the blockade line were the four merchant ships that carried the sixteen SS-5 IRBM launchers, their twenty-four ballistic missiles, and more support equipment. They had halted to avoid a confrontation with the U.S. Navy.

As tensions continued to build over the possible confrontation at sea, tempers began to flare ashore. The unlikely source of one of the first such altercations was the normally soft-spoken Chief of Naval Operations, Admiral George Anderson, facing off against the icy and mercurial Secretary of Defense, Robert McNamara. There are two totally irreconcilable versions of what took place between the two men on October 24 in the Pentagon. Joint Chiefs of Staff historian Walter S. Poole wrote,

> According to [Admiral] Anderson, when McNamara, Deputy Secretary [Roswell] Gilpatrick and two public affairs [PA] officials came to Flag

Plot [in the Pentagon], McNamara persisted in asking why a destroyer had left the quarantine line. Anderson took him to a secure area, explained that the destroyer was shadowing a submarine through the use of intelligence for which the PA men were not cleared, and then said in what he thought was a jocular manner, "Why don't you go back to your quarters and let us handle this?"[32]

Admiral Anderson recalled his own words differently. He believes he said, "Well, Mr. Secretary, you go back to your office and I'll go to mine, and we'll take care of things," or words to that effect, which apparently was the wrong thing to say to somebody of Secretary McNamara's personality.[33]

Anderson knew that Admiral Dennison and his subordinates were fully versed in the procedures to be followed. The Chief of Naval Operations certainly was not going to dictate to destroyer captains how to carry out their duties.

Poole related, "According to Gilpatrick, McNamara asked what would happen if a Soviet ship refused to stop or resisted boarding. Anderson answered angrily, 'This is none of your goddamn business. We've been doing this since the days of John Paul Jones, and if you'll go back to your quarters, Mr. Secretary, we'll handle this.'"

Kevin Costner's popular feature film *Thirteen Days* gives yet another version, showing McNamara and Anderson having words over whether U.S. destroyers would "clear their guns" by firing when in the vicinity of Soviet merchant ships. *That* fictional action was certainly *not* the cause of their confrontation. The *real* issue—the destroyer leaving the quarantine line—could not be discussed with the public affairs officers present. Still highly classified at the time was the U.S. Navy's seafloor-installed Sound Surveillance System (SOSUS), used to detect submerged Soviet submarines.[34]

One thing was true, however; the physical and mental strain of the around-the-clock nature of the crisis was beginning to show on various members of the president's inner circle. Secretary McNamara was among the first to show signs of fatigue (and perhaps sleep deprivation), possibly due to his having decided to stay in the Pentagon for most of the crisis. Like many others on both sides of the crisis, McNamara had taken to sleeping on a couch in his office, something sure to guarantee a poor night's sleep. Though nobody was yet thinking about such fatigue affecting the judgment of senior leaders, it is likely that the confrontation in the Pentagon Flag Plot that day was one of the first indicators that people were beginning to "run out of gas."

Significantly, concern over the submarine issue rapidly dissipated as U.S. aircraft and destroyers intensively harassed the submarines (see chapter 10).

The First Intercept

After some delay, fourteen Soviet merchant ships turned away from the quarantine line shortly after the blockade was announced. Among those that continued toward Cuba was the tanker *Bucharest*. Completed earlier in the year, the 32,030-deadweight-ton tanker of the Soviet merchant marine was obviously not carrying missiles or aircraft. At about 6 A.M. (Washington time) on October 25, the first interception of the quarantine took place: the destroyer *Gearing* stopped the *Bucharest*. After a brief exchange of signals—with the *Bucharest* responding that she carried only petroleum products and was bound for Havana—she was allowed to proceed.

In ExComm, there was discussion about "changing the rules" of the blockade. With the Soviets continuing to prepare the missiles in Cuba and assemble Il-28 bombers, it seemed that tankers should be put on the quarantine list as, in the president's words, "we're about to spread that quarantine."[35]

The Soviet-chartered, Lebanese-flag freighter *Marucla* was approaching the blockade line and was targeted for boarding. Being a "Third World" ship, she was unlikely to be carrying Soviet weapons. Destroyers were dispatched for the intercept. Abruptly, it appeared that the *Marucla* was slowing or stopping. The next ship to reach the line would then be the East German–flag *Völkerfreundschaff*, a combination passenger-cargo ship, believed to be carrying almost two thousand Soviet workmen and Czech technicians. McNamara explained the predicament:

> The question is, should we ask it to halt and submit to inspection? If it did not halt, should we pass it without forcing it to halt, or should we force it to halt? If we were to force it to halt, should we use [gun]fire, or should we put a Navy ship in front of it? If we use [gun]fire, and damage the ship, with 1,500 people on board, and find that it's hard to explain, does not include items on the prohibited list, have we not weakened our position? And these considerations led me to conclude this afternoon that I should recommend to this group and to you that we not ask this ship to stop.[36]

The *Völkerfreundschaff* was allowed to pass unmolested. But everyone on ExComm realized that a merchant ship *would* have to be stopped

The U.S. destroyer *Joseph P. Kennedy, Jr.*, approaches the
Lebanese-flag freighter *Marucla* on October 26. The *Marucla* was
boarded, although she was known not to be carrying offensive
weapons by virtue of being a foreign-flag ship.

to prove that the blockade was being enforced. During the night of October 25–26, reconnaissance aircraft sighted the Lebanese-flag *Marucla*
again proceeding toward Cuba. The next morning the destroyers *Joseph
P. Kennedy, Jr.*—named for the president's late brother—and *John R.
Pierce* signaled the *Marucla* to stop.[37] The Greek crew of the *Marucla*
complied and, after her cargo was inspected by U.S. Navy personnel, the
ship was permitted to continue to Havana. Admiral Dennison recalled of
the *Marucla* intercept, "I did it to show that we could and would do it.
Of course, they didn't know that we already knew what was in that ship.
It was little more than a stunt, a demonstration that we were effective."[38]

More ships were coming toward the quarantine lines, the Soviet-flag
merchant tanker *Grozny* among them. If the blockade were expanded to
include fuels, the *Grozny* would bring a direct confrontation. If the ship
carried aviation fuels, usable by the Il-28 bombers, the case could be
made that the cargo was for offensive weapons. But what if she carried
commercial-grade fuels? Another complication was that the *Grozny*
appeared to be carrying deck cargo as well.

Khrushchev had said that the blockade was illegal. How would the
Soviets react to their ships being stopped and boarded? Meanwhile, on
October 26, a U.S. destroyer challenged the Swedish ship *Coalangatta*,
under charter to the Soviet Union, which refused to stop and continued
toward Cuba. Again, the possibility of a foreign-flag ship carrying offensive weapons was unlikely.

The *Grozny* was of more concern. The ship was lost for a brief period
but was again found on Saturday, October 27, by an Air Force RB-47H
from MacDill Air Force Base.[39] Some ExComm members now believed

that a confrontation at sea should be avoided so as not to trigger a Soviet military response in view of disturbing news that Soviet officers appeared to be taking command of all Cuban air defenses. Heretofore, no SA-2 SAMs had been fired at the high-flying U-2 spyplanes, although Cuban-manned anti-aircraft guns had fired—without effect—at the low-level photo aircraft. So far, there had been no casualties in what had become a very tense situation. Unfortunately, that situation was about to change.

Shoot Down, Saturday, October 27

The previous evening, during Chairman Khrushchev's meeting with his Kremlin advisors, there had been a discussion about the specific defensive measures that General Pliyev in Cuba would be allowed to use in the event of an American air attack or invasion. In particular, there was intense discussion about the status and location of the nuclear warheads for the ballistic and the tactical missiles. The decision was made to hold the release authority for these weapons at the Kremlin level, rescinding (at least, temporarily) the earlier oral guidance Khrushchev had given Pliyev prior to the Anadyr deployment. However, guidance allowing Pliyev to defend the Soviet forces deployed to Cuba against aerial intrusion by American reconnaissance or strike aircraft had *not* changed.[40] This particular Kremlin oversight was to have tragic consequences the following day when the next set of U-2 missions was flown the next morning.

Taking off from McCoy Air Force Base in Florida, Major Rudolf Anderson headed south in a U-2 on a regular overflight of the already identified missile and military bases—Mission 3127 (see appendix B). Below, the air defense situation had changed a great deal from his first mission over Cuba on October 15. The SA-2 missiles had taken many weeks to bring into service and were now finally operational.

Soviet military doctrine placed great importance on denying an enemy exact knowledge of military intentions and dispositions. In times of political tension, extensive reconnaissance by a potential enemy was considered a warning sign of imminent attack and a threat requiring an immediate armed response. This point was hammered into the mind of every officer in the Soviet Air Defense Forces, including Captain N. Antonyets, the commander of an SA-2 SAM battery located near the port of Banes.[41] At approximately 10 A.M. local time, Antonyets reported up the chain of command to General Pliyev's headquarters that a U-2 had been detected near Guantánamo, and he was requesting instructions.

The wreckage of the U-2 flown by Major Rudolf
Anderson Jr., which was shot down by an SA-2 missile as
he overflew Cuba on October 27. It was the third U-2 shot
down by an SA-2 missile, the others being an American
U-2 flown by Francis Gary Powers and one flown by a
Taiwanese pilot.

Although General Pliyev was not at his command post, Lieutenant
General Stephan Grechko, Pliyev's deputy commander, and Major General
Leonid Garbuz, Chief of Staff for Military Preparedness, took the
call. They tried to reach Pliyev by phone but were unsuccessful, and unit
commanders were forbidden to launch SA-2s without his authorization.
Fearing that inaction would be worse than violating standing orders, the
two generals called Captain Antonyets's missile battery and authorized
him to engage the high-flying spyplane.[42] At 10:22 A.M., Antonyets's
SA-2 battery launched a pair of missiles at Anderson's U-2. At least one
of the weapons exploded close to its target, apparently killing Major
Anderson instantly. The aircraft crashed to earth, surprisingly intact for
its violent, fourteen-mile descent into the Cuban countryside.[43] When
General Pliyev arrived at his headquarters, he immediately ordered his
two subordinates to submit a report, which he quickly forwarded to
Moscow. Neither officer was punished, and there was never any formal
reprimand for their actions. The Cuban Missile Crisis had just claimed
its first combat casualty, and it was an American.[44]

Cuban political and military commanders could not understand why
the SA-2 missiles had not engaged the U-2 aircraft earlier. The Cubans
believed that the massive installation of SA-2 missiles in Cuba had been
undertaken specifically to stop the U-2 overflights from discovering the
deployment of ballistic missiles. "They were not toys," said Jorge Risquet, Secretary of the Cuban Communist Party in Oriente Province.

The failure to destroy U-2s on the earlier overflights was a major mistake of the Soviets, according to Risquet and his colleagues. After all, the Cubans observed, the SA-2 missile system was universally praised for having shot down a U-2 over the Soviet Union two years earlier.[45] When the ExComm members learned that Anderson's U-2 was overdue, they were also informed that several thousand miles from Cuba another U-2 incident had occurred that also threatened escalation. An Air Force U-2A piloted by Major Charles (Chuck) Maultsby had taken off from Eielson Air Force Base in Alaska, on a high-altitude atmospheric-sampling mission to the North Pole. These missions sought intelligence on Soviet nuclear weapons tests by using special filters to trap airborne radioactive bomb residue. Analysis of the particles trapped by the filters could tell American scientists details about Soviet nuclear weapons, including the yield, the fissile materials used, and even details about the design of the device being tested.[46]

Major Maultsby reached the North Pole and, in total darkness, turned back toward Alaska. Maultsby was unable to rely on magnetic compass data in the Arctic region latitudes, and his navigation became faulty. He flew southward on an incorrect course—toward the Chukotski Peninsula, the easternmost part of the Soviet Union. The error was detected only when a supporting C-54 rescue aircraft flying to the east reported seeing the start of the sunrise. When the Alaskan command post called Maultsby to check whether he could see the sunrise, the answer was negative. He was too far west and was entering Soviet air space.

U.S. radar installations in Alaska then detected a pair of Soviet MiG-19 fighter aircraft climbing from a Siberian airfield in an effort to intercept the U-2. Now aware of his navigation error, Maultsby immediately turned toward U.S. territory. At the same time, two U.S. Air Force F-102 fighters—armed with nuclear-tipped GAR-11 Falcon air-to-air missiles—scrambled to help the wandering U-2 find its way home and to protect Maultsby from the Soviet fighters.[47] The F-102s were on "Zulu Alert"—armed and fueled inside of special shelters with the crews standing by—and were in the air in just a few minutes.

The fighters were carrying the nuclear-tipped GAR-11s because the Air Defense Command, like SAC on October 22, had gone to DEFCON-2. Under DEFCON-2, nuclear weapons—if available—were loaded and could be used at the discretion of surprisingly low-level officers.[48] This was hardly a unique situation, as throughout the U.S. military, tactical nuclear weapons—from the tiny GAR-11 Falcon with a ¼-Kiloton warhead to the mighty Nike-Hercules SAM with a 40-Kiloton explosive yield—were normally controlled by junior officers without any real sort of supervision of their use. This meant that if the F-102s and MiG-19s engaged, nuclear weapons would likely have been used by the U.S. fighters.

By the time the MiGs and F-102s were airborne, Maultsby had burned too much fuel to return safely to Eielson and barely managed a dead-stick landing at a small Alaskan airfield. He had been airborne for ten hours, twenty-five minutes, a record for an unrefueled U-2 mission. Fortunately, both the Soviet MiGs and the American F-102s were too slow in reacting for Maultsby to turn around and head home. Thus, the U.S. nuclear-armed F-102s did not encounter the MiG fighters, and the first "bumping" incident between American and Soviet forces armed with tactical nuclear weapons did not take place by a margin of just minutes.

Nevertheless, the Arctic incident still sent shock waves in both Moscow and Washington, D.C. To Soviet officials, the U-2 flight might have appeared to be a last-minute reconnaissance before the SAC bombers on airborne alert streaked past their "fail-safe" points and struck targets in the Soviet Union. Khrushchev protested the U-2 transgression to President Kennedy on the 28th: "How should we regard this? What is this, a provocation? One of your planes violates our frontier during this anxious time we are both experiencing, when everything has been put into combat readiness. Is it not a fact than an intruding American plane could be easily taken for a nuclear bomber, which might push us to a fateful step; and all the more so since the U.S. Government and Pentagon long ago declared that you are maintaining a continuous nuclear bomber patrol?"[49]

President Kennedy was forced to apologize to the Soviet leader. He called Maultsby's flight—in an aircraft without arms or cameras—"a serious navigational error" and expressed his regret for the incident, declaring that he would "see to it that every precaution is taken to prevent recurrence."[50] In private, the president declared, "There's always some sonofabitch who doesn't get the message!" Privately, Khrushchev suspected that the U-2 flight toward Siberia had been the result of a navigational error and decided not to make an major issue of the incident. Given what else he had to deal with on this busy Saturday, it ranks as one of the Chairman's better decisions during the crisis.[51]

In the wake of the twin U-2 incidents, activity on the naval blockade line suddenly seemed far less important to ExComm deliberations. The ExComm members, sitting in the White House Cabinet Room, seemed to be moving toward full approval of an assault against Cuba. This, however, did not mean that important events were not under way in the Caribbean.

The U.S. air and naval buildup continued. More tactical aircraft were being readied at airfields in the southeastern United States, while the naval armada was growing to the largest U.S. assembly of warships since World War II. The Fast Carrier Attack Force (Task Force 135) soon numbered three aircraft carriers and sixteen destroyers, plus replenishment ships. The Quarantine Force (Task Force 136) would have three antisubmarine carriers and thirty-three surface warships, plus replenishment ships. The Amphibious Force (Task Force 128) would consist of four helicopter carriers and sixty other amphibious ships (see appendix C).

The quarantine continued, although there were no more boardings after the *Marucla*. There were intercepts, but all ships that passed through the blockade line declared to their U.S. interrogators that they carried nonprohibited cargoes. The quarantine had the effect of demonstrating American resolve and willingness to commit military forces to confront Soviet merchant ships. Most important, the "message" was clearly visible to the Kremlin and to other world governments. But while the quarantine was a message, it was not a means of resolving the crisis peacefully. That would require talking, across a very slow, unreliable, and confusing connection.

10

Crisis beneath the Waves

*I think these few minutes were the time of gravest concern for the Presi-
dent. . . . I heard the President say: "Isn't there some way we can avoid
having our first exchange with a Russian submarine—almost anything
but that?"*

Robert F. Kennedy
Thirteen Days[1]

As the first Soviet merchant ships approached the quarantine line, a
Soviet submarine was detected in the immediate vicinity of the vessels. Nikita Khrushchev and the Soviet military leadership had decided
as early as September 25 not to send a major naval force of surface ships
and submarines to the Caribbean, as originally planned for Operation
Anadyr. Instead, a number of submarines were dispatched with the osten-
sive mission of protecting the merchant ships from interference by U.S.
warships.

Only six Soviet conventional (diesel-electric) submarines participated in the crisis of October 1962. That was particularly remarkable,
considering that the Soviet Union had the world's largest undersea fleet
with almost four hundred submarines in commission in the fall of 1962.
What resulted from this small deployment was one of the most dangerous moments of the Cuban Missile Crisis.

Russian interest in submersible craft dated back to the early 1700s, the
era of Peter the Great, the irrepressible tsar whose government sponsored
primitive submarines and founded the Russian Navy. Thanks to their continued interest in submarines, in 1905–1906, the Russians purchased
American-built submarines designed by Simon Lake, later building the

world's first minelaying submarines and developing primitive snorkel-like breathing tubes for sustained underwater operations. Russian interest in submarines continued until the Bolshevik Revolution and the Russian Civil War (1917–1921) brought a halt to all naval development in the country.

When the Soviet Union initiated its first shipbuilding programs in the early 1920s, the Soviets provided for the construction of submarines as a major component of the fleet. During the next decade, Soviet shipyards produced more submarines than did the yards of any other country, giving the Soviet Union the world's largest undersea fleet when World War II began in Europe in September 1939—168 submarines compared to 57 for the German Navy.[2]

During World War II, the Soviet submarine force accomplished little, mostly because the Germans were able to close the Baltic Sea and capture much of the Black Sea coast. Also, Soviet submarine construction came to an almost complete halt during the war, with production of other weapons such as tanks and aircraft taking priority.

After World War II, building on captured German technology—as did the U.S. Navy—the Soviets again initiated a massive submarine construction program. Some statements indicated that a fleet of a thousand submarines was planned, most to be based on advanced German designs such as the Type XXI. The first postwar, ocean-going submarine—the Project 613 (NATO Whiskey)—went to sea in 1951, and by the fall of 1962, the force of approximately 400 Soviet submarines included 284 ocean-going submarines of postwar construction. Sixteen of those were nuclear propelled, although not all were fully operational (see the following table).

Soviet Nuclear-Propelled Submarines, 1962

Number in Service	Type	Soviet Project Number	NATO Code Name
7	Torpedo-Attack	627/627A	November
5	Ballistic Missile	658	Hotel
4	Cruise Missile	659	Echo I

At that time the U.S. Navy had twenty-five nuclear-propelled submarines in commission, of which nine were Polaris ballistic missile submarines of the *George Washington/Ethan Allen* classes.

The first Soviet nuclear-propelled submarine, Project 627 (NATO November), went to sea in July 1958. That was less than four years after the USS *Nautilus*, the world's first nuclear-propelled vehicle, got under way. This Soviet achievement was especially impressive, considering the massive space, missile, and nuclear weapons construction programs occurring at the time, and the lack of intelligence on U.S. submarines being provided by Soviet spies (in marked contrast to the massive spy effort against the U.S. atomic bomb program).

The Soviet nuclear-propelled submarines were highly advanced in design. The November torpedo-attack submarine was faster, could dive deeper, and was quieter than the contemporary USS *Nautilus*. Furthermore, the Soviet Union initiated the series production of nuclear submarines at an earlier stage than did the U.S. Navy and put to sea the world's first nuclear-propelled cruise (guided) missile and ballistic missile submarines.

However, Soviet industry could not adequately support the nuclear submarine construction program, and a number of near disasters befell early Soviet "nukes." Problems with reactor design and production quality control, along with shortages of key materials and equipment, all combined to make early Soviet nuclear boats as dangerous for their crews as were potential enemies. For example, the first Soviet nuclear-propelled ballistic missile submarine, the *K-19*, suffered a serious accident when a primary coolant pipe burst while the submarine was operating off Greenland on July 4, 1961. She was at a depth of 660 feet, and the entire crew suffered excessive radiation exposure before the submarine was able to reach the surface. Her crew was evacuated with the help of two diesel-electric submarines, and she was taken in tow. Of the 139 men in the *K-19* at the time, 8 men died almost immediately from radiation poisoning, and several more succumbed over the next few years—a total of 14 near-term fatalities.[3]

The official commission that investigated the *K-19* incident determined that poor welding on the reactor was the cause of the failure, and ordered that the submarine's reactor plant be replaced and those of every other Soviet nuclear submarine inspected and repaired as required. Later, the *K-19* suffered additional problems, and other serious troubles befell early Soviet nuclear submarines, which all shared the same basic nuclear reactor plant.

By the start of Operation Anadyr, the reactor inspection-and-repair program was still underway and the Soviet nuclear submarine force not fully operational yet, hence none were sent to the western Atlantic-Caribbean areas to support the missile deployment. This was a serious loss to Operation Anadyr, as the original operation plan had included deployment of a force of both November torpedo-attack and Hotel ballistic-missile boats.

Foxtrot and Slow Dances

While the Soviet Navy was unable to provide the planned force of nuclear submarines for Operation Anadyr, it did supply diesel-electric boats as stand-ins.[4] The Cuban Missile Crisis of 1962 demonstrated that Soviet diesel-electric submarines could operate at great distances and could have an influence on world events. As the U.S. Navy initiated the quarantine, there was considerable concern among the service's leaders that Soviet submarines might seek to interfere with the blockade. They had reason to be anxious, because Soviet submarines were on the way to Cuba.

On October 24, two days after President Kennedy announced the quarantine, the president of Westinghouse International, William E. Knox, met with Khrushchev in Moscow at the Soviet leader's request. Reportedly, Khrushchev stated that stopping and searching Soviet merchant ships on the high seas "would be piracy" and that "the United States could stop and search one or maybe two, but if we did, he would instruct his submarines to sink the American naval vessels."[5] Knox passed along the message.

Significant U.S. Anti-Submarine Warfare (ASW) forces were assigned to support the blockade operations and, if necessary, protect the amphibious forces, as well as the aircraft carriers, in the event of an assault against Cuba. These ASW forces included—at the height of the crisis—three ASW aircraft carriers with specialized, sub-hunting aircraft on board, destroyers, and land-based maritime patrol aircraft. The land-based aircraft flew from bases in the United States and at Argentia, Newfoundland, in Canada. Canadian maritime patrol aircraft joined U.S. aircraft on ASW patrols. U.S. Air Force RB-47 and RB-50 reconnaissance aircraft, as well as U.S. Coast Guard planes—all without specialized ASW equipment—briefly joined in the search.

When the Cuban Missile Crisis began, most U.S. anti-submarine forces concentrated on finding Soviet submarines already in the Caribbean area. But on October 27, a barrier line was established in the North Atlantic with seventeen U.S. and Canadian aircraft and ten submarines to intercept additional Soviet submarines moving westward. This ensured that no additional Soviet submarines would be able to reach Cuba to support Operation Anadyr.

In addition to forces that could "hunt and kill" Soviet submarines, to use the vernacular of the trade, the U.S. ASW "forces" included the highly secret Sound Surveillance System (SOSUS), the seafloor hydrophone arrays that sought out submarine sounds in the ocean. SOSUS provided timely cross bearings on submarine noises that would be used to cue ASW ships and submarines, along with being able to detect some status information (snorkeling on diesel power, engineering problems, etc.) about what the targets were doing.

Thus, the U.S. Navy and those NATO navies with which it shared ASW/SOSUS intelligence were well aware that several Soviet diesel-electric submarines were in the Western Atlantic by mid-October 1962. SOSUS could easily detect the relatively noisy nuclear submarines of the era, which had steam plants and hence pumps, water flowing through pipes, and other noise sources. However, diesel submarines—when submerged and drawing their power from electric batteries—were (and still are) very difficult to detect. Rather, it was when the conventional submarine came to the surface or extended a snorkel breathing tube and operated its diesel engines (to recharge batteries) that it could be easily detected by SOSUS and other means.

The Cuban crisis reached a critical point a few minutes after 10 A.M. Eastern time on Wednesday, October 24, when Secretary of Defense Robert S. McNamara advised President Kennedy at the ExComm meeting that two Soviet freighters were within a few miles of the quarantine line, where they would be intercepted by U.S. destroyers. Each merchant ship was accompanied by a submarine. "And this is a very dangerous situation," added McNamara.[6]

Robert F. Kennedy recalled, "Then came the disturbing Navy report that a Russian submarine had moved into position between the two ships."[7] The decision was made at the White House to have the Navy signal the submarine by sonar to surface and identify itself. If the submarine refused, small explosives would be dropped near the submarine (by a helicopter or a destroyer) as a signal. Robert Kennedy recalled the concern over that single Foxtrot submarine: "I think these few minutes were the time of gravest concern for the President. . . . I heard the President say: 'Isn't there some way we can avoid having our first exchange with a Russian submarine—almost anything but that?'"

At 10:25 that morning, word was received at the White House that the Soviet freighters had stopped and the crisis abated for the moment. The president's trepidation was based on the assumption by Secretary

McNamara and other members of ExComm—as well as by the U.S. Navy's leadership—that the Soviet submarine carried torpedoes with high-explosive warheads (as had Kennedy's PT-boat in World War II). A "spread" of several such torpedoes launched by a submarine could easily sink an American destroyer and possibly one of the large cruisers or even an aircraft carrier enforcing the quarantine.

Unknown to President Kennedy—or anyone else in the U.S. government or the Navy—the Soviet submarine that had been detected between the two merchant ships also carried a torpedo with a nuclear warhead. So did the other Soviet submarines in the area. Once again, "small" battlefield nuclear weapons were about to cast their dangerous shadow across the Cuban Missile Crisis.

Westward Ho!

On October 1, 1962, four Soviet Project 641/Foxtrot submarines of the 69th Brigade departed bases on the Kola Peninsula en route to the Caribbean in support of Operation Anadyr. Another Foxtrot and one older Project 611/Zulu submarine were already in the Western Atlantic.[8]

The Foxtrots were advanced, long-range, diesel-electric submarines, the first of the type having entered service in late 1958. Each had six bow and four stern torpedo tubes and normally carried up to twelve reload torpedoes, in addition to the ten in the tubes.

Along with their conventional torpedoes, each of the submarines that departed its base on October 1 had one Type 53-58 nuclear torpedo on board.[9] The nuclear torpedo, developed under the designation T-5, could be fired from a standard 21-inch-diameter torpedo tube. Its RDS-9 warhead had demonstrated an explosive force of 10 kilotons in tests—more than half the destructive power of the Hiroshima and Nagasaki atomic bombs.[10]

Rear Admiral Georgi Kostev, a veteran Soviet submarine commander and a historian, later said, "Khrushchev believed that it was proper for the submarines, if the convoy would be stopped, to sink the ships of the other party."[11] When asked how he believed a nuclear war could have been sparked at sea, Admiral Kostev replied, "The war could have started this way—the American Navy hits the Soviet submarine [with a torpedo or a depth charge] and somehow does not harm it. In that case, the commander would have for sure used his weapons against the attacker."

One of the Foxtrot commanding officers, Captain 2nd Rank Aleksey F. Dubivko of the *B-36*, recalled that each submarine had been given instructions in a sealed envelope. The commanding officer could open them only after a special radio signal was received, and with the submarine's three senior officers present. Dubivko recalled, "I had my orders to use my weapons and particularly [the] nuclear torpedo only by instructions from my base. As far as I'm concerned, having received an order to use my nuclear torpedo, I would surely have aimed it at an aircraft carrier, and there were plenty of them there, in the area."[12]

Years later, another of the submarine commanders, Captain 2nd Rank Ryurik Ketov of the *B-4*, said that their orders were "Use the special weapon [nuclear torpedo] in the following cases: first, if they bomb and hit you; second, if they force you to surface and shoot at you on the surface; third, on orders from Moscow."[13]

The U.S. Navy had initially planned to use a heavy cruiser to intercept the first Soviet ship to reach the quarantine line, the 6,500-deadweight-ton *Komiles*, on October 24. But the proximity of a submarine to the merchant ship led to the decision to intercept the ship with a destroyer—a smaller warship—because it had sonar and ASW weapons. The intercept was set to take place some 500 miles from Cuba.

As ExComm members waited for clarification as to whether the merchant ships had halted or were proceeding through the barrier, the submarine threat continued to dominate their conversation. Secretary McNamara explained, "The plan . . . is to send anti-submarine helicopters [from the ASW carrier *Essex*] out to harass the submarine. And they have weapons and devices that can damage the submarine. And the plan, therefore, is to put pressure on the submarine, move it out of the area by that pressure, by the pressure of potential destruction, and make the [merchant ship] intercept. But this is only a plan, and there are many, many uncertainties."[14]

Secretary McNamara also explained some of those uncertainties as he informed his fellow ExComm members about the difficulties of sonar detection and the relative range of submarine torpedoes. (At the afternoon ExComm meeting on the 24th, McNamara added, "Our knowledge of submarines, Soviet Union submarines, in the Atlantic is the most highly classified information we have in the Department [of Defense]." The primary source of that knowledge, of course, was SOSUS.)

Intensive U.S. search operations located all six Soviet submarines, albeit two of them on the surface and returning to their bases on the Kola Peninsula—one Foxtrot and an older Zulu-class submarine (see the following table).

Soviet Submarines Identified
During the Cuban Missile Crisis

First Sighting*	Position	Type	Notes
22 Oct. 1024Z	42°55′N 39°30′W	611/Zulu	Returning to USSR
24 Oct. 1929Z	25°25′N 68°10′W	641/Foxtrot	Returning to USSR
25 Oct. 2211Z	27°30′N 68°00′W	641/Foxtrot	Northeast of Cuba
26 Oct. 1048Z	21°31′N 69°14′W	641/Foxtrot	East of Cuba
26 Oct. 1908Z	24°40′N 72°15′W	641/Foxtrot	Northeast of Cuba
26 Oct. 2105Z	18°05′N 75°26′W	641/Foxtrot	North of Cuba

*Greenwich Mean Time (Z).

The Foxtrot (pennant no. 945) from the group that had departed on October 1 had suffered mechanical difficulties; she was sighted on the surface, en route back to the Kola Peninsula in company with the naval salvage tug *Pamir*.[15] The Zulu was also sighted on the surface, refueling from the naval tanker *Terek*.

The voyage of the Soviet 69th Submarine Brigade to Cuba—known as Operation Kama—in October 1962 was a journey fraught with difficulties and hardships.[16] Much of its troubles centered on the Soviets' lack of experience operating in the tropical waters of the Caribbean Sea, conditions that few Soviet sailors had ever encountered. Their inexperience with so-called out-of-area operations meant that the submariners of the Soviet Northern Fleet were used to operating in the Arctic depths of the Barents Sea, not in the warm waters of the Western Atlantic. Also, the Cuban deployment was one of the longest in the history of the Soviet Navy, stretching the endurance of both submarines and crews to the breaking point and—in come cases—beyond.[17]

A key problem for the Soviet submariners was fresh water or, more precisely, the shortage of it. As in all diesel-electric submarines, living conditions aboard the Project 641/Foxtrots were extremely cramped and spare. Known as "Pig Boats" by their crews, they always had a short supply of every creature comfort and even some necessities. This included fresh water, which had to be distilled from seawater and rationed to support drinking, sanitary, and some engineering needs.

The last of those fresh water needs was where the trouble came from, due to the warmer-than-expected conditions of the Western Atlantic. The tropical conditions caused a buildup of heat and humidity inside the submarines, which caused their batteries to begin drying out. This meant

Officers of the Foxtrot-class submarine *B-130* watch as they are overflown by a U.S. aircraft during the missile crisis. At the time, most Soviet submarines had large pennant numbers painted on the sail or the fairwater structure.

that water needed for the crew had to be diverted to refresh the batteries, which were also suffering storage capacity problems from the heat, which caused further difficulties while submerged. The crewmembers began to dehydrate, resulting in severe health problems that included skin lesions and rashes. Added to this were further difficulties from equipment break-downs caused by the extended use dictated by the long voyage to Cuba. By the time the submarines of the 69th Brigade got into the area being quarantined by the U.S. Navy in late October, they were barely able to function, much less be combat ready.[18]

On October 27, with her batteries running low, the submarine *B-59*, commanded by Captain 2nd Rank Valentin Savitsky, was forced to surface by U.S. destroyers. His account of the ordeal is spellbinding:

> . . . [O]nly emergency lighting was functioning. The temperature in the compartments was 45–50 C [113° F to 122° F], up to 60 C [140° F] in the engine compartment. It was unbearably stuffy. The level of CO2 in the air reached a critical practically deadly for people mark. One of the duty officers fainted and fell down. Then another one followed, then the third one. . . . They were falling like dominoes.[19]

The account, as told to a Russian journalist, continued:

> . . . [T]he totally exhausted Savitsky, who in addition to everything, was not able to establish [a radio] connection with the General Staff, became furious. He summoned the officer who was assigned to the nuclear tor-pedo, ordered him to assemble it to battle readiness. "Maybe the war has already started up there, while we are doing somersaults here"—screamed emotional Valentin Grigorievich [Savitsky], trying to justify his order. "We're going to blast them now! We will die, but we will sink them all—we will not disgrace our Navy!"

The Soviet Project 641 submarine (NATO Foxtrot) *B-59*
underway on the surface during the Cuban crisis with a
U.S. Navy HSS-1 Seabat helicopter hovering nearby. The
Foxtrot was a modern, long-range submarine that had first
entered Soviet naval service in 1957.

Suddenly, the deployment of the four Project 641/Foxtrots had become deadly serious, with a nuclear weapon assembled, armed, and loaded
into a launch tube. All that stood between tense peace and a small nuclear
war in the Caribbean Sea was a rattled, exhausted, dehydrated, and desperate submarine captain. But Savitsky did not fire any torpedoes.

Calming slightly, Savitsky had "discussions" with his second in command and the submarine's political officer about the situation, and he
made the decision to come to the surface. Upon surfacing the *B-59*,
Savitsky observed that one of the destroyers had a jazz band playing on
deck, while the USS *Cony* communicated by a flashing light, inquiring
whether the submarine required assistance. Tongue-in-cheek communications between the *B-59* and her adversaries followed, with Savitsky
identifying his submarine by different names to each of the nearby U.S.
destroyers.

The *B-59* apparently remained on the surface until the evening of
October 29, when the deck log of the U.S. destroyer *Barry* noted that the
craft submerged "without warning."

Another Foxtrot, the *B-36* (pennant no. 911), was forced to the surface after thirty-six continuous hours of sonar contact and harassment by
the U.S. destroyer *Charles P. Cecil* and maritime patrol aircraft on October 30–31. The *Cecil* made contact with the submarine some 200 nautical miles north of Haiti on the night of October 29. The submarine dived,
but the *Cecil*, coordinating other surface ships as well as ASW aircraft,

This Foxtrot-class submarine is caught on the surface by a U.S. destroyer and a P2V Neptune patrol aircraft during the missile crisis. Aggressive tactics forced all Soviet submarines in the area to the surface.

held the contact until the submarine was forced up, apparently having depleted her battery after thirty-six hours of evasion efforts. The commanding officer of the destroyer, Commander Charles P. Rozier, was awarded the Navy Commendation Medal for maintaining contact during that period, "despite repeated and extreme attempts by the submarine to escape."

Upon surfacing, Captain 2nd Rank Aleksey Dubivko of the *B-36* found helicopters hovering nearby and a signal light from the *Cecil* asking, "Do you need help?" Dubivko responded that he did not and asked that the U.S. forces not interfere with his actions.

Code Name CUBEX

The submarine/ASW aspects of the Cuban Missile Crisis provided the U.S. Navy with considerable insight into Soviet submarine capabilities and tactics, as well as problems. However, as the official U.S. analysis of the ASW operations—given the code name CUBEX for Cuban Exercise—states:[20]

> The reliability of results of CUBEX evaluation is affected by small sample size and biased by two major artificialities. The factitious aspects of the operation included the non-use of destructive ordnance and the priority scheduling of aircraft during daylight hours for the visual/photographic needs of the Cuban quarantine force. The unnatural case of not carrying a contact through "to the kill" affected the tactics of both the hunter and hunted, as did the unbalanced day/night coverage.[21]

The Soviet submarines sought to evade detection by short bursts of high speed and radical maneuvering—which included backing down and stopping, taking advantage of thermal layers, turning into the wakes of ASW ships, and releasing "slugs" (bubbles) of air and acoustic decoys. But *at times* knowing that they probably were safe from attack with lethal weapons, and not being required to carry out attacks against U.S. ships, the Soviet submarine captains were not realistically tested in a conflict situation. Also, the submarines made considerable use of radar, which they might not employ to the same extent in wartime. Extensive snorkeling also occurred, with durations of one-half hour to eleven hours being detected by U.S. forces. Undoubtedly, in a true wartime environment, the submarines would have practiced less frequent and shorter-duration snorkel operations.

Despite the "peacetime" environment of the CUBEX, with large numbers of ASW ships and aircraft available, uninhibited communications, and the lack of counterattacks by their prey, U.S. anti-submarine forces were hard-pressed to track down and force identification of the Soviet submarines. The SOSUS seafloor detection system was available to U.S. forces, but, according to one Navy after-action report, the "SOSUS signature library contents on USSR submarines are understandably meager. Further, the signatures [of Soviet submarines] were found to be significantly different from the expected."[22]

During the missile crisis, the Soviets made no effort to deploy their force of nuclear- or diesel-propelled missile submarines to within striking range of the continental United States. And the few first-generation nuclear submarines were still suffering continual mechanical problems at that time. Still, in his December 1962 report to the Supreme Soviet, Premier Khrushchev stated that "Our submarine fleet, including atomic submarines, occupied assigned stations during the crisis."

The four Soviet Foxtrot-class submarines that did operate in the Caribbean area during the crisis were harassed continually by U.S. naval forces following imposition of the quarantine. Being kept underwater—unable to snorkel—for days at a time exhausted their batteries, which meant that air was not being effectively circulated, and the submarines lacked air-conditioning. In some boats, the carbon dioxide built up to dangerous levels as the boats were unable to draw in fresh air. In spite of these terrible conditions, they continued their missions until being recalled on October 31.

Because of the need to reduce tensions with the United States, the submarines of the 69th Brigade were ordered to return to the Soviet Union, rather than continue on to Cuba. While the voyage home was somewhat less harrowing than their outbound journey, their crews were still thin and weak. It took until early December for the four boats to return to their base near Murmansk, where they were subjected to an intense debriefing, ordered to keep the events of Operation Kama secret, and quietly given leave. The leaders of the Soviet Navy knew that the submariners of the 69th Brigade had done all that could have been asked of them and more and had performed honorably.[23]

Despite these conditions, there were no U.S. attacks on Soviet submarines, nor did any of the Soviet submarines fire on U.S. warships. But it was a close-run "game"—sometimes referred to as "cat and mouse," although more often by journalists than by naval officers.

The adrenalin was pumping in U.S. sailors on destroyers and the pilots of ASW helicopters and fixed-wing aircraft as they sought the Soviet undersea craft. The harassment took a great toll on the Soviet submariners. A sudden, unexpected maneuver by a destroyer captain or the release of a decoy by a submarine—believed to be a torpedo launch by a destroyer sonarman—could have led to a deadly nuclear exchange. Those "minutes" were properly "the greatest concern for President Kennedy."[24]

11

The View from the Kremlin

In the heart of Moscow, its massive red walls jutting from the bank of the Moscow River stood the somber medieval citadel of Russian power, the Kremlin. Not a single building but an entire walled city, it seemed to a romantic Frenchman no less than a mirror of Russia itself: "This curious conglomeration of palaces, towers, churches, monasteries, chapels, barracks, arsenals and bastions; this incoherent jumble of sacred and secular buildings; this complex of functions as fortress, sanctuary, seraglio, harem, necropolis, and prison; this blend of advanced civilization and archaic barbarism; this violent conflict of crudest materialism and most lofty spirituality; are then not the whole history of Russia, the whole epic of the Russian nation, the whole inward drama of the Russian soul?"

Robert K. Massie
Nicholas and Alexandra[1]

For all the efforts of the Kennedy administration to clearly state its case for removal of the Soviet missiles from Cuba during the second week of the crisis, it failed to make any real impression on the one group that mattered: the leadership of the Soviet Union. Rather than Soviet leaders opening a dialogue following President Kennedy's speech on October 22, the sudden announcement and the establishment of the naval quarantine caused them to see the United States as threatening, rather than accommodating, in its intentions. This lack of direct communication between the White House and the Kremlin was a result of each nation misunderstanding the character of the men on the other side and the nations they led. There was also a very real ignorance on both sides of the other's political system, which was exacerbated by the still-closed and secretive nature of Soviet society as it emerged from the nightmare of Josef Stalin's "Great Terror" in the 1950s.

In the 1960s, American views of Soviet leaders and the political system they worked within were shaped by the misconception that Nikita Khrushchev was simply another version of Josef Stalin, acting in the same dictatorial and unilateral ways. Few senior leaders, including President Kennedy, understood that in 1959, the communist world had been split asunder when China and the Soviet Union had broken their ten-year partnership.[2] In fact, the Soviet Union had changed a great deal in the decade following Stalin's death in 1953, although it was hardly the idealized collective structure that had been envisioned by the communist visionaries Karl Marx and Vladimir Lenin.[3]

By 1962, the Soviet leadership was based on a committee structure—a political coalition headed by Nikita Khrushchev. While officially there was a president, a system of governmental ministries, and a parliamentary body known as the Supreme Soviet, the real power lay within the group known as the Presidium of the Central Committee of the Communist Party of the Soviet Union (CPSU).[4] In fact, the Soviet Union after Stalin had evolved into a relatively balanced system of shared power centered on the CPSU, the armed forces, and the state security apparatus (KGB). After the death of Stalin, any group or person desiring political supremacy in the Soviet Union required at least two of the three power bases to rule or to take over power.[5]

Inside the Kremlin: Khrushchev's Inner Circle

The five years prior to the Cuban Missile Crisis had seen a great deal of change and turnover within Khrushchev's inner circle, mostly due to an attempted coup that he had fended off in June 1957. The attempted coup was in fact the result of hard-line elements of the government, reacting to Khrushchev's secret speech denouncing Stalin's excesses at the 20th CPSU Party Congress in 1956 and his policy of rehabilitation that followed.[6] In June 1957, senior members of the armed forces and the KGB tried to oust him, failing when Khrushchev rapidly mobilized his power base, which included the World War II hero and Marshal of the Soviet Union Georgi Zhukov.[7] After surviving the coup attempt, Khrushchev spent the next few years restructuring the top leadership positions around him, and the men he took into the Cuban Missile Crisis reflected both his political thinking and his desire to survive future upheavals.

One of Khrushchev's first moves after the coup attempt was to sack his colleague Marshal Zhukov and replace him as Minister of Defense with Marshal Rodion Yakovlevich Malinovsky.[8] Born in Odessa in 1898, Malinovsky was a veteran of World War I (in both France and Russia), the Russian and Spanish Civil Wars, the Great Patriotic War (the Eastern Front in World War II), and the brief conflict against Japan in 1945. Promoted to Marshal of the Soviet Union in 1944, he was one of the Red Army's longest serving and most decorated officers.[9]

Despite his age, Malinovsky was a most progressive military leader, bringing guided missiles, supersonic aircraft, and nuclear-propelled submarines into service during his tenure as minister. Under Khrushchev, Malinovsky also presided over a systemic downsizing and restructuring of the Soviet armed forces, emphasizing the use of nuclear missiles in the place of conventional armed forces to deter aggression against the Soviet Union. This included creation of the Strategic Rocket Forces (SRF). Malinovsky also had a reputation as a brilliant staff officer, using brutal honesty in dealing with his peers within the Presidium.

Another important Presidium personnel change came with Khrushchev's appointment, as his foreign minister, of the man who became one of the longest-lived senior officials in Soviet history: Andrei Andreyevish Gromyko. Born in 1909 in what is today Belarus, Gromyko entered the Soviet foreign service in 1924 and quickly caught the eye of Stalin's foreign minister, Vyacheslav Molotov, who became his mentor. Gromyko was unusual for a Soviet diplomat of his era, in that he had significant experience working with and living in the United States, having been ambassador to the United States from 1943 to 1946, followed by a tour as Soviet United Nations ambassador from 1946 to 1949. When Molotov was removed as foreign minister following the 1957 coup attempt, Gromyko was named as his replacement despite his mentor's treachery, so great and obvious were his diplomatic skills. A true intimate of Khrushchev, he would serve as Soviet foreign minister for *every* remaining Soviet leader through Mikhail Gorbachev in the 1990s.[10]

A more recent appointment was Vladimir Yefimovich Semichastny as Chairman of the Committee for State Security (KGB). Born in 1924, Semichastny replaced his mentor Aleksandr Shelepin in 1961, who himself had been appointed KGB chairman in 1958 following the coup attempt. Semichastny was not a particularly strong or talented KGB chairman, which in all likelihood was exactly Khrushchev's intention.[11] Having allowed Shelepin to purge the KGB of anti-Khrushchev elements between 1958 and 1961, Semichastny appears to have been a nonthreatening choice to head a greatly weakened agency.[12] Colonel Oleg Penkovsky did almost all of his spying for the British and the Americans on their watch, which was characterized by the KGB's poor development of an intelligence collection network in the West.[13]

While the Presidium normally had about two dozen members at any given time—both voting and "candidate" nonvoting—only a handful had power during Khrushchev's reign.[14] Interestingly, in 1962 this did *not* include KGB chairman Semichastny. After the 1957 coup attempt, Khrushchev packed the Presidium with men of his own choosing, trying to carefully balance the political character and the politics of the committee. He included two former Stalin supporters, Leonid Ilyich Brezhnev and Aleksei Nikolayevich Kosygin. An engineer by training, Brezhnev held a number of party posts, though his most important duties were to oversee the Soviet nuclear and missile programs.[15] Kosygin was an industrial planner and an economist, who was a key contributor to the Soviet "Five-Year Plans" during Khrushchev's tenure as premier.[16] Most of the remaining Presidium members had only secondary roles in the Cuban Missile Crisis.

Premier Khrushchev shared the personal quality with President Kennedy of keeping his own counsel. Just two other men became Khrushchev's personal sounding boards for ideas and policies, along with carrying out special errands. The first was Anastas Ivanovich Mikoyan, a peer of the Soviet premier and one of his closest advisors. Born in 1895 in Armenia, Mikoyan was both salesman and survivor, having spent much of his life around Stalin and other senior Soviet leaders. A generalist and a natural diplomat, he held Khrushchev's absolute trust for the most discreet tasks, which ranged from investigating Stalin's crimes to conducting the early negotiations with Fidel Castro and the Cuban leadership for Operation Anadyr.[17]

The other man Khrushchev could talk to and trust implicitly was his son Sergei, a missile guidance engineer at the Chelomi Design Bureau. Although not a politician per se, the younger Khrushchev was present on many of his father's trips, and he attended many important meetings. Born in 1935 to Khrushchev's second wife, Nina Petrovna, Sergei became a regular partner on his father's evening walks, providing a useful sounding board for the Soviet premier at the end of his long days in the Kremlin.

The Boss: Nikita Sergeyevich Khrushchev

At the center of the Soviet political and government structure in 1962 was Nikita Sergeyevich Khrushchev, who had taken power after the

Nikita Khrushchev with his son Sergei. The younger Khrushchev, a missile guidance engineer and a historian, is now a professor at Brown University in Providence, Rhode Island.

death of Josef Stalin in 1953 and the subsequent power struggle. Born in southwestern Russia in 1894 as the son of an itinerant miner and the grandson of a serf, Khrushchev received little formal schooling and began working as a pipe fitter at age fifteen. Something of a labor activist, he joined the Communist Party in 1918. He was brought to Moscow by Stalin, where he began a steady rise to the heights of the Soviet leadership. Khrushchev survived Stalin's purges to become one of the top CPSU political officers during the Great Patriotic War (World War II on the Eastern Front), serving at the battles of Moscow, Stalingrad, and Kursk. After the war, Khrushchev managed to avoid Stalin's renewed purges during his final years and was the Moscow party boss when Stalin died on March 5, 1953.

Though initially considered something of a "lightweight" among Stalin's inner circle, Khrushchev was among the several Soviet officials who took the reins of power at Stalin's death. But within months he emerged as the "first among equals," outmaneuvering Kremlin insiders like Lavrenty Beria (Stalin's sadistic NKVD chairman) and Georgi Malenkov, who took over the jobs of premier and, briefly, CPSU chairman. Khrushchev quickly assumed the important post of First Secretary of the Communist Party in September 1953 and soon became the de facto head of the Soviet government. In 1958, he was also named premier of the Soviet Union.

Although Khrushchev had spent much of his life ruthlessly carrying out the policies and orders of Stalin, he had a sincere desire to undo the excesses of his mentor and try to make the Soviet Union into something more than a Third World police state with nuclear weapons. A generation before Mikhail Gorbachev's *Perestroika* and *Glasnost* movements took hold, Khrushchev attempted a similar set of reforms in a much tougher world environment with far more potential enemies.[18] Among his earliest efforts were the halting of Stalin's huge conventional buildup of armed forces, the downsizing of the Soviet Army and Navy, and a shift to a policy of deterrence by developing long-range guided missiles. Khrushchev also attempted to heal some of the social damage done by Stalin by denouncing his excesses at the 1956 CPSU Party Congress and releasing thousands of political prisoners from gulags and other detention facilities. Khrushchev's long-range goal was to create a consumer economy with standards of living comparable to those in the West, while avoiding another devastating foreign invasion like Napoleon's and Hitler's.

As logical as these goals seem in the post–Cold War world, they represented a radical change of direction for the Soviet Union in the 1950s, and supporters of Stalin's regime had to be placated for Khrushchev to keep his position. Thus, Khrushchev could denounce Stalin in 1956 and still allow the 1957 coup plotters to remain alive and to quietly retire. Nevertheless, there was still a ruthless side to Khrushchev, manifested in his maintaining the closed society of the Soviet Union and his willingness to invade Hungary when a minor democracy movement took hold there in late 1956.

By contemporary standards, Khrushchev was an odd hybrid: a visionary who could see the Soviet Union as a world-class military and economic superpower, while still maintaining his personal commitment to Communism and its spread around the world. A man of little education and knowledge of the world outside the Soviet Union, Khrushchev had the vision to give the Soviet Union the world's first intercontinental ballistic missile force and earth-orbiting satellites. Most of all, Nikita Khrushchev was a natural politician, able to charm guests and competitors one minute, yet able to outrage the world the next.

By the spring of 1962, when Premier Khrushchev had decided to send strategic missiles to Cuba, he was the unchallenged head of the Soviet regime. While some members of the ruling Presidium were opposed to Khrushchev's policies and actions, he invariably enjoyed their total support when critical votes were cast.

Still, life was difficult for Khrushchev in the spring and the summer of 1962. The previous year, the aborted American-sponsored invasion of Cuba at the Bay of Pigs had demonstrated how tenuous communist expansion was beyond the distance that could be marched by the Red Army. The Soviets had supported East Germany's decision to erect the Berlin

Wall to stop the hemorrhage of workers and scientists to the West, a move that many—some within the Soviet Union—believed had vilified the communist regime. Earlier, a meeting in Vienna in June 1961 with John F. Kennedy, the new American president, had not gone well. Sergei Khrushchev later wrote, "It's not especially important who looked gloomier: Father and the president both understood that something unfortunate was happening, but both sides envisioned a final victory over the adversary."[19]

The threat of an American invasion of Cuba loomed in 1962, and issues over Berlin and the unification of Germany remained major problems for Khrushchev. The problems with the Soviet domestic economy, the buildup of U.S. conventional military forces, and the increasing imbalance of strategic nuclear forces that favored the United States weighed on Khrushchev.[20] Khrushchev's daring stratagem for placing nuclear missiles, accompanied by a massive conventional military force armed with tactical nuclear weapons, in Cuba was seen as a means of protecting the Cuban Revolution, as well as of helping to redress the strategic imbalance.

On August 26, 1962, Ernesto Che Guevara and Emilio Aragonés Navarro, a close associate of Fidel Castro, arrived in Moscow for talks with Soviet defense officials. On August 30, they met with Khrushchev at his dacha in the Crimea, where Guevara delivered Castro's amendments to the Soviet-Cuban agreement on the deployment of missiles in Cuba. Guevara urged Khrushchev to announce the missile deployment publicly, which would bring Castro the prestige of being an international "player." Khrushchev quickly explained to the thirty-four-year-old Cuban official that such an announcement before the missiles were in place would be premature.

After negotiations, the decision was made to put off formal ratification of the treaty until the end of the year, when the signing ceremonies would take place in Havana. Khrushchev had visited the Western Hemisphere in September 1959, when he toured the United States as President Eisenhower's guest, and again in September 1960, for the opening session of the United Nations. During the latter trip, he had met and, literally, embraced Castro in New York City. In December 1962, Khrushchev planned to again cross the ocean to visit the first socialist state in the New World. There he intended to announce that his missiles were in Cuba and were ready to launch to deter American aggression. But he wanted to wait until after November, when the Anadyr buildup was completed and after the U.S. congressional elections.

*   *   *

Khrushchev believed that American duplicity in the U-2 overflights of the Soviet Union from 1956 to 1960 entitled him to employ similar deceptions. Using the more personal communications link established after their meeting in Vienna in 1961, the superpower leaders used trusted aides to pass messages. Robert Kennedy and White House Press Secretary Pierre Salinger were messengers on the American side, and Ambassador Anatoly Dobrynin, the head of the press department of the Foreign Ministry Mikhail Kharlamov, and the Washington-based journalist and military intelligence officer Georgi Bolshakov worked directly for Khrushchev. Using this communications back channel, Dobrynin assured Robert Kennedy, and hence the president, as late as September 1962 that no offensive missiles had been placed in Cuba, especially not ballistic missiles that could strike the United States. In Moscow's desire for secrecy, the *maskirovka* plan meant that Ambassador Dobrynin knew nothing of the missile deployment.

The perceived success of the *maskirovka* effort apparently led Khrushchev not to order the use of the SA-2 missiles that had been rushed to Cuba to down U.S. reconnaissance flights. The U-2 flight of August 29 had provided conclusive evidence of SA-2 sites at eight locations in Cuba. Two days later, President Kennedy had been informed of the presence of the surface-to-air missiles in Cuba. (That same day, Kennedy, at a news conference, had declared that there was no evidence of Soviet troops in Cuba and "no information as yet" about the possible presence of air-defense missiles on the island.)

It was now September. With the chill of fall in the air and clouds in the sky over the Kremlin, Khrushchev could look with pride on the apparent success of Operation Anadyr. In early September, despite intensive surveillance flights by U.S. and other NATO aircraft, there was no evidence that the missiles or the large number of heavily armed troops being sent to Cuba had been detected. But on September 4, Kennedy released a statement to the American public revealing that SA-2 missiles and substantially more military personnel than previously estimated had been detected in Cuba. Still, Kennedy tempered his comments by adding, "There is no evidence of any organized combat force in Cuba from any Soviet Bloc country; of military bases provided to Russia; of a violation of the 1934 treaty relating to Guantánamo; of the presence of offensive ground-to-ground missiles; or of other significant offensive capability. . . . Were it otherwise the gravest issues would arise."[21] On the same day, using back-channel communications, Khrushchev assured Kennedy that the Soviet Union would not deploy ballistic missiles or other offensive weapons to Cuba.

On September 7, as Soviet Ambassador Dobrynin was assuring Adlai Stevenson, the American ambassador to the United Nations, that only defensive weapons were being sent to Cuba, President Kennedy asked Congress to call fifteen thousand reservists to active military service.

Possibly in response to continued U.S. questions about offensive weapons in Cuba, the Soviet news agency TASS released a government statement on September 11 condemning U.S. overseas bases and denying any intention of introducing offensive weapons into Cuba. The statement declared: "The arms and military equipment sent to Cuba are intended solely for defensive purposes. . . . There is no need for the Soviet Union to set up in any other country—Cuba, for instance—the weapons it has for repelling aggression, for a retaliatory blow."[22]

In mid-September, Khrushchev returned to Moscow from another holiday on the Black Sea. Western intelligence agencies—which tried to keep track of the Soviet leader's movements—must have felt that his vacationing was a clear signal that no crisis was building. After a few days in Moscow, on September 26, Khrushchev again departed his capital, flying to Ashkhabad in Central Asia to assess the cotton harvest. He visited farms and cities in the area before coming back to Moscow on October 10.

The reports from General Issa Pliyev in Cuba were all positive. Ships were arriving on schedule, with their cargoes and troops being moved under cover of darkness to the preselected sites. Pliyev reported that all was proceeding as planned and that the missiles would be installed and ready by October 31—*except* that the SS-5 (R-14) missiles had not yet arrived. Those weapons had always been planned to follow the SS-4 (R-12) missiles because they required the construction of concrete launchpads and more elaborate support facilities.

Soviet commanders in Cuba had been warned to keep their weapons and troops out of sight from spying American U-2s (and, after October 23, from low-flying F8U-1P reconnaissance aircraft). However, the volume of equipment, with thousands of troops and hundreds of vehicles, and the large size of the SS-4 missiles made it difficult to hide all activity. Furthermore, although Soviet troops were considered masters at camouflage techniques, the camouflage netting provided was not immediately used. Early on October 14, a U.S. Air Force U-2 flying over western Cuba took photographs of missile equipment at San Cristobal, some sixty miles west of Havana, igniting the missile crisis. As the U-2's cameras recorded the scene, the Kremlin leaders were enjoying a leisurely Sunday afternoon, blissfully unaware that their secret was about to be revealed.

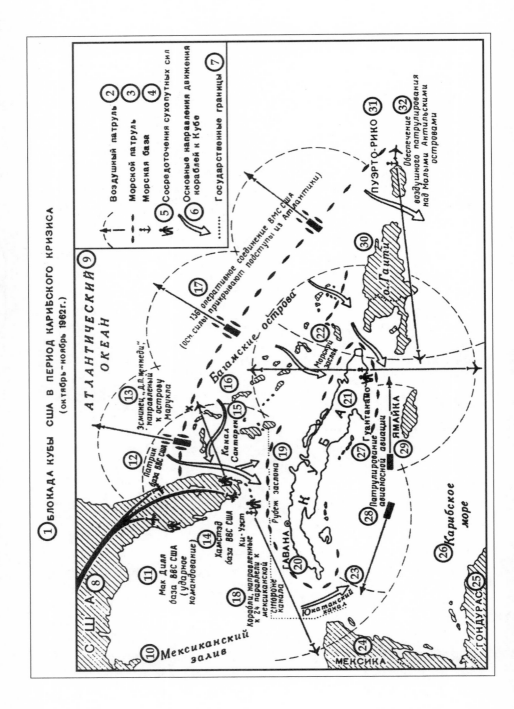

Блокада Кубы США в период Карибского кризиса (октябрь–ноябрь 1962 г.)

① БЛОКАДА КУБЫ США В ПЕРИОД КАРИБСКОГО КРИЗИСА (октябрь–ноябрь 1962 г.)

Условные обозначения:
- Воздушный патруль ②
- Морской патруль ③
- Морская база ④
- ⑤ Сосредоточения сухопутных сил
- ⑥ Основные направления движения кораблей к Кубе
- Государственные границы ⑦

⑨ АТЛАНТИЧЕСКИЙ ОКЕАН

⑧ США

⑩ Мексиканский залив

⑪ Мак Дилл база ВВС США (ударное командование)

⑫ Патрик база ВВС США

⑬ Эсминец „Д.Л.кеннеди" направленный к острову Марукла

⑭ Хамстэд база ВВС США

Ки-Уэст

⑰ 138 оперативное соединение ВМС США (осн. силы прикрывают подступы из Атлантики)

⑯ Бахамские острова

⑮

⑱ Корабли, направленные к 24 параллели к мексиканской каналы

⑲ Рубеж заслона

⑳ ГАВАНА

Канал Санторен

Старый Багамский канал

К У Б А

Юкатанский канал

㉔ МЕКСИКА

㉒ Морской заслон

㉓

㉑ Гуантанамо база авиационной

㉗

㉙ ЯМАЙКА

㉘ Патрулирование авианосной авиации

㉚ о. Гаити

㉛ ПУЭРТО-РИКО

㉜ Обеспечение воздушного патрулирования над Малыми Антильскими островами

㉖ Карибское море

㉕ ГОНДУРАС

176

English Translations for Russian text on Anadyr Map

① BLOCKADE OF CUBA BY THE USA IN THE PERIOD OF THE CARIBBEAN CRISIS (OCTOBER - NOVEMBER OF 1962)

② Air patrol (USA)

③ Sea patrol (USA)

④ Sea base (USA)

⑤ Concentration of land forces (USA)

⑥ Basic direction of ships to Cuba (Soviet)

⑦ State frontier (Cuba)

⑧ USA

⑨ Atlantic Ocean

⑩ Gulf of Mexico

⑪ MacDill base of the USA Air Force (Strike Command)

⑫ Patrick base of the USA Air Force

⑬ Destroyer J. Kennedy directed to Marucla

⑭ Homestead base of the USA Air Force

⑮ Santaren Channel

⑯ Bahama Islands

⑰ 136th Operational [task] Force USA Navy (basic forces which cover the approaches from the

⑱ Ships sent to the 24th parallel to the Mexican side of the channel

⑲ Sea Blockade Line (USA)

⑳ Havana

㉑ Cuba

㉒ Sea covering detachment (USA)

㉓ Yucatan Channel

㉔ Mexico

㉕ Honduras

㉖ Caribbean Sea

㉗ Guantánamo (USA base)

㉘ Patrolling aircraft (USA)

㉙ Jamaica

㉚ Haiti

㉛ Puerto Rico

㉜ Providing air patrols above the Antilles Islands (USA)

A Soviet view of the situation and of U.S.-Soviet forces deployments in the Caribbean area at the height of the missile crisis.

177

Thursday, October 18: The First Indications

Not until Thursday, October 18, did the Kremlin have any indication that something was amiss. That afternoon, at five o'clock, Andrei Gromyko, the Soviet minister of foreign affairs, had his previously scheduled meeting at the White House with President Kennedy. Gromyko had been the first person with whom Khrushchev had discussed his proposal for sending missiles to Cuba and thus was the first senior Soviet leader with knowledge of Operation Anadyr who met with his American counterparts. The foreign minister had given his support to the idea, believing that the United States would not risk nuclear war over such a Soviet action. Now he delivered the most bald-faced of lies, under the gilded veil of diplomacy.

Minister Gromyko told President Kennedy that Premier Khrushchev planned to visit the United Nations following the U.S. congressional elections in November, and he believed that a meeting with Kennedy at that time would be useful. After Kennedy agreed to meet with Khrushchev, Gromyko raised the subject of Cuba and charged that the United States was "pestering" that island nation. Because he was knowledgeable of the missile deployments to Cuba, Gromyko played a careful game with Kennedy, expressing concern about the stories in the American press describing Soviet aid to Cuba. He explained that the merchant ships traveling to Cuban ports were bringing agricultural and other civilian experts, tractors and other farm equipment, and materials to construct a major fishing port. The weapons that were being brought into Cuba were for defensive purposes only, he said. Gromyko then reiterated Khrushchev's previous declarations that no offensive weapons were being delivered to Cuba.

President Kennedy responded that "there was no intention to invade Cuba."[23] But he was not complacent. The Soviet arms shipments to Cuba, said Kennedy, without mentioning offensive missiles, were leading to "the most dangerous situation since the end of the war [World War II]."

Kennedy and Gromyko discussed other contentious issues, including the status of Berlin and nuclear testing. Gromyko also assured Kennedy that the Soviets would do nothing related to Berlin until after the U.S. congressional elections in November. Their meeting ended at 7:08 P.M. Gromyko then went on to a dinner hosted by Secretary of State Dean Rusk. Khrushchev later recalled Gromyko's report of the dinner: "The conversation was polite, but Rusk kept insisting: the military are giving us data proving that you are installing missiles. You should take into account the fact that we can't accept that. The president cannot ignore the reaction developing inside our country. A dangerous situation is being created, and it would be better if you get out of Cuba."[24]

Rusk's statement was not a warning so much as a request not to aggravate the situation. Later that night, ExComm continued its deliberations.

Saturday, October 20: The Missiles Are Ready

There was still no alarm in the Kremlin. On October 20, General Pliyev reported to Moscow that the first regiment of SS-4 ballistic missiles was operational. It was located near San Cristobal in western Cuba, approximately sixty miles west of Havana. "Operational" meant that the missiles were being maintained at Readiness Level 4: about two and one-half hours from firing.[25] This readiness included, according to then-Colonel Anatoli Burnov, technical officer of one of the SS-4 regiments in Cuba, an estimated one hour to transport the nuclear warheads to the launch sites and to mate them with the missiles.[26]

Years later, Burnov recalled, "As military people we certainly were supposed to fulfill our mission and we were ready to do that." He added, "But deep inside, as human beings, we of course knew all of the possible consequences of the use of nuclear weapons . . . we as human beings thought it was unthinkable to use those weapons and that we were hopeful very much . . . that some sort of a compromise would be found."

Monday, October 22: Concern

By Monday, the Soviet Foreign Affairs Ministry and the intelligence organs had learned that President Kennedy would make a major speech that evening and that the *Washington Post* reported an unusual amount of activity in the White House over the weekend, probably having to do with the Cuban situation. People driving along Shirley Highway or Washington Boulevard in northern Virginia saw an unusually large number of cars in the Pentagon's parking lots for a weekend, and a great number of lights were seen burning at night in the building. At the same time, the Kremlin had received reports of major U.S. warship movements toward the Caribbean. And, for the first time, there was concern about the *Alexandrovsk*, the second merchant ship loaded with nuclear warheads. She was still at sea, scheduled to reach Cuba on the 23rd.

To his son Sergei, Khrushchev said, "In Washington they've announced that the president will deliver an important speech tonight. They've probably discovered our missiles. We can't assume anything else. In Berlin everything's quiet, and if they were getting ready to invade Cuba they wouldn't be saying anything."[27]

Elaborating, the senior Khrushchev added, "Most of the missiles aren't operational as yet. They are defenseless and everything could be destroyed from the air at one blow." It seemed as if the Soviet leader had forgotten about his vaunted air defense divisions of SA-2 missiles, the regiment of state-of-the-art MiG-21 interceptors, and the mass of anti-aircraft guns provided to the Cubans and with the Soviet ground forces deployed to the island.

An hour before President Kennedy's television appearance, Secretary of State Rusk met in his office with Ambassador Dobrynin. Calling the Soviet missile deployment "a gross error," Rusk handed the Soviet ambassador a copy of the president's speech. Rusk later recalled that Dobrynin, who did *not* know of the missiles in Cuba, aged "ten years right in front of my eyes." The text of Kennedy's speech was transmitted by embassy radio to the Kremlin. In Moscow, Ambassador Foy Kohler received an encrypted copy of the president's speech from the White House, which he was to present to Khrushchev one hour before the speech was made. But it was 2 A.M. Tuesday in Moscow, and the duty officer at the Ministry of Foreign Affairs told Kohler that he must wait until morning to see an official. When President Kennedy spoke to the world via television and radio at seven on Monday night, it was 3 A.M. the following day in Moscow.

Also on October 22 in Moscow, KGB officers arrested Colonel Oleg Penkovsky. An officer in Soviet Military Intelligence (GRU), Penkovsky had passed a massive amount of secret information to the United States and Britain since April 1961. At that time, Penkovsky had suggested that Khrushchev might soon send ballistic missiles to Cuba, which had just successfully resisted the American-sponsored invasion at the Bay of Pigs.

Penkovsky, forty-three years old at the time of his arrest, was the son of a tsarist army officer who had fought for the Bolsheviks during the Russian Civil War (1917–1921). After attending an artillery school, the younger Penkovsky became an officer in the Red Army in 1939 and fought in the 1940 war against Finland, and in the bitter conflict with Germany, he was wounded. In 1948, he graduated from the Frunze Military Academy, where he learned English, and was sent to the Military-Diplomatic Academy to study Strategic Intelligence. He then became a GRU officer, and in 1955, as a military attaché in Turkey, he became angry about his treatment by a superior (whom he anonymously reported to Turkish intelligence). After a course on rockets and missiles at the Dzerzhinsky Military Academy, he became disillusioned with the Soviet state and in 1960 made contact with British intelligence (MI6). He soon became an agent for the CIA and MI6 (who ran him jointly), passing along secrets in Moscow and during GRU-sanctioned trips to Great Britain and France.[28]

He accepted no payment, but his Western "handlers" stroked his ego, one time photographing him in the uniforms of the U.S. Army and the British Army with the rank insignia of a colonel. The CIA gave him the code name "Hero," and to the British he was "Yoga" with his invaluable products being given the code-word designation "Ironbark." Penkovsky produced so much material that the CIA had a team of twenty translators and analysts to handle the flow of Ironbark, while MI6 had ten officers working on the documents Penkovsky had photographed. Among his most important deliveries were data on actual Soviet missile production and their technical characteristics, even field manuals for their operation.

Reports allege that upon learning that he was about to be arrested, Penkovsky sent a signal to Western intelligence *that a Soviet attack on the West was imminent.*[29] A year earlier, Penkovsky and his handlers had secretly met in Paris where they devised a signal—code-named "Distant"—wherein if he learned that an attack on the West was imminent, he would call one of two telephone numbers at the American Embassy in Moscow. When someone answered the phone, Penkovsky was to blow into the mouthpiece, wait one minute, hang up, and then repeat the procedure.[30] Penkovsky was told that he should use the signal only if he learned that the Soviet Union had decided to attack or that the Soviets had decided to attack if the West were to take a specific action or fail to undertake specific actions.[31]

The Distant signal was in fact received at the American Embassy on *November 2—after* the missile crisis was over and Penkovsky had been arrested.[32] KGB officers apparently made the call to see whether it would provoke someone to visit the Moscow "dead drop" where Penkovsky had left messages.[33] After brutal interrogation by the KGB to learn what he had sent to the West, Penkovsky was tried for espionage and executed in 1963.

Shortly before President Kennedy's October 22 speech, a call came from the Foreign Ministry to Presidium members assembled in the Kremlin. The text of Kennedy's speech was slowly read to one of Khrushchev's assistants, who made notes and then relayed the president's words to the members. There was some discussion about the precise meaning of the word *quarantine*. Indeed, the Soviets were concerned that Americans would possibly board Soviet ships, some of which were covertly armed. They were also concerned about the ships that had the last of the SS-5 missiles on board and for the warhead-laden *Alexandrovsk*.[34] Reflecting on Khrushchev's reaction, his son wrote, "One thing was clear: they were threatening us." He elaborated that the Soviet answer "should demonstrate a determination to answer force with force and warn that we possessed a nuclear strike force no less powerful than the U.S. one."[35] That, of course, was a lie, but one that they would continue to broadcast publicly throughout the crisis.

The Presidium members remained at the Kremlin through Tuesday morning, meeting and then resting. There was an effort not to reveal the early morning session to journalists and "intelligence agents prowling around near the Kremlin."

Tuesday, October 23: To Stop or to Continue?

Premier Khrushchev's immediate response to President Kennedy's speech was to radio orders to all ships at sea carrying arms to Cuba. He initially ordered the ships' captains to ignore the American threat and to continue on to their Cuban destinations. At 8 A.M. on Tuesday morning, TASS produced another statement declaring that the weapons being shipped to Cuba were defensive. At the same time, the Soviet Foreign Ministry summoned U.S. Ambassador Kohler and gave him a copy of the TASS statement and a letter from Khrushchev addressed to Kennedy. The Soviet leader stated: "I must say frankly that the measures indicated in your statement constitute a serious threat to peace and to the security of nations. . . . We reaffirm that the armaments which are in Cuba, regardless of the classification to which they may belong, are intended solely for defensive purposes in order to secure [the] Republic of Cuba against the attack of an aggressor."

In his transmittal letter, Ambassador Kohler said that both the TASS statement and Khrushchev's letter "avoid specific threats and are relatively restrained in tone." Also, the letter did not deny the existence of strategic weapons in Cuba, the first sign that the Soviets might be willing to admit publicly to placing them there. Meanwhile, merchant captains whose ships carried offensive weapons and troops now received orders not to cross the quarantine line.

At 4 P.M., Moscow radio announced that (1) all personnel scheduled to leave active duty in the Strategic Rocket Forces (SRF), the National Air Defense Forces, and the submarine force would be retained on active duty; (2) all military leaves were canceled; and (3) all military forces were being placed at a higher state of alert. Significantly, the SRF's intercontinental ballistic missiles were readied for launching. At the Baikonur (Tyuratam) missile test facility, the first Soviet unmanned probe toward Mars was being prepared for launch on the following day.[36] The General Staff ordered that an operational SS-6 ICBM immediately replace the probe on the launch stand, as well as on Baikonur's second SS-6 launch position.[37] Similar arrangements were ordered for two test pads for the new R-9A (NATO SS-8 Sasin) ICBM.[38] Heavily armed troops were deployed at the launch facility in case of an attack by U.S. paratroopers.

Throughout the USSR at ICBM launch centers like Pletesk and Yurya, SRF launch crews began to prepare the Soviet Union's handful of operational SS-6 and SS-7 missiles for launch.[39] Other SRF crews assigned to the MRBM and IRBM regiments around the perimeter of the Soviet Union also went on alert, particularly those aimed at targets in Western Europe. Long Range Aviation units prepared the Soviet Union's few strategic bombers for staging to forward air bases for arming and fueling. Meanwhile, construction work also continued at the missile sites in Cuba to get the two remaining SS-4 regiments ready to fire as quickly as possible.

In Moscow, Premier Khrushchev and other Soviet leaders stressed that there was no panic. That evening, after having slept fully clothed for a few hours in his office in the Kremlin, Khrushchev and several other Presidium members accompanied a Romanian delegation to the Bolshoi Theater to see an American production of *Boris Godunov*. Khrushchev recalled, "We were trying to disguise our own anxiety, which was intense."[40]

In response to his son's question, "Will there be war?" the senior Khrushchev replied, "It's one thing to threaten with nuclear weapons, quite another to use them."[41] Yet it was Khrushchev who had warned the West of the strength of his nuclear weapons during the Suez crisis of 1956. Because the West was ignorant of Soviet nuclear capabilities, Khrushchev got away with making that threat when he had at most a handful of deliverable weapons able to be targeted at Europe and almost none at the United States. By 1962, with the advent of satellite surveillance by Corona reconnaissance satellites, Khrushchev could no longer make such bluffs work.

Khrushchev went into the "public" phase of the crisis with very few nuclear weapons that could reach the United States. Kennedy had thousands. Khrushchev's force of SS-4s and SS-5s could devastate all of Western Europe. Both Kennedy and Khrushchev knew the balance of terror between their respective nations, and they knew that it was in their best respective interests to find a way back from the nuclear brink.

President Kennedy's response to Khrushchev's message was transmitted to Moscow at 6:51 P.M. on October 23. The president stressed in his reply that it was important for both sides to "show prudence and do nothing to allow events to make the situation more difficult to control than it already is." He asked Khrushchev to direct Soviet ships to observe the quarantine line.

At a reception that evening at the Soviet Embassy in Washington, Lieutenant General Vladimir Dubovik indicated that the captains of Soviet merchant ships steaming toward Cuba were under orders to defy the American blockade. Arriving late to the reception, Ambassador Dobrynin declined to refute Dubovik's comments, saying, "He is a military man, I am not. He is the one who knows what the Navy is going to do, not I."

At 9:30 on the night of the 23rd, Robert Kennedy, at the president's suggestion, met privately with Dobrynin at the Soviet Embassy. Kennedy called the Soviet missile deployment "hypocritical, misleading, and false." Dobrynin responded that so far as he knew, there were no missiles in Cuba. As Kennedy was leaving, he asked whether Soviet ships were going to go through the blockade to Cuba. Dobrynin replied that this had been their instructions, and he knew of no changes.

Less than one hour after his meeting with Dobrynin, Robert Kennedy reported his conversation to the president and British Ambassador David Ormsby-Gore, who were meeting in the White House. It was at this meeting that Ormsby-Gore suggested that the quarantine intercept line be changed from 800 miles from Cuba to 500 miles, in order to give the Soviet side more time to consider the situation. President Kennedy called the change in to Secretary McNamara and told him to so advise the Navy.[42]

Wednesday, October 24: Approaching the Line

The next morning, the Soviet merchant ships *Yuriy Gagarin* and *Komiles* neared the quarantine line. As U.S. warships approached the merchant ships, and as American officials in the White House and the Pentagon prepared for the worst, the two merchant ships were receiving encrypted messages from Moscow. The messages were brief: the captains were to turn away from the blockade line. A short time later, the Soviet-flag merchant tanker *Bucharest* passed through the blockade line without difficulty. Moscow had directed sixteen ships approaching the blockade line to halt or to reverse course at what appeared to be the last possible moment. Other ships, those not carrying missile-related cargoes or aircraft, were told to proceed through the barrier of U.S. warships.

Construction of the missile bases in Cuba continued. That evening, at 9:24 P.M., the State Department in Washington received Khrushchev's letter that had been sent earlier that day. Minutes later, it was read to President Kennedy: "If you coolly weigh the situation which has developed, not giving way to passions, you will understand that the Soviet Union cannot fail to reject the arbitrary demands of the United States." Khrushchev warned Kennedy that he viewed the blockade as "an act of aggression" and that he would not instruct Soviet ships bound for Cuba to observe the quarantine.

Thursday, October 25: The United Nations Appeal

President Kennedy's response to Khrushchev's second letter arrived at the U.S. Embassy in Moscow late on the morning of October 25, for delivery to the Soviet premier. Kennedy stated, "I regret very much that you do not appear to understand what it is that has moved us in this matter." Again saying that he had earlier received "solemn assurances" that no offensive missile bases were being established in Cuba, he explained that he was required to undertake the responses that he had directed.

Meanwhile, UN Secretary General U Thant addressed letters to both Kennedy and Khrushchev in an effort to defuse the situation, which he called "highly dangerous and requiring . . . immediate interference by the United Nations." But neither leader, with his own national interests— and survival—at stake would pay heed to Secretary General U Thant's efforts.

The same day, the second regiment of SS-4 ballistic missiles in Cuba became operational, five days after the first. One battalion of the third regiment was also ready. A total of twenty launchers with thirty missiles was operational and could strike the southeastern United States. Nuclear warheads for the missiles were available in Cuba, ready to be mated to the SS-4s and launched in a few hours.

Friday, October 26: The Back Channel

On October 26 in Washington, John Scali, the State Department correspondent for ABC News, lunched with Aleksandr Fomin at the Occidental
Restaurant in Washington, an excellent eatery with a clublike atmosphere
less than two blocks from the White House. Officially, Fomin was the
Soviet Embassy's public affairs counselor, but he was widely acknowledged to be the KGB's Washington station chief. "Fomin" was the cover
name of Alexander Feklisov, who had earlier handled the atomic spies
Julius and Ethel Rosenberg.[43] They were meeting in response to Fomin's
urgent request, the two men having known each other for some time.

Noting that "war seems about to break out," Feklisov asked Scali to
contact his "high-level friends" in the State Department to ascertain
whether the United States would be interested in a possible solution to
the crisis. According to Scali's notes, Feklisov's proposal ran along the
following lines: "[Soviet] bases would be dismantled under [U]nited
[N]ations supervision and [C]astro would pledge not to accept offensive
weapons of any kind, ever, in return for [a U.S.] pledge not to invade
Cuba."[44]

Following their lunch, Scali went directly to the State Department to
report on the meeting to Roger Hillsman, the assistant secretary for intelligence and research. Scali's meeting with Feklisov opened yet another
line of communications between the two superpowers. Realizing that
Khrushchev might be reaching out through a new back channel untainted
by the lies of the Soviet *maskirovka*, Hillsman got his staff working to
evaluate the offer. They spent a frantic afternoon checking every scrap of
information on Feklisov and even getting a positive evaluation from
Sherman Kent over at the CIA regarding the offer and its delivery method.
At 4 P.M., Scali called Feklisov and arranged a second meeting to clarify
details of the Soviet offer. Deciding that this represented a new and genuine "back channel," Hillsman sent Scali to brief Dean Rusk of Feklisov's proposal at 6:45 that evening.

Meanwhile, in the Kremlin, Khrushchev, touched by the sincere tone
of Kennedy's second letter, began looking toward a compromise to the
crisis. At the afternoon session of the Presidium, Khrushchev for the first
time raised the issue of removing the missiles already in Cuba. But he
proposed that the United States match the withdrawal by removing the
Jupiter missiles from Turkey and Italy. The decision was reached not to
raise the issue of the Thor ballistic missiles in Britain. The compromise
letter from Khrushchev was dispatched to the United States. At the same
time, reports were arriving from Soviet intelligence agencies that U.S.

military readiness was being increased, and that U.S. orders were being sent "in the clear" so that Soviet agencies would intercept and read them.

At 6 P.M., the State Department began receiving a message from the U.S. Embassy in Moscow containing another letter from Premier Khrushchev to President Kennedy. The message arrived in four sections. The final portion arrived at 9 P.M., some twelve hours after the text had been delivered to the U.S. Embassy. The letter, composed by Khrushchev himself, was, in Robert Kennedy's words, "very long and emotional." It contained a proposal for a settlement: "I propose: we, for our part, will declare that our ships bound for Cuba are not carrying any armaments. You will declare that the United States will not invade Cuba with its troops and will not support any other forces that might intend to invade Cuba. Then the necessity of the presence of our military specialists in Cuba will disappear."

Later that same night, John Scali met again with Feklisov and recited a message from Secretary Rusk. Scali said, "I have reason to believe that the [U.S. government] sees real possibilities and supposes that the representatives of the two governments in New York could work this matter out with U Thant and with each other. My impression is, however, that time is very urgent." Feklisov assured Scali that his remarks would be communicated immediately to the "highest Soviet sources."

Feklisov remains one of the enigmas of the missile crisis. While the letter from Khrushchev offering to remove the missiles from Cuba in return for a U.S. pledge not to invade the island reflected the Scali-Feklisov discussions, the Soviet KGB officer has maintained in his autobiography and in an interview in 2002 that he was not instructed to initiate contact with the Kennedy administration, nor was he authorized to make any offers for settlement of the crisis.[45] However, his refutation is consistent with his position. KGB *Rezidents*, especially someone with Feklisov's decades of experience, do not just make diplomatic offers on a whim. His own comments have been confusing if not self-contradictory, while Sergei Khrushchev, reflecting on his extensive conversations with his father, as well as personal research in Soviet archives, has observed, "There is much that is unclear in the history of the meetings between Fomin and Scali." And, recalling Feklisov's participation in a 1989 conference in Moscow, the younger Khrushchev wrote, "I had the distinct impression that his memory had really deteriorated."[46] Most likely, Feklisov was a personal back channel reporting directly to Nikita Khrushchev.

At 10 P.M. on the night of the 26th, ExComm reconvened in an extraordinary session to consider Khrushchev's latest (third) letter. ExComm ordered a textual analysis of the letter, and two Soviet specialists, Helmut Sonnenfeldt and Joseph Neubert from the State Department, were directed to analyze the letter alongside the proposal from Feklisov.

On the same night—unknown to any other ExComm members—Robert Kennedy and Anatoly Dobrynin again met in secret at the Soviet Embassy on 16th Street. Dobrynin has since disclosed that when he defended the Soviet missile deployment in Cuba by citing the Jupiter missiles being placed in Turkey, Robert Kennedy offered to introduce the Turkish missiles into a potential agreement to defuse the crisis. Reportedly, Robert Kennedy left their meeting room to telephone the president. When he returned, he told Dobrynin, "The president said that we are ready to consider the question of Turkey, to examine favorably the question of Turkey."

Dobrynin reported the conversation to the Kremlin.

At about the same time, according to Nikita Khrushchev, "we received information from our Cuban comrades and from other sources which directly stated that this attack [on Cuba] would be carried out within the next two or three days." Khrushchev's statement may have referred to a cable from Fidel Castro that was transmitted from Havana on the evening of Friday, October 26. Fearing that an American invasion was imminent, Castro reportedly composed the message—dictating in Spanish to Soviet Ambassador Aleksandr Alekseyev, who translated the letter into Russian—while spending the night in a bomb shelter in the Soviet Embassy in Havana.

Castro's message began: "From an analysis of the situation and the reports in our possession, I consider that the aggression is almost imminent within the next 24 to 72 hours." The Cuban leader then expounded, "There are two possible variants: the first and likeliest is an air attack against certain targets with the limited objective of destroying them; the second, less probable although possible, is invasion. I understand that this variant would call for a large number of forces and is, in addition, the most repulsive form of aggression, which might inhibit them."

Castro then proposed that if U.S. forces did invade—"in violation of international law and morality—that would be the moment to eliminate such danger forever through an act of clear and legitimate defense, however harsh and terrible the solution would be for there is no other." To Khrushchev, this passage was an appeal for a Soviet nuclear first-strike attack on the United States.

According to an unpublished portion of his memoirs, Khrushchev recalled Castro warning that "an American invasion would take place within a few hours. Therefore, he was proposing to preempt the invasion and inflict a nuclear strike on the U.S." At a conference in Havana in January 1992, Castro stated that his letter had been mistranslated; he was suggesting that if Cuba were invaded, the Soviet Union would need to defend itself from attack by using nuclear weapons.

Also on October 26, Castro ordered his anti-aircraft guns to fire on low-flying U.S. reconnaissance aircraft that had been flying over Cuba since the 23rd. Earlier in the day, Castro had met with his senior commanders and advisors; they were unanimous that the U.S. reconnaissance flights over Cuba should not be allowed to continue.[47] They also looked at the flights as a prelude to an American invasion and feared that the morale of the men and the women at the anti-aircraft guns, as well as of other Cuban troops, would suffer if they could not fire at the intruders. The decision was reached to begin shooting the next day, and the Soviet commanders were so informed.

Several hours earlier, General Pliyev had sent a coded message to Moscow seeking permission to fire on the low-flying U.S. reconnaissance aircraft if it appeared that U.S. forces were preparing for an invasion. Pliyev had been given permission to open fire in response to a "massive" air attack and now wanted that authority expanded.[48] Meanwhile, Soviet Ambassador Alekseyev apparently had asked Castro to rescind his order for Cuban forces to fire on U.S. reconnaissance aircraft, but the Cuban leader rebuffed him.

During the night of October 26–27, General Pliyev ordered that nuclear warheads be moved from their temporary storage sites to positions close to their missiles. U.S. reconnaissance flights kept careful watch on the permanent nuclear bunkers being built in Cuba—which were never used.

Saturday, October 27: Flash Points

At 9 A.M. Eastern time on October 27, another message was received from Moscow. Shortly after 11 A.M., it was read in the White House: "You are disturbed over Cuba. You say that this disturbs you because it is ninety miles by sea from the coast of the United States of America. But . . . you have placed destructive missile weapons, which you call offensive, in Turkey, literally next to us."

In contrast to Feklisov's private message sent to Kennedy the day before, Khrushchev's new message called for the United States to dismantle the missiles in Turkey in return for the removal of the Soviet missiles in Cuba. The result of this transmission was that negotiations would enter a new phase as the ExComm began lengthy discussions throughout the day of possible responses to the Soviet proposal.

But there would be severe complications on the 27th as new flash points arose. Two of them related to U-2 spyplanes: the shooting down of Anderson's U-2 over Cuba and the Alaska-based U-2 lost over the Arctic that flew toward Soviet Siberia. Robert Kennedy wrote in *Thirteen Days* of his brother's reaction when news of the U-2 shoot down reached the White House:

> "How can we send any more U-2 pilots into this area tomorrow unless we take out all of the SAM sites?" the President asked. "We are now in an entirely new ball game."[49]
>
> At first, there was almost unanimous agreement that we had to attack early the next morning with bombers and fighters and destroy the SAM sites. But again the President pulled everyone back. "It isn't the first step that concerns me," he said, "but both sides escalating to the fourth and fifth step—and we don't go to the sixth because there is no one around to do so. We must remind ourselves we are embarking on a very hazardous course."[50]

After the shoot down, there was some trepidation among the senior Soviet commanders in Cuba, especially when someone had to contact Moscow with the news. Castro was delighted and so informed General Pliyev. In Moscow, when Khrushchev was told of the shoot down, he was inwardly pleased but concerned about American reaction. "It was at that very moment—not before or after—that Father felt the situation was slipping out of his control," recalled his son Sergei.[51] And, "As Father said later, that was the moment when he felt instinctively that the [ballistic] missiles had to be removed, that disaster loomed. Real disaster."

When Secretary McNamara learned that the Alaska-based U-2 had intruded into Soviet air space, he predicted, "This means war with the Soviet Union." President Kennedy's laconic reaction when he heard of the incident was to laugh and remark, "There is always some S.O.B. [son of a bitch] who doesn't get the word."

Khrushchev protested the U-2 transgression to President Kennedy on the 28th:

> How should we regard this? What is this, a provocation? One of your planes violates our frontier during this anxious time we are both experiencing, when everything has been put into combat readiness. Is it not

a fact that an intruding American plane could be easily taken for a nuclear bomber, which might push us to a fateful step; and all the more so since the U.S. Government and Pentagon long ago declared that you are maintaining a continuous nuclear bomber patrol?[52]

General Pliyev reported on the morning of the 27th to Moscow that all twenty-four SS-4 launchers and their thirty-six missiles would be ready to launch against the United States within a few hours.

That afternoon, while ExComm considered the deteriorating situation and how to respond to Anderson's shoot down, four U.S. Navy F8U-1P Crusader photo planes streaked low over Cuba. Cuban troops opened fire with anti-aircraft guns, but none of the low-flying photo planes were hit.[53]

Despite the events in Cuba, President Kennedy and ExComm concentrated their efforts on responding to Khrushchev's letters. ExComm reached the decision to ignore Khrushchev's proposal to remove missiles from Cuba in exchange for the U.S. removal of missiles from Turkey and to instead respond to his more friendly letter of the 26th.

While ExComm was deliberating, the ABC correspondent Scali and the Soviet KGB officer Feklisov continued their exchanges, meeting at 4:15 that afternoon on the street between the White House and the Soviet Embassy, which were five blocks apart on 16th Street. When Scali asked Feklisov about Khrushchev's last-minute introduction of the Jupiter missile issue into the discussions, Feklisov said that the change was the result of "poor communications." Feklisov expected clarification at any moment. Scali, concerned and frustrated, warned the Soviet official, "The invasion of Cuba is only hours away."

After the ExComm meeting broke up, President Kennedy and a smaller group of advisors decided that their response to Khrushchev would be reinforced with an oral message sent through Ambassador Dobrynin.[54] Khrushchev would be informed that the United States would take military action if the missiles were not removed from Cuba. Secretary Rusk proposed that Khrushchev be assured that upon resolving the Cuban question, the Jupiter missiles would in turn be removed from Turkey; *however*, there could be no public or explicit agreement about the Jupiter withdrawal. Rusk's proposal was accepted.

At 7:45 P.M., Robert Kennedy met once more with Ambassador Dobrynin at the Justice Department on Pennsylvania Avenue. The attorney general told the Soviet ambassador that "We had to have a commitment by tomorrow that those [missile] bases would be removed. I was not giving them an ultimatum but a statement of fact. He should understand that if they did not remove those bases, we would remove them."[55]

The formal U.S. response to Khrushchev was transmitted at 8:05 P.M. It was just after four o'clock the following morning in Moscow. ExComm continued meeting into the night, addressing various military, as well as political, options that could be executed the following day if the Kremlin made no move to withdraw its missiles from Cuba.

Meanwhile, that night in Havana, Ambassador Alekseyev briefed Castro. The Cuban leader received the contents of the messages between the Kremlin and Washington.

Sunday, October 28: "Obey No Orders to Launch"

The following morning, October 28, at 9 A.M., Radio Moscow broadcast a public message from Premier Khrushchev declaring that "the Soviet government, in addition to previously issued instructions on the cessation of further work at the building sites for the weapons, has issued a new order on the dismantling of the weapons which you describe as 'offensive,' and their crating and return to the Soviet Union."

Because of difficulties in rapidly transmitting messages between the two capitals, Khrushchev had decided to publicly broadcast the message, as well as send it by official channels.

Meanwhile, Khrushchev was becoming increasingly concerned about the possibility of an "accidental" launch of nuclear weapons in Cuba. On the afternoon of the 27th, at Khrushchev's direction, Marshal Malinovsky had signaled General Pliyev: "We categorically confirm that you are prohibited from using nuclear weapons from missiles, FKR [cruise missiles], 'Luna' and aircraft without orders from Moscow."[56,57] The following afternoon, the 28th, Khrushchev directed that another message be sent to Pliyev. As recounted by his son Sergei, it ordered: "Allow no one near the [ballistic] missiles. Obey no orders to launch and under no circumstances install warheads."[58]

Work on dismantling the missile sites began at 5 P.M.[59] The crisis, though, would have many more twists and turns before it was solved.

12

"Until Hell Freezes Over!"

A great nation such as yours would not take such a serious step if there was any doubt. I need no such evidence. For our purposes, the missiles are there.

President Charles de Gaulle
October 22, 1962[1]

From the first moments of the Cuban Missile Crisis, secrecy had been at the core of the Kennedy administration's response to the Soviet missile deployment to Cuba. Then, on the evening of October 22, 1962, and with almost no public warning, President Kennedy's television address had thrown a nuclear confrontation into the public forum. Within the United States, the reaction ranged from deep concern to extreme fear, including panic buying at some supermarkets in the southeastern part of the country. There was also great skepticism regarding the validity of Kennedy's charges in foreign newspapers, on radio, and on television. It was a matter of public record that the CIA had used the media and United Nations Ambassador Adlai Stevenson as part of the cover plan for the failed Bay of Pigs invasion in April 1961. The Kennedy administration's decision to make secrecy the overriding consideration during the ExComm deliberations the previous week now required a major public relations effort.

Public relations campaigns were central to John Kennedy's approach toward politics and life, as they were to most of the men surrounding him. Throughout his career, Kennedy had believed that one should be able to justify action with a good legal case. Debate skills come naturally to lawyers and politicians, and it was not surprising that many in the Kennedy administration would view the diplomatic effort to remove the Soviet missiles from Cuba as a sort of contest.[2] Now they would have to sell the public on the reality of the missiles in Cuba and on the rightness of U.S. actions in forcing their removal. The challenge was difficult because much of the world already viewed American intentions toward Castro and Cuba with great suspicion after the Bay of Pigs fiasco.

Former U.S. ambassador to the Soviet Union Llewellyn Thompson is generally credited with pointing out during the ExComm sessions that the Soviets respected a good legal case. This idea became the core of the worldwide American sales effort to get the missiles out of Cuba.[3] The task fell mainly to individuals and organizations that were completely uninformed of the crisis prior to Kennedy's speech on October 22. These people had to alert the international community to the danger of the Anadyr missile deployment and to the absolute need to remove the weapons from Cuba.

Tuesday, October 23: The Morning After

In 1962, the press still respected the privacy of political leaders, resulting in a much more intimate intercourse between the two communities. President Kennedy often called reporters, like Hugh Sidney of *Time* magazine, for their opinions and reactions. Kennedy actively socialized with journalists. In return, the reporters chose not to report on Kennedy's alleged extramarital affairs and liaisons, most of his health problems, and other matters of private interest; it was a level of regard almost unthinkable in today's journalism.[4] The *New York Times* had held up publication of the story on the Cuban situation by Scotty Reston the previous weekend in a display of such deference. Over the next dozen years, the Vietnam War and the Watergate scandal would change that relationship.

White House Press Secretary Pierre Salinger was denied information on the crisis until just before the announcement on October 22. President Kennedy would later say that he did not want to put Salinger in the position of having to knowingly lie to the press. However, of greater concern was maintaining discretion and security with the press. Senior members of the administration questioned Salinger's ability to do so, as Salinger was extremely close to the Washington press corps. A passionate card player, Salinger was a regular at a weekly foursome that included the legendary columnist Art Buchwald.

President Kennedy's senior advisors need not have worried about Salinger. Throughout the crisis, Salinger produced nearly emotionless, no-nonsense press statements and kept his mouth shut to friends and family about what was being done in the White House. Ironically, Salinger's only security lapse may have occurred over the weekend of October 20–21, when he canceled the weekly poker game. Buchwald, knowing of Salinger's love of cards and of the good cigars smoked at the games, immediately deduced that something important was happening, and thus began to pursue the story.[5]

Buchwald was not alone. Around the world, newsmen began to cover the crisis with an interest and excitement unrivaled since World War II. Even before Kennedy's speech on October 22, reporters had made surprising headway against the Kennedy administration's screen of secrecy. With the president's announcement of the existence of Soviet missiles in Cuba and the pending quarantine, many reporters knew the dangers that might be involved, having covered World War II and Korea from the front lines. This time, though, the dangers were more personal; their friends and families were potentially at risk from the Soviet missiles that were just ninety miles off the American coast. Significantly, the leaders of both superpowers often trusted veteran newsmen more than their own intelligence and foreign ministry personnel, something unimaginable today.[6]

Informing the Allies

After Kennedy's speech on Monday evening, the Department of State flashed a message at 10:55 P.M. to American embassies around the world to officially inform the host governments about the crisis. While most nations received a polite diplomatic note and a visit from their respective American ambassadors, several countries had already received more attention. Obviously, Latin American nations would have to be specially briefed if Secretary of State Dean Rusk were to obtain a resolution of support from the Organization of American States. In addition, Canada, France, Germany, and Great Britain had "special" relationships with the United States. President Kennedy would ask a great deal of those countries in the coming weeks, and they deserved to be shown the best evidence of the Soviet missile deployment in Cuba. That meant widely sharing U-2 photography, an idea never even considered just a few days earlier. Nevertheless, the support of Latin America and of key NATO nations was critical to successfully resolving the crisis in America's favor. Teams led by senior U.S. diplomats and intelligence officers, armed with sets of U-2 photographs and NPIC briefing boards, would have to be sent from Washington to brief foreign leaders.[7]

Code word "Talent" materials—derived from U-2 and Corona satellite overhead photography—were among the most sensitive of America's secrets and were rarely shared even within the senior ranks of the U.S. government. In 1962, less than fifteen hundred men and women worldwide, including military analysts and contractors, were cleared to see the Corona-based Talent-Keyhole photos.[8] In fact, when President Eisenhower had viewed the first U.S. satellite photos in 1960, he had decreed that they should never be released in any form. U-2 photography was handled in a similar fashion. The sudden need to publicly prove that the missiles in Cuba were both real and dangerous changed that policy. Finding verifiable proof would require more of the special talents of the Central Intelligence Agency and the National Photographic Interpretation Center (NPIC).

The weekend before Kennedy's October 22 speech, NPIC staff under Art Lundahl produced four sets of briefing packages for presentations in Ottawa, London, Paris, and Bonn (then the capital of West Germany). The packages consisted of eleven briefing boards carried in portfolios, each with photos and location maps of Soviet equipment in Cuba. Highlights included photos of the ballistic missile sites, SAM sites, the MiG-21 and Il-28 aircraft, along with coastal cruise missile sites and missile boats. Another set of briefing materials was produced for Adlai Stevenson at the United Nations. The ambassador's request for a personal briefing by Lundahl was deferred because NPIC was already being stretched to fulfill the many requests from government and military users for photographs and other materials to support operations in and around Cuba.[9] In short, NPIC personnel were beginning to suffer from the same stress and exhaustion as the senior leaders they briefed each day. With daily briefings to the president, ExComm, JCS, and other agencies, the twenty-four-hour-a-day pace was beginning to take its toll on NPIC staff, as additional U-2 and low-level missions delivered ever more photographs for analysis. Lundahl and NPIC senior staff personnel were too valuable to let them depart for New York, and Stevenson had to do with one of the overseas briefing sets and a thorough presentation by Air Force Colonel David Parker, Lundahl's military deputy. Parker would continue to work with Stevenson and his staff throughout the crisis, providing powerful evidence for the ambassador.

The plan for briefing the British, the German, and the French leaders was designed to compensate for not having conferred with them earlier about the Soviet missile deployment to Cuba. The men heading each nation were legendary political figures in their countries, and Prime Minister Harold Macmillan was already openly hostile because Kennedy had not formally consulted with him earlier. In addition, U.S. ambassadors to

Briefing boards like these were used thoughout the missile crisis to brief ExComm, government and military leaders, foreign diplomats and heads of state, and even reporters and spies.

France, Canada, and Germany were away from their posts and initially unable to present the American evidence personally.[10] Thus, the briefings had to deliver maximum impact and incite a minimum of anger among the target audience.

To help smooth things over with the sometimes testy French President Charles de Gaulle, President Kennedy decided to send an American who might best be able to look him in the eye and make the case for the quarantine: former Secretary of State Dean Acheson. Although Acheson had been among the strongest of the air strike supporters in the ExComm meetings, Kennedy now wanted him to act as a special envoy to France to present the American case. Similarly, Kennedy recalled Ambassador Walter Dowling to lead the briefing team to Bonn. To provide the best possible technical presentation, Sherman Kent, Director of the CIA Board of Estimates, went along, as did three CIA briefers and an armed courier to carry the bags of classified materials. All assembled at Andrews Air Force Base on Sunday, October 21, for a flight to Europe on the president's personal VC-137.[11] Since the U.S. ambassador to Britain David Bruce was available in London to lead the briefing team for the British, the first stop was a short one, just to deliver the presentation materials to Bruce before continuing on to the European continent. The errand to England completed, the VC-137 made the short flight to Paris, where Dean Acheson and Sherman Kent deplaned to brief President de Gaulle.

At midday on October 22 at the Admiralty buildings in Whitehall, Ambassador Bruce and the CIA's Chester Cooper briefed an unhappy Prime Minister Macmillan, who was accompanied by Foreign Secretary Lord Home. While Macmillan was unconditionally supportive of the

U.S. position toward the Soviet deployment to Cuba, he expressed severe reservations about the American response and the necessity of showing the U-2 photos to the media.[12] Macmillan also asked that the British political opposition leadership—known as the "Shadow Cabinet"—be briefed as well, which was quickly done. In response, members of the political opposition expressed disdain for American sensitivity to the Soviet nuclear weapons, something that Europeans had been living with for years.

More than any other European leader, Charles de Gaulle was the personal embodiment of his nation and its character. A rough and tumble leader, de Gaulle was a formidable challenge in the mind of the American government.[13] The audience, which took place in de Gaulle's office late on the afternoon of October 22, was initially limited to Acheson and American chargé d'affaires Cecil Lyon, who described the scale and scope of the Soviet deployment to Cuba. Surprisingly, when the two men offered to show de Gaulle the briefing photos, the old general deferred, telling them that he trusted their integrity, and that Acheson would never have been sent to misinform him.[14]

However, when Acheson offered de Gaulle an opportunity to look at the materials as a matter of professional interest, the president relented, and Kent was admitted with his briefing boards. The general was soon examining the photos with a large magnifying hand lens, stunning his audience by identifying various pieces of Soviet equipment from memory. Kent immediately realized that he was briefing a seasoned consumer of intelligence, and he found the French president's questions insightful, especially when de Gaulle asked about the U-2 and its operating altitude. When de Gaulle was informed that the photographs in front of him had been shot from an altitude of fourteen miles, de Gaulle replied, *"C'ést formidable! C'ést formidable!"*

When asked whether France would support America's efforts to get the Soviet missiles out of Cuba, de Gaulle matter of factly replied in the affirmative and added, "It's exactly what I would have done."[15] The de Gaulle interview was a rare pleasant surprise in a month full of unhappy notices for the Americans.

While in Europe, Acheson and Kent also briefed the North Atlantic Council (the parent organization of NATO) and members of the French press on October 23. As in the presentation to the British press, selected U-2 photos were shown to provide background information, and copies were released for publication in the press on the 24th.[16] In Bonn,

Ambassador Dowling and the CIA briefer R. J. Smith caught up with Chancellor Konrad Adenauer, who had been campaigning in Hannover earlier in the day. Although they had to wait until late afternoon of the 22nd to deliver their briefing, Adenauer was attentive and curious. In particular, the West German chancellor wanted to know about the readiness of the SS-4 missiles in Cuba, eventually commenting to Dowling and Smith, "You may assure your President that I will be useful."[17]

While the European briefings were taking place on the 22nd, Canadian Prime Minister John Diefenbaker, Secretary of State for External Affairs Harold Green, and Defense Minister Douglas Harkness received a briefing in Ottawa. Since a newly appointed U.S. ambassador was not due to arrive in Canada until after New Year's 1963, the duty of briefing the Canadian officials fell to the special emissary Livingston Merchant and the CIA's William Tidwell. The three Canadians were fascinated by the briefing photos and were supportive of America's reaction to the Soviet weapons in Cuba, but they were concerned about the tone of President Kennedy's planned speech for that evening, especially its personal attack on the Soviet government for lying about the missile deployment. The Americans then briefed another half-dozen Canadian cabinet officers, and flew back to Washington that evening.[18]

Rusk's Masterpiece: The OAS Vote

While the four NATO briefings did much to ensure allied support for the American quarantine, they did not establish Latin American solidarity for the effort. The American quarantine may have been intended to be a "short of war" measure, but in international circles, it could easily appear to be a hostile act. Therefore, the Kennedy administration believed that Latin American nations should speak with one voice about their outrage over the Soviet missile deployment to Cuba and should support American efforts to remove the weapons. The venue for such a statement would be the Organization of American States (OAS), headquartered on 17th Street in Northwest Washington, just three blocks from the White House. Known by some cynics as "the Latin American branch of the State Department," the OAS was rarely a united body on any issue. Now the Kennedy administration wanted the OAS to "rubber-stamp" the quarantine plan and then to support it with an on-the-record vote for the entire world to see.

President Kennedy and the ExComm members wanted to get at least two-thirds of the OAS nations to endorse a statement on the crisis. Secretary of State Dean Rusk personally led the drive to deliver an OAS resolution. His diplomatic career in the Kennedy administration had been decidedly mixed to that point.[19] Now the State Department under Rusk had only twenty-four hours to get the votes to make the OAS resolution credible. The effort began on the afternoon of the 22nd, when Deputy Under Secretary of State U. Alexis Johnson and Assistant Secretary of State for Latin American Affairs Edwin Martin briefed the ambassadors of the OAS nations. The OAS military attachés in Washington were similarly informed at the Pentagon.

The meeting to consider, debate, and vote on the U.S. proposal on Cuba was scheduled to convene at 9 A.M. the next day, the earliest time that the senior OAS representatives could be gathered in Washington.[20] Secretary Rusk personally led the U.S. delegation into the OAS hall that morning, having spent the previous twenty-four hours privately lobbying the Latin American diplomatic community to support the resolution. The OAS membership now understood that an affirmative vote authorized the United States not only to quarantine Cuba, but also to use force as necessary to remove the missiles.

Interestingly, instead of using the Monroe Doctrine as justification, Rusk invoked the language of the 1947 Rio Pact, which provided for mutual hemispheric defense. President Kennedy had set a precedent for acting on the pact when he had extended the nuclear umbrella of the United States to the rest of Latin America. The passage in his October 22 speech stating that if Soviet missiles from Cuba struck any target in the region, that action would be treated as an attack on the United States made support of the resolution more palatable for the Latin American countries.

The result was startling. The OAS vote was unanimous: 19 to 0, with a single abstention from Uruguay, whose delegate was unable to get voting instructions from Montevideo in time. The resolution was the high point of Dean Rusk's tenure as Secretary of State, and it provided a solid base of regional support for the upcoming United Nations Security Council debate, which had already begun in New York. However, worldwide public support for America's action in the Caribbean was still soft, resulting as much from the absence of publicly available knowledge on the missiles as from any other factor. That absence of information would change two days later in the Security Council of the United Nations.[21]

Thursday, October 25: Stevenson versus Zorin

Ambassador Adlai Stevenson was one of the most gifted and well-loved politicians of his era. He retained his humanity and sensitivity despite years of bare-knuckles political battle in Illinois. The heir to the Democratic Party's progressive movement following President Harry S. Truman's retirement in 1953, Stevenson had only one shortcoming: bad timing. He suffered the ill fortune of losing the presidency in 1952 and again in 1956 to Dwight Eisenhower, effectively ending his hopes to lead the United States into the 1960s. Nevertheless, Stevenson, wishing to serve his country, offered himself (and his considerable political machine) to John F. Kennedy during the election of 1960. While Stevenson aspired for the Secretary of State position, he settled for the ambassadorship to the United Nations when Kennedy nominated Dean Rusk to be the Secretary of State. Stevenson had endured almost two years of thankless duty on New York's East 44th Street, often fronting bad policies and actions from his president and government because it was his sworn duty. But October 25, 1962, would be his finest hour as a servant of the American people, as he showed his personal mettle for the entire world to see.

For almost two days since the OAS vote, the UN Security Council had been debating a resolution regarding American accusations of Soviet missiles in Cuba. In reality, what was occurring was a personal battle between Stevenson and Soviet UN ambassador Valerian Zorin. Stevenson's goal was to get Zorin to commit to whether or not there were Soviet ballistic missiles in Cuba. If Zorin confirmed that the missiles in Cuba existed, then a Security Council resolution on the Soviet weapons in Cuba could go forward. On the other hand, if Zorin denied their presence in Cuba, Stevenson had a diplomatic ambush planned, though there would be challenges.

In October 1962, Zorin held the rotating monthly chairmanship of the Security Council and thus controlled the tempo and the focus of the debate. Wily and experienced, Zorin had survived as a diplomat in the bizarre years of Josef Stalin's reign. However, Zorin had no support from Moscow; he had not been given information on Operation Anadyr and had no real instructions other than to deny the existence of the missiles in Cuba. Zorin came into the October 25 debate blind and ignorant, and Adlai Stevenson was waiting for him to make a mistake.[22]

Zorin's gaffe came in the early evening with the entire world watching the proceedings on live television. The Soviet ambassador allowed Stevenson to make a statement, which led to the thrust and parry: "All right, sir, let me ask you one simple question: Do you, Ambassador Zorin, deny that the USSR has placed and is placing medium- and intermediate-range missiles and sites in Cuba? Yes or no—don't wait for the translation—yes or no?"[23]

Realizing that Stevenson had finally gotten his key question in the open and on the record, Zorin attempted to delay the proceedings. He

After taunting the Soviet ambassador to the United States to admit that strategic weapons were being introduced into Cuba, Ambassador Adlai Stevenson (lower center) revealed the aerial photography that demonstrated Soviet duplicity.

then tried to brush the question aside with a procedural deferral to the Chilean ambassador. Stevenson insisted on an answer amid chuckles of light laughter in the Security Council chamber. Defying the earlier assessment by some Kennedy administration officials that he was somehow too soft for the brinkmanship required during the crisis, Stevenson struck like the Illinois political warlord of his youth. When Zorin refused to directly answer the question, Stevenson went in for the kill: "You can answer yes or no. You have denied they exist. I want to know if I understood you correctly. I am prepared to wait for my answer until hell freezes over, if that's your decision. And I am also prepared to present the evidence in this room."[24]

Before Zorin or any other member of the Soviet delegation could react, Stevenson signaled for Colonel Parker of NPIC to bring forward an easel with photos of the missile sites mounted on briefing boards. Not missing a beat, Stevenson personally led the Security Council representatives through something that the Soviets had never expected: enlarged U-2 and F8U-1P photographs showing the critical details of the Anadyr deployment. At Stevenson's insistence, President Kennedy and his advisors had decided to rescind the restrictions on publicly showing Talent photography and had sent a copy of the overseas briefing package to New York. Now the U-2 photos were used to destroy the last shreds of the Soviet *maskirovka*.[25] When Stevenson had finished going though the briefing boards, he completed his statement with a challenge to Ambassador

Zorin: "And now I hope that we can get down to business, that we can stop this sparring. We know the facts, and so do you, sir, and we are ready to talk about them. Our job here is not to score debating points. Our job, Mr. Zorin, is to save the peace. And if you are ready to try, we are."[26]

In a matter of minutes, Stevenson had given President Kennedy the worldwide public relations victory that he had wanted. Having shown that the Soviets had clandestinely introduced strategic nuclear weapons into the Western Hemisphere, Kennedy and his senior advisors had won the battle *they* had considered most critical to eventual resolution of the crisis. The only shortcoming to Stevenson's victory was that it produced nothing substantial.

Premier Khrushchev and the Soviet leadership had no concern about what any nation or organization thought of Operation Anadyr. The dramatic debates at the OAS and the UN had no effect whatsoever on the Soviet plans and intentions, nor did the public embarrassment change their minds about the validity of their actions. While the various briefings of foreign leaders helped to shore up international support for possible U.S. military action against the Soviets in Cuba, that was hardly the outcome Kennedy and his advisors had wanted. They wanted a solution and wanted Khrushchev to back down under the burden of international scrutiny. The main achievement of the public debates was to embarrass and humiliate the Soviet leadership, something that rarely generated positive results during the Cold War. In the end, the path to a solution of the Cuban Missile Crisis would come not from highly educated diplomats debating in parliamentary halls and chambers. The honor of finding a path back from the brink would go to a handful of American reporters and Soviet spies and would occur in the bars and the restaurants of downtown Washington, D.C.[27]

13

Back Channels and Telegrams

Mr. President, we and you ought not now to pull on the ends of the rope in which you have tied the knot of war, because the more the two of us pull, the tighter that knot will be tied. And a moment may come when that knot will be tied so tight that even he who tied it will not have the strength to untie it, and then it will be necessary to cut that knot, and what that would mean is not for me to explain to you, because you yourself understand perfectly of what terrible forces our countries dispose.

Nikita Khrushchev, letter to President John F. Kennedy,
October 26, 1962[1]

While the public diplomacy of Ambassador Adlai Stevenson at the United Nations was compelling to watch on television, it had little or no effect on the eventual outcome of the Cuban Missile Crisis. Even the efforts of Secretary of State Dean Rusk, Dean Acheson, and Sherman Kent at coalition and consensus building contributed nothing toward convincing Nikita Khrushchev to remove the Soviet missiles from Cuba. What members of the Kennedy administration did not realize was that their counterparts in the Kremlin were not men who were easily intimidated. In fact, the Americans had little idea about just what kind of men they were facing, most of all Nikita Khrushchev.

History has rarely presented two leaders whose lives contrasted more than did those of John F. Kennedy and Nikita Sergeyevich Khrushchev. While Kennedy had been raised in wealth and privilege, Khrushchev had known only hardship and turmoil during his rise to the top of the Soviet political apparatus.[2] At the time that the future president was studying at Oxford and writing his first book, the future Soviet leader was the Communist Party boss of Moscow and surviving Stalin's purges of the 1930s. Where Kennedy's military experience had been limited to commanding a dozen men on a tiny torpedo boat, Khrushchev had been Stalin's personal commissar at some of the largest land battles in the history of warfare. Even the difference in their ages defined the gulf between the two men: Kennedy was actually younger than Khrushchev's older son, Sergei, a missile engineer with the Chelomi Design Bureau.[3] It is hard to imagine the two taking a common view of anything, much less finding a common course for the Cuban Missile Crisis. Nevertheless, that was the challenge that both men faced at the end of the second week of the confrontation.

The relationship between the two governments had at best been "frosty" since Kennedy's inauguration in January 1961 and had already come close to shooting during the confrontation over Berlin the previous year. Since the second Berlin crisis a year earlier, there had been only ministerial contact between Kennedy and Khrushchev, along with an occasional exchange of personal letters. Now the two men had only days—and possibly hours—to develop the personal trust and intimacy to settle the most dangerous crisis of the nuclear age. Fortunately, both of them had some key characteristics in common. Each man had certainty of his place in the world and in history. Each man clearly understood the potential consequences of their mutual actions if the crisis led to open conflict. And each had a desire to find a way out of the situation by which he could declare some sort of political "victory."

The downturn in U.S.-Soviet relations predated the Kennedy administration, having been sparked by the U-2 spyplane shoot down on May 1, 1960. Khrushchev's embracing of Castro and the Cuban Revolution and desire for greater international influence made the Soviet leader a lightning rod for American paranoia and anger.[4] Kennedy had been inflammatory during his presidency; beginning with his inaugural address just minutes after being sworn in, he laid down an ultimatum to the Soviet Union and other potential American foes:

> Let every nation know, whether it wishes us well or ill, that we shall pay any price, bear any burden, meet any hardship, support any friend, oppose any foe, in order to assure the survival and the success of liberty. . . . In the long history of the world, only a few generations have been granted the role of defending freedom in its hour of maximum danger. I do not shrink from this responsibility—I welcome it.[5]

President Kennedy had sought opportunities for direct confrontations with communist states, especially the Soviet Union. Nevertheless, Kennedy and Khrushchev both privately desired to improve U.S.-Soviet relations.

One major casualty of the public East-West conflict was the official government dialogue between the United States and the Soviet Union. Both sides had different agendas and goals in their political advances toward each other, which muddied the diplomatic waters.[6] A 1962 shuffling of personnel in the Soviet Foreign Ministry meant that Anatoly Dobrynin, the new ambassador to the United States, had to build a relationship with Secretary of State Dean Rusk. Secretary Rusk, not the most talented and assertive of foreign ministers, failed to develop any real rapport with the new Soviet ambassador.[7]

Such official friction proved to be intolerable to both Kennedy and Khrushchev, both of whom had a habit of taking shortcuts to get their way. One was the exchange of personal letters, which varied in length, subject, and frequency. Sometimes the notes were short and personal, such as an exchange referring to John Glenn's successful orbital space flight in February 1962.[8] Others were long and involved, especially one from Khrushchev supporting the Anadyr *maskirovka* on the eve of the missile crisis.[9] However, polite notes were hardly a substitute for personal meetings and established diplomatic relations.

Kennedy and Khrushchev were both men who preferred a personal touch when trying to understand a problem or making an important decision. Khrushchev, in particular, felt the need to reach out to the young American president, whose lack of maturity and experience concerned him. Hoping that Kennedy would be open to an unconventional approach, Khrushchev decided to make use of an old diplomatic tool: the back-channel contact. Such channels are trusted individuals, often midlevel civil servants, journalists, and businessmen, who are used to establish a second-person dialogue between senior leaders. Khrushchev had made use of a back-channel contact in the late 1950s to pass messages to the Eisenhower administration through the *New York Daily News* reporter Frank Holeman and Vice President Richard Nixon.

Now Khrushchev would do it again.[10] Colonel Georgi Nikitovich Bolshakov was a Red Army officer who had once been a personal aide to the famous Marshal Georgi Zhukov. Now assigned to Soviet Military Intelligence (GRU), he operated in the United States undercover as the TASS news bureau chief and editor of the English-language magazine *USSR*. Bolshakov worked alone, passing along items of interest to the GRU station chief (known as a *Rezident*) assigned to the Soviet Embassy.[11] Early in 1961, Bolshakov had contacted Frank Holeman, asking for an introduction to Attorney General Robert Kennedy. Remembering his previous experience during the 1950s, Holeman made the contact, and Bolshakov soon had a budding relationship with John and Robert Kennedy.[12] Initially kept secret even from Secretary of State Rusk, this back-channel relationship proved valuable for all parties.

Over the next few months, Bolshakov was the primary communications channel between President Kennedy and Nikita Khrushchev. He made the initial inquiries for the subsequent Vienna summit meeting, and he also helped to arrange the withdrawal of American and Soviet forces from Checkpoint Charlie in October 1961 during the second Berlin crisis.[13] By the fall of 1962, Bolshakov was a trusted and regular visitor of Robert Kennedy's. Like Ambassador Dobrynin and other Soviet personnel in the United States, Bolshakov knew nothing about the Anadyr deployment to Cuba and denied the movement of offensive weapons to the island throughout the summer months. President Kennedy was heard to yell, "That son of a bitch lied to me!" angry over what he felt was a conscious lie by Bolshakov.[14] He was only one of many communications channels damaged or discredited by the Anadyr *maskirovka*.

Every senior member of the Kennedy administration, beginning with the president, had been angered by the Soviet deception in deploying the missiles to Cuba. But no one was more upset than Robert Kennedy, who had seen not only Bolshakov discredited but also Ambassador Dobrynin, with whom he had developed his own friendship and rapport. Furthermore, the decision to make the president's announcement of the missiles in Cuba and the subsequent quarantine of the island a surprise had penalties of its own. Until Ambassador Stevenson's performance before the television cameras at the United Nations, the official position of the Soviet Union had been to deny the existence of the missiles in Cuba. Now, with the deception of the Soviets' *maskirovka* exposed, Americans were suspicious of virtually every communications channel from Moscow. At a time when dialogue between the Kremlin and the White House was most critical, the Kennedy administration had no confidence in any pronouncement from the Soviet Union.

President Kennedy's October 22 speech had not come as a particular surprise to Khrushchev. For weeks, he had known of the U-2 reconnaissance flights over Cuba. What had been unpleasant was the timing of the discovery, just as the first SS-4 missiles were becoming operational and the launchpads for the SS-5 missiles were being prepared. When he learned of the planned speech that evening, Khrushchev was at home visiting with his son Sergei. Ordering the members of the Presidium of the Central Committee into session, the elder Khrushchev told his son,

"We have to consult. Don't wait for me; I'll be late," then took a car back to the Kremlin.[15]

Within hours, he had the text of President Kennedy's speech in his hands, delivered by a courier from the American Embassy. Originally, U.S. Ambassador Foy Kohler had been tasked to give the message to Khrushchev personally. However, the ordered 6 P.M. Eastern time delivery meant that the letter arrived at 2 A.M. in Moscow, and nobody at a senior level was available at the Soviet Foreign Ministry to receive it. It was the first of many instances when the time zone difference between Moscow and Washington, along with the primitive nature of 1962-era diplomatic communications, would make the path to a solution for the crisis more difficult.[16]

The Presidium worked through the early morning hours of Tuesday, October 23, to craft a response to Kennedy's letter and speech. While Khrushchev dictated the letter, the Presidium discussed and approved the individual points of the note. The group worked until almost noon Moscow time before dispatching the letter to President Kennedy. Khrushchev's first official communication of the missile crisis took another twelve hours to arrive at the White House. When it did, the response was terribly disappointing to the Kennedy administration.

The short, belligerent note admitted nothing and offered no suggestions for a solution to the crisis. The only concession was that Khrushchev had stopped denying that offensive nuclear weapons had been deployed to Cuba. One passage in particular revealed that the Soviets knew to some extent what the Americans had found in Cuba: "We confirm that armaments now on Cuba, regardless of [the] classification to which they belong, are destined exclusively for defensive purposes, in order to secure [the] Cuban Republic from attack [by an] aggressor."[17]

The intent of the note was clear: the Soviet Union had sent military forces to the Caribbean to protect the Cuban Revolution and Fidel Castro. The October 23 message from the Kremlin also showed Soviet determination not to be influenced by the American quarantine or by the diplomatic pressures of the Organization of American States or the United Nations.

Despite Khrushchev's hostile tone, the Soviet leader knew that the deception was now finished. Khrushchev had no illusions about the probable outcome of a direct conflict with the United States. If the U.S. military bombed or invaded Cuba, Castro and his government would be destroyed, along with the entire Anadyr combat force. If Khrushchev chose to order the Cuban missiles fired at the United States, then the

Soviet homeland would be destroyed in retaliation by the far superior U.S. strategic offensive forces. While the United States and its allies would suffer massive casualties and physical damage, the Soviet Union would be turned into a thermonuclear wasteland. Most of its citizens would be dead, and the land would be rendered unlivable for generations. Everything that he and the Soviet leadership had done since the October Revolution of 1917 would be destroyed, lost like countless other dead civilizations.[18]

Khrushchev and the men around him were a pragmatic group, and none was particularly interested at the time in fixing blame for the failed attempt to hide the Anadyr deployment. The Presidium members began to make preparations for the worst, which included raising the alert levels of Soviet military forces.[19] In a move designed to show the Kennedy administration that the Soviet leadership was not rattled by the public disclosure of Anadyr or by the pending quarantine, Khrushchev took selected members of the Presidium to the Bolshoi Ballet. That night, Khrushchev joined many of his American counterparts, like Secretary of Defense Robert McNamara, in sleeping on his office couch.

By the morning of October 24, Khrushchev had more information to work with, including a note from Ambassador Dobrynin in Washington. The most important point of Dobrynin's message was that the Kennedy administration was deeply upset at having been lied to over the nature and extent of the Anadyr deployment. The information in the message was based on a meeting with Attorney General Kennedy at the Soviet Embassy late on the evening of October 23.[20] In addition to the concern over the clandestine attempt by the Soviet Union to move strategic weapons into Cuba, there also were concerns over whether Soviet merchant ships were going to challenge the American quarantine line the following day. When Dobrynin indicated that the merchant captains had not been ordered to turn around, Robert Kennedy replied simply, "But this can end in war."[21]

By that time, Khrushchev had made up his mind to initiate an additional back channel to send messages to the Kennedy administration. As the crisis was erupting, the president of Westinghouse Electric International Company, William Knox, was in Moscow examining Soviet patents for possible licensing. The two men had met previously in the United States in 1960, and Khrushchev summoned him to a Kremlin meeting on the afternoon of October 24. Knox was subjected to a tirade, during which Khrushchev explained the Soviet position in Cuba in purely defensive terms. He mixed in some Russian folk stories to leaven the emotion.

Khrushchev admitted to Knox that the Soviets had emplaced "ground-to-ground missiles" in Cuba, the first time he had said so directly. Knox returned to the United States the following day and was immediately debriefed by officials from the State Department and the CIA and the information forwarded to the president.[22] It had taken two days to get that message from Moscow to Washington.

The Information Flow

Two days into the public phase of the missile crisis, moving diplomatic notes and reports between Washington and Moscow was becoming a crisis within a crisis. One of the oddities of the nuclear age was that while the United States and the Soviet Union had built secure command-and-control systems for their strategic nuclear forces that could respond in just minutes, simple text messages between capital cities took hours or even days to arrive. The apparent delay in receiving Khrushchev's response to the speech and the message of October 22 was causing heartburn among senior Kennedy administration leaders, concerned about the lag in communications. Now it had taken two days to get the news of William Knox's meeting with the Soviet leader back to the White House. Poor communications were threatening to make the crisis even worse.

Ambassador Dobrynin's message to Khrushchev, dealing with his October 23 meeting with Robert Kennedy, clearly illustrates the difficulties of getting information quickly and securely between Moscow and Washington. As odd as it may seem, in 1962, secure overseas communications had advanced very little since the introduction of the first telegraphic service in the mid-1800s.[23] Most nations, including the United States and the Soviet Union, used commercial telegraph services like Western Union for secure messages that had to be sent between embassies. The correspondence was encrypted or encoded by the embassy communications section—part of the KGB's Eighth Directorate for the Soviet Union—and then typed onto telegram message forms. When messages were ready, a call would be made to the local telegraph office for transmission to the desired overseas station.

Ambassador Dobrynin's message took several hours just to draft and submit to the embassy's communications section for encoding. Encoding probably took an additional hour before the Western Union office in Union Station, a mile and a half from the Soviet Embassy, was called. Western Union would then sent a dispatch rider by *bicycle* to pick up the message, which would add an additional hour or more before it was ready to be sent overseas to Moscow.[24] It would then be transmitted to Moscow, where the message would be delivered to the Foreign Ministry. Following decoding, copies would be typed and distributed to Foreign Minister Gromyko, Khrushchev, and certain other members of the Presidium. Normally, this process took a minimum of twelve hours one way, not counting time for analysis or comments being added by appropriate offices.[25]

Neither government had viewed diplomatic communications message delivery times as a driver in the outcome of the crisis, but that was exactly what was happening. The fact was that in a nuclear confrontation that might last just a few days, the twelve-hour delivery time for diplomatic notes meant that only a handful of such messages could be sent. While Kennedy and Khrushchev could order the destruction of the world in a matter of minutes, it took many hours just to send a short message from the White House to the Kremlin. The issue of nuclear war or peace would ride in the message bags of minimum-wage Western Union delivery boys.

On the morning of October 23, *New York Daily News* reporter Frank Holeman invited GRU officer Bolshakov, who had been such an effective back-channel contact prior to the crisis, to a meeting.[26] When they got together, Holeman told Bolshakov that the Kennedy administration, despite the hard-line rhetoric of the president's speech the previous evening, was ready to find a way to negotiate the missiles out of Cuba. Robert Kennedy had sent Holeman with a special carrot to help sweeten the deal for the Soviets: an offer to remove the U.S.-supplied Jupiter missiles from Italy and Turkey in exchange for the withdrawal of the missiles from Cuba.[27] While there are indications from taped White House conversations that Robert Kennedy may have been "freelancing" the idea of a missile trade to defuse the crisis, Bolshakov had good reason by the end of October 23 to believe the offer was official.[28]

Almost as soon as he had finished the meeting with Holeman, Bolshakov received a call from another newsman close to the Kennedy brothers: *Chattanooga Times* columnist Charles Bartlett, whom John Kennedy knew from his playboy days in Palm Beach, Florida. Arriving for a midday meeting at Bartlett's office, Bolshakov found himself looking at U-2 photos of ballistic missiles on Cuba. It was two full days before Ambassador Stevenson's presentation to the United Nations. Bartlett was informed that Robert Kennedy had sent him to show the photos to Bolshakov, and he confirmed the offer to "trade" the Jupiter missiles in

Europe for the Soviet weapons in Cuba. A second Bartlett-Bolshakov meeting that afternoon provided further support for the idea. Bolshakov returned to the Soviet Embassy and wrote up a report for GRU headquarters in Moscow. Unfortunately, the GRU *Rezident* in Washington did not believe that the offer was real and initially refused to forward Bolshakov's report on the evening of October 23, adding another delay in critical information reaching Khrushchev.

Bolshakov was not the only Soviet intelligence officer trying to make contacts during the crisis. In addition to the GRU presence in the Soviet embassy, there was also a large contingent from the KGB, the Committee for State Security.[29] Unlike the GRU *Rezident*, the head of the KGB section in Washington was not reluctant to forward information to Moscow when he had it. The KGB *Rezident* in Washington was Alexander Feklisov, perhaps the most talented and experienced Soviet master spy ever to operate within the United States. Feklisov had spent almost a decade in New York in the 1940s and 1950s, running the spy network that had included Julius and Ethel Rosenberg. Now, as the KGB *Rezident* in Washington, Feklisov was working hard to reestablish the network of agents that the FBI had wrecked in the 1950s following his departure from the United States.[30] Arriving in Washington, D.C, late in 1960 under his cover name of Alexander Fomin, Feklisov had been given the unobtrusive title of Embassy press attaché.[31] Since that time, Feklisov had slowly built up a network of informants and contacts, and his superiors in Moscow generally thought that he was doing a good job. The Cuban Missile Crisis would be the zenith of his service to the Soviet Union.

The second week of the crisis had begun with Ambassador Dobrynin ordering Feklisov to get ready to evacuate the Washington embassy and to destroy all classified documents not required for operating under wartime conditions. Realizing that a major crisis between the United States and the Soviet Union was about to erupt, Feklisov ordered his KGB team into action and to report *everything* they heard around Washington, down to barroom gossip. As it turned out, that week Washington bars and restaurants initially proved to be Feklisov's best venues for collecting information. One of the best was located in the National Press Club at 14th and F Streets Northwest, where the bartender, Johnny Prokov, was an émigré from the Baltic region. A strident anti-communist, Prokov often passed along gossip between the various members of the press fraternity. Just before 1 A.M. on October 25, as he was getting ready to close, Prokov told Anatoly Gorsky of TASS about what he had heard

Alexander Feklisov (alias Aleksandr Fomin) was a key player in several American dramas. As an NKVD officer, he "ran" the Rosenberg atomic spy ring, and as a KGB officer, he attempted to negotiate a peaceful conclusion to the missile crisis.

that evening while tending bar. What made this idle chat so important was that in addition to being a TASS journalist, Gorsky was also a KGB officer working for Feklisov.[32]

Prokov told Gorsky that he had overheard Robert Donovan and Walter Rogers of the *New York Herald Tribune* discussing the Caribbean, and that one of them was headed south to cover the "impending invasion of Cuba." In fact, Rogers had been assigned to one of the military press pools that would go in with the marines if an invasion took place. Feklisov came to the conclusion that war was now a real possibility.[33] Unlike Bolshakov, who had to answer to his GRU superiors in the embassy, Feklisov had the ability as the KGB *Rezident* in Washington to forward reports on his own authority, either to Ambassador Dobrynin or to KGB Chairman Semichastny in Moscow. When Feklisov's report regarding the bar chat arrived in the Kremlin on the morning of October 25, it proved to be the final corroboration needed to convince Khrushchev and the Presidium that the United States would go to war if the missiles were not removed from Cuba.

Feklisov had also been given a task indirectly from Khrushchev himself. The Soviet leader built a Presidium consensus to offer to remove the missiles from Cuba if the Americans made certain concessions. The concessions included a hard promise to respect the integrity of the Castro regime and not to invade the island. Khrushchev also expressed a desire— although not yet a hard requirement—for the United States to remove at least some of the Jupiter missiles from Europe. Khrushchev, concerned over the lack of clarity and slow speed in the diplomatic communications channels, without informing Ambassador Dobrynin, ordered Feklisov to find a back-channel contact to the Kennedy administration and to raise the offer directly that same day. When he arrived for work at the embassy on the morning of the 26th, Feklisov found a message with instructions waiting for him.[34]

Feklisov had made many friends and acquaintances in Washington and quickly made contact with the Kennedy administration through the ABC State Department correspondent John Scali. The moderator of the weekly Sunday television talk show *Issues and Answers*, Scali was close to several senior Kennedy administration officials, including his next-door neighbor—the presidential advisor Ken O'Donnell. Feklisov had met with Scali on a number of occasions, most recently the Monday prior to the president's televised speech. Now he dialed Scali, who was assigned the KGB code name "MIN," and suggested that they meet for lunch at 1:30 p.m.[35]

The two men met at the Occidental Grill near the White House and next to the Willard Hotel on Pennsylvania Avenue, where over lunch they began to discuss the status of the crisis. Scali had already advised Dean Rusk at the State Department that he was going to meet again with Feklisov, something he had done periodically since their introduction some months earlier. Lunch began with Scali asking probing questions about Khrushchev. The Soviet leader had not been seen publicly for several days, something that caused certain analysts at the CIA to suspect that a coup had occurred in the Soviet Union.[36]

Scali continued the aggressive questioning and then openly threatened American action against Cuba. Feklisov later claimed that Scali told him that the only way to avoid war was for the Soviets to pull their missiles out of Cuba. Feklisov then recalled saying that "there were Russian troops there . . . thousands of them. This will not be productive . . . it will be counter-productive . . . a military quagmire."

The meeting was now stormy, with Feklisov recalling harsh words being exchanged over the consequences of an attack or an invasion of Cuba, even threatening Scali with a counterresponse in Berlin. Both men apparently calmed down after this exchange, and then one of them made the offer to have the Soviets withdraw the missiles in exchange for a peaceful solution to the crisis.[37]

After lunch, Feklisov was waiting to brief Dobrynin about his meeting when at 4 p.m. Scali asked for another meeting. Excusing himself,

John Scali, the ABC news correspondent who provided one of several back-channel links between the Kremlin and the White House.

Feklisov headed to the Statler Hotel, almost midway between the Soviet Embassy and the White House, the direction from which Scali apparently was coming. Five minutes later, the two men sat down at a hotel bar, and over coffee Scali laid out the American response. The Soviet Union would have to dismantle and remove the missiles from Cuba under UN supervision, the United States would lift the quarantine, and the American government would pledge never to invade Cuba. Writing furiously in his notebook, Feklisov decided to find out how high this American response was sponsored. When he asked Scali where the offer came from, the reporter replied, "John Fitzgerald Kennedy, president of the United States."[38] Just to make certain that he had heard it correctly, Feklisov made Scali repeat what he had just said.

Wanting to see if the American position had any flexibility, Feklisov asked whether the UN might supervise the withdrawal of American air and invasion forces from Florida and the southeastern United States. Scali's response was apparently quick and scathing: "No!" He emphasized that Kennedy was under considerable pressure to initiate military action against Cuba. Agreeing to transmit the offer, Feklisov excused himself and quickly walked back the few hundred feet to the Soviet Embassy to send a message to Moscow about his meetings and to brief Ambassador Dobrynin.

Dobrynin and Feklisov talked several times after his hasty return to the embassy, and the ambassador was apparently upset about *again* having been left out of the loop about the Cuban situation. As a result, Dobrynin was unwilling to forward the message with his endorsement, since he had never seen any written instructions on the offer from the Kremlin. This left Feklisov on his own to send a cable on the meeting through the KGB communications channel, which was dispatched via the Western Union courier around 10 P.M. (Eastern time). Knowing that the note would probably not reach the Kremlin before noon Moscow time the following day, the exhausted KGB *Rezident* headed home.[39]

The Official Letters: Mixed Messages

At the same time that Feklisov and Scali were meeting over coffee at the Statler Hotel, Khrushchev was composing the most important diplomatic message of the Cold War. Khrushchev assumed that Feklisov had been effective in contacting the Kennedy administration. Feklisov's report of the previous day, among others, told Khrushchev that the Americans were getting ready to attack Cuba, perhaps in just a matter of hours. Khrushchev began to compose a letter directly to President Kennedy, laying out for the record an official offer to withdraw the missiles from Cuba. The rest of the Presidium was present and endorsed the terms laid out in the text. Despite the unanimous reaction, Khrushchev was reluctant to sign the letter.[40]

The letter was actually a revision of a draft letter from several days earlier. It was a long note and took some time to get to the point. However, when it did, there was a troubling addition to what had been discussed between Scali and Feklisov: a request to trade the fifteen Jupiter missiles being installed in Turkey for the Soviet weapons in Cuba. The key section of the note read:

> I therefore make this proposal: We are willing to remove from Cuba the means which you regard as offensive. We are willing to carry this out and to make this pledge in the United Nations. Your representatives will make a declaration to the effect that the United States, for its part, considering the uneasiness and anxiety of the Soviet State, will remove its analogous means from Turkey. Let us reach agreement as to the period of time needed by you and by us to bring this about. And, after that, persons entrusted by the United Nations Security Council could inspect on the spot the fulfillment of the pledges made.[41]

The trade seemed reasonable to Khrushchev and the rest of the Presidium, and it had been openly discussed in newspapers around the world, particularly in the column of the American journalist Walter Lippmann. Such a trade would help take some of the humiliation out of the Soviet weapons withdrawal from Cuba, and it had been added in the final draft of a letter to Kennedy.

Once the letter was dispatched, Khrushchev settled down to await the American response. Unfortunately, the length of the note and the fragile nature of the diplomatic communications channel converged to cause a major problem at the worst possible time. Because the letter was so long, it had to be sent in multiple parts in separate telegrams and then reassembled at the Soviet Embassy in Washington. Somehow, the message became entangled in the Western Union system and was not delivered to the White House until the following morning in Washington. In the intervening hours, Khrushchev had a fitful night on his Kremlin office couch, tossing and turning while he wondered whether adding the Turkish missile caveat had been wise. Early on the morning of Saturday, October 27, he decided to rescind the Turkish missile swap, and he sent the earlier draft version of the message, which had not called for the Jupiters to be removed. This message went through smoothly and actually beat the earlier letter to the White House. What followed nearly led to a nuclear war.

The two messages gave no indication of *when* they were written or dispatched, and that situation now conspired to cause a firestorm of debate within ExComm. Late on Friday night, the 26th, what became known as "the first letter" arrived, containing Khrushchev's more lenient terms. For the first time in almost two weeks, there was reason for some optimism in the White House, and the note was reviewed for any diplomatic problems. If none were apparent, then an acceptance would be cabled to Moscow the following day and the crisis would be at an end. Most of the senior administration went home for some sleep and hoped for a peaceful outcome, spurred by the note.[42]

Then early on Saturday morning, "the second letter," actually sent first and containing the request for an exchange of missiles, arrived at the White House, making it look as if Khrushchev had gone back on the earlier offer and was playing the "Turkish card."[43] The letter was delivered at the start of the 10 A.M. ExComm meeting to discuss the contents of the "first letter" and Scali's meetings with Feklisov of the previous day.

The "second letter" hit ExComm members like a bomb, the animated discussion taking up the remainder of the two-hour meeting.[44] Clearly, the swap of the Jupiters in Turkey was a potential deal breaker, and the optimism of the previous evening was shattered. Suddenly, just as a solution seemed within reach, a minor communications glitch had taken both sides back to the brink of nuclear war.

14

OPLAN 316: Invasion!

The reference . . . OPLAN [Operations Plan] provides for air and sea blockade and/or simultaneous airborne and amphibious against the Havana area, employing relatively large forces and heavy equipment in order to defeat the Cuban military forces, gain control of the Havana area, and overthrow the Castro regime.

Situation Analysis, Operations Plan 314[1]

While John F. Kennedy and Nikita Khrushchev were stumbling toward a solution to the Cuban Missile Crisis, the military forces on both sides continued to make plans in the event that their commanders-in-chief could not achieve peace. Military options for the Soviet Union in October 1962 were decidedly limited: nuclear missile and bomber strikes on Western Europe and the United States, and perhaps taking over West Berlin in retribution for American action in the Caribbean.[2] This limited set of options had been one of the reasons Khrushchev favored Operation Anadyr in the first place: to have greater strategic security and flexibility to deal with the growing military might of the United States and its NATO allies. Now, with Anadyr an open book to U.S. reconnaissance and intelligence activities and only partially completed, the full power of the American military establishment was about to fall on Cuba.

The fact that the Kennedy administration desperately wanted to be rid of Fidel Castro was no secret in 1962. What was not generally known is the extent to which President Kennedy was willing to have the U.S. armed forces do the job for him. While most historians have focused on the CIA's covert Cuban activities—Operation Mongoose—the main thrust of U.S. operations against Castro in 1962 was oriented toward a more final solution. Throughout 1962, U.S. military staffs in the Pentagon and various combat commands were putting the final touches on OPLANs 314 and 316, the war plans to invade and "free" Cuba.[3] Both plans had been created to provide President Kennedy with military options if a political opportunity arose that would allow the United States to invade and occupy Cuba, and to finish off Castro once and for all. Thus, as Kennedy and Khrushchev tried to reach out to each other and avoid a war, the American military commands prepared to fight one in Cuba.

A military maxim states that one learns more from failure than from victory. The thinking behind OPLANs 314 and 316 reinforced the maxim.[4] Bitterly won lessons from the CIA's abortive invasion at the Bay of Pigs were key to preparing the two OPLAN options. The first lesson was the most obvious one: employ massive amounts of tactical air power. More than any other factor at the Bay of Pigs, the lack of adequate and timely air strikes and protective air cover led to the annihilation of Brigade 2506 in the swamps of Bahia de Cochinos. The second lesson was the need for overwhelming numbers and arms. Castro's fast-moving troops rapidly killed or captured the fifteen hundred Cuban expatriates. The third lesson was a requirement that military professionals, not clandestine operatives of the CIA, would command the invasion. These lessons, along with others, were part of the massive planning effort that went into the creation of the two OPLANs.[5]

Admiral Robert L. Dennison, the Commander-in-Chief U.S. Atlantic Command (CINCLANT) and in 1962 one of the most experienced U.S. military professionals, was in charge of the U.S. armed effort against Cuba. Dennison had watched in frustration as ships of his Atlantic Fleet had been ordered to stand by while Brigade 2506 was chopped to pieces in April 1961. Within a year of the Bay of Pigs disaster, the CINCLANT staff, along with support from the Joint Chiefs of Staff, the CIA, and other government agencies, had created OPLANs 314 and 316 to make certain that an invasion of Cuba would oust Castro.

Both plans shared a common operational concept, with only a timing difference. OPLAN 314 assumed that the invading forces would have four or more days to assemble, equip, and move to their staging areas, OPLAN 316 was designed to be executed within just forty-eight hours of an alert order, meaning that the initial landings would take place with fewer men and fewer weapons in trade for the more rapid response time.[6] For 1962, the two OPLANs were surprisingly "joint" in their concept and vision. Ironically, the target date for both plans was October 1962.

Admiral Dennison's forces were broken into several components, each responsible for various warfare operations. In addition to his CINCLANT

NPIC analysts construct a model of a military target in Cuba, based on aerial photography. These models were to be used by U.S. invasion forces, which were poised to assault the island.

responsibilities, Dennison was also his own naval component comman-der (Commander-in-Chief Atlantic Fleet), including command of the Marine forces. Army General Herbert B. Powell of the U.S. Continental Command at Fortress Monroe, Virginia, would command the Army units.[7] General Walter C. Sweeney of the Tactical Air Command (TAC) at Lang-ley Air Force Base, Virginia, headed the Air Force component.

The units that would take part in the invasion of Cuba included the Second Fleet, 2nd Marine Division, Ninth and Nineteenth Air Forces, and the Army's XVIII Airborne Corps. Formed into an overall organiza-tion known as Joint Task Force (JTF) 122, the various component com-mands had their own task force (TF) numbers based upon function: TF-123 was the naval force, TF-125 the Army, TF-126 the Air Force, and TF-127 the "unconventional" force for special operations. Many of the combat units were given special training in the summer of 1962, including a rehearsal landing on the island of Vieques near Puerto Rico by Atlantic Fleet marines.

In general, both plans projected an assault by two Marine Corps divisions and two Army airborne divisions within the first days of an invasion. The Marine formations would be drawn from the 1st Marine Division at Camp Pendleton, California, and the 2nd Marine Division at Camp Lejeune, North Carolina. The Army airborne units would be the 82nd and the 101st Airborne Divisions from Fort Bragg, North Carolina, and Fort Campbell, Kentucky, respectively. Follow-on Army forces would include the 1st Armored Division and the 3rd Armored Cavalry Regiment, along with supporting units.

Whichever version of the Cuban invasion plan was executed, the landing would be preceded by an extensive air campaign flown from airfields in the southeastern United States and from aircraft carriers of the Atlantic Fleet. Over a period of days, several hundred strike and fighter aircraft would soften up the Cuban armed forces, while paving the way for the amphibious and airborne assaults. Then, on D-Day, the invasion forces would strike with their primary focus on seizing airfields, ports, communications centers, and, of course, the capital city of Havana.[8]

The planned invasion would have been the largest U.S. forced entry operation since World War II. The amphibious landings would be the largest since Okinawa in April 1945, with more than a hundred naval vessels participating. There was little subtlety to the plans: both were big and powerful, reflecting their American roots in concept of operations and scope. Prior to the landing, Army Special Forces "A" Teams would be inserted into Cuba, to conduct sabotage, reconnaissance, and unconventional warfare missions, working with anti-Castro insurgents. In western Cuba, Army airborne units would drop onto and capture airfields, while the Marine Corps amphibious units would drive inland to capture Havana and other large cities. In the east, the Marines at Guantánamo Bay would break out of their perimeter and drive into central Cuba. While the terrain would favor the Cuban defenders, there was little doubt that the U.S. forces would overwhelm Castro's forces. The fight would be bloody and nasty, but that would be the price of eliminating the only communist regime in the Western Hemisphere.[9] At least, that was the idea before Operation Anadyr and Soviet military forces began arriving in August 1962.

When word came to ready the Navy quarantine forces, there were also instructions issued to all units to prepare for executing OPLAN 316. The instructions included significant modifications to accommodate the rapidly changing military situation on the ground in Cuba.[10] Obviously, the introduction of Soviet ground forces meant that elements of OPLAN 316 would have to be greatly enlarged to deal with the new forces in Cuba. Some of the main alterations included moving portions of the 1st Marine Division from Camp Pendleton, California, through the Panama Canal and into the Caribbean aboard amphibious ships. Additional follow-on Army units were mobilized and prepared for movement to embarkation ports—primarily, Beaumont, Texas, and Savannah, Georgia.

As the crisis developed, Admiral Dennison realized that there would not be time to establish the various task force headquarters and staffing called for in OPLAN 316. He decided to retain component commands with Generals Powell and Sweeney for Army and Air Force operations, respectively, and to hold naval and Marine commands at his own head-quarters.[11] The three commanders established a forward headquarters in Florida, from which much of the coming operations in the Caribbean were directed in the weeks that followed.

On October 20, Dennison had one of his staff call Vice Admiral Alfred Ward, commander of the Atlantic Fleet's amphibious forces, to tell him that he would be relieved of his command the next day. Before Ward could protest, he was told that his new assignment would be to command the Second Fleet, the principal naval command in the Atlantic. Dennison did not even have time to attend his subordinate's relief-promotion ceremony the next day; he was in Washington discussing invasion preparations with President Kennedy.[12] Ward was replaced in the amphibious force command by Vice Admiral Horacio Rivero Jr.[13]

To accommodate the enlarged target list for air strikes against Cuba, General Sweeney of TAC began to move additional Air Force units into the southeastern United States, mostly to borrowed SAC bases like MacDill Air Force Base near Tampa, Florida. One of the most engaged Air Force units was the 363rd Tactical Reconnaissance Wing, normally based at Shaw Air Force Base in South Carolina but moved en masse to MacDill. The 363rd was TAC's premier reconnaissance unit, flying both the RF-101 Voodoo and the RB-66 Destroyer. The Voodoos were not equipped with cameras designed for low-altitude work. The RF-101, once refitted with improved U.S. Navy–developed cameras, proved to be an excellent low-level photographic aircraft and was used to augment the Navy and the Marine Corps F8U-1P Crusaders that began low-level photo flights over Cuba following President Kennedy's speech on October 22.[14]

The RB-66s, flying off the coast of Cuba, provided electronic "order of battle information" on Soviet and Cuban radar, including real-time warning of hostile enemy action through the electronic emissions of SAM-related radars. The 363rd was joined in the reconnaissance duties by a few RB-47s of SAC's 55th Strategic Reconnaissance Wing and helped begin the process of building a tactical intelligence picture of Soviet and Cuban military forces. Meanwhile, TAC was busy moving units to and from bases in and around Florida and creating a special "Peninsular" command to control aircraft movements around the state.

These preparations took time and had begun several days prior to President Kennedy's speech on October 22. Unfortunately, moving ground divisions and fighter wings is about as easy as hiding an elephant under a thorn bush, and journalists throughout the United States noticed the movements. Rail lines and roads throughout the southern United States were commandeered and rapidly became jammed with military

An Air Force RF-101 Voodoo photo plane shows the sharp lines of the aircraft. Both the Voodoo and the Crusader reconnaissance aircraft were later used in the Vietnam conflict.

traffic. At ports from Norfolk to San Diego, Navy warships and amphibious ships rapidly assembled their crews and sailed to support the coming operations in the Caribbean. To help cover these movements, the Navy announced that they were part of an exercise known as PHIBRIGLEX-62, an amphibious practice session at Vieques involving forty Atlantic Fleet ships. All would be part of the planned quarantine and invasion operations, hence the subterfuge was both useful and practical. However, once the president's announcement had been made, all concerns about operational security went by the wayside, and PHIBRIGLEX-62 was officially canceled.

As JTF-122 was finally assembled at the end of the second week of the crisis, the assembly of men, ships, and aircraft was impressive. More than 500,000 military personnel were now committed to planned operations in the Caribbean, with 180 ships; about 1,000 land-based aircraft; 40,000 marines; 14,500 Army paratroops; and some additional 100,000 soldiers now ready to carry out the assault on Cuba. The problem was that nobody on the American side had a good idea of what they would be facing when they hit the beaches and the landing zones in Cuba. As it turned out, that ignorance almost became the spark plug for World War III.

Defending the Beaches

In fewer than four years, Castro and his supporters had built an impressive defensive capability for Cuba, which had been greatly improved with the addition of the Soviet equipment and now the troops of Operation Anadyr. In 1962, the Cuban military was a mix of World War II–era American weapons left over from the Batista years and a sizable supply

Fidel Castro visits an anti-aircraft gun site manned by the militia. The Cuban leader continually visited his troops during the crisis, both to encourage them and to ascertain the state of Cuban defenses.

of new Soviet equipment delivered over the previous year. The fully mobilized Cuban Army could deploy about 270,000 soldiers, regular and militia. Armed with some 160 T-34 and T-54 tanks, the Cuban Army had been good enough to knock off Brigade 2506 in a few days with minimal losses. Less powerful was the Cuban Air Force, equipped with sixty MiG-17 (NATO Fresco) and MiG-19 (NATO Farmer) fighters; some Cuban pilots had combat experience from the Bay of Pigs. Backed by a growing network of ground control radar and more than seven hundred anti-aircraft guns of various calibers, the Cuban air defenses could have been a shock to anyone trying to repeat what the CIA had attempted at the Bay of Pigs in 1961. However, even the most optimistic of Cuban patriots would have been hard-pressed to imagine their armed forces standing up to the might of a U.S. military assault in full fury. For that, Castro's military needed help, which it found beginning in August 1962 with the arrival of the Group of Soviet Forces in Cuba.

With the assistance of four decades of hindsight, it now becomes clear just how much Khrushchev was willing to risk in order to sustain Castro and his regime in Cuba. Along with a significant percentage of the Soviet Union's ballistic missiles and nuclear warheads, the Soviet Union committed some of its finest combat units to help defend Cuba and the strategic weapons. The Soviet commitment included four motorized rifle regiments, some of the world's most powerful and best-balanced combat units in 1962. Two full divisions of SA-2 surface-to-air missiles were deployed to provide an air defense shield over the ballistic missile sites and other forces. The Soviet Air Forces sent a regiment of forty-two MiG-21 (NATO Fishbed) fighters and a regiment with forty-two Il-28 (Beagle) medium jet bombers, as well as two FKR-1 (NATO SSC-2a Salish) battlefield cruise missile regiments armed with nuclear warheads. The Soviet Navy contributed additional Il-28 bombers and a dozen Komar missile

"My father is in the trenches," reads the hat on this toddler, as threats of a U.S. invasion kept Cuba's armed forces—both regulars and the militia—on continuous alert during most of the month of October.

patrol boats, as well as a number of land-based Sopka (NATO SSC-2b Samlet) anti-ship cruise missile batteries.

Prior to the beginning of the Anadyr deployment, Khrushchev made the decision to deploy tactical or battlefield nuclear weapons to Cuba. These weapons included a dozen Luna (FROG) rockets and eighty FKR cruise missiles, all with nuclear warheads. Finally, six atomic bombs for Il-28s were sent to Cuba.

Even with the last-minute changes reflecting new intelligence that the CINCLANT-Joint Chiefs of Staff planners were able to include in OPLAN 316, a vast array of the Soviet force was missed or identified late. One revelation was the discovery by a low-level reconnaissance mission on October 25, when one of the tracked FROG rocket launchers was photographed. While it took two days to identify the tracked launch vehicle and report it to senior military commanders, this finally woke up the American military leadership to the possibility that tactical nuclear-capable systems *could* be in Cuba.[15] The evaluation, by several intelligence committees and NPIC staff, noted: "Photography . . . confirmed the presence of a FROG missile launcher in a vehicle park near Remedios. (The FROG is a tactical unguided rocket of 40,000 to 50,000 yard range and is similar to the U.S. Honest John)." The analysis repeated a now-frequent line: "we still lack positive evidence that nuclear weapons are deployed in Cuba."

Admiral Dennison responded to the report by requesting the inclusion of tactical nuclear weapons in his invasion force, although it is questionable whether they would have been available by the planned D-Day of November 4.[16] He requested that his assault forces take nuclear-capable weapons into Cuba, for example, 8-inch howitzers and Honest John rockets. The Joint Chiefs of Staff approved his request to take *launchers* but did not authorize him to take the actual weapons (warheads) into

Cuba. "Dennison was told he could have them [the weapons] if required but they were not released to him," recalled an aide to JCS Chairman Maxwell Taylor.[17]

The attitude of the Joint Chiefs of Staff—and of most senior U.S. commanders—was summed up by Taylor's aide, then-Major William Y. Smith: "We didn't think about tactical nuclear weapons in Cuba."

OPLAN 316: Prescription for Armageddon

As conceived, OPLAN 316 was to have commenced on Monday, October 29, if there were no negotiated solution to the crisis. The first air strikes would have been aimed at the five ballistic missile launch sites and twenty-four SA-2 SAM sites. Those attacks would have been carried out by F-100 Super Saber and F-105 Thunderchief fighter-bombers armed with conventional "iron" bombs, napalm canisters, and rockets, as well as their 20-millimeter cannon. At the same time, F-104 Starfighters armed with 20-millimeter Gatling guns and AIM-9 Sidewinder air-to-air missiles would have been flying MiG sweeps, trying to destroy Soviet and Cuban interceptors that might take off to stop the attackers. Finally, Navy and Marine Corps aircraft would begin to bomb landing beaches and other objectives in preparation for the amphibious and airborne landings that would have subsequently taken place. U.S. aircraft losses would probably have been heavy to the large numbers of SA-2 missiles and anti-aircraft guns, based upon U.S. experience over North Vietnam later in the 1960s.[18]

The air strikes were planned to last for several days, until the bomb damage assessments showed that the Soviet and the Cuban defenses were "soft" enough for the amphibious and airborne landings to take place. The landings were planned to begin about Sunday, November 4. Assuming that none of the Soviet Foxtrot-class diesel submarines in the area had managed to put a nuclear torpedo into an aircraft carrier or an amphibious group, the first opportunity for the Soviets to use their battlefield atomic weapons would have been during the initial landings.

The OPLAN 316 amphibious landings in Cuba would have taken place along the northern coast of western Cuba, with most of the marines hitting beaches around Tarana, east of Havana. The narrow mountain passes and the beaches on the north side of Cuba greatly limit the beaches that are open to amphibious assault, and the marines would have had only a handful of places they could have landed. Simultaneously, the parachute assault elements of the 82nd and 101st Airborne Divisions, delivered by Air Force transport aircraft, would be dropped on the José

Martí airfield (near Havana), Los Banos airfield, the Mariel naval air station, and the airfield at Baracoa.[19] Each airfield would be assaulted by at least a regiment of paratroopers. Finally, the reinforced Marine garrison at the Guantánamo naval base would have tried to break out of its perimeter. Marines and Army paratroops would have been concentrated into several areas, and the beach landings would have assembled a hundred amphibious transport ships just offshore. This would have made the entire invasion force extremely vulnerable to the Soviet trump card: the tactical or the battlefield nuclear and coastal weapons that were initially under General Pliyev's control.

When General Pliyev received his final instructions for Operation Anadyr on September 8, he had been given liberal rules of engagement for the use of nuclear weapons in Cuba. The launch authority memorandum read:

> In a situation of an enemy landing on the island of Cuba, and of the concentration of enemy ships off the coast of Cuba and in its territorial waters, when the destruction of the enemy is delaying [further actions] and there is no possibility of receiving instructions from the USSR Ministry of Defense, you are permitted to make your own decision and to use the nuclear means of the "Luna," Il-28 or FKR-1 as instruments of local warfare for the destruction of the enemy on land and along the coast in order to achieve the complete destruction of the invaders on the Cuban territory and to defend the Republic of Cuba.[20]

General Pliyev was free to use any means or weapons necessary to defend Cuba and the Soviet units on the island, with the exception of the SS-4 and the SS-5 ballistic missiles (for which launch authority was to come from the Kremlin). It was Soviet national and military doctrine to *never* allow nuclear weapons or their delivery systems to fall into the hands of enemy forces for *any* reason. Faced with a "use them or lose them" situation, the general planned to execute his orders and use the battlefield nuclear systems for maximum effect. However, with the exchange of diplomatic notes late in the second week of the crisis, Khrushchev rescinded release authority on the battlefield nuclear systems, deciding to control them at the national level in the Kremlin.[21]

The U.S. Marines and the airborne troops in the OPLAN 316 assault force would have been confronted by well-trained and well-armed Soviet troops, along with large numbers of dedicated Cuban troops. While the Cuban and the Soviet air forces would have been easily destroyed, the SA-2 SAMs could have taken a high toll of American aircraft, and the defending ground forces would have been more difficult and tenacious opponents, even without their tactical nuclear weapons. Particularly in the early hours of the invasion, the American airborne and Marine units would have been bunched up, with thousands of troops almost elbow-to-elbow, waiting for follow-on forces prior to moving out to their strategic objectives. These bunched-up units would have been prime targets for Soviet battlefield nuclear weapons.

Indeed, one of the most troubling aspects of the Soviet tactical nuclear doctrine was the apparently "seamless" transition from conventional to *tactical* nuclear weapons that was observed in Soviet exercises, according to a senior U.S. intelligence specialist, Rear Admiral Thomas A. Brooks. "That transition was unlike anything that we contemplated in our own theater nuclear forces," he added.[22] Such a Soviet nuclear attack would be retaliatory against the United States without directly threatening the U.S. homeland. Of course, the American view might not have been so reasonable.

Given General Pliyev's orders, his battlefield nuclear weapons—the Lunas and the FKR-1s—would have been ideal for his purposes. Assuming that Khrushchev would have reinstated his release authority, General Pliyev would have quickly applied his hundred or so battlefield nuclear weapons against the American forces. This likely would have resembled a modified version of Field Marshal Erwin Rommel's "on the beaches" strategy for defending Normandy against Operation Overlord in June 1944.[23] Given that the Americans would probably have achieved air supremacy by the start of the airborne and the amphibious landings, Pliyev would likely have taken a "use them or lose them" attitude toward his supply of Lunas and FRK-1s, using them quickly in preplanned strikes.

More than any other factor, timing and target position would have determined the effectiveness of the Soviet tactical nuclear strikes had they occurred. For example, the Lunas with their 2-kiloton warheads would have devastated an area of 1,000 to 2,000 yards from the center of the blast. Exposed troops would have been killed instantly by the heat and the blast, while personnel in amphibious tractors and armored vehicles might have survived for a few days before dying of radiation effects. Anyone looking directly at the impact point at the moment of detonation would have suffered retinal damage and possible long-term blindness.

In practical terms, each Luna warhead potentially could devastate a battalion landing beach or zone if the unit were bunched up directly under the blast. Also, the area around each blast center would remain a radioactive "dead zone" for several weeks, restricting mobility of the surviving American forces.[24] While each Luna launcher had reload rockets, it is unlikely that more than one or two could have ever launched a second nuclear strike. The retribution by American strike aircraft would have been swift and devastating, likely ending in a hail of rocket fire and flaming napalm.

As bad as the Lunas might have been, the FKR-1 cruise missiles would have probably been worse. Basically an unpiloted MiG-15 fighter, the FKR-1 carried a 14-kiloton warhead out to a range of about fifty to sixty miles. The last forty-four warheads for the FKR-1s had just made it to Cuba aboard the *Alexandrovsk* on October 23, mere hours before the naval quarantine went into effect. This meant that Pliyev had eighty of the FKR-1s and sixteen launchers in two regiments (compared to just a dozen Lunas for six launchers), which had more than three times the range and seven times the explosive yield. The FKR-1 warhead footprint would be between four and five miles in diameter and would immediately kill at least half of any exposed personnel within that area. Any buildings or trees would have been flattened or burned out and every window shattered for miles around.[25]

Almost certainly, the 584th FKR Regiment near Holguin would have been tasked to destroy the American base at Guantánamo Bay, where a Marine regimental combat team was preparing to break out into central Cuba. Guantánamo Bay was also home to a large port facility and an air base, where close air support missions were to be flown from. A single properly placed FKR-1 could have devastated much of the base; the Soviets would likely have fired as many as needed to overcome the batteries of Hawk SAMs protecting the area.

On the western end of the island, FKR-1s from the 561st Regiment could have blanketed the Marine landing beaches and airborne drop zones, perhaps as follow-up strikes to the initial Luna attacks. The larger 14-kiloton warheads of the FKR-1s would have made targeting the American units much easier than with the Lunas, and the larger supply of missiles would have allowed for salvo firing for some hours. FKR-1s could also have been fired against groups of amphibious ships offshore.

The only Soviet tactical nuclear weapons that would not have made it to their targets would have been the six Il-28 Beagle jet bombers, each armed with a 20-kiloton warhead. Assuming that the aircraft had not been destroyed by the preinvasion air strikes, once airborne they would have been sitting ducks for U.S. fighter aircraft, Hawk SAMs, or the Navy's ship-based SAMs offshore.

Only the intrusion of American airpower would have stopped the Soviet nuclear barrage. There can be little doubt that news of Soviet tactical nuclear weapons killing American troops by the thousands in Cuba would have elicited a vicious response from President Kennedy. The realization that the Soviet Union had covertly based battlefield nuclear arms, on top of the other Soviet deceptions used in Anadyr, just would have made the decision to respond in kind that much easier.

The most likely nuclear weapon of choice for the Navy and the Air Force would have been the Mk 28 gravity bomb, which could be configured with yields from 70 kilotons to 1.5 megatons.[26] Nuclear strikes against Cuba would have been flown from U.S. Air Force *tactical* strike aircraft based in the southeastern United States and the two Navy attack carriers in the Caribbean, the *Enterprise* and the *Independence*. Then-Commander Edward L. (Whitey) Feightner, on the carrier division staff embarked on the "Big E," recalled, "We had some 40 nuclear weapons on board [the *Enterprise*] and we were prepared to use them. The nearby 'Indy' had a similar load of nuclear bombs and both ships had scores of A4D Skyhawks as well as other nuclear-capable aircraft ready to fly against Cuban targets with conventional or nuclear weapons."[27]

While the nuclear bombs were stored in magazines on board the aircraft carriers, with Marines providing tight security, the nuclear cores for the weapons were carried aboard cruisers operating with the carriers. When called for, Navy helicopters were prepared to transfer the cores to the carriers, with nuclear assembly teams standing by in the carriers to assemble and check out the weapons. Exercises demonstrated that the first cores could reach the carriers within ten minutes of the "go" order to attack, and the first bombs could be assembled and ready for loading onto aircraft within twenty minutes.[28]

Thus, with relatively short notice, the carriers *Enterprise* and *Independence* could add their nuclear-strike capabilities to the land-based strike forces of the Tactical Air Command. But there was also a *strategic* bomber force being readied to strike Cuba. Concerned that conventional or tactical nuclear strikes would not destroy all of the Soviet SS-4 and SS-5 ballistic missiles, SAC made plans for a limited attack by B-47 Stratojets. Approximately six of the jet bombers were designated to strike Cuba with 10- to 20-megaton weapons. Although Cuba is approximately the size of England—the Caribbean island is almost 43,000 square miles— a half-dozen B-47s, each carrying two gravity bombs, would have devastated the western portion of the island (and probably subjected the U.S. naval base at Guantánamo on the southeastern coast to radioactive fallout).[29] In all likelihood, these would have been the first of thousands of strategic thermonuclear weapons that would detonate around the world in what would have become World War III.

15

From SIOP to Dr. Strangelove

There was, definitely, a time when we could have destroyed all of Russia (I mean by that, all of Russia's capability to wage war) without losing a man to their defenses. The only losses incurred would have been the normal accident rate for the number of flying hours which would be flown to do the job. This period extended from before the time when the Russians achieved The Bomb, until after they had The Bomb but didn't yet own a stockpile of weapons. During that same era their defenses were at low ebb. As for their offensive capacity: no one bomb or missile, in that day, could have hit the United States.

General Curtis E. LeMay
Mission with LeMay[1]

While U.S. conventional military forces were preparing for air strikes and an invasion of Cuba, the U.S. strategic nuclear forces—those that could rain nuclear devastation on the Soviet homeland—were also preparing for war. In the fall of 1962, those U.S. strategic forces had massive nuclear superiority over their Soviet counterparts.

The Soviet Union had surprised the U.S. military and political leaders when it had detonated an atomic bomb on August 25, 1949. The explosion occurred three years before most U.S. intelligence and nuclear experts predicted that the USSR would have an atomic bomb. According to Rear Admiral Lewis Strauss, one of the first commissioners of the U.S. Atomic Energy Commission, "The majority opinion set the time substantially further in the future, while not a few believed it beyond Soviet capacity in *any* time scale likely to be of much concern to us."[2] The Soviet detonation of an atomic bomb in 1949 did not immediately provide a nuclear strike capability. That came in the early 1950s, when the Soviet first-production atomic bombs could be delivered by the Tu-4 (NATO Bull), a long-range, four-engine bomber that was a direct copy of the U.S. B-29 Superfortress. The U.S. reaction to the Soviet atomic test, as well as to the Berlin Blockade of 1948–1949, was to increase U.S. defense spending, particularly for nuclear weapons development.

An even greater surprise to the West came in August 1953, when the USSR detonated its first thermonuclear (hydrogen) device. While there had been a four-year interval between the first U.S. and Soviet nuclear detonations, there was less than ten months between their respective hydrogen bomb detonations. Subsequently, large numbers of advanced bombers were being displayed at air shows on Soviet national holidays, and increasingly in the United States there was concern that the Soviet advances in this area were creating a "bomber gap" unfavorable to the United States.

Then, on August 3, 1957, a Soviet R-7 intercontinental missile (NATO SS-6 Sapwood) rocketed several thousand miles from a launchpad in central Asia to impact in Soviet Siberia. In guarded words, the Soviet news agency TASS announced that "a super-long distance intercontinental multi-stage ballistic rocket flew at an . . . unprecedented altitude . . . and landed in the target area." Not for another sixteen months would a U.S. Atlas ICBM be tested over its full range. American concern over a possible "missile gap" was exacerbated on October 4, 1957, when the USSR orbited *Sputnik 1*, the world's first artificial satellite. The initial U.S. efforts to orbit a satellite failed. The Soviets soon set mark after mark with their satellites and deep space probes.[3] Obviously, large rocket boosters were needed to lift those payloads, portending a major military advantage for the Soviets.

But neither the "bomber gap" nor the "missile gap" existed. Despite their spectacular technical achievements, the Soviets were lagging far behind the United States in the production of manned bombers and intercontinental missiles, as well as of lightweight nuclear weapons. The truth was revealed to those who had access to the photography of the twenty-three successful U-2 spyplane flights over the Soviet Union from 1956 to 1960. Although then senator John F. Kennedy had received top-secret CIA briefings on the true state of Soviet bomber and missile developments in 1960 while he campaigned for the presidency, he had attacked the Eisenhower administration—and by inference his opponent, Vice President Richard M. Nixon—contending that the United States was falling behind in these important areas.

When he entered the White House in January 1961, President Kennedy knew the true state of the balance between U.S. and Soviet strategic forces. The "gaps" were a myth, perpetuated by Air Force leaders seeking more funding for strategic weapons and by Democratic politicians seeking to attack the Eisenhower administration. Major U.S. weapons development programs were already in hand that would soon make the apparent strategic imbalance overwhelmingly in favor of the United States. The development of the new-generation Minuteman ICBM was under way, and the first missiles would become operational in November 1962. The Minuteman, unlike the earlier U.S. Atlas and Titan ICBMs, was a solid-propellant missile, which meant that it could be launched on short notice. The first U.S. Polaris submarines were at sea, with U.S. shipyards producing the new boats at a rate that would peak at one per month, with each submarine carrying sixteen solid-propellant missiles.

And although American manned bomber production had halted in October 1962, by that time, the Strategic Air Command had almost sixteen hundred manned bombers based in the United States and periodically rotating to twenty overseas bases. When added to the nuclear strike aircraft on the five forward-deployed U.S. aircraft carriers, the missiles at sea in the two deployed Polaris submarines, and the two Regulus cruise missile submarines, the U.S. strategic force in the fall of 1962 was overwhelming. Indeed, by any measurement—aircraft, missiles, throw-weight (the weight of warheads delivered), megatonnage (the total explosive yield of the warheads delivered), or accuracy—the U.S. strategic forces were more capable than those of the world's other nuclear powers combined.[4]

SAC: The House That LeMay Built

To the president of the United States and most officials of the Kennedy administration, the Strategic Air Command (SAC) was *the* U.S. strategic striking force. The manned bombers and ICBMs controlled by SAC personified American nuclear striking power and were much more visible than the Navy's Polaris or Regulus missiles in submerged submarines or nuclear-capable aircraft on carriers in distant waters.

SAC had been created in 1946 to consolidate the several bomber commands of the Army Air Forces into a single, unified organization. What started as a collection of leftover aircraft and units from World War II began to rapidly evolve when Lieutenant General Curtis E. LeMay became the commanding general of SAC in October 1948.[5] LeMay was an innovative and aggressive U.S. bomber commander, as well as a charismatic leader. He had begun his flying career as a fighter pilot, but in the 1930s he became a strong advocate of strategic bombing and established a reputation as one of the most skillful bomber navigators of the Army

Air Corps. In World War II, he gained recognition as a master of bomber strategy, first while commanding B-17s in the European theater and then commanding the B-29 bomber force in the Pacific. Under LeMay, SAC would become the most powerful killing machine ever created by man.

Beginning in 1946, SAC planners had developed war plans for attacking the Soviet Union. Their plans had prosaic code names: Halfmoon, Broiler, Frolic, Grabber, Fleetwood, Doublestar, Trojan, Offtackle, Shakedown, and Crosspiece. The early plans included SAC bombers that had little chance of reaching their targets, using routes that were not accurately known, to deliver bombs that were not in military custody. During his tenure, General LeMay overcame those limitations.

General LeMay held command of SAC for a decade. When he left the command on June 30, 1957, he had personally influenced every aspect of SAC—promotion policy, base security, housing for his flight crews, laundry services, the design and procurement of the aircraft SAC operated, its attack plans, and the release authority for nuclear weapons.[6] The last was a critical issue, as LeMay had strong ideas about who should be able to order the use of nuclear weapons in time of war.

The Atomic Energy Act of 1946 established the Atomic Energy Commission (AEC), which, in January 1947, took control of all U.S. nuclear programs from the Manhattan Project. This meant that the military services had neither custody nor control of nuclear weapons. The concern of military leaders like LeMay was that an enemy might be able to mount a Pearl Harbor–style surprise attack before the nuclear bombs could be delivered to SAC bomber bases. Like every other senior American military officer of his generation, LeMay was haunted and driven by the memory of Pearl Harbor.

In July 1948, as B-29s were departing U.S. bases for England and West Germany during the Berlin Blockade, Secretary of Defense James Forrestal raised the issue with President Harry S. Truman of transferring custody of atomic bombs from the Atomic Energy Commission to the Pentagon's control. Truman, according to Forrestal's diary, "wanted to go into this matter very carefully and he proposed to keep, in his own hands, the decision as to the use of the bomb, and did not propose 'to have some dashing lieutenant colonel decide when would be the proper time to drop one.'"[7]

A week later, on July 21, President Truman met with Secretary Forrestal, the Secretaries of the Army and the Air Force, and members of the AEC. Forrestal and others believed that the Berlin crisis could lead to conflict between the Soviet Union and the United States. The Secretary of Defense sought an executive order from the president to have military custody of the available bombs turned over to the Pentagon, the chief reasons being: "(1) that the user of the bomb, who would ultimately be responsible for its delivery, should have custody of it with the accompanying advantages and familiarity, etc., which this would bring, and (2) concentration of authority—unified command."[8]

After listening to the various positions on the custody issue, President Truman was reported to have stated, "I don't think we ought to use this thing unless we absolutely have to. It is a terrible thing to order the use of something that . . . that is so terribly destructive, destructive beyond anything we have ever had. You have got to understand that this isn't a military weapon. It is used to wipe out women and children and unarmed people, and not for military uses. So we have to treat this differently from rifles and cannon and ordinary things like that."[9]

President Truman's final words at the time, as recorded by David Lilienthal, the Chairman of the AEC, were: "You have got to understand that I have got to think about the effect of such a thing on international relations. This is no time to be juggling an atomic bomb around." With that, Truman, the only man to have ever directed the use of nuclear weapons against an enemy, said he would review the papers submitted by the participants. The meeting was over. On July 23, Truman announced his decision that the AEC would continue to have custody of nuclear weapons; his public statement declared: "Since a free society places the civil authority above the military power, the control of atomic energy properly belongs in civilian hands."

Thus an awkward and time-consuming system was established whereby in times of crisis—and when authorized by the AEC—Air Force planes would load the fissionable material (cores or "pits") for atomic bombs at domestic AEC depots and fly them to SAC bases in the United States and overseas where the nonnuclear bomb casings were held. Only at those bases would the bombs be assembled and loaded into aircraft. Air Force planes would deliver the cores to forward bases for the Navy, where specially modified TBM-3C Avenger torpedo planes would fly them out to the carriers to be inserted into the bomb casings.

General LeMay, among others, felt that this delivery scheme would take too long in time of crisis, and he became a leader in the fight to give the military custody of the complete weapons. A 1954 briefing by SAC officials, as recorded by an attending naval officer, includes the passage:

> SAC is not much concerned over current or prospective [Joint Chiefs of Staff] allocations of weapons "because we know we will get the weapons when the bell rings," or words to that effect. [The general]

stressed, however, that their primary concern is: *"Where are these weapons* which they expected to be allocated?" That is, in what sites are they located so that SAC can plan his pick-up schedules accordingly. This aspect of SAC's philosophy, indifference to JCS allocations, was repeated later by General LeMay.[10] [Emphasis in original.]

Finally, in 1959, President Eisenhower approved transferring the custody of nuclear weapons that were held by the AEC to the Department of Defense. Meanwhile, General LeMay trained SAC and increased the readiness of the nation's manned bombers and ICBMs. He also selected their targets and developed their attack plans. The plans were very "close hold"; the information was shared with only his own senior commanders and a few others in the Department of Defense.

General LeMay sought ways to win and prevail in a future war through the use of atomic weapons, a doctrine that made him suspect in the eyes of some senior officers and politicians.[11] He advocated the preemptive first use of nuclear weapons on the communist world, believing that conflict with those enemies was inevitable and hence it should be prosecuted on terms favorable to the United States. In an interview following his retirement, LeMay talked about the effects of a nuclear strike on the Soviet Union:

> Let us assume that the order had been received this morning to unleash the full weight of our nuclear force. (I hope, of course, that this never will happen.) Between sunset tonight and sunrise tomorrow morning the Soviet Union would likely cease to be a major military power or even a major nation: the bulk of its long-range air power would be shattered, its centers of industry and control devastated. Communications would have been disrupted and much of their economic strength depleted. Dawn might break over a nation infinitely poorer than China—less populated than the United States and condemned to an agrarian existence perhaps for generations to come.[12]

That the concept of such unilateral action would have been morally repugnant to America's allies and the rest of the world meant little to LeMay. His job was to make certain that a Pearl Harbor–style attack on the United States would never happen again. Therefore, LeMay kept SAC on a constant war footing.[13]

As a means of increasing the readiness and survivability of SAC bombers, especially against the threat of Soviet ICBM attacks on his bomber bases, LeMay's successor, General Thomas S. (Tommy) Power, conducted an airborne alert exercise in 1959. One of the new B-52 Strato-

A U.S. Air Force KC-135 Stratotanker refuels a B-52 Stratofortress. At the time of the missile crisis, this was the standard and oft-repeated procedure as the Strategic Air Command kept bomb-laden B-52s on airborne alert, ready to streak across their "fail-safe" lines to strike targets in the Soviet Union as part of U.S. nuclear deterrence. To counter such attacks, the Soviet Union made a massive investment in air-defense forces.

fortress bombers assigned to the 99th Strategic Bombardment Wing (Heavy) took off from Westover AFB in Massachusetts. The seven-man crew, with a mattress and a stack of box lunches, remained aloft for about twenty-five hours. In the plane's bomb bay were two Mk 39 thermonuclear bombs.[14] Subsequently, six B-52s were kept aloft on a sustained basis—called an airborne alert—proving that SAC could keep bombers continuously in the air.

The airborne alert bombers, flying prescribed routes, had target folders on board, and upon receipt of an encoded message—a "go code" authenticated by two or more crew members—the planes would pass though a "fail-safe" line and proceed toward their preassigned targets. This procedure meant that a percentage of SAC's bombers would streak toward the communist world even if there were a surprise attack on SAC bases by Soviet intercontinental missiles, long-range bombers, submarine-launched missiles, submarine-based aircraft, or saboteurs.[15]

The airborne alert was expensive. It required an entire wing of thirty to forty-five B-52s to keep just six Stratofortresses airborne. Each airborne B-52 had to be refueled at least twice during the twenty-four-hour flight, placing a strain on SAC's aerial tanker fleet and consuming vast quantities of jet fuel. Nevertheless, the airborne alert effort was continued, and by the time of the Cuban Missile Crisis about sixty of SAC's six hundred–plus B-52s were on continuous airborne alert. Simultaneously, one-half of the remaining B-52s and one-half of the command's almost nine hundred B-47 Stratojet bombers were on ground alert, armed with nuclear weapons, and ready to begin rolling toward takeoff within fifteen minutes after being "scrambled."

General Power, testifying before Congress, explained, "We in the Strategic Air Command have developed a system known as airborne alert where we maintain airplanes in the air 24 hours a day, loaded with bombs, on station, ready to go to the target. . . . We must impress Mr. Khrushchev that we have it, and that he cannot strike this country with impunity."[16]

General LeMay became Chief of Staff of the Air Force and a member of the Joint Chiefs of Staff in 1961, a position from which he continued to support a strong and aggressive posture for SAC led by General Power. Formerly LeMay's chief of staff at SAC, Power held strong convictions that his bombers and ICBMs must be ready to strike the communist world at a moment's notice. Where LeMay had built SAC, Power polished it to a razor's edge of effectiveness and readiness. At times, Power also displayed a bizarre personality. One of his wing commanders recalled,

> General Power . . . was demanding; he was mean; he was cruel, unforgiving, and he didn't have the time of day to pass with anyone. A hard, cruel, individual . . . I would like to say this. I used to worry about General Power. I used to worry that General Power was not stable. I used to worry that he had control over so many weapons and weapons systems and could, under certain conditions, launch the force. Back in the days before we had real positive control, SAC had the power to do a lot of things, and it was in his hands, and he knew it.[17]

While SAC's image was primarily one of large, graceful bombers, SAC also had several hundred reconnaissance, electronic surveillance, and command aircraft, as well as just over 1,000 aerial tankers. In 1962, its strength totaled more than 2,700 aircraft. The command also controlled the nation's ICBMs. By 1962, this part of the strategic force consisted of 142 Atlas ICBMs of several models and 62 Titan ICBMs, all located in the United States.[18]

The Atlas was America's first ICBM, and although its development was troubled, this 1962 strength compared to a Soviet ICBM force of just six R-7 (NATO SS-6 Sapwood) and about twenty R-16 (SS-7 Saddler) missiles.[19] The Atlas, with a range of some 6,300 miles, used liquid-propellant fuel that had to be loaded shortly before launch. The missile carried either a W38 warhead (3- to 4-megaton yield) or a W49 warhead (1.45 megatons). The Atlas launch facilities differed for each model. Some were aboveground; others were partially "hardened" to resist a nuclear blast. The larger and more-advanced Titan I missile had a similar range, propellant, and warhead, but all sixty-two of these ICBMs were in hardened underground silos that were believed to be capable of surviving a Soviet nuclear attack.

And, of course, there were the overseas-based Intermediate-Range Ballistic Missiles (IRBMs) that could strike the Soviet Union: the sixty Thor missiles in Britain, the thirty Jupiter missiles in Italy, and the Jupiter missiles being installed in Turkey. Those missiles were all labeled "two-key" weapons because they were under joint control of the U.S. Air Force and the host countries.

By law, this massive array of SAC weapons, as well as the Navy's missile submarines and carrier-based nuclear aircraft, was under the president's control. In 1962, President Kennedy's control was exercised through use of the *SIOP Decision Handbook*. The handbook, apparently with drawings, walked the president through the process of secure identification and transmission of the orders for the release of nuclear weapons to the Pentagon. The president would choose an option from the *SIOP Decision Handbook*. The decision would then be sent to SAC headquarters and to other major commanders who controlled nuclear weapons, through a variety of special radio links that were always available to the president. In 1962, however, the president's authority over SAC and its thousands of nuclear weapons was ambiguous.

The "Little Nukes"

The United States also deployed thousands of atomic weapons for "other" requirements, such as air defense, anti-submarine warfare, and theater/battlefield combat. In 1962, these weapons were assigned to the Army, Navy, Air Force, and Marine Corps and included tactical/theater ballistic missiles, artillery shells, surface-to-air missiles, atomic demolitions, depth charges, anti-submarine rockets, and submarine-launched torpedoes. Perhaps the most bizarre tactical nuclear weapon of this era was the Davy Crockett, fielded by the Army in 1961 at the *battalion* level. Davy Crockett was a 150-pound rocket that looked like a futuristic mortar shell. It could loft a small nuclear warhead (the W54 with a yield of 1/5th of a kiloton) to a range of *only two and one half miles*!

Significant to the Cuban Missile Crisis, the Air Force also deployed a number of air-to-air weapons with nuclear warheads. They were assigned to the Air Defense Command (ADC) for use against formations of Soviet bombers approaching the United States. There were two weapons in this category: the Genie was a large, unguided rocket, fitted with the small W25 (1- to 2-kiloton) warhead. The GAR-11 Falcon guided missile, armed with the same small W54 warhead as the Davy Crockett, was a more discreet system, capable of being guided to a specific enemy aircraft.

Closer to "home," Army-manned Nike-Ajax and Nike-Hercules and Air Force Bomarc surface-to-air missiles stood ready to shoot down incoming Soviet bombers. These missiles were installed around numerous U.S. cities and industrial complexes, as well as at two sites in Canada. The Nike-Hercules and Bomarc missiles had nuclear warheads, the former with the W31 warhead with a variable yield of 1 to 40 kilotons, the latter with the W40 warhead rated at 10 kilotons.

Should Soviet bombers penetrate the squadrons of defending air-defense fighters, the missiles would be launched against them; the effects of the nuclear warheads on the bombers would be devastating. The probable impact of the SAM's nuclear detonations over the United States and southern Canada was less clear. Depending upon the location of the missile launch sites, altitudes of the nuclear detonations, winds, and other atmospheric conditions, there would be electromagnetic blackouts of radio and television over wide areas and possibly radioactive fallout on large portions of North America.

The United States had more than six thousand theater and tactical nuclear weapons at the time of the Cuban Missile Crisis, many more than the entire stockpile of nuclear weapons of the rest of the world combined. Other than the IRBMs shared with the British, Italians, and Turks, however, there were virtually no "controls" on these weapons other than the reliability of the humans working on, loading, and launching them.[20] No special security devices protected against an accidental or unauthorized arming or firing of these tactical nuclear weapons. Around the world in 1962, thousands of these weapons were being protected only by what was known as the Personnel Reliability Program, or PRP, a process of psychological tests and monitoring to certify that the individuals handing nuclear weapons and their release were both responsible and emotionally stable. Highly successful during the Cold War, PRP was a lock made of paper and hope in a world filled with stressed and fearful people handling thousands of nuclear weapons.[21]

SIOP: Road Map to Armageddon

In the late 1950s, as the U.S. Navy's Polaris submarine program was given the highest national priority (as were other strategic missile programs), General LeMay sought control of these sea-based missiles. He argued that it would be inefficient, counterproductive, and dangerous to have two different missile forces, that is, SAC and the Navy, simultaneously launching against the Soviet Union. The Navy argued that the operation and control of submarines was totally different from with land-based bombers and missiles and should remain under the control of the Atlantic and the Pacific Commands, whose commanders-in-chief at the time were both admirals.

Up to that point, the Navy's carrier-based nuclear-strike aircraft were targeted against "naval targets" in the Soviet Union. Those targets included shipyards, submarine bases, airfields for naval aviation, and even factories that produced submarine batteries. Obviously, some of these targets were contiguous to major population centers, and some were relatively far inland.

The debate over Polaris control continued for a year until, in August 1960, Secretary of Defense Thomas S. Gates made what he considered to be the most important decision of his career in defense: he ordered the establishment of the Joint Strategic Target Planning Staff (JSTPS).[22] Gates, a former Secretary of the Navy, deferred accepting the Air Force proposal for a single unified strategic command. Rather, he desired improved coordination and the development of a single attack plan for all U.S. nuclear weapons, although Gates did believe that SAC had the best facilities and the most competent staff to undertake that effort.[23]

The result was JSTPS, a separate Department of Defense agency, directly under the jurisdiction of the Joint Chiefs of Staff and responsible for the integrated target planning of all of the nation's strategic and theater strike weapons. The JSTPS would be located at SAC headquarters at Offutt Air Force Base in Nebraska; its director would be the commander-in-chief of SAC (that is, an Air Force general) and the deputy director a Navy vice admiral. Although most of the key billets in the JSTPS went to Air Force officers, the Navy was represented, as were the Army and the Marine Corps.[24]

The JSTPS developed the National Strategic Target List (NSTL), which enumerated targets in the Soviet Union, Eastern Europe, North Korea, and China that had been selected for attack. It also designed the Single Integrated Operational Plan (SIOP) for attacking the NSTL targets with specific aircraft and missiles. Secretary Gates approved the first target list and SIOP in December 1960, less than four months after the JSTPS was established. By 1962, the JSTPS challenge was to most efficiently use the large numbers of nuclear weapons available in the U.S. arsenal. Between 1955 and 1960, the U.S. inventory grew from one thousand to more than ten thousand nuclear weapons of all sizes, providing war planners with options in the prosecution of nuclear war.

Prior to the introduction of the SIOP, U.S. nuclear strategy had been the policy of "massive retaliation," meaning that U.S. strategic nuclear weapons would be used in a single massive attack against an aggressor (assumed to be the Soviet Union). Under SIOP—at least, in theory—the nuclear strike forces of the United States would be task organized and scheduled so that the maximum number of targets would be attacked and destroyed. Rather than a single massive attack, the nuclear strikes would continue for days, allowing the bombers that survived the first set of strikes against the Soviet Union to return to base, refuel, reload, and fly additional missions. Similarly, the Polaris submarines would, after having fired their missiles, return and rearm from tenders in foreign ports or from U.S. reload facilities.[25]

The JSTPS delivered a revised version of this targeting plan—known as SIOP-62—about the time that President Kennedy was inaugurated in January 1961. It went into effect in October 1962. While the operative parts of SIOP-62, including the full target list, still remain classified more than four decades later, a number of aspects of the plan are known. One is that SAC bombers would have generated the vast majority of the nuclear strikes under the SIOP. The strategic nuclear "Triad" of land-based ICBMs and bombers and sea-based Polaris missiles had not yet been fully developed in 1962, and the crews of the almost 1,600 SAC bombers would have delivered most of the nuclear devastation on the planned SIOP targets. SIOP-62 reportedly consisted of 1,077 targets, 480 of which were to have been hit by the first wave—known as the alert force—of SAC bombers and ICBMs, with 1,447 nuclear weapons being launched against them.[26] The follow-up attacks would have delivered an additional 1,976 nuclear weapons by 1,778 bombers and missiles.

Several features of SIOP-62 were disturbing. For all of its detail and organization, SIOP-62 had just one strike option—the so-called "Major Attack Option." This option was a throwback to the massive retaliation doctrine of the 1950s, providing virtually *no* choices for the president in the event that strikes on a more limited target set were required or desirable. This problem first became apparent during the Berlin crisis of

1961, when President Kennedy and his advisors were discussing possible first-strike options in the event of a Soviet move against West Berlin.[27] Then-Major William Y. Smith, on the staff of the Joint Chiefs of Staff, wrote to General Maxwell Taylor that

> Flexibility in SIOP-62 came only from the ability to withhold preprogrammed strikes. Once the alert force is launched, however, selective withholding of its forces is not presently possible. . . . SIOP-62 is a rigid, all-purpose plan, designed for execution in existing form, regardless of circumstances. Rigidity stems from . . . belief that winning general war means coming out relatively better than the USSR, regardless of the magnitude of losses. . . . SIOP-62 is a blunt instrument, and its tactics almost make certain fulfillment of prophecy that enemy will be able to launch some weapons.[28]

That was not the most appalling fact about SIOP-62. There was also the matter of just *who* and *what* it would have hit. When General Power had the JSTPS planners put together SIOP-62, he advised them to plan to strike *every* strategic target in the communist world. Therefore, in addition to the basic target set in the Soviet Union, SIOP-62 had a large number of targets in China, North Korea, North Vietnam, and most of the Eastern European nations.[29] These other nations were not involved with the Cuban Missile Crisis. The People's Republic of China, with the world's largest population, could have seen up to one-half—hundreds of millions—of its people killed. The irony of such an attack was that just three years earlier, the Soviet Union and China had suffered a political split, leading to ideological competition between the two communist nations for the remainder of the Cold War.[30]

The 1961 Berlin crisis caused a major review of SIOP-62 in late 1961, and the revised plan—SIOP-63—was ready just in time for the Cuban Missile Crisis. SIOP-63 provided five quick-reaction options for nuclear strikes, ranging from an attack specifically at Soviet strategic weapons and forces and not at population centers—called a "counterforce" strike—to the complete destruction of the USSR. The option to attack China and other communist nations was still retained in SIOP-63, but such attacks could be conducted without linkage to strikes against the Soviet Union. Thus, if President Kennedy had chosen to use strategic nuclear weapons, he would have had a limited number of specific options with regard to which countries and target sets would have been hit.

The SIOP assigned more than one nuclear weapon per target. With the relatively large number of weapons now available to U.S. strategic planners, specific targets were assigned several warheads, possibly one from an ICBM, one from a bomber, and one from a submarine-launched missile or a European-based IRBM.[31] This multiple attack scheme, which became known as "overkill," was undertaken to compensate for the possible failure of an attacking system, such as a bomber being shot down, and shortfalls in accuracy. (In future years, the increased number of warheads carried by submarine-launched missiles and, to a lesser degree, by ICBMs would provide many thousands of additional warheads for SIOP planners.[32])

The Alert: "This Is General Power"

Along with the rest of the American military establishment, SAC had received the DEFCON-3 alert on Monday night, October 22. The alert had confirmed what General Power had known since the early hours of October 15, when Airman 1st Class Michael Davis had discovered the SS-4 missiles in Cuba. SAC policy kept its bombers and missiles at a high state of alert. General Power immediately increased his command's readiness, recalled reservists, opened warstocks of weapons and spare parts, and pushed his maintenance and operations personnel to ready every possible aircraft and missile for combat.

In 1962, SAC was one of a small group of commands that had a level of independent authority to adjust readiness levels. General Power was a truly extreme personality who tended to bring out the worst in people. At a conference in December 1960, Power had snapped at Professor William Kaufmann, declaring, "Restraint! Why are you so concerned with saving *their* lives? The whole idea is to kill the bastards!"[33] Then the angry general said, "Look. At the end of the war, if there are two Americans and one Russian, we win!" Kaufmann snapped back, "Well, you'd better make sure that they're a man and a woman," referring to the American survivors. Reportedly, Power angrily left the room following Kaufmann's remark.

Much of SAC's authority stemmed from the earlier efforts of General LeMay, who argued that the SAC commander should have what was called "release authority." In 1957, a series of discussions at the highest government levels led President Eisenhower to authorize the SAC commander to have an extraordinary degree of freedom of action in certain circumstances. A memo on the meetings explained: "The proposed authorization would require that Strategic Air Command retaliation for an attack on the United States will be on the order of the President *except in cir-cumstances where communications between the President and the Com-mander of SAC is impossible because of the results of enemy attack*"[34] [emphasis added].

In effect, this policy meant that if the United States were attacked with nuclear weapons, and the commander of SAC had made a good faith but unsuccessful effort to contact the president and been unable to reach him because of communications problems, the Commander-in-Chief of SAC was authorized to launch a full-scale retaliation upon the attacker. (This type of policy was the model for the fictional Plan "R" depicted in Stanley Kubrick's 1963 classic Cold War film *Dr. Strange-love, Or How I Learned to Stop Worrying and Love the Bomb.*)[35]

The Kennedy administration endorsed the existing nuclear release policy in 1961 and took it into the Cuban Missile Crisis essentially un-changed. The preauthorized release policy would have also granted the SAC commander a number of other powers, some of which General Power put into effect just two days after the DEFCON-3 alert on October 22. At 10:30 A.M. Eastern time on Wednesday, October 24, General Power moved SAC to DEFCON-2 on his own authority as the naval quarantine of Cuba became effective.[36] While Power never fully ex-plained his reasoning for declaring the heightened alert, his authorization to do so clearly came from the preauthorized release authority granted by the 1957 policy decision. That President Kennedy might not want to elevate SAC beyond DEFCON-3 or have the Soviets know of the com-mand's heightened alert status never seems to have occurred to Power.

When General Power declared DEFCON-2, a whole sequence of events came into play, some of which drove the United States and the Soviet Union closer to nuclear war. The first was that the DEFCON-2 order was transmitted unencrypted over SAC's worldwide broadcast sys-tem.[37] It was unquestionably intercepted by the Soviet military intelli-gence monitoring station at its military attaché office on Belmont Road in northwest Washington, D.C. Power undoubtedly knew this.[38] In all likelihood, he was trying to send a personal message to Nikita Khrush-chev and the Soviet leadership that SAC was getting ready to strike.

Beyond sending a message to the Soviets, the DEFCON-2 alert had very real effects on SAC itself. The first was that the command sus-pended its normal training and maintenance schedules and went on a heightened alert and security posture. Normal administrative and other peacetime support functions were put aside, allowing the affected per-sonnel to strengthen security units and other combat support functions.

SAC training units emptied out their schoolhouses so that instructors, trainees, and aircraft could be readied for combat operations.[39] This provided additional bomber crews and aircraft to maximize SAC's striking power.

DEFCON-2 also meant that each SAC bomber wing began what was called a "Reflex" deployment, in which bombers and tanker aircraft dispersed to regional military bases and civilian airports to reduce their vulnerability to a surprise attack. One such unit was the 100th Bombardment Wing (Medium) based at Pease Air Force Base in New Hampshire. Flying B-47 Stratojet bombers and KC-97 tanker aircraft, the 100th conducted twelve Reflex deployments during October 1962, sending men, equipment, and planes to other bases.[40] Some of the wing's bombers and tankers were forward deployed to Torrejon, Spain. Ironically, one of the main problems encountered by the units on Reflex deployment was a shortage of cars and light trucks. As a result, SAC ran up a massive bill for rental cars and trucks, much to the liking of rental car companies.

The increase in SAC's airborne alert force, operating under the program known as "Chrome Dome," was more ominous than a simple dispersion of planes and crews. One of the Chrome Dome units flying during the DEFCON-2 alert was the 306th Bombardment Wing (Heavy), based at McCoy AFB near Orlando, Florida.[41] Under Chrome Dome, the wing's airborne B-52s continuously flew missions to its "fail safe" point over the eastern Mediterranean Sea. Each mission lasted some twenty-four hours and required four in-flight refuelings from tanker aircraft to keep the bombers "topped off." At any moment during the DEFCON-2 alert, at least sixty—and, reportedly, at times up to eighty—B-52s were flying on Chrome Dome airborne alert missions.

Within hours of the DEFCON-2 announcement, General Power decided to send an additional message in the clear to his command. Again using the SAC worldwide broadcast network, he issued a voice address that began, "This is General Power . . ."[42] What followed was a long message declaring that SAC was ready to strike, and that he expected every man to do his duty. Of course, Soviet radio intercept stations picked up the message and passed it to the Soviet leadership. The message also reached President Kennedy and the members of ExComm, who were outraged by Power's elevation of SAC's alert level on his own authority, as well as by his personal broadcast to anyone who cared to listen.[43,44] The United States was now on the brink of nuclear war.

Executing the SIOP

As the crisis continued, a key question was how a nuclear exchange between the United States and Soviet Union might begin. The most likely triggers for releasing U.S. strategic nuclear forces would have been the launching of SS-4 MRBMs that survived the initial air attacks against targets in the United States. This would have undoubtedly fulfilled any legal or moral requirement for retaliation in President Kennedy's mind. Nevertheless, the decision to initiate SIOP-63 would not have been an easy one.

Time and events allowing, several steps would have likely preceded the order for U.S. strategic strikes on the Soviet Union. One of the first would have been to initiate a plan known as Continuity of Government (COG), to rapidly move selected leaders and staff personnel from the federal government to classified and secure locations away from Washington, D.C.[45] The Office of Civil and Defense Mobilization, a predecessor to the present-day Federal Emergency Management Agency, administered the COG program.[46]

By 1962, almost every federal agency had some sort of COG team that would evacuate personnel to bunker complexes in the countryside and mountains of Virginia, West Virginia, Pennsylvania, and Maryland. President Kennedy, his staff, and key personnel from the various federal departments would have been at Mountain Weather, Virginia, where a large underground bunker complex (known as "High Point") was built into the Blue Ridge Mountains. Similar facilities for the Pentagon (Raven Rock, Maryland) and even the Federal Reserve (Mount Pony near Culpeper, Virginia) were constructed in the 1950s and 1960s.[47]

In 1962, the largest such facility was the enormous congressional relocation facility under the famed Greenbrier Resort Hotel at White Sulphur Springs, West Virginia. With 112,000 square feet of bunkered space, the Greenbrier complex had been completed just prior to the outbreak of the crisis. It was large enough to support operations of the House of Representatives and the Senate, with accommodations for all 535 members of Congress and a reduced staff.[48] Like all the other sites supporting the COG program, the Greenbrier was part of a sophisticated and survivable communications system, controlled by another large bunker facility known as Site R, located at Fort Ritchie, Maryland.

The actual evacuation to the COG sites would have been based upon the Joint Emergency Evacuation Plan (JEEP). The president, key administration and congressional leaders, the Joint Chiefs of Staff, and a skeleton staff would have been transported on a fleet of helicopters to the various COG sites.[49] Buses and trucks would have moved most of the rest of the personnel selected for COG duty, over roads secured by military police and Army National Guardsmen.[50] The largest contingent, Congress with its reduced staff, would have been transported to the Greenbrier facility aboard a special train of the Chesapeake and Ohio Railroad, which also owned and ran the resort.[51] One grim fact permeated all of the planned COG operations: no wives, children, or other family members would have gone to the bunkers. Government and military dependents would have been on their own, having only the facilities and services of the Civil Defense system to see them though a nuclear exchange.[52]

Actual execution of the JEEP plan would likely have caused as many problems as it solved. The JEEP plan involved dozens of helicopter sorties, hundreds of military trucks and buses, and long lines of trains leaving Washington's Union Station. Along with maintaining civil order, one major consequence of the JEEP evacuation would have been that KGB agents under Alexander Feklisov at the Soviet Embassy would have seen the relocation and reported to Moscow. This was one of the top "warnings and indications" that Feklisov had been tasked to look for, and, undoubtedly, it would have caused great concern with Nikita Khrushchev and the Kremlin leadership.[53]

Reality Check

Obviously, both Soviet and U.S. leadership would desperately seek to avoid a nuclear exchange that would threaten retaliation against their homelands. But the overwhelming U.S. advantage in strategic weapons that could reach the Soviet Union might come into play. Certainly, General Power, and possibly General LeMay and other members of the Joint Chiefs of Staff, would have argued for exploiting the U.S. strategic advantage. Indeed, even within the membership of ExComm, there were those who supported a hard line toward the Soviets when they began to back down. Discussing General Power wanting to exploit the U.S. advantage, Assistant Secretary of Defense Paul Nitze recalled, "I felt that way myself at the time."

When asked directly whether he felt that the United States "should strike the USSR," Nitze, who had advised seven different U.S. presidents, responded, "Yes."[54] Nitze recalled that others on ExComm supported that view. "I think [Roswell] Gilpatric and a few others." In more diplomatic language, Nitze recalled for the postmortem of the crisis performed by officials from the Defense and the State Departments: "I believe that we should have pushed our advantage with greater vigor. . . . With the nuclear balance heavily in our favor, I believed we should have pushed the Kremlin in 1962 to give up its efforts to establish Soviet influence in this hemisphere."[55]

Whichever SIOP-63 option President Kennedy might have chosen would have involved an attack on the strategic nuclear forces of the USSR. The few Soviet ICBMs would have been given early priority for attack by U.S. land-based ICBMs and possibly by Polaris submarine-launched missiles, all of which could probably reach the Soviet launch sites before the ICBMs could be fired. The flight time would have been very short. The Soviets would have had little warning, as the missiles would have emerged over the polar regions of the Soviet Union with no possible way to stop them in 1962. Much of the Soviet ICBM and bomber force would probably have been caught on the ground. Still, a few Soviet missile-launched nuclear warheads might have made it to the United States.

While the Soviet Union had perhaps one hundred Tu-20 Bear and Mya-4 Bison strategic bombers that could reach the United States, all of them would not be immediately available. Those bombers would have to stage through Arctic bases, which could be targeted by U.S. missiles, and, after flying across the polar region, would be confronted by a large percentage of the forty-two squadrons of U.S. and five squadrons of Canadian air-defense fighters. Batteries of nuclear-tipped Nike-Hercules and Bomarc surface-to-air missiles that surrounded a number of U.S. cities and other strategic sites would confront the Soviet bombers that survived the fighters. The U.S. fighters carried nuclear air-to-air missiles, the Genie and Falcon. The Canadian CF-101 Voodoo interceptor could also carry the Genie air-to-air rocket with a nuclear warhead.[56]

If the SIOP counterforce option had been activated, the first strategic targets in the Soviet homeland for U.S. nuclear missiles would be Soviet ICBM, IRBM, and MRBM launch sites, along with the bomber bases. The Soviet intermediate- and medium-range missiles would be targeted in an effort to protect U.S. NATO allies and Japan from Soviet nuclear strikes. Additional U.S. ICBMs and available submarine-launched Polaris missiles would then be targeted against Soviet air defenses—command centers, radars, SAM batteries, and fighter bases. This would be an effort to help the U.S. manned bombers reach their targets.

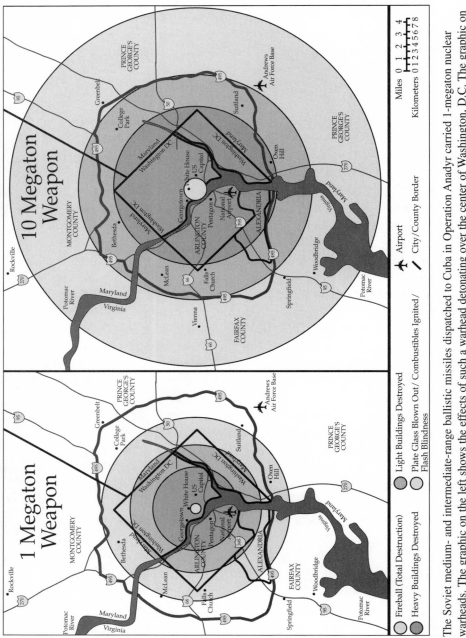

The Soviet medium- and intermediate-range ballistic missiles dispatched to Cuba in Operation Anadyr carried 1-megaton nuclear warheads. The graphic on the left shows the effects of such a warhead detonating over the center of Washington, D.C. The graphic on the right shows the effects of a 10-megaton bomb, like the B41 gravity bombs carried by SAC bombers during the crisis. Note that the affected area is not ten times greater.

The U.S. intermediate-range Thor and Jupiter missiles in Europe would have been an unknown factor in a developing nuclear conflict. Their counterparts on the other side of the Iron Curtain, several hundred SS-4 MRBMs and SS-5 IRBMs in fixed sites, would have been equally destabilizing. Depending upon the decisions of the British government, which were possibly influenced by Soviet promises not to strike Britain if Americans were denied the use of British bases and the Thor missiles were not launched, Her Majesty's government might have decided not to launch the Thor missiles under the two-key system. Similarly, the launch of the thirty Jupiters in Italy would be a NATO political decision, which could take considerable time to reach. The single Turkish-based Jupiter missile that became operational during the Cuban crisis would have had no role. The U.S. fighter-bombers at Turkish airfields, however, would be armed with nuclear weapons, probably drawing salvos of Soviet ballistic missiles onto targets in Turkey.

U.S. bomber losses would undoubtedly have been heavy in strikes on the Soviet Union, these bombers being subjected to intense air defenses. The B-47 and B-58 strategic bombers and Navy carrier–based planes would mostly strike targets that would be too far from their home bases, or even from forward bases, to return safely. But Lieutenant General Keith Compton, who had served as head of operations for SAC, as well as being a B-47 wing commander, stated explicitly that "we never designed a one-way mission."[57] Aircraft that could not reach their home bases when returning from a mission—possibly because they failed to rendezvous with an airborne tanker—had instructions to attempt to land in friendly or neutral countries, have the crews bail out, or reach positions at sea where their crews would be rescued by U.S. submarines. However, many SAC pilots—as well as Navy pilots assigned to nuclear strike missions—have told the authors of this book that they considered many targets reachable only on "one-way" missions. Commander Edward L. Feightner commanded a squadron of nuclear-armed F2H Banshee fighter-bombers aboard the carrier *Coral Sea* in the Mediterranean in 1954:

> While in the Mediterranean, all squadron pilots were assigned specific targets in case a nuclear attack was ordered. Target assignments and the weapons to go on them were carefully controlled by a small select team of nuclear specialists. . . . Feightner recalled that one of his targets was a fighter airfield in Hungary. "It would be a one-way mission as far as I was concerned. There were no tankers to bring the pilots

home. That 'one-way mission' thought seemed to be a general view among squadron pilots."[58]

One reason for these one-way missions was a lack of refueling aircraft, even though in 1962 SAC had more than a thousand tankers.[59] Because of the Chrome Dome airborne alert and the increased bomber readiness during the Cuban Missile Crisis, the readiness of those tankers was deteriorating and, with some sixteen hundred SAC bombers, there were insufficient tankers for the entire bomber force. Some attacking aircraft would have been lost to fuel starvation, and their crews left to fend for themselves in the middle of a nuclear battlefield. The bomber crews knew this.

As powerful as the U.S. strategic forces were, nobody in the West was under any illusions that they could emerge from a nuclear war untouched. During such a nuclear exchange, the Soviets would most likely strike Britain, Italy, Spain, and Turkey because of their U.S. missiles and strategic air bases. The air defenses of those countries were impotent against ballistic missiles and would have had only limited success against Soviet nuclear strike aircraft.

In the same manner that President Merkin Muffley of the movie *Dr. Strangelove* (played by Peter Sellers in one of his three roles in the film) stopped George C. Scott from launching a preemptive strike against the USSR, General Power's preparations—or proposals—for such an attack in the real world were negated by the Kennedy administration *and* by Nikita Khrushchev. Those men feared a nuclear conflagration, even one that would destroy "only" a fraction of their homelands, most likely a smaller fraction of the United States than of the Soviet Union.

In the end, Fidel Castro was the only leader who wanted to use nuclear weapons to resolve the Cuban Missile Crisis. Fearing the imminent destruction of his nation and revolution, Castro wrote a letter to Khrushchev urging the use of the SS-4s. The Soviet leader decided not to act on the suggestion.[60] In a recent interview about the Cuban Missile Crisis, Castro said of the letter:

> Later, on 30th October, [Khrushchev] wrote to me trying to square accounts with me for my letter of the 27th. It's three pages long, but I will read you only one paragraph. It says: "In your cable of 27th October, you proposed that we should be the first ones to deal a nuclear strike against enemy territory. You realize, of course, where this would

lead. This would not be a simple strike, but rather the start of a thermonuclear world war. Dear Comrade Fidel Castro, I consider this proposal of yours incorrect, although I understand your motivation."

But in substance, he [Khrushchev] was making reference to a message in which I was actually telling him that in the event of an invasion, he should not give the enemy the possibility of dealing a first nuclear strike against his country. I was advising him. And of course, I took it for granted that by that time [Cuba] would have disappeared from planet Earth.[61]

16

The Deal: The Turkish Card

President Kennedy said that in exchange for the withdrawal of our mis-siles, he would remove American missiles from Turkey and Italy. We knew perfectly well that this pledge was of a symbolic nature; the American rockets in Turkey and Italy were already obsolete, and the Americans would promptly replace them with more modern ones. Besides, the US was already equipping its navy with Polaris missiles. Nevertheless, by agreeing even to symbolic measures, Kennedy was creating the impression of mutual concessions.

Nikita Khrushchev
Khrushchev Remembers: The Last Testament[1]

Nikita Khrushchev sent ballistic missiles to Cuba primarily to ensure that the spark of communist revolution in the Americas would succeed. And, of course, missiles only ninety miles from the United States would help to redress the increasing imbalance of Soviet and U.S. strategic weapons. As the crisis evolved, Khrushchev also sought the removal of U.S. Jupiter ballistic missiles from Turkey and Italy. To Khrushchev, their removal would benefit the political interaction between the Soviet Union and the West and would help to counter the growing U.S. superiority in nuclear weapons.

The development of Intermediate-Range Ballistic Missiles (IRBMs) in the West was circuitous. The first U.S. effort was the Army's Jupiter, begun in 1954 by the Redstone Arsenal in Alabama as a successor to the Redstone *battlefield missile*, which had a range of about 175 miles. The Jupiter would be a 1,000-mile-range weapon. Both Redstone and Jupiter carried nuclear warheads. By the time of the Cuban Missile Crisis, the Jupiter missiles in Turkey—just becoming operational—were already obsolete. Still, those IRBMs became a major factor in the resolution of the crisis.

In 1955, the U.S. Air Force initiated the Thor as a *tactical ballistic missile*. It was envisioned that Thor would have a range of possibly as much as 1,500 miles carrying a nuclear warhead. Like the Jupiter, Thor used a mix of kerosene and liquid oxygen propellants. Thus, neither Jupiter nor Thor was initiated as a strategic missile, nor were they derivatives of ICBMs.

In October 1955, in response to a report of increased Soviet strategic bomber developments, the U.S. Joint Chiefs of Staff recommended development of both the Jupiter and Thor missiles, making the former a joint Army-Navy program, with the Navy to arm surface ships with the Jupiter-S variant of the IRBM. A month later, Secretary of Defense Charles Wilson assigned to the IRBM effort "a priority equal to the ICBM but with no interference to the valid requirements of the ICBM program." On December 1, 1955, President Eisenhower approved assigning the ICBM and IRBM programs the highest national priority. By early 1956, the Navy gained approval to withdraw from the Jupiter effort, eschewing the use of liquid propellants aboard ship. Instead, the Navy developed the highly successful Polaris solid-propellant missile, which was based on nuclear-propelled submarines.[2] In 1956, because of controversies over duplication of U.S. strategic weapon efforts, the Department of Defense limited the Army's missile program to ranges of less than 200 miles. Thus, the U.S. Air Force would control the Jupiter when it became operational.

However, the rapid march of missile technology was actually moving faster than the weapons could be built and deployed. Perhaps the most telling example of this came when the U.S. Navy's SLBM program was able to rapidly push certain key technologies so quickly that the Polaris A-1 missile and its launch submarine were able to go *operational* before the Jupiter.[3] In the case of Thor and Jupiter, this meant they were obsolete before they were installed in their European launchers. Still, in the rush to build up nuclear forces that could hit the Soviet Union, development and deployment of both systems continued into the 1960s.

The dramatic Soviet launching of *Sputnik 1*, the world's first artificial satellite, on October 4, 1957, further accelerated U.S. development of strategic missiles, as well as of manned bombers. Thor entered service first, with four squadrons totaling sixty missiles being established in Britain beginning in December 1959.[4] These missiles were operated by

A Jupiter intermediate-range ballistic missile on the launchpad at Cape Canaveral, Florida, prior to a test launch. The installation of Jupiter IRBMs in Turkey, the first of which became operational during the missile crisis, was a key factor in Premier Khrushchev's decision to undertake Operation Anadyr. U.S. Thor IRBMs were already operational in Britain, and Jupiter IRBMs were in Italy.

the Royal Air Force, although U.S. Air Force officers retained control of their W49 warheads, each of which had an explosive force of 1.45 megatons. They were aimed at targets in Eastern Europe.

The first deliveries of the Jupiter combat missiles, also to carry W49 warheads, took place in August 1958.[5] With a range of 1,750 miles, the Jupiter would have to be based overseas to reach targets in the Soviet Union. Several NATO nations were invited to participate in the Jupiter program. The missiles would be based on their territory—within range of Soviet targets—and their launch would be controlled by a "two-key" procedure: a U.S. officer and a host country officer would have to simultaneously insert keys into a control panel for the missiles to launch. However, their warheads would be under control of only U.S. officers until the missiles were ready to launch, in effect giving the United States a veto over the use of the missiles.

Negotiations with the French government led to an agreement for three squadrons of Jupiters—forty-five missiles—to be sent to France sometime in 1959–1960. But when General Charles de Gaulle became president of France in June 1958, he was determined to have an independent nuclear striking force under absolute French control. When he refused the Jupiters, the U.S. Air Force initially turned to alternate sites in Greece and Spain. However, negotiations with those NATO nations failed.

Subsequently, on March 26, 1959, the Italian government signed an agreement to accept two squadrons with thirty Jupiter missiles, and on October 28, 1959, the Turkish government agreed to accept one squadron of fifteen missiles. Turkey, a founding member of NATO, had staunchly supported the United States in the Korean War, and in December 1950 had allowed U.S. forces to begin work on nuclear storage facilities at several sites in the country. As a result, several hundred nuclear warheads for artillery and Honest John rockets, as well as nuclear bombs for tactical aircraft, were stored in Turkey, under U.S. control.[6]

Turkey would also provide a major base for U-2 spy flights over the Soviet Union and the Middle East. When the U-2 became operational in July 1956, the spyplanes were initially based in Britain but were soon moved to a base in West Germany. On May 1, 1956, the U.S. chargé d'affaires in Ankara, Foy D. Kohler, approached Prime Minister Adnan Menderes on this matter.[7] Kohler told the Turkish prime minister that the U-2 effort was a continuation of the Genetrix program, in which camera-carrying balloons had been released from Turkey to overfly the Soviet Union. Menderes gave his approval immediately for a U-2 basing arrangement in Turkey.

Entering the Soviet Union across its southern borders, Turkey-based U-2s could spy out Soviet missile test centers and weapon test ranges. Most of these U-2 flights were from Incirlick (Adana) in southern Turkey. Other NATO reconnaissance aircraft, including electronic intelligence-collection planes that flew along the Soviet border, were also based there. The bases in Turkey were invaluable to the United States and NATO.

In 1962, preparations to install the Jupiter IRBMs in Turkey, at Cigli airfield at Izmir, were accelerated. The first missile became operational at the height of the Cuban Missile Crisis, on October 22. With a range of some 1,750 miles, a nuclear-armed Jupiter launched from Turkey could strike the Soviet Union along an arc that included the country's major cities—Moscow, Leningrad, Kiev, and Gor'kiy.

The U.S. intelligence community had earlier looked into "probable" Chinese and Soviet reactions to the deployment of Jupiter and Thor IRBMs along the periphery of those countries.[8] The 1958 analysis concluded: "We believe that the [Sino-Soviet] Bloc, while taking vigorous diplomatic and propaganda measures aimed at preventing or delaying these deployments, and making them politically costly, would not resort to the use of force to do so."[9]

The analysis included a highly perceptive comment about Soviet fear that in the long run, IRBMs in the territories of the U.S. allies would probably come, in fact, under the sole control of the recipient countries. For this reason, the Soviets might look upon the initial U.S. IRBM deployment as marking an important step toward growth of an independent European nuclear capability. The achievement of such a capability would, in their view, further reduce Western European susceptibility to Soviet threats and would increase the number of countries that were able to trigger a nuclear war.[10]

Ironically, the increasing availability of other nuclear weapons within the U.S. and British arsenals soon made the Thor and Jupiter missiles superfluous. In 1962, planning was already under way for the withdrawal of the IRBMs from all three countries in the near future.

Trading Missiles

The installation of Jupiter missiles in Turkey was a particularly painful reminder to Khrushchev of the increasing American encirclement of the Soviet Union with nuclear-capable ballistic missiles ashore and at sea, as well as land-based and carrier-based nuclear strike aircraft. Turkey, however, was the first country that bordered on the Soviet Union in which the United States was emplacing nuclear missiles.

In July 1962, the KGB reported to Andrei Gromyko, the Minister of Foreign Affairs, that there were seventeen Jupiter missiles in Turkey. Soviet military intelligence reported that American ballistic missiles in Turkey were close to becoming operational. Khrushchev, in his memoirs, wrote, "The United States had already surrounded the Soviet Union with its own bomber bases and missiles. We knew that American missiles were aimed against us in Turkey and Italy, to say nothing of West Germany. Our vital industrial centers were directly threatened by planes armed with atomic bombs and guided missiles tipped with nuclear warheads."[11]

Reportedly, when at his Black Sea holiday dacha, Khrushchev was fond of pointing out to sea toward Turkey and claiming that he could almost see the American missiles.

As the missile crisis intensified in October 1962, there was some concern in the White House and the Pentagon over those U.S. nuclear weapons that were partially under foreign control. The deployment of sixty Thor missiles in Britain had been completed in June 1960. There was little concern over the control of those missiles, given the long "special relationship" between the two countries. The two Jupiter squadrons in Italy had become operational in 1961, and those in Turkey were nearing operational status.

In Washington, early on the afternoon of Monday, October 22, at the president's urging, the Joint Chiefs of Staff Chairman Maxwell Taylor sent a message to the Commander-in-Chief U.S. forces in Europe, who had the additional duty of being NATO's Supreme Allied Commander Europe. Taylor wanted to "make certain that the Jupiters in Turkey and Italy will not be fired without specific authorization from the president. In the event of an attack [by the Soviets], either nuclear or non-nuclear . . . U.S. custodians are to destroy or make inoperable the weapons if any attempt is made to fire them."[12] The U.S. commander was also to make certain that the order to U.S. officers at the missile sites was kept secret from the Italian and the Turkish governments. Charles de Gaulle had opposed joining with the United States in placing nuclear weapons on French territory because of concern that this very situation would occur— when solely U.S. interests would interfere with even the consideration of using such weapons.

On October 24, as the U.S. blockade of Cuba went into effect, the issue of a "trade" of Jupiter missiles in Turkey for Soviet missiles in Cuba was voiced for the first time in the White House by Ambassador Adlai Stevenson. Soon, variations of such a trade were being voiced in the Kremlin as well, while columnist Walter Lippmann devoted a column to the subject, advocating a missile swap to end the crisis.

The Soviet leadership had not previously held significant discussions about the missiles in Turkey. But with the "negotiations" over the Soviet missiles in Cuba essentially deadlocked, "the Jupiter missiles in Turkey, now presented the Kremlin with a means of snatching a victory from the jaws of defeat," wrote historians Aleksandr Fursenko and Timothy Naftali.[13]

The crisis worsened on October 27 when Khrushchev's letter arrived at the White House, demanding that the United States agree to remove its Jupiter missiles from Turkey in exchange for Soviet removal of missiles from Cuba. U.S. officials viewed the letter as a hardening of the Soviet position from Khrushchev's message of the previous day, which had not mentioned the U.S. missiles in Turkey. President Kennedy initially chose to ignore the letter proposing a trade. What had happened was that the two messages had arrived in the wrong order, making it appear that the Soviet position was hardening.

Soon Kennedy could not ignore the proposal, and a missile trade became a part of the bargaining between the Kremlin and the White House, as many parties took up support for such a "swap." Such an exchange, however, ignored the many dissimilarities between the two missile deployments. First, the missiles in Turkey were a small fraction of the U.S. nuclear weapons that ringed the Soviet Union, while nuclear missiles in Cuba would represent a major portion, perhaps upward of 50 percent, of the Soviet nuclear warheads that had a high probability of striking the United States. Second, the installation of U.S. missiles in Britain, West Germany, Italy, Turkey, and elsewhere was being undertaken in the full light of public knowledge, compared to the clandestine character of Operation Anadyr. And, third, while the nuclear missiles in Cuba were totally under Soviet control, those in Turkey ostensibly had a two-nation control policy.

There was one important similarity in the missile deployments to Cuba and Turkey: *both* host nations *wanted* the missiles. Castro had *almost* immediately accepted Khrushchev's proposition to base nuclear missiles in Cuba and later would strongly oppose their withdrawal. The Turkish government would be equally adamant on the subject. The idea of a "nuclear umbrella" was terribly seductive during the Cold War.

As early as October 24, the U.S. State Department—in the cryptic language of classified telegrams—had advised the American ambassador in Ankara that

> Soviet reaction to Cuban quarantine likely to involve efforts to compare missiles in Cuba with Jupiters in Turkey. While such comparison refutable, possible that negotiated solution for removal Cuban offensive threat may involve dismantling and removal Jupiters. Recognize this would create serious politico-military problems for US-Turkish relations and with regard to Turkey's place in NATO Alliance. Therefore need prepare carefully for such contingency order not harm our relations with this important ally.[14]

The response from the American ambassador in Paris was rapid and pointed; the message, for the Secretary of State's "eyes only," cited the Turkish representative in Paris having

> Consistently made it clear that Turks set great store in Jupiters placed in Turkey. He makes very clear that Turkey regards these Jupiters as symbol of Alliance's determination to use atomic weapons against Russian attack on Turkey whether by large conventional or nuclear forces, although Turks have been most reluctant admit presence IRBM's publicly. Fact that Jupiters are obsolescent and vulnerable does not apparently affect present Turkish thinking. My impression is that symbolic importance represents a fixed [Government of Turkey] view.[15]

The U.S. ambassador then made a most perceptive observation:

> [S]ince Cuba is by definition outside NATO area, [the U.S. government should] offer [to] close down some US nuclear-capable base outside NATO area rather than making deal involving Turkey or Italy. Such a deal would then be strictly US-USSR trade rather than involving one of our NATO allies in any deal.

But it was already too late. A few days after this exchange between Paris and the Secretary of State, the White House and the Kremlin—through their back-channel intermediaries—had both embarked on a course to remove the missiles from Turkey as an *unacknowledged* exchange for the removal of the missiles in Cuba.

At the same time, proposals were being put forth in Washington meetings for U.S. Polaris missile submarines to be sent into the Mediterranean as "replacements" for the Jupiter missiles in Turkey. By October 1962, there were nine Polaris submarines in commission and another score under construction.[16] Each nuclear-propelled Polaris submarine carried sixteen missiles. The missiles could be launched while the submarine was fully submerged and, each carrying a Mk 47 warhead of approximately 600 kilotons, the missiles could reach targets at distances of 1,380 miles for the A-1 version of the missile or 1,725 miles for the subsequent A-2 version.

There were also reports circulating that the United States would transfer Polaris missile submarines to Turkey.[17] Those accounts said that the Turkish Navy would be trained to operate the nuclear submarines, while the Polaris missiles and their nuclear warheads would be retained under U.S. control. But such reports were spurious—the U.S. Navy would certainly not transfer nuclear-propelled submarines to another country.[18]

(Interestingly, as the crisis was evolving into a "trade"—Cuban security and Turkish missiles in return for Soviet missiles being removed from Cuba—the United States was already sponsoring a program to develop a multination Polaris missile force. Being developed under the name Multilateral Force [MLF], this NATO program was to deploy surface ships carrying Polaris missiles that would be jointly manned by several NATO navies. The British, Dutch, West German, Greek, Italian, and Turkish governments agreed to participate in the MLF program with the U.S. Navy. However, the MLF program was canceled by the United States in December 1964.[19])

Removing the Missiles

The Jupiter missiles would be removed from Turkey, although such a trade was never put in writing to the Soviet government. Significantly, when the Jupiter missiles were removed, the United States would still have large numbers of *tactical* nuclear weapons in Turkey. Beyond nuclear warheads for artillery and Honest John short-range rockets that were stored in Turkey, there was a store of B28 nuclear bombs. With each bomb rated at a yield of approximately 1 megaton, the B28 stockpile was kept in Turkey for the U.S. Air Force F-105 Thunderchief strike aircraft based at Turkish airfields. The F-105s could reach targets in the southern areas of the Soviet Union. But there was no two-key arrangement for these weapons—the artillery warheads, bombs, and Polaris missiles were totally under U.S. control. Withdrawal of the Jupiter missiles from Turkey, with removal of the Jupiters from Italy most likely to follow, would deprive all members of NATO except for the three NATO nuclear powers—Great Britain, France, and the United States—of any real influence in the use of strategic weapons.

Beyond the Jupiters, there were the Thor IRBMs in Britain. On the evening of October 26, at about six thirty, President Kennedy put through his by then daily telephone call to Prime Minister Harold Macmillan. After a brief discussion of the United Nations' role in the crisis and the quarantine, Macmillan said, "There is just a third point that occurred to us. If we want to help the Russians to save face, would it be worthwhile our undertaking to immobilize our Thor missiles which are here in England?"[20]

Kennedy responded, "I think we don't want to have too many dismantling. But it is possible that that proposal might help. They might insist on Greece [sic], on Turkey, on Italy. But I will keep in mind your suggestion here. . . . it may be advantageous."[21]

The installation of the last of sixty Thor missiles in Britain had been completed in June 1960. The 1958 U.S.-British agreement on the Thor deployment had stipulated a five-year deployment of the missiles in Britain—that is, through 1964. The deployment could have been extended by mutual consent. A "firm decision" had already been made in May 1962—before the missile crisis—that the Thor missiles would be dismantled in 1963.[22] Britain had had its own nuclear weapons since July 1955, when the Blue Danube atomic bomb became available on a limited basis for use with Valiant strategic bombers. Other nuclear bombs had since entered service, and more strategic weapons were under development in Britain, while the Skybolt air-launched nuclear missile, under development in the United States, was to be used by both U.S. and Royal Air Force bombers. Macmillan's offer was therefore meaningless, because the Thor missiles were already scheduled to be dismantled.

The concerns of Turkey and Italy were swept away in the meeting rooms of the Pentagon and the White House as the "trade" was discussed and agreed upon. Meanwhile, construction of the Jupiter missile sites in Turkey continued at Cigli airfield near Izmir on Turkey's west coast. (A total of five Jupiter launch positions became operational by March 1963.)

On January 17, 1963, the U.S. government officially announced the phaseout of Jupiter IRBMs from Turkey and Italy. The withdrawals began on April 1, 1963; by April 23, all thirty missiles in Italy had been disassembled. The five operational Jupiters in Turkey were taken off alert by April and were withdrawn from Turkey in July. The Thor IRBMs were also withdrawn from Britain in 1963.

The Kennedy administration decided to send three Polaris submarines into the Mediterranean Sea beginning about April 1, 1963, to coincide with the removal of Jupiter IRBMs from Turkey. The USS *Sam Houston*, armed with sixteen A-2 Polaris missiles, was the first submarine to enter the "Med." All interested parties knew of the Polaris submarine's presence when, on April 14, the *Sam Houston* entered the port of Izmir.[23]

The promised withdrawal of Jupiters from Turkey—but not from Italy— had been a key factor in resolving the Cuban Missile Crisis. But it also demonstrated American willingness to ignore the emotions and interests of principal allies. At the height of the crisis, the American ambassador to Turkey, Raymond Hare, had advised the State Department, "Turks deeply resent any coupling of Turkey and Cuba on [the] ground that situations [are] completely different and that suggestions to that effect, especially when coming from Western sources, are both inexcusable and seriously damaging; and all the more so when associated with [the] idea that [the] Turkish relationship with US can be equated with stooge status of Cuba with USSR."[24]

17

Withdrawal

The withdrawal of the missiles by Moscow . . . did not come on the heels of the President's speech, in which he warned of full retaliation on the Soviet Union, nor did it come after the SAC alert that followed. It came only after noncombatant measures had been applied, and we had made it unmistakably clear that the United States was on the verge of destroying the missiles in Cuba or invading the island, or both, and was obviously capable of doing so.

Paul H. Nitze
From Hiroshima to Glasnost [1]

The missile crisis was not over when the Soviet and U.S. governments agreed that the Soviet missiles would be withdrawn from Cuba and the U.S. missiles would be withdrawn from Turkey. The Soviet announcement on Radio Moscow on the morning of October 28, saying that the USSR would dismantle and withdraw the missiles, was merely the start of a new phase in a confrontation. The Strategic Air Command, for example, remained on high alert for several more weeks into November. At the National Photographic Interpretation Center, Art Lundahl and his photo interpreters continued to work around the clock, as the reconnaissance planes brought back the photos that would prove whether the Soviets were removing the missiles. And the Soviets had their own problems, which included dealing with a now-furious Fidel Castro.

The Kremlin's effort to assuage Fidel Castro's growing anger and frustration was needed because while Premier Khrushchev and President Kennedy had negotiated their deal to get the missiles out of Cuba, nobody had consulted the Cuban leader. That finally happened on the evening of Saturday, October 27, when Ambassador Aleksandr Alekseyev met with Castro at the Soviet embassy in Havana to brief him on the situation between the United States and the Soviet Union. Around noon on Sunday, October 28, Castro transmitted a letter to UN Secretary U Thant,

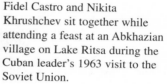

Fidel Castro and Nikita Khrushchev sit together while attending a feast at an Abkhazian village on Lake Ritsa during the Cuban leader's 1963 visit to the Soviet Union.

declaring that the reported U.S. pledge of nonaggression against Cuba was unacceptable unless it included what he called his "five points" (1) an end to the U.S. economic blockade of Cuba; (2) an end to subversive activities—Operation Mongoose—against Cuba being carried out by the United States; (3) a halt to attacks being carried out by U.S. military forces from bases on Puerto Rico; (4) an end to the U.S. reconnaissance flights over Cuba; and (5) the return of the Guantánamo naval base to Cuban sovereignty.

Ambassador Alekseyev, a KGB officer, a former journalist, and a personal friend of Castro, was rebuffed by the Cuban leader. Moscow then sent Castro a lengthy telegram explaining the Soviet decisions. Any other action, the cable explained, could have led to "global conflagration and consequently the destruction of the Cuban revolution." The cable also stressed that "the Soviet government under no circumstances would refuse to fulfill its international duty to defend Cuba."

On Sunday morning, October 28, ExComm met at the White House. President Kennedy decided to continue withholding U-2 overflights of Cuba, because of fear of another SA-2 shoot down like that of the previous day. He did authorize additional low-level flights by Navy F8U-1P Crusader and Air Force RF-101 Voodoo photo aircraft. The president also decided to maintain the quarantine force in position.

Beginning in the summer of 1962, every major Cuban port was employed for the unloading of Operation Anadyr forces. This photo of a ship alongside a pier at Mariel was taken by an RF-101 Voodoo aircraft, whose shadow is caught in the photo.

At the same time, ExComm began to discuss the issue of the Il-28 Beagle light bombers that had been shipped to Cuba. The ambiguity over the bombers—including their roles—came from Khrushchev's letter of October 28, in which he told President Kennedy that he would remove from Cuba "those weapons you describe as offensive." The Americans assumed that those aircraft had a nuclear strike capability, which placed them in the arbitrary category of offensive weapons. In fact, of the fifty-six Il-28s shipped to Cuba, only six were configured to carry nuclear bombs, although that detail was unknown to U.S. intelligence.

Raymond Garthoff, a State Department analyst whose memorandum recommended that the Il-28s be considered in the same category as the ballistic missiles, wrote that the United States could not "reasonably insist" on the withdrawal of the MiG-21 fighters, surface-to-air missiles, or ground forces that the Soviet Union had sent to Cuba. Neither Garthoff nor his colleagues realized the actual size of the Soviet deployment of ground combat forces to Cuba, nor that they were armed with tactical nuclear weapons.

While these issues were being discussed in Washington, in an effort to confirm the dismantling of the ballistic missiles and the withdrawal of offensive weapons, U Thant and several of his staff flew to Havana on the afternoon of October 30. The UN secretary general was cordially received by Castro and other Cuban officials. U Thant proposed the on-site inspection by a UN team, an International Red Cross team, or by aerial inspection from UN aircraft. The last would be a U.S. C-130 Hercules fitted with cameras, manned by a U.S. or another nation's flight crew, with UN observers on board.[2] Castro declared that *all* of the proposals were "intended to humiliate the Cuban state." Despite offers from several parties to verify the removal of the missiles by on-site inspection, Castro was adamant in rejecting all such efforts.

This lack of progress, which U Thant reported to all parties, led President Kennedy at the ExComm meeting on October 31 to order the continuation of low-level flights while still withholding the U-2 overflights. In a strange turn of events, U Thant and his aides again met with Castro on the 31st in Havana, where the Cuban leader agreed to a request from the secretary general to return the body of Major Rudolf Anderson, the pilot of the U-2 spyplane shot down by a Soviet SA-2 missile on the 27th. But Castro claimed to U Thant that *Cuban anti-aircraft guns* had shot down the high-flying U-2, rather than Soviet missiles.

Complaining about the continuing U.S. aerial reconnaissance, Castro warned U Thant that "the Cuban people can no longer tolerate such daily provocations," and that Cubans would destroy any aircraft that intruded into Cuban air space. U Thant was unable to obtain Castro's approval for any form of monitoring of the Soviet missile withdrawal. Upon learning this, President Kennedy confirmed that low-level reconnaissance would continue over Cuba, but he still kept the U-2s grounded.

On November 1, Castro met with Ambassador Alekseyev for the first time since October 27. That evening, Castro reported to the Cuban people by radio and television on his meetings with U Thant and his differences with the Soviet government. Still—adopting a conciliatory tone—Castro explained, "we have confidence in the leadership of the Soviet Union. . . . More than ever, we should remember the generosity and friendship that the Soviets have shown us."

Inside Cuba

As Castro spoke, U.S. photo interpreters studied the film brought back from the latest low-level reconnaissance missions. The photos revealed that the SS-4 medium-range missiles and their associated equipment had been removed from the missile sites, and that the areas were being bulldozed. Construction at the SS-5 intermediate-range sites had also halted, and those facilities, never completed, were also being dismantled.

The evidence concerning the missiles was incontrovertible, although reports continued to come out of Cuba that some missiles were being hidden.[3] The following evening, in a brief television address—his first since the quarantine speech—President Kennedy informed the nation that "on the basis of yesterday's aerial photographs . . . the Soviet missile

The Soviet merchant ship *Anosov* shortly after she departed Cuba on November 6, with eight canvas-covered missile transporters for the SS-4 MRBM. Only Soviet-flag merchant ships carried missiles, aircraft, troops, and nuclear warheads to Cuba.

bases in Cuba are being dismantled, their missiles and related equipment are being crated, and the fixed installations at these sites are being destroyed." However, at the San Julián Asiento airfield, where the Il-28 bombers were being assembled, work was continuing. It was not clear, however, whether the Soviet mechanics were assembling or dismantling the bombers.

At the November 2 morning ExComm meeting, President Kennedy confirmed that the United States would press the Kremlin for removal of the Il-28s from Cuba. He added that the blockade would continue, but while merchant ships entering the quarantine area would be questioned, they would not be stopped or boarded.

With White House guidance, Ambassador Adlai Stevenson was able to provide on November 2 a definitive list of "offensive weapons" to Anastas Mikoyan, who was in New York en route to Havana. The list included:

1. Surface-to-surface missiles including those designed for use at sea and including propellants and chemical compounds capable of being used to power missiles;
2. Bomber aircraft;
3. Bombs, air-to-surface rockets, and guided missiles;
4. Warheads for any of the above weapons;
5. Mechanical or electronic equipment to support or operate the above items such as communications, supply and missile launching equipment, including Komar-class motor torpedo boats.[4]

With the list in hand, Mikoyan flew to Havana on the 2nd and immediately announced the Kremlin's support of Castro's "five points."[5] Castro, already angry over the missile withdrawal, was said to have initially refused to meet with Mikoyan, but Ambassador Alekseyev eventually convinced him to do so.

The next day, in Castro's Havana apartment, Mikoyan met with the Cuban leader, Ambassador Alekseyev, and a Soviet interpreter. Their discussion was interrupted almost immediately by a message that Mikoyan's wife of more than forty years had died in the Kremlin hospital. After an anguishing recess in the talks, Mikoyan decided to remain in Havana. His son Sergo, a historian who had accompanied him to act as a personal secretary, returned to Moscow, and Mikoyan reentered the discussion.

With unambiguous evidence of the Soviet dismantlement of the missile sites in Cuba, the withdrawal issue now centered on the Il-28 bombers, not more than twenty of which had actually been assembled, and on the issue of inspection and verification of the removal of offensive weapons.[6] Even as Mikoyan and Castro were meeting, President Kennedy replied to Khrushchev's letter of October 30. He wrote on November 3 that before the naval quarantine could be lifted, the verification and bomber issues had to be resolved, citing "very serious problems" if Castro could not be convinced to allow on-site verification.

At the afternoon ExComm meeting in the White House on November 3, the discussion again centered on the bombers. President Kennedy said that the United States should announce publicly that the Il-28s were offensive weapons and that they had to be withdrawn from Cuba, but he agreed that such a statement should be delayed until the next day. That evening, at 8:44 P.M., the president issued additional instructions to all involved with the negotiations: "We have good evidence that the Russians are dismantling the missile bases. . . . [But] the assembly of Il-28s continues. There is some evidence of an intent to establish a submarine-tending facility. The future of the SAM sites is unclear. We have no satisfactory assurances on verification. . . . In blunt summary, we want no offensive weapons and no Soviet military base in Cuba, and that is how we understand the agreements of October 27 and 28."[7]

At his Stamford, Connecticut, home, presidential confidant John McCloy met with Deputy Foreign Affairs Minister Vasily Kuznetsov on November 4 to discuss the crisis. Kuznetsov, who had been dispatched to New York to help the Soviet UN delegation, assured McCloy that all missile construction sites had been dismantled as of November 2.

In continuing discussions with Adlai Stevenson and McCloy, Kuznetsov proposed that the United States conduct "at-sea inspections" to verify the removal of missiles from Cuba. Under that scheme, U.S. warships (and aircraft) would come alongside Soviet merchant ships en route from Cuba to observe their deck cargoes. In return, Kuznetsov explained that the Soviet government wanted the quarantine lifted. In addition, he wanted formal assurances that the United States would not invade Cuba, would not encourage other Latin American countries to do so, and would cease all subversive activities against Cuba.[8]

The following day, November 5, the exchange between Washington and Moscow continued as another of Khrushchev's letters arrived at the White House. The Soviet leader said that he was "seriously worried" about the manner in which the United States defined "offensive weapons." Khrushchev labeled the U.S. requirements for withdrawal of the Il-28s and the twelve Komar missile boats as "additional demands" and explained that the Soviet Union viewed them as "a wish to bring our relations back again into a heated state in which they were several days ago."

With the crisis still unresolved, President Kennedy advised Secretary of Defense Robert McNamara on November 5 that the U.S. forces still being readied for invading Cuba were, in his opinion, too "thin" and recommended calling up three Army Reserve divisions for a possible invasion. And, thinking further ahead, Kennedy sent a memo dated November 5 to McNamara warning that "the Russians may try again" to introduce offensive weapons into Cuba, and that they could be prepared to use force at sea to overcome any U.S. blockade.

Getting the Bombers Out

Discussions between U.S. and Soviet representatives continued, both official and back channel, in Washington and in New York. The Soviets insisted that the Il-28s were outside of the Kennedy-Khrushchev understanding, while the Americans insisted that they were offensive weapons and hence were included in the terms. At the highest level, the Kennedy-Khrushchev exchange continued, and on November 6, Kennedy raised for the first time the issue of the four reinforced Soviet rifle regiments in Cuba. He also expressed concern that a submarine base might be established in Cuba.

Throughout this tense period, low-level reconnaissance photos from the F8U-1Ps and RF-101s left no doubt that the Soviets had been dismantling the SS-4 and SS-5 missile sites. The missiles and their support equipment were crated and loaded aboard ships in Cuban ports and were readied for transport back to the USSR. In response to reports that the missiles were being withdrawn, on the evening of November 7, President Kennedy advised ExComm members that the United States "wouldn't invade with the Soviet missiles out of Cuba." But he suggested that a public noninvasion commitment be withheld until the Il-28s were also

VOLGOLES ENR USSR 9 NOVEMBER

A U.S. Navy P2V Neptune and the destroyer *Vesole* take a close look at the missile-laden merchant ship *Volgoles* as she departs Cuba on November 9. The departure of strategic weapons was closely watched after Castro refused on-ground observers.

removed. There was still uncertainty about how to handle the Il-28 issue. Kennedy requested that ExComm convene again on November 8 to "decide whether we should go to the mat on the Il-28 bombers or whether we should say that the Soviets have now completed their agreement to remove the missiles and move on to other problems." Meanwhile, U.S. negotiators were directed to drop the issue of the Komar missile boats—which could not be armed with nuclear weapons—and to concentrate on the Il-28 bomber issue.[9] The SA-2 surface-to-air missiles were not mentioned.

At the afternoon ExComm meeting on November 8, the discussion centered on how the United States could force the Soviets to remove the Il-28s. President Kennedy was inclined not to reimpose a blockade, but he did favor pressuring U.S. allies to keep their merchant ships out of Cuba. Other proposals were made during the ExComm session, including covert operations against Cuba and even air attacks against the Il-28 aircraft.

The following day, the final ballistic missiles departed Cuba on Soviet ships. As the ships reached the open sea, they were inspected by U.S. Navy ships and aircraft; the crewmen pulled back canvas covers to permit the Americans to photograph the missiles. There was at least one humorous incident. According to Admiral Robert Dennison, "A destroyer closed to speak to this Soviet ship and we had put Russian-speaking officers in each one of these quarantine ships. So this Russian-speaking officer in the destroyer hailed this ship in Russian—'Where are you from? Where are you bound . . . ?' And the answer came back from the Soviet ship's bridge in perfect English!"[10]

Assistant Secretary of Defense Arthur Sylvester later told reporters at a Pentagon news conference that the "responsible people of this government are satisfied" that the merchant ships were in fact carrying missiles. U.S. surveillance efforts did not confirm whether the less noticeable tactical missiles—FROG and FKR-1—were shipped back to the Soviet Union.[11]

Although U.S. reconnaissance aircraft had sighted the construction of storage bunkers for nuclear warheads at several sites, the CIA reported that "no nuclear weapons or missile nose cones have been identified in Cuba." These storage bunkers—at each of the SS-4 and SS-5 sites—consisted of structures "about 35 feet in width and are about 80 feet in length at the MRBM [SS-4] sites and 112 feet in length at the IRBM [SS-5] sites."[12] Significantly, the CIA memorandum stated, *"If nuclear weapons are in Cuba* they are probably in an unlocated facility between the entry port of Mariel and the [missile] sites" [emphasis added].

The negotiations over the Il-28 bombers continued. On November 12, Ambassador Stevenson reported to ExComm that negotiations in New York over the Il-28 removal were deadlocked. Almost simultaneously, President Kennedy received a letter from Premier Khrushchev dated the previous day. The long, friendly note referred to the removal of missiles from Cuba, observing, "We, the Soviet side, have carried out our obligations and thereby have created possibility for complete elimination of tension in the Caribbean. Consequently, now it is your turn, it is for your side to carry out precisely your obligations." Khrushchev—mentioning former Vice President Richard Nixon's defeat in the California gubernatorial race, which "did not draw tears from our eyes"—did address the Il-28 issue. Denying that the Il-28s were an offensive weapon, Khrushchev continued,

> However, if you do not agree—and this is your right—ask your intelligence after all and let it give you an answer based not on guesswork but on facts. If it really knows anything it must tell you the truth and namely that it is long since the Il-28's have been taken out of production and out of use in our armed forces. And if some planes still remain now—and a certain number of them have been brought by us to Cuba—that was done as a result of your action last year when you increased the budget and called up the reservists. We on our part had to take measures in response at that time, having postponed taking those planes out of use as well.[13]

Khrushchev added that the planes were defensive weapons, also outdated, and would be flown only by Soviet pilots. The implication was that they were closely controlled from the Kremlin. He did not mention that six of the Il-28s were configured for nuclear bombs and that the bombs had been brought to Cuba.

Then, giving his "gentleman's word," Khrushchev agreed that "we will remove the Il-28 planes with all the personnel and equipment related to those planes, although not now but later. We would like to do that some time later when we determine that the conditions are ripe to remove them. We will advise you of that." That night, the president told his brother Bobby that he should inform Ambassador Dobrynin that Khrushchev's "gentleman's word" on the bombers was acceptable and that the United States would not insist on the immediate withdrawal of the aircraft. Robert Kennedy met with Dobrynin that night to say that the U.S. government hoped that the bombers will be removed "within, say, 30 days."

Meeting the next morning, November 13, ExComm continued to discuss the Il-28 issue, including a proposal to send a "last chance" message to Khrushchev, warning that further actions could be taken shortly if the bombers were not removed. ExComm members also addressed what those actions might be. Suggestions included blockade, low-altitude reconnaissance flights as a means of psychological warfare, and having friendly Latin American countries bring pressure against Cuba. One other option was considered: "provoking" an attack on U.S. reconnaissance planes, leading to retaliatory U.S. air attacks on Cuban targets, primarily the bombers.

Three days later, the Joint Chiefs of Staff recommended that if the bombers were not withdrawn, the quarantine should be expanded to petroleum products, and if that did not have the desired effect, the United States "should be prepared to take them out by air attack."[14] The Joint Chiefs of Staff also observed,

> Even if the Il-28's are negotiated out of Cuba, there will remain weapons systems of significant military importance; the MiG's, the SAM's, the air defense control system, and the large stocks of modern Army equipment. . . . The air defense weapons will be a constant threat to our air surveillance of Cuba while the army weapons may be used against Guantánamo or against any invasion attempt. But more important than this equipment are the thousands of Soviet military personnel who remain in Cuba to man it.

Meanwhile, Khrushchev responded to the Robert Kennedy-Dobrynin meeting with another letter on the 14th: "The question of the withdrawal of the Il-28's within the mentioned 30 days does not constitute any complicated question. Yet this period will probably not be sufficient. As I already said in my oral message I can assure the President that those planes will be removed from Cuba with all the equipment and flying personnel. It can be done in 2–3 months."

Khrushchev also complained in his letter that the United States was "not carrying out its commitments" to end the overflights of Cuba or the quarantine, nor had the United States given its written pledge not to invade Cuba.

President Kennedy could not immediately come to a decision on how to handle the Il-28 issue. Still, with the missiles removed from Cuba, the Soviet Union and the United States had moved away from a potential nuclear conflagration.

The Bomber Crisis Resolved

Castro continued to belligerently warn U Thant on November 15 that his anti-aircraft guns would fire again on U.S. reconnaissance aircraft violating Cuban air space. He also continued to reject any on-the-ground inspection of Cuban territory.

That same day, President Kennedy wrote again to Premier Khrushchev, complaining that "three major parts of the undertakings on your side—the removal of the Il-28s, the arrangement for verification [of the removal of missiles], and safeguards against introduction [of more offensive weapons]—have not been carried out."

Ambassador Dobrynin was informed that the Il-28 issue must be resolved, or the Soviet Union and United States would "soon find ourselves back in the position of increasing tension." In New York, Stevenson and McCloy continued to meet with Zorin and Kuznetsov in an effort to resolve the Il-28 issue. The Soviet diplomats were adamant in declaring that the Il-28 bombers were not offensive weapons and could not threaten the United States.

The bomber crisis was coming to a climax. Four days later, at 10 A.M. on November 19, President Kennedy authorized resumption of the high-altitude U-2 spy flights over Cuba. Later in the day, Robert Kennedy met with journalist-GRU officer Georgi Bolshakov to warn him that the low-level reconnaissance flights would resume unless the Il-28 issue was quickly resolved. He told Bolshakov that he needed a response from the Soviet side before the president's press conference scheduled for the next day.

That evening, President Kennedy sent messages to Britain's Harold Macmillan, France's Charles de Gaulle, and West Germany's Konrad Adenauer to advise them that if the Il-28s were not withdrawn from Cuba, the United States might take further actions. He noted, however, that the overall situation was "somewhat less dangerous than it was in October."

There was a breakthrough of sorts on November 19 when Castro advised U Thant that the Cuban government would not object if the Soviet Union removed the Il-28s from Cuba. After describing the aircraft's speed and altitude limitations, Castro observed, "It is clear that the position of the government of the United States in demanding the withdrawal of these planes merely constitutes a pretext for maintaining tension, prolonging the crisis, and continuing its policy of force."[15] Castro still warned that he would fire on aircraft invading Cuban air space and again rejected inspections on Cuban territory.

In another lengthy letter to President Kennedy dated November 19 and received the following day, Khrushchev formally agreed to remove the Il-28s from Cuba "within a month's term and maybe even sooner since the term for the removal of these planes is not a matter of principle for us." Like Castro, Khrushchev also belittled the Il-28s, noting that they "are twelve years old and by their combat characteristics they at present cannot be classified as offensive types of weapons."

Khrushchev then asked about the American "commitment not to invade Cuba" and for the immediate lifting of the quarantine and the withdrawal of U.S. naval and other military units from the Caribbean area. He also suggested the United States terminate reconnaissance flights over the island.

The fourteen-page letter concluded: "I wish to stress that much time has already passed since an agreement was reached between us and it is not in the interests of our countries, not in the interests of peace to delay the fulfillment of the agreement that has been reached and the final settlement of the Cuban crisis. Such is our conviction."

After discussing Khrushchev's letter, ExComm agreed the next day, November 20, to lift the quarantine. However, U-2 missions would continue to verify that the Il-28 bombers were being disassembled. And at the end of the day, the Joint Chiefs of Staff canceled the DEFCON-2 alert of the Strategic Air Command at 11:21 P.M. With this, the world moved a big step back from the brink of nuclear war.

Seamen open a container to reveal the fuselage of an Il-28 Beagle bomber on the Soviet merchant ship *Kasimov* on December 15 after the ship's departure from Cuba. The *Kasimov* carried fifteen of the controversial aircraft.

That evening, at six o'clock, President Kennedy opened a White House press conference with the statement: "I have today been informed by Chairman Khrushchev that all of the Il-28 bombers now in Cuba will be withdrawn in thirty days. He also agrees that these planes can be observed and counted as they leave. Inasmuch as this goes a long way toward reducing the danger which faced this Hemisphere four weeks ago, I have this afternoon instructed the Secretary of Defense to lift our naval quarantine."

The president explained the U.S. position on Cuba: "If all offensive weapons are removed from Cuba and kept out of the Hemisphere in the future . . . there will be peace in the Caribbean. And as I said in September, we shall neither initiate nor permit aggression in this Hemisphere." President Kennedy did not mention that the Strategic Air Command had stepped down from DEFCON-2. Indeed, his statement mentioned neither nuclear readiness nor nuclear weapons.

The next day, President Kennedy sent a brief letter to Khrushchev welcoming the decision to remove the Il-28 bombers. Kennedy wrote, "There need be no fear of any invasion of Cuba while matters take their present favorable course."

Secretary of Defense McNamara ordered the release of reservists called to active duty and other military stand-down procedures. In Moscow, Minister of Defense Rodion Malinovsky ordered a stand-down of Soviet and other Warsaw Pact forces from their levels of increased readiness.

Still in Cuba were four well-equipped rifle regiments, the dozen Komar missile boats, coastal defense missiles, and the elaborate SA-2 and MiG-21 air-defense systems. A CIA report on November 29 observed, "We have no evidence of any preparations in Cuba to withdraw these elements."[16]

The U-2 flights over Cuba continued; they were immune to Cuban anti-aircraft guns at their operating altitude. The Soviet-operated SA-2 missile batteries were ordered not to engage the U-2s. Still, some U.S. aircraft were kept ready to retaliate against Cuban (or Soviet) anti-aircraft sites if a U.S. plane were shot down. Eventually, reconnaissance satellites and the more-capable SR-71 Blackbird spyplanes would replace the U-2s.[17] Meanwhile, U.S. spy ships, operating in international waters, continued to keep Cuba under electronic surveillance.

At a press conference on December 10, 1962, President Kennedy told reporters that it appeared that all strategic missiles and Il-28 bombers had been removed from Cuba. Although the exchange of letters between Kennedy and Khrushchev on the Cuban situation continued, the United States never issued a formal guarantee not to invade Cuba. The Cuban Missile Crisis had ended.

18

Legacy: The Anadyr Effect

Khrushchev miscalculated. Whatever his failings may have been, John Kennedy did not lack courage in the face of imminent danger. Kennedy, of course, was supported at the time by the vastly superior U.S. conventional military capabilities around Cuba as well as by a superior strategic nuclear position. He also had an able group of men assisting him. But without that peculiar quality of courage that enabled him to call Khrushchev's bluff, subsequent history could have been quite different.

Paul H. Nitze
From Hiroshima to Glasnost[1]

The Soviet Union and the United States came perilously close to nuclear war in October 1962, closer than at any other time during the forty-five years of superpower confrontation known as the Cold War. Neither nation wanted a nuclear conflict; both national leaders, John Kennedy and Nikita Khrushchev, knew that there would be no true "winner" in a nuclear exchange. Even if only a *few* nuclear warheads fell on either country, there could be millions of direct casualties, plus incalculable material devastation.

How, then, could the world have come so close to such a conflict? Nuclear war almost occurred during the fall of 1962 because of a combination of factors: (1) Premier Khrushchev lying to President Kennedy; (2) U.S. political and military leaders, along with intelligence analysts, refusing to believe that the Soviets would send nuclear weapons and a large combat force across an ocean, far beyond Soviet borders; (3) the failure of U.S. intelligence to detect the nuclear warheads actually in Cuba; (4) the harassment by U.S. naval forces of Soviet submarines that were carrying nuclear torpedoes; and (5) the dispatch of two nuclear-armed U.S. fighter aircraft to stop Soviet fighters from approaching an errant U-2 spyplane.

Despite a continued U.S. threat of invasion of Cuba and numerous specific incidents, including a Soviet SA-2 missile shooting down a U-2 spyplane over Cuba and the death of its pilot, both Khrushchev and Kennedy, along with several of their subordinates—at sea, under the sea, in the air, and in Cuba—showed restraint at critical moments.

Eventually, as the United States stood firm on most issues, the crisis ended as Khrushchev backed down and ordered the offensive nuclear missiles removed from Cuba, as well as, after some additional delays, the Il-28 Beagle bombers, which constituted only a minimal threat (only six were configured to carry atomic bombs, and their effectiveness in reaching major U.S. cities was questionable). As U.S. Secretary of State Dean Rusk had remarked, "We're eyeball to eyeball and I think the other fellow just blinked." That "blink"—and the withdrawal from Cuba—was caused primarily by the overwhelming U.S. superiority in nuclear weapons in the fall of 1962, along with the diplomatic and political skills of the president and certain members of his administration.

What We Knew . . . and Didn't

During the Cold War, the Soviet Union had generally outperformed the United States in both intelligence and counterintelligence operations. This trend was evident during the missile crisis as well. For example, even the usually perceptive Director of Central Intelligence John A. McCone *never* predicted that the Soviets would flood Cuba with tactical nuclear weapons. Ignorant of those short-range, nuclear-tipped weapons, the United States planned a massive airborne-seaborne assault on Cuba. Most U.S. military commanders—perceiving overwhelming U.S. air, naval, and troop superiority—believed that such an invasion would be an unqualified success. The Chief of Naval Operations, Admiral George W. Anderson, predicted,

> Unquestionably, if we had gone in with an invasion, unquestionably we would have been successful.
>
> It could have been rather bloody but I would say with a relatively low degree of casualties on the part of the American forces.
>
> I think the Cuban people would have immediately rallied to our support and I think we could have installed a good government in Cuba, and I think with proper warnings to the Russians and care on our part, my belief is that there would not have been a military confrontation between Russian troops that were there and ours, because there were relatively few Russians there.[2]

One can only wonder what his opinion would have been had he known of the nuclear arsenal the Soviets had ashore and aboard the submarines in the area.

On several occasions during the crisis, the Kennedy administration was within hours of initiating such an assault, which would certainly have been contested with tactical nuclear weapons, especially if the U.S. forces appeared to have been on the verge of capturing or destroying the ballistic missiles already in Cuba. Soviet military doctrine placed an almost manic emphasis on nuclear weapons security, and the Soviets would likely have taken a "use them or lose them" attitude toward their weapons in Cuba. Combined with the fact that U.S. intelligence agencies had given the Kennedy administration no warning of the large numbers of battlefield nuclear weapons equipping the Group of Soviet Forces in Cuba and the shock of their unexpected use on U.S. troops, the result cannot be properly gauged. At the very least, there would have been a concerted American effort to hunt down the remaining Soviet nuclear weapons and destroy them.

Another scenario in which the crisis could have erupted into nuclear conflict was the at-sea submarine situation. The four Soviet diesel-electric submarines that had been dispatched to Cuba each carried a single nuclear torpedo. On the first day of the blockade, one of those submarines was detected in close proximity to the first two Soviet merchant ships to approach the quarantine line.[3] If those two Soviet merchant ships had not received last-minute instructions not to penetrate the barrier, a confrontation would have occurred that could easily have evolved into a nuclear exchange because the submarines had orders to protect the merchant ships.

A cornered Soviet submarine might well have launched its nuclear torpedo; the U.S. anti-submarine destroyers and the carrier-based and land-based ASW aircraft could have employed nuclear weapons as well.[4] Thus, an at-sea confrontation could have evolved into a nuclear exchange. A nuclear exchange at sea, or even Soviet use of nuclear missiles *in* Cuba, most probably would not have led directly to a strategic nuclear exchange between the United States and the Soviet Union. Other scenarios were possible—all of which could have brought the world to the brink of a nuclear holocaust. General Pliyev in Cuba had orders not to allow the strategic missiles—the SS-4s—to be captured or destroyed. Would he have received permission from Moscow to launch those weapons against American cities if their loss appeared imminent? *That* action would have most certainly led to a U.S. retaliatory strike against *some* targets in the

Soviet Union. Just how many targets in the Soviet Union would have been attacked, and with how much force, remains unknown. However, given the immature and still-evolving configuration of the American nuclear attack plans (the SIOP) in 1962, there is a real possibility that President Kennedy and his advisors would have considered a full-scale nuclear strike against the Soviet homeland.

Combat Fatigue

The weeks-long and round-the-clock character of the crisis caused exhaustion among a number of the senior American leaders and their Soviet counterparts. The president and members of ExComm spent many hours every day in White House meetings, in addition to carrying out some of their normal duties. In the case of Robert Kennedy and a few others, there were additional late-night, back-channel meetings with Soviet diplomats, KGB officers, and others.

After one of his nocturnal meetings with the younger Kennedy, Soviet Ambassador Anatoly Dobrynin reported to Khrushchev: "Robert Kennedy looked exhausted. One could see from his eyes that he had not slept for days. He himself said that he had not been home for six days and nights. 'The president is in a grave situation,' Robert Kennedy said, 'and he does not know how to get out of it. We are under very severe stress.' "[5]

Secretary of Defense Robert McNamara slept in his E-ring Pentagon office for most of the crisis. He and other members of ExComm worked around the clock, sometimes missing a night's sleep entirely. "We were all exhausted by the end of it," recalled Paul Nitze.[6]

In Moscow, the burden of the crisis fell mainly on Khrushchev. Although he met regularly with his fellow Presidium members, he appears to have held his own council far more than did President Kennedy. Sometimes Khrushchev slept on a couch in his Kremlin office, not wanting to travel the few miles to his residence. Khrushchev later recalled, "And I kept my clothes on. I didn't want to be like that Western minister who was caught literally with his pants down by the Suez events of 1956 and who had to run around in his shorts until the emergency was over."[7] (Kennedy could walk the short distance between his living quarters in the White House residence to his West Wing office.)

The effects of sleep deprivation on decision making are better understood today than they were in 1962, when physical and mental stamina was seen as a quality of strength and manhood in a Cold Warrior. This quality even had a name—"brinksmanship"—which was much touted on the Washington cocktail circuit prior to the crisis. By the end of the crisis, however, senior officials within the Kennedy administration were beginning to lose the qualities that had made them *"the best and brightest"* when President-elect Kennedy had selected them for service. Secretary of defense Robert McNamara's concerns about "seeing another Saturday night" (see chapter 1) were a clear sign that his ability to sustain and provide useful advice to the president was deteriorating.[8] In a crisis that was coming to a head, with a possible decision to go to war in the offing, this kind of exhaustion might well have led to disastrous consequences.

Physical impediments may also have contributed to the crisis. Admiral Anderson, speaking of the Joint Chiefs of Staff communications with the White House and ExComm, said, "I think we lacked in some measure a flow of information on the deliberations at the special group [ExComm] . . . partially perhaps because [General] Maxwell Taylor had a hearing impediment. [General Curtis] LeMay also had a hearing impediment."

Anderson continued, "When General LeMay went up to the White House, he put in a hearing aid, which Maxwell Taylor would never do, I guess through some quirk of vanity or something. LeMay never missed anything but I'm quite certain that Taylor did miss or chose not to pass on or didn't have time to pass on some of the things that took place [in ExComm]."

Men under strain, living in a crisis situation and going without sleep, often miss nuances, which can lead to mistakes. In a world where people control the decisions to go to war and which weapons will be used to fight those conflicts, such mistakes can be catastrophic.

The Anadyr Effect—Never Again, Again

The Cuban Missile Crisis also had a number of long-term effects on the participants, not all of which can be considered positive in the context of twenty-first-century hindsight. On the Soviet side, despite the removal of the Jupiter missiles in Turkey, the crisis was a humiliating affair that led to a "Never again, again!" mentality for the Presidium members and the military leaders who had participated. The result was a major military buildup of almost every component of the Soviet military establishment, especially the Strategic Rocket Forces and the Navy. The massive military buildup began even before Leonid Brezhnev and Aleksei Kosygin took power in October 1964, to lead the Soviet Union down the road to eventual bankruptcy and, ultimately, the breakup of the Soviet Union in 1991.

In the Soviet Union, Khrushchev's ignominious withdrawal of the ballistic missiles from Cuba was viewed by most knowledgeable Russians as a humiliating defeat. Although Khrushchev could point to the American-assured survival of the Castro regime, he could not put a positive spin on either the withdrawal of the strategic missiles or the dismantling of the Jupiter missiles in Turkey. The strategic nuclear balance in late 1962 was too greatly in favor of the United States.

Ultimately, the Cuban Missile Crisis cost Khrushchev his political career and almost his life. Faced with several other foreign and domestic problems, Khrushchev found that his position became increasingly tenuous, and in October 1964 he was ousted in a bloodless coup. Khrushchev was permitted to retire—without being incarcerated, exiled, or killed. Leonid Brezhnev and Aleksei Kosygin took over his positions as First Secretary of the Communist Party and as prime minister, respectively. Brezhnev eventually consolidated all government and Party power in his own hands, a partial step back to the days of Josef Stalin's absolute control of the Soviet Union. Reportedly, Brezhnev plotted not only Khrushchev's ouster but also his death. KGB Chairman Vladimir Semichastny, while supporting the coup, firmly refused to participate in the murder of Khrushchev, and the Soviet leader, at age seventy, was simply retired and isolated.[9,10]

After the missile crisis, the Soviet leadership was determined to never again be humiliated by the West by inferiority in strategic or conventional military forces. Khrushchev and then Brezhnev were in a catch-up situation for some years, but they persistently pushed forward until the Soviet Union achieved parity with the West. Following the missile crisis of 1962, the United States rapidly deployed large numbers of land-based Minuteman missiles and submarine-based Polaris missiles—a total of 1,000 and 656 missiles, respectively, within just a few years. In the same period, U.S. strategic bomber production ended and the intercontinental bomber force declined, from almost 1,600 aircraft in 1962 to only 460 by the end of the decade. The last U.S. strategic bomber of the era, the 744th B-52 Stratofortress, was delivered in October 1962.[11]

The United States then extended the strategic imbalance in its favor when it added multiple warheads, known as Multiple Independently targeted Reentry Vehicles (MIRVs), to its ICBMs and SLBMs. The Minuteman III missile, which entered service in 1970, was fitted with a three-MIRV warhead (550 missiles deployed, armed with 1,650 warheads); the

Poseidon submarine-launched missile, operational from 1971 on, could carry up to fourteen MIRVs (496 missiles deployed with potentially 6,944 warheads).[12]

Immediately following the Cuban Missile Crisis, the Soviet Union accelerated its existing ICBM and SLBM programs and initiated new ones. Like his predecessor, Brezhnev strongly supported ballistic missiles in preference to manned strategic bombers with an intercontinental strike capability.[13] The Soviet Union also continued to procure both theater ballistic missiles (MRBMs and IRBMs) and manned bombers (such as the Su-24 Fencer and Tu-22M Backfire) for theater strikes against Western Europe and China, along with targets in the Far East.

The Soviet Union overtook the United States in numbers of ICBM launchers in 1969. A short time later, the USSR overtook the United States in the number of submarine-launched ballistic missiles. Furthermore, the Soviet Union held a considerable advantage in both types of missile "throw weight" and hence in "equivalent megatons." Only in the number of MIRV warheads did the United States retain a clear superiority over the Soviet Union. But the Soviet Union deployed land- and submarine-based MIRV missiles, and the two nations' MIRV warhead inventories were very close to one another in 1970 (just under two thousand MIRV warheads each). Until the end of the Cold War, the United States did retain an advantage in ballistic missile accuracy and in the numbers of intercontinental bombers.[14,15]

The first nuclear arms limitation treaty—SALT I in 1972—essentially froze the two sides in a fairly even thermonuclear balance, which lasted until the demise of the Soviet Union in 1991.

The embarrassing odyssey of the submarine of the 69th Submarine Brigade during its voyage to Cuba badly stung the Soviet Navy, which had been cut back considerably in the 1950s after Khrushchev came to power. Following the missile crisis, Khrushchev, and then Brezhnev, approved the Soviet Navy's massive expansion into a world-class fleet. In 1962–1963, the decision was made to resume the construction of ballistic missile submarines, and the lead submarine of Project 667A (NATO Yankee) was laid down at the Severodvinsk shipyard in the Arctic on November 4, 1964. This was the beginning of an unprecedented ballistic missile submarine construction effort.

The Soviet Union surpassed the United States in modern nuclear-propelled ballistic missile submarines and the number of submarine-launched ballistic missiles in 1973 (when each nation had 41 submarines with 656 missiles).[16] Also approved were massive surface warship construction programs, which provided the Soviet Navy with aircraft carriers and nuclear-propelled battle cruisers, as well as with lesser warships. The decisions to approve those military programs have their basis in the Soviet backdown in the Cuban Missile Crisis. The humiliation of the 69th Submarine Brigade had a lasting effect, and the United States found itself well matched when the two navies occasionally faced off—for example, in the Mediterranean Sea in October 1973 during the Yom Kippur War.[17,18]

As bad as the embarrassment of the Cuban Missile Crisis had been for the Soviet Union, it was nothing compared to the long-term damage done by the Soviets' continuing arms buildup afterward. Khrushchev had realized upon taking power in the 1950s that the only way to build a better life for his people was by having a reduced military that would not place such a heavy strain upon the manpower and resources of the Soviet Union. Khrushchev had radically downsized and transformed the Soviet armed forces and had made significant progress toward that goal. Operation Anadyr was undertaken in part as the interim solution to the Soviet strategic weapons shortfall until the problems with the SS-7 ICBMs and Hotel-class nuclear ballistic missile submarines could be corrected.

Instead, the 1962 missile crisis undid all of Khrushchev's efforts to nudge the Soviet economy toward a consumer-oriented system and allowed the Cold War to continue for almost three more decades. Leonid Brezhnev and his generation of Soviet leaders would have to die in their beds before a true Soviet reformer, Mikhail Gorbachev, would come to power and take up where Nikita Khrushchev had been before the 1964 coup. By then, it was too late, and even the enlightened policies of *Perestroika* and *Glasnost* could not preserve the Soviet Union.

The Soviets were not the only participants of the missile crisis to suffer consequences when it was over. For senior American leaders, particularly those who had endured the lengthy ExComm sessions, the memories of the crisis were a continuing concern for the rest of their lives. Afterward, there were too many reminders of those days in 1962 to ever allow them to forget the stress, strain, and genuine terror of being on the brink of nuclear war. One such touchstone held special significance for the ExComm members.

After the crisis was resolved, President Kennedy wanted a special commemorative gift for everyone who had been at his side during those difficult days. He ordered for each individual a custom-made plaque

The commemorative plaque given by President Kennedy to his wife, Jackie, for her support during the Cuban Missile Crisis. The plaques were custom made by Tiffany's for the president to give to ExComm members and other selected individuals in thanks for their service during the crisis. Mrs. Kennedy later commented that it was the only time the president ordered something from Tiffany's that was not directly out of its catalog.

from Tiffany's thanking them for their service. On every plaque was an engraved calendar sheet of October 1962, with the thirteen days of the crisis highlighted. While each recipient was unquestionably proud to be recognized for his service, many saw a darker significance to the gift.[19]

For the Americans, particularly those who had endured the lengthy ExComm sessions, the crisis was a source of continuing concern. None of them ever wished to duplicate what they had gone through in October 1962, and this probably explains much of the American reluctance to aggressively react to international incidents during the remainder of the 1960s.[20] The crisis also appears to have influenced U.S. policy for conducting the war in Vietnam, with President Johnson constantly concerned about possible Soviet or Chinese intervention in the war.[21] It would take the election of Richard Nixon in 1968, and the retirement of the last of John Kennedy's senior advisors from public service, before the U.S. government overcame the aftereffects of the Cuban Missile Crisis.

This American reluctance for confrontation and action in the international area may have actually worked in the Soviet Union's favor in the years immediately after the crisis. As the United States increased its role in the Vietnam War in the 1960s, a sense of the Anadyr effect on its American counterparts may have led to the Soviet government's decision to provide massive economic and military assistance to North Vietnam. But only military advisors and instructors were sent to North Vietnam—combat troops were not dispatched, nor were fighter pilots (as occurred in the Korean War and in Cuba). Undoubtedly, the Soviets did not want another direct encounter with U.S. military forces. Consequently, military equipment sent to North Vietnam was moved by railroad (through China) and not by sea.[22] There was never any question raised within the Soviet ruling circles of sending nuclear weapons to Vietnam—or elsewhere beyond the borders of the Soviet Union and its satellite Warsaw Pact states.[23]

The Forces Left Behind

The Soviet backdown in Cuba was complete. Not only were the offensive missiles withdrawn, but so were the relatively benign Il-28 Beagle light bombers, the nuclear-capable tactical missiles, and subsequently, most of the ground combat forces.

However, one regiment-sized ground combat group remained in Cuba. A force of several thousand heavily armed troops was maintained on the island until the end of the Cold War. Periodically, transport aircraft arrived in Cuba with replacement troops, while cargo ships brought in updated weapons. This combat force—usually referred to in the Western press as a "combat brigade" of some twenty-five hundred troops—was "discovered" by President Jimmy Carter in 1979, who accused the Soviets of breaking the terms of the 1962 agreement by keeping combat troops on the island. Tensions built until the Soviet Union assured the White House that its troops in Cuba had neither the intention nor the capability of invading American territory.

President Carter had it wrong, however. Ground forces were never a part of the 1962 agreement between the Soviet Union and the United States. The remaining brigade served as a symbol of the Soviet relationship with Cuba and—to a limited degree—was a practical deterrent to U.S. military action against Cuba.

Far more significant than the combat brigade was a massive signals intelligence facility near Havana at Lourdes, which the Soviet intelligence community established in 1962.[24] Called the most sophisticated Soviet "spy base" outside of the Eastern Bloc when it was publicly revealed by the U.S. government in March 1985, Lourdes was credited with being able to monitor telephone conversations in the southeastern United States; space activities at Cape Canaveral, Florida; and transmissions by U.S. commercial and military satellites.[25] At that time, the facility was operated by more than 2,000 Soviet military and civilian technicians.[26]

In the mid-1980s, including the combat brigade and the Lourdes facility, the Soviets had an estimated 5,600 military personnel and 7,000 civilians in Cuba. The civilians sought to help the Cuban infrastructure and economy, with the Soviet Union supporting the latter from the early 1960s through the end of the Cold War. Cuba was almost completely dependent upon Soviet petroleum, which was purchased with crops, as the Cuban economy was short of hard currency. For much of the Cold War, the Soviet Union spent the equivalent of $1 million per day to sustain the Castro regime. Many Soviets who supported the Cuban Revolution and appreciated Castro allowing offensive missiles to be deployed to the island in 1962 felt that the economic and political support of Cuba was important for the prestige of the Soviet Union, as well as for the Socialist brotherhood. And Cuba provided other forms of payment to the Soviet Union. Cuban combat troops—armed, supplied, and transported by the Soviet government—fought for Soviet causes in Angola and Ethiopia with significant successes.

In the Western Hemisphere, Cuban paramilitary forces, initially led by Che Guevara, attacked the political systems and the governments of several South and Central American countries.[27] Furthermore, Cuba sponsored the takeover of the Caribbean island of Grenada by a Marxist government. Cubans subsequently expanded the island's airfield and stockpiled arms there, most likely for other adventures in the area.[28] Although most Cuban overseas ventures were thwarted, the Castro regime remained a problem for the United States and other democratic states in the Western Hemisphere.

From the Soviet viewpoint, there were no more inroads into South and Central America. The United States had challenged the Soviet effort to defend a revolutionary government; the U.S. government had agreed not to invade Cuba but had sent the Soviets packing. It was a major Cold War victory for the United States.

The Castro Factor

While the missile crisis was fundamentally a confrontation between the United States and the Soviet Union, the focus of the confrontation was Cuba. The largest island in the Caribbean, Cuba at its closest point is ninety miles from U.S. territory. The United States, both directly and through surrogates, sought to destroy the Castro government, although it was obvious that the overwhelming majority of the island's almost 7 million people had rejected the deposed Batista regime and did support Castro.

Fidel Castro took control of the country on January 1, 1959. While he initially espoused a pro-American policy, efforts of pro-Batista refugees in the United States to hurt and embarrass the new Cuban government and Castro's establishment of a socialist state, including the nationalization of foreign commercial interests, soon alienated the United States. The Eisenhower administration exacerbated the estrangement by freezing Cuban assets in the United States, imposing trade sanctions, preventing Cuba from obtaining weapons from Western Europe, and, in January 1961, breaking off diplomatic relations.

This last action led to an immediate Cuban military alert against a feared U.S. invasion. The April 1961 landing at the Bay of Pigs confirmed these fears. The Cuban victory over the invaders served to demonstrate the unity of the country, while Castro, seen commanding from a Soviet-provided self-propelled gun, became an icon of defiance against American imperialism.[29] In response, Castro gladly accepted massive Soviet military assistance—as well as economic support—and stepped up the readiness of his nation to repel an assault by American military forces. The periodic raids against Cuba carried out by the CIA under Operation Mongoose, coupled with continual reports of American preparations for overt military action against Cuba, confirmed the validity of Havana's concerns.

Thus, Premier Khrushchev's proposal to base strategic missiles in Cuba to deter an American assault was quickly accepted by Castro. The acceptance, according to José Fernández, a key Castro lieutenant, would "show Cuba was with the socialist countries in the battle with the USA."[30] Jorge Risquet, another Castro confidant, recalled that "the people were behind us" in accepting the missiles.[31] "The peasants knew that these were big weapons . . . and would help defend us."

However, according to Carlos Lechuga, also a Castro confidant and Cuba's ambassador to the United Nations during the missile crisis, "Castro has said that if he had known of the United States' strategic lead over the Soviet Union, Cuba wouldn't have agreed to having the missiles and would have advised the Soviet government to be more prudent."[32]

The Soviet capitulation and withdrawal of the ballistic missiles shocked the Cuban leadership: "The Cuban people's frustration was deep and vociferous," wrote Lechuga. He added, "The Soviets who were in

Cuba, risking their lives, also felt bitter about what Moscow had done."[33] Khrushchev had not discussed the withdrawal with Castro beforehand; Cuban officials contend that Castro first learned of the U.S.-Soviet agreement over the radio. At that time, "the Soviets did not say a word about it," declared Risquet.[34]

Castro went on the radio to announce that the Cuban people would defend themselves even without the Soviet missiles. But "we felt that we had been left alone," recalled Fernández. Soviet-Cuban relations were severely damaged, and it would take many years—and a visit by Castro to the Soviet Union in 1964—to heal that damage. The removal of the Soviet ballistic missiles and, subsequently, the Il-28 bombers did not quell Cuban fears that the United States would invade the island. Fernández felt that there was a threat of invasion with President Kennedy under pressure from "the Pentagon and political leaders" to do so. Cuban forces remained on high alert until late November 1962.

Also, Castro would not allow UN inspectors to visit the missile sites, as demanded by the United States. In the view of the Cuban leadership, there was never a formal agreement by the United States not to invade the island. There was strong feeling by many Cubans that the United States still planned an invasion even after the missiles and the bombers had been removed. In the Cuban view, only the U.S. engagement in Vietnam and the massive commitment of forces to that war stopped the Americans from coming to Cuba.

Had the United States invaded Cuba, it would be a "very costly war for Cuba . . . but we would prevail," said Risquet.[35] He—and other Cubans—use the example of the American defeat in the Vietnam War as an example of how Cuba would prevail over an assault by the United States after the Soviet Union withdrew the missiles.

The Nuclear Factor

As U.S. and Soviet forces went to lesser degrees of readiness after the missile crisis, there was extensive speculation in several spheres about how close the two superpowers may have come to a nuclear exchange. As time passed, participants—in their memoirs and at public conferences—revealed the extent of nuclear readiness, especially the number of nuclear warheads that were sent to Cuba. After tensions receded, there were efforts to reduce the probability of a future nuclear exchange by addressing the mutual concerns of both the United States and the Soviet Union.

A first-order concern for both sides was the slow speed of diplomatic communications between the White House and the Kremlin—twelve hours or more for a simple text message to be exchanged between the superpower leaders. Accordingly, a "hot line" was established in 1963 to facilitate communications between the two capitals. The Washington terminal is in the Pentagon, the Moscow terminal in the Kremlin. As established, the Kremlin terminal used earth satellite stations near Lvov and Vladivostok, with the system using both land-sea cable routes and satellites to ensure rapid and reliable transmissions. In both locations, Soviet and U.S. high-speed teletypes—not voice telephones—are installed side by side. Initially, the two nations alternated transmitting test messages every hour, 24 hours a day, 365 days per year. While "operational" messages sent between Washington and Moscow have been classified, the hot line existed to reduce tension when possible. By all accounts, it has functioned well and represents the top priority for diplomatic communications in times of crisis.

Satellite surveillance has also abetted calm during a crisis. Supplementing other air, ground, and naval intelligence-collection systems, satellites have provided the national leaders with increased confidence in understanding a potential enemy's intentions. For example, during the Middle East War of 1973, the Soviet Union undertook a large buildup of naval forces in the Mediterranean. This was the largest Soviet force yet assembled in the Mediterranean. (By October 31, there were ninety-six Soviet ships, including twenty-three submarines and thirty-four surface combatants.)[36]

The Sixth Fleet Commander, Vice Admiral Daniel Murphy, wrote, "The U.S. Sixth Fleet and the Soviet Mediterranean Fleet were, in effect, sitting in a pond in close proximity and the stage for the hitherto unlikely "war at sea" scenario was set. This situation prevailed for several days. Both fleets were obviously in a high readiness posture for whatever might come next, although it appeared that neither fleet knew exactly what to expect."[37]

Meanwhile, in Washington, D.C., intelligence analysts pored over satellite photography; their quest was to determine whether the Soviet Union was readying its strategic missiles or bomber force—in other words, going to a higher state of combat readiness. While the images revealed greatly increased activity at the bases of several Soviet airborne divisions, there was no increase in activity at the ICBM missile sites, the strategic submarine bases, and the long-range bomber bases. There were absolutely no indications that the Soviets were considering a possible nuclear exchange in 1973. Supported by several exchanges of messages over the hot line, the 1973 Yom Kippur War went into the history books as a war between Arabs and Israelis, not between Americans and Soviets.

The same perspective was not always true on the Soviet side. In May 1981, Soviet leader Leonid Brezhnev and KGB Chairman Yuri Andropov made a joint appearance before a closed session of senior KGB officers. Brezhnev took the podium first and told the assembled intelligence officers of his concerns about U.S. policy under President Ronald Reagan, who had entered the White House four months earlier. Andropov then asserted that the United States was making preparations for a surprise nuclear attack on the Soviet Union. The KGB and the GRU, he declared, would join forces to mount a new intelligence-collection effort to monitor indications and provide early warning of U.S. war preparations. The effort was given the code name RYAN—an acronym from the Russian *Raketno-Yadernoye Napadenie* (Nuclear Missile Attack).

Supporting the Soviet paranoia, an armada of eighty-three U.S., British, Canadian, and Norwegian ships, led by the nuclear-propelled aircraft carrier *Dwight D. Eisenhower*, had managed in an August–September 1981 exercise to transit from the Atlantic into the Norwegian Sea undetected. The naval force used a variety of carefully crafted and previously rehearsed concealment and deception measures. A combination of passive measures (maintaining radio silence and operating under emissions-control conditions) and active measures (radar-jamming and transmission of false radar signals) turned the allied force into something resembling a stealth fleet, which even managed to elude a Soviet low-orbit, active-radar satellite that was launched to locate it.[38] The exercise—with the *Eisenhower* carrying nuclear-capable strike aircraft—was of great concern to the Soviet leadership.

Soviet concerns were raised another notch on March 23, 1981, when President Reagan announced his plan for a national missile defense system—which the press promptly dubbed "Star Wars," after the series of films produced by George Lucas. Four days after the president's announcement—and in direct response to it—Andropov lashed out. Having succeeded to the head of the Soviet leadership upon Brezhnev's death in November 1982, the career KGB officer accused the United States of preparing a first-strike attack on the Soviet Union and asserted that President Reagan was "inventing new plans on how to unleash a nuclear war in the best way, with the hope of winning it."[39]

In March 1982, the senior KGB officer in charge of coordinating requirements at the agency's headquarters was sent to Washington to oversee the collection of indications-and-warning intelligence. Furthermore, RYAN intelligence was placed in the daily briefing books for members of the Politburo. On February 17, 1983, KGB headquarters notified all senior officers in foreign embassies (*Rezidents*) that RYAN had "acquired an especial degree of urgency" and was "now of particularly grave importance."[40] The KGB *Rezidents* received new orders instructing them to organize a "continual watch" using their entire operational staffs.[41]

In April–May 1983, forty ships of the U.S. Pacific Fleet conducted another major exercise, with a high degree of stealth. Those ships came within 450 miles of the Kamchatka Peninsula and Petropavlovsk, the main Soviet missile submarine base in the Pacific Theater. The U.S. carriers *Midway* and *Enterprise*—the latter a veteran of the Cuban crisis—both had nuclear-capable strike aircraft embarked. Once again, Soviet leaders were deeply concerned over what they considered to be an intrusion into their home waters, and tensions rose.

Then, in the fall of 1983, a NATO command post exercise called Able Archer included a practice drill that took NATO forces through a large-scale simulated release of nuclear weapons. In response, on November 8 or 9, KGB headquarters sent a flash cable to West European operatives advising them—incorrectly—that U.S. forces in Europe had gone on alert and that troops at some bases were being mobilized. The cable speculated that the (nonexistent) alert might have been ordered in response to the recent bomb attack on the U.S. Marine barracks in Beirut that had killed more than two hundred Americans, or that it was related to impending U.S. Army maneuvers, *or that it was the beginning of a countdown to a surprise nuclear attack.* The cable recipients were asked to confirm the U.S. alert and evaluate these hypotheses. Soon, in the tense atmosphere generated by the crises and the rhetoric of the past few months, some KGB officials concluded that American forces had been placed on alert—and might even have begun the countdown to war.

A short time later the alert dissipated, in part because President Reagan reduced his rhetoric against the USSR in light of indications that the Soviets were reacting poorly to U.S. stimuli. Andropov's death, at age sixty-nine, in February 1984 also contributed to the resolution of the threat.

The alert was a crash program to create a strategic warning system in response to new threats and challenges the Soviets saw looming on the horizon. That response was panicky but not paranoid. The historian William Fuller, rejecting the paranoia thesis that has often been used to explain the Soviet reaction to technologically superior Western military power, captured the point when he wrote: "At various times Russian strategists were acutely fearful. But those fears, although at times extreme, were scarcely insane."[42]

President Reagan said in his memoirs—without reference to British intelligence reports or Able Archer—that in late 1983 he was surprised to learn that "many people at the top of the Soviet hierarchy were genuinely afraid of America and Americans," and "many Soviet officials feared us not only as adversaries but as potential aggressors who might hurl nuclear weapons at them in a first strike."[43]

The former KGB officer Oleg Gordievsky later wrote: "The world did not quite reach the edge of the nuclear abyss during Operation RYAN. But during Able Archer 83 it had, without realizing it, come frighteningly close—certainly closer than at any time since the Cuban missile crisis of 1962."[44]

Significantly, in comparison to the 1962 missile crisis, the RYAN crisis two decades later found the Soviet Union with strategic weapons parity and, in some categories, superiority. While the Soviet Union had gone to a high state of strategic forces alert in 1983, the United States did not. Never again after the Cuban Missile Crisis did U.S. strategic forces go to the DEFCON-2 alert.

There is one other aspect of President Reagan's hard-line pronouncements. His condemnation of the Soviet Union and threats—both veiled and direct—to defeat communist advances in the Third World led Fidel Castro to again fear an attack against his island bastion of communism in the Western Hemisphere. Sometime in 1981, Castro met with a visiting Soviet general and urged that the Soviet Union prevent the United States from deploying a new generation of theater nuclear missiles to Western Europe.

These were ground-launch cruise missiles, a variant of the U.S. Navy's highly successful Tomahawk, and ground-launch Pershing II ballistic missiles. The Reagan administration initiated a massive deployment of these weapons to counter the earlier Soviet deployment of SS-20 multi-warhead ballistic missiles that could target European NATO countries.

Castro then proposed that if the U.S. missile buildup in Western Europe continued, the Soviet Union should again establish strategic missile bases in Cuba as a counter move. So far as is known, Castro's proposal received no consideration in the Kremlin.

Intelligence Successes and Failures: Lessons Unlearned

One other aspect of Operation Anadyr warrants attention in reviewing the Cuban crisis: the successes and failures of intelligence operations on both sides. The Soviet Union, in great secrecy, made the decisions to pursue Operation Anadyr. The Soviets prepared the plans; moved the missiles, troops, and equipment to ports; and embarked and transported them to Cuba—all without the watching U.S. ships and aircraft being able to accurately determine the nature of their cargoes. The size and complexity of Anadyr, coupled with it being a joint or multiservice operation undertaken in a few months, make it one of the most remarkable military achievements of the Cold War by either superpower. That a failure of intelligence policy by the Kennedy administration almost allowed Anadyr to succeed is a lesson that today's political, military, and intelligence community leaders would be well advised to take heed of.

During the late summer of 1962, the Kennedy administration had its focus on places other than Cuba. Racial integration of schools in the American South was being pushed, there was growing concern over a possible war between India and China, and the United States hoped to negotiate with the Soviet Union a treaty banning aboveground testing of nuclear weapons. This last item was a priority for Secretary of State Rusk and National Security Advisor Bundy. Finally, the status of Berlin remained a perennial Cold War problem.

When the first of the SA-2 missile sites appeared in western Cuba in late August 1962, the intelligence community took the view that a closer look at western Cuba with continuing U-2 overflights was needed. However, concern over a possible U-2 shoot down by an SA-2 missile led the Kennedy national security team to recommend to the president that additional overflights be withheld. The result was a moratorium of more than six weeks on U-2 overflights over western Cuba, during which all three of the Soviet SS-4 ballistic missile regiments were unloaded and moved to their basing areas.

Since that decision about the U-2 flights, there has been a combative discussion on how the intelligence community failed to warn President Kennedy of the growing threat of nuclear-armed ballistic missiles in Cuba. In fact, the opposite is true, as President Kennedy and his national security team chose to turn a blind eye to the emerging threat in Cuba. This "intelligence failure" has been the subject of books and articles for four decades, although rarely has the finger of responsibility been aimed at those actually responsible: President Kennedy and his national security advisors. What had occurred was a failure of intelligence policy, *not* a failure of the intelligence community.[45]

Only the continued efforts of the intelligence community over the following six weeks eventually provided the information necessary to convince President Kennedy of the need for at least one U-2 mission over western Cuba. That overflight—Mission 3101—took the photos that quickly and positively allowed Airman Michael Davis, Art Lundahl, and Lundahl's NPIC team to determine the true state of affairs in Cuba.[46] Quite simply, President Kennedy and his closest advisors had not been able to imagine Nikita Khrushchev lying to them about something that they had specifically warned him not to do. That bit of naive political trust very nearly led to a nuclear war.

Fortunately, John McCone and other intelligence professionals not only could imagine such an act by Khrushchev but also saw the threat of Soviet missiles in Cuba as a real possibility. Members of the intelligence community kept up a relentless surveillance of the ships headed to Cuba and electronic signals coming from the island until they found the crucial piece of information that turned the tide: the discovery on September 28 of ten crated Il-28 Beagle bombers on the Soviet freighter *Kasimov*. The Il-28 was listed as an "offensive" weapon because of its nuclear capability, and that fact triggered Mission 3101 on October 14. President Kennedy had been lucky and as a result had the critical week from October 16 to October 22 to work out a strategy to try to end the crisis peacefully.

But what if the intelligence community had missed the September 28 sighting of the crated bombers on the deck of the *Kasimov*? The available records indicate that the next known detection of material related to offensive weapons on Cuba came more than three weeks later, on October 21. The U.S. spy ship *Oxford* detected a radar signal specific to the SS-4 missile system and flashed the news to NSA headquarters at Fort Meade, Maryland. So key was that intercept that a U.S. Navy helicopter was sent out to pick up the tape recordings from the *Oxford* later that day to confirm the assessment.[47] Combined with Ironbark material supplied by Oleg Penkovsky, that radar emission enabled NSA analysts to determine that an SS-4 regiment had probably become operational, ready to fire its missiles if ordered.

It would have taken another day for NSA to confirm the initial assessment and brief the president and ExComm. Undoubtedly, Kennedy would have ordered a full-scale reconnaissance effort to confirm the NSA assessment, probably with U-2s followed a day or two later by low-level F8U-1P Crusaders. Given the usual delays for planning, flying the missions, processing the film, and assessing the "take," the earliest that ExComm would have had confirmation of the true scale and intent of the Anadyr deployment would have been October 26 or 27. By then, the situation in Cuba would have looked like this:

- All three SS-4 regiments would have been operational, with twenty-four launchers and thirty-six missiles ready to fire.

- The freighter *Poltava* with the twenty-four SS-5 IRBMs on board would have reached Cuba, allowing those missiles to be ready for firing sometime in November.
- The SA-2 missile systems and the MiG-21 interceptors would have been fully operational, making aerial reconnaissance of Cuba very hazardous.
- All four of the Soviet ground battle groups—including their supporting artillery, FROGs, and FKR-1s—would have been deployed and fully operational.
- The submarines of the 69th Brigade would have made landfall in Cuba, allowing them to make repairs, refuel, and restock, and be ready to go to sea when required.

This would have left President Kennedy and his advisors with few options and very little time to react. The most likely solution would have an immediate implementation of either OPLAN 314 or 316, with the air campaign beginning about November 1 (see chapter 14). This would have been followed a few days later by the invasion, assuming that General Pliyev did not receive instruction to fire the SS-4s that survived the early air strikes. That would have caused an immediate counterforce strike by the SAC ready force of B-47s, which would have carpeted central and western Cuba with 10- and 20-megaton thermonuclear bombs.[48] One thing is certain, however: the Cuban Missile Crisis would probably have turned into a shooting war, with thousands and possibly millions of lives lost. Whatever the developments from there, the results would have certainly branded John Kennedy's policy not to have the U-2s overfly western Cuba in the late summer of 1962 as the worst intelligence policy decision in history.

However, the U.S Navy patrol planes *did* find the *Kasimov* and photographed the crates with the Il-28s packed inside. This forced President Kennedy and his senior advisors to allow Mission 3101 to go forward and bought them a full week to consider their plans and options. In the end, only "one shot," the SA-2 fired at Major Anderson's U-2 on October 27, was exchanged between the United States and the Soviet Union, with but one combat death resulting.

Still, it is likely that the brothers Kennedy were thinking about the consequences of possible inaction on the evening of October 22 after the president's speech when Bobby said, "Well, there isn't any choice. I mean, you would have been, you would have been impeached." The president's reply was, "Well, I think I would have been impeached."[49]

He had the professionals of the U.S. intelligence community to thank for the time to have that moment of introspection at the height of the Cuban Missile Crisis.

Others may have been thinking about the judgment of history as well. In early 1963, the Kennedy administration was already beginning to develop cover against any criticism of the U-2 overflight moratorium. A memorandum circulated on February 27, 1963, stated:

> It should be noted that mission planning and Go-No Go decisions for high-altitude missions over Cuba had to be based on weather forecasts for targets as much as 48 hours in advance of take-off-time.
>
> Weather forecasts used in connection with mission planning are provided by the Global Weather Center at SAC Headquarters, Offutt Air Force Base, Nebraska. Between 5 September and 14 October, poor to bad weather prevailed over target areas in Cuba for 30 of 40 days.[50]

Clearly, senior Kennedy administration officials were nervous about questions regarding Cuba overflights during the moratorium period and were trying to use poor weather as an excuse to cover poor intelligence policy. What nobody mentioned at the time, and the memo does not address, is that overflights of western Cuba were not allowed during this period. That fact has waited four decades to be properly addressed.

Another critical lesson from the 1962 Cuban crisis is that intelligence assets need to be properly designed, sized, and staffed; otherwise, their performance will be "hit or miss" at best. The success of the entire intelligence community in uncovering the true intent of the Anadyr deployment, despite the limitations imposed upon it by President Kennedy and his advisors, was one of its greatest successes. However, almost as quickly as that success had exposed the Soviet missile deployment on Cuba, those same intelligence agencies began to miss crucial details that could have been disastrous.

Following Mission 3101 on October 14, eight additional U-2 missions (numbers 3102 through 3109) were flown over the next two days to provide complete coverage of Cuba. Thirteen additional U-2 missions were successfully flown before the shoot down of Major Rudolph Anderson on October 27 (Mission 3127). In addition, beginning on October 23, dozens of additional low-level photoreconnaissance missions were flown by Commander Ecker and his F8U-1P pilots.[51] This sudden glut of imagery caught Art Lundahl's NPIC short of personnel and resources,

A Soviet-erected nuclear warhead bunker, one of several installed in Cuba. U.S. reconnaissance aircraft kept close watch on the bunkers, but the large number of nuclear warheads brought into Cuba were never placed in the bunkers.

unable to glean much of the critical information contained in the photos. Similar problems developed at other offices within the CIA, the NSA, and various branches of military intelligence, as they reached their maximum capacity to assess the incoming data flow. Like someone trying to take a drink from a fire hose, there was no way to effectively sift the key bits of intelligence data from the flood of incoming information.

Missed were most of the dozens of battlefield nuclear weapons deployed to support the Group of Soviet Forces in Cuba defending the SS-4 ballistic missile regiments. The eighty FKR-1 cruise missiles were *never* identified by American intelligence. Worse, none of the warheads for the SS-4s were *ever* reported by any U.S. intelligence agency, although several nuclear storage bunkers were located while under construction. The status of the SS-4 regiments and SA-2 surface-to-air missile sites was carefully monitored throughout the crisis, and the Kennedy administration never lacked for data on these critical targets. The problem was that anything "below" that level of interest rarely was reported to the ExComm participants. Even the one known report of FROG battlefield rockets failed to have any impact, and the fact that they might be armed with nuclear warheads was never emphasized in either the daily briefing documents or the briefing boards from NPIC.[52] There simply was not the base of personnel, equipment, and facilities to handle the intelligence flow from a crisis as large and complex as the Cuban Missile Crisis.

Strangely, the responsibility for this failure was the same as that which allowed the Soviet ballistic missiles to be discovered in the first place: Art Lundahl and his NPIC establishment. When the U-2 and Corona satellite programs began in the 1950s, the creation of the organization to analyze the photos that were generated was left to Lundahl and just five other CIA employees. The result was that while NPIC grew to accommodate the expanded need for information across an increasing number of areas around the world in the late 1950s and early 1960s, the organization was totally unprepared for what it had to deal with during the Cuban Missile Crisis.

So while NPIC in the late summer of 1962 was perfectly designed and sized to provide strategic warning about a possible nuclear strike against the United States, it was never designed to deal with the flow of information (tactical, operational, *and* strategic) that came with the Cuban Missile Crisis. It's not that Lundahl and his subordinates were negligent in their creation and design of NPIC. Art Lundahl, Dino Brugioni, and the hundreds of dedicated men and women at NPIC are owed a debt for their efforts that cannot possibly be paid by the American people. No one in the CIA or anywhere in the U.S. intelligence community imagined that a situation like the one in Cuba that summer might ever develop, and this led to a severe capacity and capability shortfall at NPIC and other agencies to handle to flow of photography and other data that was produced during the crisis.

Such failures of imagination are often the cause of mass disaster. This disaster might have occurred in Cuba in October 1962. It would behoove individuals who have the job of structuring intelligence agencies and their capabilities to spend time and effort imagining just what kinds of threats must be monitored in the future and what tools should be used to accomplish these tasks.

One more crucial intelligence lesson can be learned from the 1962 Cuban crisis: technology is not the entire answer to the problem of timely and useful intelligence collection. *People* on the ground in Cuba gave the first indications that the United States had reasons to be concerned in the summer of 1962. Using technology alone and forbidden to fly the U-2s over western Cuba by President Kennedy, the prime U.S. intelligence gathering establishment—the Central Intelligence Agency—concluded and reported that "no nuclear weapons or missile nose cones have been identified in Cuba."[53] U.S. intelligence failures in Vietnam, Iran, Iraq, Lebanon, and Central America show that human intelligence collection, no matter how costly and potentially repugnant it might be, is a priority in a capable and balanced intelligence community.

This is particularly relevant in the twenty-first century, as surreptitious entry into unsuspecting countries is a topic of continuing concern. Just nineteen men with box cutters and pepper gas, none of whom had committed an overt illegal act prior to boarding their flights, conducted the 9/11 attacks. Tragically, $40 billion a year of expenditures in the U.S. intelligence budget had not guaranteed that the necessary human assets for detecting those terrorists, including translators and field personnel, were ready on September 11, 2001. It remains to be seen whether this vital lesson will ever be learned.[54]

One more point about people goes back to the very origins of the crisis. President Kennedy and Premier Khrushchev had, prior to the crisis, only one face-to-face meeting: the tempestuous June 1961 summit meeting in Vienna. Following that unpleasant introduction, neither man felt the desire for a follow-up meeting before the Cuban Missile Crisis. In fact, that mutual decision may have been the reason the crisis occurred. While the two leaders conducted an extensive and frequent exchange of notes and letters, they were never intellectually intimate or genuinely friendly. At best, the two became thermonuclear "pen pals," often sending trivial notes while plotting to gain an advantage against the other.

Both Kennedy and Khrushchev made significant mistakes in the year following the Vienna summit, creating the conditions that drove the United States and the Soviet Union into the crisis. Kennedy, stinging from the Bay of Pigs fiasco, the Vienna summit, the building of the Berlin Wall, and the United States falling behind in the space race, actively confronted Khrushchev on a number of fronts, while also trying to kill or overthrow Castro. Khrushchev, on the other hand, sought to redress the strategic forces imbalance with the United States while protecting the Castro regime from what appeared to be an inevitable U.S. invasion. The result was that in the spring of 1962, Khrushchev initiated Operation Anadyr with little insight into Kennedy's likely reaction if he discovered strategic weapons in Cuba.

The meeting of Nikita Khrushchev and John F. Kennedy in Vienna in June 1961 did not go well. Still, it helped to establish links between the two leaders, both of whom relied on confidants for direct exchanges of communications.

While it is unlikely that the two men ever could have become friends, a greater understanding and insight into each other could not have helped but to foster more understanding of the other's motivations and potential reactions. Khrushchev might have realized that Kennedy was serious when he warned of the consequences of moving offensive weapons into Cuba and that he was willing to go to the brink of nuclear war to enforce his policy. Kennedy, on the other hand, might have realized that Khrushchev considered protecting the Castro regime a top foreign policy objective, one worth moving powerful offensive weapons and almost fifty thousand troops thousands of miles to preserve. Neither man did, and the result was nearly a nuclear war.

It is worth noting that with the exception of Lyndon Johnson, every president since then has made face-to-face meetings and even social events an important part of the dialogue between the superpowers. Even Ronald Reagan, who faced the challenge of having three Soviet premiers die during his first four years in office, met Mikhail Gorbachev as soon as he had consolidated his position in the Kremlin. The two men became genuine friends and signed the first true nuclear disarmament treaty, the Intermediate Nuclear Forces accords, to eliminate the very class of weapons that had almost brought the world to the brink in 1962.[55]

The United States had a significant superiority over the Soviet Union in strategic weapons at the time of the missile crisis. Here, President Kennedy watches a Polaris missile launch from a submarine one week before his assassination. Rear Admiral I. G. (Pete) Galantin, the head of the Polaris program, is at left.

* * *

Despite being "enemies" for the remaining twenty-nine years of the Cold War, neither the United States nor the Soviet Union was ever so reckless as they were in 1961 and 1962. While mistakes and missteps did occur, there has never been a crisis that came as near to nuclear war as that of October 1962. Choosing not to engage in nuclear confrontations may well be the ultimate legacy of Khrushchev's gamble with Operation Anadyr in 1962. As President Kennedy said in his famous speech at American University on June 10, 1963, "For in the final analysis, our most basic common link is that we all inhabit this small planet. We all breathe the same air. We all cherish our children's future. And we are all mortal."[56]

APPENDIX A

The Membership of ExComm

The Executive Committee of the National Security Council was established on October 22, 1962, under NSC Action Memorandum No. 196, as an advisory body to President Kennedy. Previously, the body was referred to as "the group" and "the war council" of the National Security Council. Its members included the following:

George Ball, *Under Secretary of State*
McGeorge Bundy, *National Security Advisor*
C. Douglas Dillon, *Secretary of the Treasury**
Roswell Gilpatrick, *Deputy Secretary of Defense*
U. Alexis Johnson, *Deputy Under Secretary of State*
Robert Kennedy, *Attorney General**
Edwin Martin, *Assistant Secretary of State for Latin America*
John McCone, *Director of Central Intelligence*
Paul Nitze, *Assistant Secretary of Defense for International Security Affairs*
Walter Rostow, *State Department policy planner*
Dean Rusk, *Secretary of State**
Theodore Sorenson, *Special Counsel to the President*
General Maxwell Taylor, U.S. Army, *Chairman, Joint Chiefs of Staff*
Llewellyn Thompson, *Ambassador at Large for Soviet Affairs*

The following individuals attended some ExComm meetings at the invitation of President Kennedy:

Henry H. Fowler, *Under Secretary of the Treasury*
Roger Hillsman, *Assistant Secretary of State for Intelligence and Research*
Lyndon B. Johnson, *Vice President*
Robert Lovett, *Former Secretary of Defense*
Edward A. McDermott, *Director of the Office of Emergency Preparedness*
Kenneth O'Donnell, *Assistant to the President*
Adlai Stevenson, *Ambassador to the United Nations*
Donald Wilson, *Acting Director, U.S. Information Agency*

---

*Member of the Cabinet

APPENDIX B

U-2 Missions Flown
during Operation Anadyr

Date	Interval in Days between Missions	Mission Number	Coverage	Results
Aug. 5, 1962		3086	Overflight of entire island (CIA mission)	Located early Anadyr deployment of equipment and personnel
Aug. 29, 1962	24	3088	Overflight of entire island (CIA mission)	Eight SA-2 SAM sites identified in western Cuba
Sept. 5, 1962	7	3089	Overflight of eastern and central Cuba only; western area restricted due to SAM threat (CIA mission)	Three additional SA-2 SAM sites and MiG-21 interceptors identified
Sept. 26, 1962	21	3093	Peripheral flight (CIA mission)	Additional SA-2 SAM sites identified
Sept. 29, 1962	3	3095	Peripheral flight with short overflight of Isle of Pines and south-central Cuba (CIA mission)	Additional SA-2 SAM sites identified
Oct. 5, 1962	6	3098	Peripheral flight (CIA mission)	Additional SA-2 SAM sites identified
Oct. 7, 1962	2	3100	Peripheral flight (CIA mission)	Additional SA-2 SAM sites identified
Oct. 14, 1962	7	3101	Overflight of western Cuba (USAF mission)	Located first regiment of Soviet SS-4 MRBMs near San Cristobal
Oct. 15, 1962	1	3102 and 3103	Multimission coverage of entire Cuban land-mass (USAF missions)	A total of 5 SS-4 MRBM and 23 SA-2 SAM sites are confirmed; possible SS-5 IRBM equipment identified
Oct. 17, 1962	2	3104, 3105, 3106, 3107, 3108, and 3109	Multimission coverage of entire Cuban land-mass (USAF missions)	Three SS-4 MRBM and 2 SS-5 IRBM regiments, along with 24 SA-2 SAM sites, located and confirmed

Date	Interval in Days between Missions	Mission Number	Coverage	Results
Oct. 18, 1962	1	3111	Coverage of entire Cuban landmass (USAF mission)	First indications of SS-4 missiles ready to fire, nuclear warhead storage site, 6 SA-2 support sites, and 12 Komar-class missile patrol boats
Oct. 19, 1962	1	3113 and 3114	Multimission coverage of entire Cuban landmass (USAF missions)	Indications that up to half of the SS-4s may be ready to fire
Oct. 20, 1962	1	3115, 3116, and 3117	Multimission coverage of entire Cuban landmass (USAF missions)	Twenty-three of 24 SA-2 SAM sites estimated to be fully operational
Oct. 22, 1962	2	3118, 3119, and 3120	Multimission coverage of entire Cuban landmass (USAF mission)	Two of 3 SS-3 regiments now estimated to become operational on October 25
Oct. 23, 1962	1	3121, 3122, and 2123	Multimission coverage of entire Cuban landmass (USAF missions)	Soviet personnel beginning to make use of camouflage at several SS-4 sites
Oct. 25, 1962	2	3125	Coverage of entire Cuban landmass (USAF mission)	Additional use of camouflage at SS-4 sites; 5 of 6 SS-4 launch sites fully operational, though readiness of final SS-4 site estimated as being delayed due to heavy rain; a single FROG rocket launcher is located
Oct. 27, 1962	2	3127(?)	Coverage of entire Cuban landmass (USAF mission)	First of 6 scheduled U-2 missions, shot down by SA-2 site near Banes and pilot Major Rudolf Anderson Jr. killed; all further U-2 missions canceled for duration of crisis and withdrawal

U.S. Naval Forces in the Caribbean

The composition of U.S. naval forces in the Caribbean changed almost daily; what follows is a "snapshot" of the forces about the time the crisis reached its peak in mid-October 1962.

Task Force 135: Fast Carrier Attack Force

Task Group 135.1	Task Group 135.2	Task Group 135.3
Carrier Group CVA *Independence* 4 destroyers	*Carrier Group* CVAN *Enterprise* 4 destroyers	*Logistics Group* 1 ammunition ship 2 fleet oilers 1 destroyer
Later Arrivals 3 destroyers	*Later Arrivals* CVA *Saratoga* 2 destroyers	*Later Arrivals* 2 ammunition ships 10 fleet oilers 2 destroyers

Task Force 136: Quarantine Force

Task Group 136.1	Task Group 136.2	Task Group 136.3
Surface Combatants 2 heavy cruisers 14 destroyers	*ASW/HUK Group* CVS *Essex* 4 destroyers	*Logistics Group* 1 ammunition ship 1 fleet oiler 2 destroyers
	Later Arrivals CVS *Randolph* CVS *Wasp* 7 destroyers	*Later Arrivals* 2 store ships 3 oilers 1 gasoline tanker 4 destroyers

Task Force 128: Amphibious Force

LPH *Boxer*	3 Amphibious Command Ships (AGC)
LPH *Iwo Jima*	12 Amphibious Cargo Ships (AKA)
LPH *Okinawa*	12 Amphibious Transports (APA)
LPH *Thetis Bay*	3 High-Speed Transports (APD)
	15 Dock Landing Ships (LSD)
	15 Tank Landing Ships (LST)

Abbreviations
CVA = Attack Aircraft Carrier; CVAN = Attack Aircraft Carrier (nuclear);
CVS = Anti-Submarine Carrier; LPH = Helicopter Carrier; ASW = Anti-Submarine
Warfare; HUK = Hunter-Killer

Soviet Missile Characteristics

All characteristics are converted from metric measure.

FKR-1 METEOR (NATO SSC-2a Salish)

This frontal rocket—*Frontoviye Krilatiye Raketi* (FKR)—was a long-range battlefield missile, carried and launched from a towed trailer. It was similar to the naval Sopka (NATO SSC-2b Samlet), which led U.S. intelligence to mistake them both for coastal defense weapons.

Two Soviet Air Force regiments, the 561st and the 584th Frontal Cruise Missile (FKR) Regiments, were deployed to Cuba during Operation Anadyr. Each regiment had eight launchers and forty nuclear-capable missiles—a total of sixteen launchers and eighty missiles. Warheads for the missiles were brought to Cuba in the merchant ship *Indigirka* (thirty-six warheads), which arrived on October 4, and the *Alexandrovsk* (forty-four warheads), which docked in Cuba on October 23.

The FKR-1 was in Soviet service into the late 1960s.

Design: The FKR-1 resembled a diminutive MiG-15 turbojet fighter. It had a subsonic speed.

Design:	Mikoyan
Operational:	1955
Weight:	approx. 6,700 lb.
Length:	23 ft.
Wingspan:	15 ft., 5 in.
Diameter:	approx. 35 in.
Propulsion:	turbojet
Range:	approx. 50–60 mi.
Guidance:	inertial
Warhead:	nuclear (14 KT)

3R9/10 LUNA (NATO FROG-3/5)

The Luna/FROG (Free Rocket Over Ground) was a short-range battlefield missile widely used by the Soviet Ground Forces and by many Soviet allies and neutral nations. The FROG-3/5 versions were produced in the largest numbers of the FROG family of rockets.

In 1962, the Soviet weapons sent to Cuba included a Luna battalion, which contained three FROG batteries, each with a pair of mobile launchers and six missiles (a total of twelve nuclear FROG-5s and twenty-four conventional FROG-3s). Twelve nuclear warheads were available, four per battery. The warheads arrived in Cuba on October 4 in the *Indigirka*.

Design: The basic missile had four small cruciform fins at the tail; the nuclear version had a warhead section with a larger diameter than the body of the rocket. The missile was spin stabilized. The missile launcher was mounted on a PT-76 tank chassis, providing a high degree of battlefield mobility.

Operational: FROG missiles were first seen publicly on parade in Moscow's Red Square on November 7, 1957. FROG-3/7 missiles with conventional warheads were employed by Egyptians in 1973 to support their crossing of the Suez Canal. When the Israeli counteroffensive crossed the canal, FROGs were used against the bridgehead. The Syrians fired twenty to twenty-five FROG-2/3 missiles with conventional warheads against Israel in the 1973 war; the Syrian FROGs failed to hit any military targets (and two landed in Jordan).

Design:	Unknown
Operational:	1961
Weight:	2,821 lb.
Length:	34 ft., 5 in.
Wingspan:	ballistic
Diameter:	16 in. body
	22 in. warhead
Propulsion:	2-stage solid-propellant rocket
Range:	approx. 18 mi.
Guidance:	Unguided (ballistic trajectory)
Warhead:	nuclear (2 KT) or conventional-chemical
	(1,100 lb.)

P-15 (NATO SS-N-2 Styx)

The Styx was a ship-launched missile, developed to provide an anti-ship capability for small combat craft operating in the coastal defense role.

Soviet doctrine appeared to call for launching the SS-N-2a variant at a range of approximately eleven to fifteen miles, or about one-half of its maximum range. Maximum speed was approximately Mach 0.9. The Square Tie radar was used to detect targets. Once launched, there was no data link to the SS-N-2a version; the missile's terminal radar seeker automatically switched on approximately five miles from the estimated target position; the missile homed in on the largest target within a group of ships.

The SS-N-2a was first deployed on Soviet Komar-class missile boats.

Design: The original Styx missile had fixed wings, compared to folding wings in later variants that extended as the missile departed the launch tube. The missile was launched with a rocket booster that fell away after leaving the tube.

Operational: Including Third World sales, the Styx was the world's most widely used anti-ship missile prior to the appearance of the French Exocet in 1973 and the U.S. Harpoon in 1977. The Styx gained international attention after Egyptian Komar boats, from inside the Port Said harbor, sank the Israeli destroyer *Eilat* that was steaming 13.5 nautical miles offshore on October 21, 1967. The weapon was subsequently used by the Indian Navy to sink a number of Pakistani ships, including the destroyer *Khaiber*, in the 1971 Indo-Pakistani conflict.

Design:	Raduga
Operational:	1958
Weight:	approx. 5,500 lb.
Length	19 ft.
Wingspan:	9 ft., 2 in.
Diameter:	29 in.
Propulsion:	turbojet with solid-fuel booster
Range:	approx. 29 mi.
Guidance:	active radar homing
Warhead:	high explosive

R-12 (NATO SS-4 SANDAL)

The SS-4 was a road-transportable Medium Range Ballistic Missile (MRBM) that had an extraordinary three-decade service life. This was the first Soviet ballistic missile to employ storable-liquid propellant, meaning that once fueled, it could be held in a state of readiness for launching for at least several days. The SS-4 was produced in large numbers, with Nikita Khrushchev boasting in 1958, after visiting the production plant in Dnepropetrovsk, that "they are making them like sausages."

Design of the SS-4 began in 1949–1950.

The 1962 Soviet deployment to Cuba consisted of the 79th, the 181st, and the 664th Missile Regiments. Each regiment had eight SS-4 launchers and twelve missiles, an aggregate of twenty-four launchers and thirty-six nuclear-armed missiles. Warheads for the missiles arrived in Cuba on the merchant ship *Indigirka* on October 4. These were 1-megaton warheads (a 2-megaton warhead was in production for the SS-4 MRBM).

A single unarmed training missile, one of several sent to Cuba in 1962, remains on display in Havana.

Design: The missile had a thick cylindrical body with a pointed nose cone. There were four small steering vanes at the tail, in line with the engine exhausts.

The reentry vehicle was 13 feet, 7 inches long, and weighed an estimated 3,300 pounds. The missile had an RD-214, four-chamber engine; it produced 135,300 pounds of thrust.

The early SS-4s had radio command guidance; all were converted to inertial guidance by 1962. The missiles were deployed at soft sites in the USSR from 1958 on and at semihard sites from 1962 on. The SS-4 served as the basis for the SL-7 space-launch vehicles, employed from 1962 to 1977. The SL-7 was used in 177 space launches to carry a variety of Soviet satellites.

Operational: The first test flight occurred on June 22, 1957. The SS-4 was first publicly displayed at a Moscow parade in November 1960. Peak deployment occurred in 1965 with 576 launchers—492 at soft sites and 84 at semihard sites. (In theory, the aboveground launch sites could be reused within four to six hours.) The SS-4 was being retired as the SS-20 Saber missile was being deployed; its retirement was accelerated by the Intermediate-range Nuclear Forces treaty, with the last SS-4 being destroyed on May 23, 1990. The INF treaty listed sixty-five SS-4 missiles and seventy-nine launchers deployed as of December 1987, although the number may have been higher; additional missiles were probably in storage and repair facilities.

Total missile production was estimated at twenty-three hundred by Western sources.

Design:	Yangel
Operational:	1958
Weight:	62,000 lb.
Length	74 ft., 8 in.
Wingspan:	ballistic
Diameter:	65 in.
Propulsion:	liquid-propellant rocket (storable)
Range:	1,300 mi.
Guidance:	radio-command/inertial
Warhead:	nuclear (1 MT)

R-14 (NATO SS-5 SKEAN)

The SS-5 was an Intermediate Range Ballistic Missile (IRBM), probably representing the final Soviet development of the German A-4 (V-2) ballistic missile design. The missile was fired from a fixed position and required the installation of a concrete launchpad.

Two missile regiments, the 665th and the 668th, with a total of sixteen SS-5 launchers and twenty-four missiles, were en route to Cuba at the time of the confrontation. The ships carrying the two regiments were ordered to turn back to the USSR. The Soviet cargo ship *Alexandrovsk* had already reached Cuba carrying twenty-four nuclear warheads for these IRBMs, but they were never unloaded, remaining on board the ship at the port of La Isabela. These were

1-megaton warheads (a warhead with a yield of 2.3 megatons for the SS-5 missile was in production at the time).

Although no longer in service, the SS-5 was included in the December 1987 INF agreement between the United States and the Soviet Union because of missiles remaining in storage; the last of those was destroyed on October 2, 1989.

Design: The missile had a storable-liquid propellant; still, it required up to eight hours to prepare for launching from a soft site; the hard-site preparation time was about fifteen minutes. In theory, the aboveground launchpads could be reused six to eight hours after a launch.

Two different reentry vehicles were tested for the SS-5, each with an estimated weight of 3,500 pounds. The Mod 1 RV had a length of 9 feet, 4 inches, and was intended for soft-site missiles; the Mod 2 RV was 7 feet, 6 inches long, and was employed for hard-site missiles. Missile CEP was approximately 1,000 yards. The SS-5 engine produced a thrust of 460,000 pounds. The missile served as the basis for the SL-8 space-launch vehicles employed from 1964 to 1987 to carry a variety of Soviet satellites. An estimated 345 missiles were used in this role.

Operational: The first flight test of the SS-5 occurred in June 1960. The first public view of the SS-5 was in Moscow's Red Square parade on November 7, 1964.

A reported ninety-seven SS-5 missiles were deployed in the Soviet Union, forty-six on aboveground launchpads and, from 1962 on, an additional fifty-one in underground silos. The aboveground pads were "soft," and the silos had minimum hardening. The phasing out of the soft-site missiles began in 1969 and of the hard-site missiles in 1971.

Design:	Yangel
Operational:	1961 (soft sites)
Weight:	216,500 lb.
Length	76 ft.
Wingspan:	ballistic
Diameter:	96 in.
Propulsion:	liquid-propellant rocket (storable)
Range:	2,800 mi.
Guidance:	inertial
Warhead:	nuclear (1 MT)

SOPKA (NATO SSC-2b SAMLET)

This was a coastal defense missile developed from the air-launched KS-1 missile (NATO AS-1 Kennel). The missiles were transported on a specialized trailer but had to be unloaded and placed on a rail-type launcher for firing. The Sopka was deployed in East Germany and Poland, as well as in the USSR.

A naval coastal defense regiment with six missiles was sent to Cuba during the missile crisis. Only conventional warheads were provided for those missiles.

Design: The Sopka resembled a small MiG-15 turbojet fighter, that is, similar to the FKR-1. It had a subsonic speed.

Design:	Mikoyan
Operational:	1957
Weight:	approx. 6,700 lb.
Length	26 ft., 3 in.
Wingspan:	15 ft., 3 in.
Diameter:	approx. 35 in.
Propulsion:	turbojet with solid-propellant booster
Range:	50 mi.
Guidance:	Probably inertial
Warhead:	nuclear or conventional

V-75 DVINA (NATO SA-2 GUIDELINE)

The SA-2 was the most widely used surface-to-air missile of the Cold War. The first SA-2 launchers were installed in 1957–1958 around Baku, Moscow, and Leningrad. Launch sites were rapidly provided to defend other industrial centers, with SA-2 deployment in the Soviet Union peaking at about 4,800 launchers by 1968.*

During the Cuban Missile Crisis, two anti-aircraft divisions were sent to Cuba with a total of 144 launchers. The Soviets deployed twenty-four firing battalions or launch sites of six launchers each. The missile battalions each had about a hundred men assigned. Each battalion launch site was centered on a (NATO) Fan Song—in 1962, it was called "Fruit Stand"—engagement radar, supported by a P-12 (NATO Spoon Rest) target acquisition radar. The designation V-75 Dvina indicated the entire missile system, including radar, launchers, and support equipment. The actual missile was designated V-750.

Design: The SA-2 was a two-stage missile with solid-propellant engines providing a Mach 3 speed.

Operational: An SA-2 missile downed the U.S. U-2 spyplane piloted by Francis Gary Powers near Sverdlovsk on May 1, 1960. The next U-2 to fall victim to an SA-2 was a Taiwanese-piloted CIA aircraft over eastern China on September 8, 1962. The third U-2 loss to an SA-2 was the aircraft flown by Major Rudolf Anderson, USAF, over Cuba on October 27, 1962, during the Cuban Missile Crisis.

---

* Steven J. Zaloga, *Soviet Air Defense Missiles: Design, Development and Tactics*. Coulsdon, Surrey, U.K.: Jane's Information Group, 1989.

SA-2s were probably responsible for shooting down four additional CIA U-2s flown by Taiwanese pilots over China, the last in 1967. China also used the SA-2 to down other Taiwanese aircraft, and Egyptian SA-2 missiles have shot down a number of Israeli aircraft.

Several thousand SA-2s were used against U.S. aircraft overflying North Vietnam from 1965 to 1973. (The U.S. aircraft shot down by SA-2s included fifteen B-52 Stratofortress strategic bombers.)

Design:	OKB-2
Operational:	1957
Weight:	5,040 lb.
Length	34 ft., 9 in.
Wingspan:	8 ft., 2 in.
Diameter:	$19\frac{2}{3}$ in. missile
	25 in. booster
Propulsion:	2-stage solid-propellant rocket
Range:	approx. 25,000 ft. altitude
Guidance:	radio command
Warhead:	high explosive (420 lb.)*

---

* Nuclear only in variant designated SA-2E Guideline Mod. 4 by NATO.

NOTES

Chapter 1. Most Dangerous Moments

1. Raymond L. Garthoff, *Reflections on the Cuban Missile Crisis* (Washington, D.C.: Brookings Institution, 1989), p. 9. Garthoff was a leading analyst at the Department of State during the missile crisis. A prolific author on Soviet political and military subjects, he was a senior advisor at the Strategic Arms Limitation Talks from 1969 to 1973 and the U.S. Ambassador to Bulgaria from 1977 to 1979.

2. The U.S. code-breaking effort was given the names Bride and, subsequently, Venona.

3. In SAC at the time, there were fewer than forty B-29s modified to deliver nuclear weapons, with an inventory of approximately fifty atomic Mk 3 bombs, all that the United States had produced from 1946 to 1948.

4. Despite some claims to the contrary, the first Soviet atomic bomb was not a pure copy of the American Mk "Fat Man" device. The espionage of spies like Klaus Fuchs, Donald Hall, and members of the Rosenberg spy ring provided Soviet scientists with a road map to the use of plutonium as fissile material and a template for the use of explosives to create an "implosion" design for the bomb itself. David Holloway, *Stalin and the Bomb* (New Haven, Conn.: Yale University Press, 1994), pp. 106–8.

5. The Tupolev design bureau used a trio of damaged American B-29s that had been interned after raids on Japan as the templates for designing the Tu-4. While some systems were of Soviet design, such as the engines and the defensive guns, the Tu-4 was an almost perfect copy of its American precursor. Approximately thirteen hundred were built and served until the mid-1950s. Von Hardesty, "Made in the USSR," *Air & Space* (February/March 2001), pp. 68–79. Also available at www.airandspacemagazine.com/ASM/Mag/Index/2001/FM/TU-4.html.

6. The congressional bunker complex at the Greenbrier Resort was closed shortly after the appearance of an article by Ted Gup, "The Ultimate Congressional Hideaway," *Washington Post Magazine* (May 31, 1992), p. W11. The article can also be found at www.washingtonpost.com/wp-srv/local/daily/july/25/brier1.htm.

7. These ships were the converted cruiser *Northampton* and the converted aircraft carrier *Wright*. A third carrier conversion was halted before completion. The conversion of the large nuclear-propelled submarine *Triton* to an underwater presidential command post was proposed but not undertaken.

8. The North Atlantic Treaty Organization (NATO), the first peacetime military alliance in which the United States participated, was established on April 4, 1949.

9. The Pentagon is a five-sided building with five concentric "rings" emanating from an open courtyard in the center. The inner ring is called the A-ring and the outermost is called the E-ring.

Chapter 2. Imbalance of Terror

1. Nikita Khrushchev, *Khrushchev Remembers* (Boston: Little, Brown, 1970), p. 408. Khrushchev made the comment at an April 1956 reception hosted by Britain's First Lord of the Admiralty in London.

2. Richard Overy, *Russia's War: Blood upon the Snow* (New York: TV Books, 1997), pp. 94–103.

3. Ibid., pp. 345–46.

4. Soviet naval policy and strategy in this period are examined extensively by Comdr. Robert Waring Herrick, USN (Ret.) in his *Soviet Naval Strategy: Fifty Years of Theory and Practice* (Annapolis, Md.: U.S. Naval Institute Press, 1968); *Soviet Naval Theory and Policy: Gorshkov's Inheritance* (Annapolis, Md.: Naval Institute Press, 1989); and other works.

5. Vladislav Zubok and Constantine Pleshakov, *Inside the Kremlin's Cold War: From Stalin to Khrushchev* (Cambridge, Mass.: Harvard University Press, 1996), pp. 138–73.

6. Ibid., pp. 174–209.

7. American dead at Pearl Harbor numbered 2,340 military personnel.

8. Norman Polmar, *Spyplane: The U-2 History Declassified* (Osceola, Wisc.: MBI, 2001), pp. 1–4.

9. Norman Friedman, *The Fifty Year War: Conflict and Strategy in the Cold War* (Annapolis, Md.: Naval Institute Press, 2000), pp. 193–210.

10. Ibid., pp. 231–40.

11. Michael R. Beschloss, *Mayday: Eisenhower, Khrushchev, and the U-2 Affair* (New York: Harper and Row, 1986), pp. 6–11.

12. Sergei N. Khrushchev, *Nikita Khrushchev and the Creation of a Superpower* (University Park: Pennsylvania State University Press, 2000).

13. The German V-2 could deliver a 2,145-pound high-explosive warhead to a distance of about 200 miles with an accuracy of about 2 miles. Some 4,320 V-2 missiles were fired operationally, many of them failures; however, a reported 1,190 missiles struck England and 1,610 missiles fell on Antwerp, Belgium. Another 600 missiles were fired in trials and training.

14. U.S.-NATO designations for Soviet missiles are used in the text. The SS-6 had the NATO name Sapwood (S indicating surface-to-surface missile). The Soviet designation was R-7 for the missile system, with the code 8K71 for the missile.

15. When the SS-7s finally began to be deployed in 1961, they were initially based in regiments, each with eight "coffin-style" launchers. The coffin launchers allowed the missiles to be stored sideways and provided a minimal level of blast protection against enemy nuclear attack. To launch the SS-7, the coffin shelter doors were opened and the empty missile erected to the vertical position, then fueled. This made for a fairly long launch cycle, which further increased the SS-7's vulnerability and drove the development of silo launchers, which began to be used in the mid-1960s. Stephen Zaloga, *Target America* (Novato, Calif.: Presidio Press, 1993), pp. 192–99.

16. Sergei N. Khrushchev, *Nikita Khrushchev*, pp. 416–29.

17. The first Soviet submarines capable of launching ballistic missiles had been the diesel-powered Project 611AB (NATO Zulu V) armed with a pair of R-11FM (NATO SS-1b SCUD-A), which began to be deployed in the late 1950s. These were followed by the Project 629 (NATO Golf) diesel ballistic missile submarines, which carried the newer

R13 (NATO SS-N-4 Sark) missile, which began patrols in 1959. None of these ballistic missile submarines were deployed during the Cuban Missile Crisis. *Source*: Zaloga, *Target America*, pp. 174–80.

18. Captain Peter Huchthausen, USN (Ret.), *K-19: The Widowmaker* (Washington, D.C.: National Geographic, 2002), pp. 61–78.

19. Jacob Neufeld, *Ballistic Missiles in the United States Air Force, 1945–1960* (Washington, D.C.: Office of Air Force History, 1989), pp. 119–48 and 185–222.

20. David K. Stumpf, *Titan II: A History of a Cold War Missile Program* (Fayetteville: University of Arkansas Press, 2000), pp. 7–36.

21. Norman Polmar and K. J. Moore, *Cold War Submarines: The Design and Construction of U.S. and Soviet Submarines* (Washington, D.C.: Brassy's, 2004), pp. 119–24.

22. Norman Polmar, *Ships and Aircraft of the U.S. Fleet*, 17th ed. (Annapolis, Md.: Naval Institute Press, 2001), pp. 61–67.

23. John D. Gresham, "NIE 11-8/1-61: The Most Dangerous Document of the Cold War," *Military History* (June 2000), pp. 22–27.

Chapter 3. The Cuban Decision: Coming to America

1. Sergei N. Khrushchev, *Nikita Khrushchev*, p. 493 (see chap. 2, n. 12).

2. Zubok and Pleshakov, *Inside the Kremlin's Cold War*, pp. 188–94 (see chap. 2, n. 5).

3. Norman Friedman, *The Fifty Year War*, pp. 231–40 (see chap. 2, n. 9).

4. Zaloga, *Target America*, pp. 194–200 (see chap. 2, n. 15).

5. Sergei N. Khrushchev, *Nikita Khrushchev*, pp. 482–483.

6. The source for this exchange is Mikoyan's son; see McGeorge Bundy, *Danger and Survival: Choices about the Bomb in the First Fifty Years* (New York: Random House, 1988).

7. Nikita Khrushchev, *Khrushchev Remembers*, p. 493 (see chap. 2, n. 1).

8. Called Operation Dominic, these U.S. nuclear tests lasted from April 25 to November 4, 1962. They consisted of thirty-six nuclear and thermonuclear weapon tests: twenty-nine weapons were dropped from aircraft, five were high-altitude missile bursts, and two were full missile-systems tests. The tests included a Navy Polaris A-1 missile and an ASROC anti-submarine rocket, the latter launched from a destroyer. Operation Dominic was the second series of nuclear tests conducted by the United States, following the breaking of a thirty-four-month voluntary test moratorium by the Soviet Union in September 1961.

9. Nikita Khrushchev, *Khrushchev Remembers*, p. 494.

10. Sergei N. Khrushchev, *Nikita Khrushchev*, pp. 484–86.

11. The deployment is described in detail in Matthias Uhl and Vladimir I. Ivkin, "'Operation Atom': The Soviet Union's Stationing of Nuclear Missiles in the German Democratic Republic, 1959," *Cold War International History Project Bulletin* (Fall/Winter 2001), pp. 299–307.

12. Sergei N. Khrushchev, *Nikita Khrushchev*, p. 486.

13. Malinovsky had close and friendly contact with Khrushchev throughout World War II.

14. Lieutenant General Anatoli I. Gribkov and General William Y. Smith, USAF (Ret.), *Operation Anadyr: U.S. and Soviet Generals Recount the Cuban Missile Crisis* (Chicago: Edition q., 1994).

15. Gribkov and Smith, *Operation Anadyr*, pp. 9–10; this wording is from Raymond Garthoff's translation for the Cold War International History Project.

16. Sergei Khrushchev, *Nikita Khrushchev*, p. 490.

17. Both the SA-2 and the SS-4 had the Soviet name Dvina (a major river in northern European Russia).

18. Characteristics of the principal Soviet missiles discussed in this volume are contained in appendix D.

19. Sergei N. Khrushchev, *Nikita Khrushchev*, p. 490.

20. Ibid., p. 490.

21. The Tu-114 was named Rossiya (Russia); the NATO reporting name was Cleat. It was the world's largest commercial airliner prior to the Boeing 747.

22. *Supplement 5 to Joint Evaluation of Soviet Missile Threat in Cuba, October 24, 1962*, in Mary S. McAuliffe, ed., *CIA Documents on the Cuban Missile Crisis 1962* (Washington, D.C.: Central Intelligence Agency, October 1992), p. 301.

23. Sergei N. Khrushchev, *Nikita Khrushchev*, p. 490.

24. James G. Blight and David A. Welch, *On the Brink: Americans and Soviets Reexamine the Cuban Missile Crisis* (New York: Hill and Wang, 1989), p. 238.

25. Sergei N. Khrushchev, *Nikita Khrushchev*, pp. 490–91.

26. Aleksandr Fursenko and Timothy Naftali, *One Hell of a Gamble: Khrushchev, Castro, and Kennedy, 1958–1964* (New York: W. W. Norton, 1997), p. 187.

27. Sergei N. Khrushchev, *Nikita Khrushchev*, p. 495.

28. Gribkov and Smith, *Operation Anadyr*, p. 25.

29. Fursenko and Naftali, *One Hell of a Gamble*, p. 189; based on the authors' interviews with Aleksandr Alekseyev, February 16, 1994, and November 15, 1995.

Chapter 4. Cuba: The American View

1. Evan Thomas, *Robert Kennedy: His Life* (New York: Simon & Schuster, 2000), pp. 119–25.

2. Tad Szulc, *Fidel: A Critical Portrait* (New York: William Morrow, 1986), pp. 19–27.

3. During the transition period between the election and the inauguration, President-elect Kennedy attempted to find the most talented minds in the Democratic Party to fill his cabinet and senior advisory posts. In some cases, he even sought out Republican members for his administration, although the majority had solid Democratic credentials dating back to the presidencies of Franklin Roosevelt and Harry Truman. *Source*: David Halberstam, *The Best and the Brightest* (New York: Random House, 1972).

4. The "Annual Message to Congress" was the direct predecessor of the present-day State of the Union Address, delivered each January by the president. The actual text that became the Monroe Doctrine was actually contained in just three long paragraphs of the address and became the basis for America's Latin American policy for the next two centuries.

5. For decades before the American Civil War, leaders in southern states had sought new territories to expand the institution of slavery, with Cuba a tempting opportunity. *Source*: James M. McPherson, *Battle Cry of Freedom* (New York: Oxford University Press, 1988).

6. The late nineteenth and early twentieth centuries were a formative period for the U.S. Navy, as it grew from a force designed for coastal defense and small expeditionary

operations into a world-class navy capable of competing directly with the great powers of Europe and Japan. *Source*: Captain Edward L. Beach, USN (Ret.), *The United States Navy: 200 Years* (New York: Henry Holt, 1986).

7. The United States was a leader in the rapid development of the all-big-gun battleship in the early 1900s. Battleships were the source of a major worldwide arms race during the years just prior to World War I. *Source*: Tony Gibbons, *The Complete Encyclopedia of Battleships: A Technical Directory of Capital Ships from 1860 to the Present Day* (New York: Crescent Books, 1983).

8. The building of the Panama Canal was the greatest engineering and scientific achievement of the early twentieth century; the epic undertaking is chronicled in David McCullough's *The Path between the Seas: The Creation of the Panama Canal 1870–1914* (New York: Simon & Schuster, 1977).

9. Major W. D. Bushnell, USMC, *American Military Intervention: A Useful Tool or Curse?* (Quantico, Va.: Marine Corps Command and Staff College, 1984); and Colonel Robert Debs Heinl Jr., USMC (Ret.), *Soldiers of the Sea* (Charleston, S.C.: Nautical and Aviation Publishing, 1991).

10. The CIA was created by the 1947 National Security Act, which created the unified Department of Defense from the previously separate Departments of the Navy and War.

11. Allen Dulles was one of two brothers who dominated American foreign policy in the 1950s. His brother, John Foster, was Secretary of State for President Eisenhower until his death from cancer in 1959.

12. Dulles drew much of the inspiration for his plans from his experience in the OSS in World War II. Headed by Brig. Gen. "Wild Bill" Donavan, the OSS had a reputation for recruiting intelligent and motivated young men, training them intensely, and then allowing them great personal latitude during field operations. *Source*: Peter Grose, *Gentleman Spy: The Life of Allen Dulles* (New York: Houghton Mifflin, 1994).

13. The Middle East and Persian Gulf regions were the center of numerous plots and great intrigue during the development of the oil industry in the twentieth century. Operation Ajax and the creation of the state of Israel in 1948 were two of the main reasons for the regional resentment toward Western powers that continues to the present day. *Source*: Daniel Yergin, *The Prize: The Epic Quest for Oil, Money and Power* (New York: Simon & Schuster, 1991), pp. 450–78.

14. The key American business involved was the United Fruit Company, which is best known for its Chiquita-brand bananas. Although there later were claims of the Dulles brothers having run PBSuccess for their own gain (they were major stockholders), the basic rationale for running PBSuccess was anticommunism. *Source*: Richard M. Bissell Jr., *Reflections of a Cold Warrior: From Yalta to the Bay of Pigs* (New Haven, Conn.: Yale University Press, 1996).

15. The stories of the CIA leaders who designed and ran the Ajax and PBSuccess operations are told in Evan Thomas's *The Very Best Men: The Early Years of the CIA* (New York: Simon & Schuster, 1995).

16. Norman Friedman, *The Fifty Year War*, pp. 102–9 (see chap. 2, n. 9).

17. Batista ran a campaign of racist oppression against mulattos and Negroes, in addition to allowing the breakdown of Cuba's public utility and health infrastructures.

18. Fidel Castro's struggle against Batista was long and involved, spanning almost a decade. A full description of his campaign and the subsequent Cuban Revolution can be found in Tad Szulc's extensive biography *Fidel* (see chap. 4, n. 2).

19. Batista initially fled to the Dominican Republic, then to the Portuguese island of Madeira, and finally to Spain, where he died in 1973.

20. Despite Castro's accusations, there has never been any proof that the CIA or any other foreign government had anything to do with the explosion aboard the *La Coubre*. In fact, like the explosion of the American battleship *Maine*, the detonation appears to have been internal. Fursenko and Naftali, *One Hell of a Gamble*, pp. 40–47 (see chap. 3, n. 26).

21. Peter Wyden, *Bay of Pigs: The Untold Story* (New York: Simon & Schuster, 1979), pp. 19–25.

22. Northwoods would have consisted of a series of staged assassinations of Cuban exiles in South Florida and sinkings of small boats on the high seas, among other ideas. There even was a plan to blame the death of astronaut John Glenn on Cuban interference, had he died during his orbital flight on February 20, 1962. James Bamford, *Body of Secrets: Anatomy of the Ultra-Secret National Security Agency* (New York: Anchor Books, 2002), pp. 82–91.

23. The CIA operatives included E. Howard Hunt, who a dozen years later would play a prominent role in the Watergate scandal that drove President Richard M. Nixon from office.

24. *Source*: "Weekly COMINT Economic Briefing, 5 Oct 60," October 5, 1960. Available from the National Security Agency's online archive at www.nsa.gov/docs/cuba/archive.htm.

25. The evidence came from an NSA communication intercept of flight-training radio traffic in Czechoslovakia on January 17, 1961. *Source*: "Spanish Speaking Pilot Noted in Czechoslovakia Air Activity at Trecin 17 January," from online National Security Agency Archive at www.nsa.gov/docs/cuba/archive.htm.

26. Wyden, *Bay of Pigs*, pp. 68–71.

27. Along with cutting off petroleum supplies and sugar purchases, President Eisenhower limited travel and exports to Cuba, except for food and medicine. Fursenko and Naftali, *One Hell of a Gamble*, pp. 56–82.

28. Peter Kornbluh, ed., *Bay of Pigs Declassified: The Secret CIA Report on the Invasion of Cuba* (New York: New Press, 1998).

29. The unit designation for the Cuban freedom fighters was Brigade 2506, from the identification number of a brigade member who died during training. Wyden, *Bay of Pigs*, pp. 51–53.

30. Castro had toured the area where the invasion occurred the previous November, on an inspection trip of several public works projects on the south coast of Cuba. Wyden, *Bay of Pigs*, pp. 104–7.

31. Wyden, *Bay of Pigs*, pp. 152–90.

32. McCone was a Republican who had headed the Atomic Energy Commission during the Eisenhower administration. While not an intelligence professional with prior OSS or CIA experience, McCone was a regular consumer of the communities' products and a superb administrator. He also had a surprising instinct for intelligence assessments, something that would pay dividends during the Cuban Missile Crisis in 1962. Norman Polmar and Thomas B. Allen, *Spy Book*, updated and revised edition (New York: Random House, 1998), p. 357.

33. W. W. Rostow, Memorandums *Notes on Cuba Policy, Steps to Isolate and Weaken Castro Regime, Draft Plan for Cuba*, and *Plan for Cuba*, all dated April 24, 1961, JFK Presidential Library.

34. President Kennedy left few notes from his presidency and kept no diary that has ever been released. This can be partially explained by his poor penmanship, which shows in his occasional personal notes and doodles on the margins of documents he reviewed while president. For example, on the cover sheet of "Draft Plan for Cuba" is the notation "How far willing to go" with further comments of "ideal" next to suggestions about involving the Organization of American States in future American dealings with Cuba. The "Plan for Cuba" cover sheet has similar tantalizing comments, listing things like, "Vulnerability" and "Pentagon—Cuban Brigade." This lack of a body of written notes may explain the decision to later tape record many of his phone calls and meetings, which has provided fresh and important insights into the workings of the Kennedy administration.

35. Thomas, *Robert Kennedy*, pp. 126–40.

36. Lansdale was made famous by his depiction in two popular novels, *The Quiet American* (Graham Greene, 1955) and *The Ugly American* (Eugene Burdick and William J. Lederer, 1958).

37. Lawrence Freedman, *Kennedy's Wars: Berlin, Cuba, Laos, and Vietnam* (New York: Oxford University Press, 2000), pp. 153–60.

38. The early development of American war plans is laid out in Edward S. Miller, *War Plan ORANGE: The U.S. Strategy to Defeat Japan, 1897–1945* (Annapolis, Md.: Naval Institute Press, 1991).

39. OPLAN 314, JTF-127 Air Force Annex, Headquarters, Nineteenth Air Force, U.S. Air Force, Seymour Johnson AFB, N.C.

Chapter 5. Operation Anadyr

1. Gribkov and Smith, *Operation Anadyr*, p. 31 (see chap. 3, n. 14).

2. Lieutenant General Gribkov interview with William Howard, Moscow, June 20, 2002.

3. Ibid.

4. The best English-language description of the SA-2 system is in Steven J. Zaloga, *Soviet Air Defense Missiles: Design, Development and Tactics* (Coulsdon, Surrey, U.K.: Jane's Information Group, 1989), pp. 36–76.

5. The 12th and 27th Anti-aircraft Divisions, like many other units assigned to Operation Anadyr, were given new designations to reflect their deployed and/or provisional status or to deceive Western intelligence agencies as to their actual function or composition. In the case of the large SA-2 divisions, the personnel and the equipment were drawn from the 10th and 11th Anti-aircraft Divisions in the Soviet Union and then formally established in Cuba. For purposes of consistency, unless the new designation was designed to hide the actual function of the unit, the new designation used during Operation Anadyr will be used. *Sources*: R. Malinovsky and M. Zakharov, *Memorandum on Deployment of Soviet Forces to Cuba, May 24, 1962*; R. Malinovsky, *Memorandum from R. Malinovsky to N. S. Khrushchev, September 6, 1962.*

6. Zaloga, *Soviet Air Defense Missiles*, pp. 36–76.

7. The 32nd Fighter Aviation Regiment was assigned to the 213th Fighter Air Division, both of which were based at Santa Clara Airfield. The 213th provided radar detection and ground control services for the 32nd, along with tying the fighter regiment into the Soviet integrated air defense system, which included the two divisions of SA-2s. The 213th also provided liaison services to coordinate with the fighter aircraft of the

Cuban Air Force. *Sources*: R. Malinovsky and M. Zakharov, *Memorandum on Deployment of Soviet Forces to Cuba, May 24, 1962*; R. Malinovsky, *Memorandum from R. Malinovsky to N. S. Khrushchev, September 6, 1962*.

8. The AA-2 was a reverse-engineered copy of the American AIM-9B Sidewinder air-to-air missile. Several early AIM-9Bs were recovered intact by China following dogfights with Sidewinder-armed Taiwanese F-86s in the 1950s and were used as a template for creation of the AA-2A. The AA-2 provided the USSR with its first effective air-to-air missile. *Source*: Piotr Butowski with Jay Miller, *OKB MiG: A History of the Design Bureau and Its Aircraft* (Stillwater, Minn.: Aerofax, Inc., for Specialty Press, 1991), pp. 166–71.

9. William Green, *The World Guide to Combat Planes*, vol. 1 (Garden City, N.Y.: Doubleday, 1967), p. 136.

10. The Il-28 first flew in 1948 and entered squadron service in 1950; it was roughly equivalent to the English Electric Canberra and the North American B-45 Tornado. *Source*: Bill Gunston with Peter Gilchrist, *Jet Bombers from the Messerschmitt 262 to the Stealth B-2* (Over Wallop, Hampshire, U.K.: Osprey Aerospace, 1994), pp. 48–59.

11. U.S. Defense Intelligence Agency, *Handbook on the Soviet Armed Forces* (Washington, D.C.: July 1969), p. 26.

12. FROG—Free Rocket Over Ground. The Soviets actually sent two types of FROG rockets to Cuba. The nuclear-armed version was the 3R10 (NATO FROG-5), while the 3R9 (NATO FROG-3) was armed with a 1,100-lb. high-explosive warhead. *Source*: Steven J. Zaloga, *The Scud and Other Russian Ballistic Missile Vehicles* (Hong Kong: Concord Publications, 2000), pp. 3–11.

13. The four motorized rifle regiments assigned to Operation Anadyr were originally designated as the 302nd, the 314th, the 400th, and the 496th Separate Motorized Rifle Regiments, meaning they were not assigned to a particular division. They were reflagged when deployed to Cuba. *Sources*: R Malinovsky and M. Zakharov, *Memorandum on Deployment of Soviet Forces to Cuba, May 24, 1962*; R. Malinovsky, *Memorandum from R. Malinovsky to N. S. Khrushchev, September 6, 1962*.

14. See Aleksandr Fursenko and Timothy Naftali, "The Pitsunda Decision: Khrushchev and Nuclear Weapons" (Washington, D.C.: *Cold War International History Bulletin 10*, Woodrow Wilson International Center for Scholars, March 1998). The full text of the article can be obtained at http://wwics.si.edu/index.cfm?topic_id=1409&fuseaction=library.document&id=82.

15. The An-8 and An-12 could each carry one R-11 and two Luna missiles but would have no space for their support equipment or crews.

16. The Soviets provided Scud missiles to at least thirteen other countries, with variants also produced by China, Egypt, Iraq, and North Korea. In August 1991, the Afghan rebel leader Jalaluddin al-Haqqani claimed that the Soviets had launched approximately 3,000 Scuds against anti-government *mujahadeen* forces since 1979. Iraq and Iran may have launched as many as 630 Scuds against each other's cities during their conflict of the 1980s. Iraq launched 43 modified Scuds against Saudi Arabia and 38 against Israel in the Gulf War of 1991. During the latter conflict, two of those fired against the Israeli Dimona nuclear facility in the Negev desert had concrete warheads, apparently intended to smash into the facility and cause a spread of radioactive material.

17. The Frontal Aviation squadron of Il-28s was originally scheduled to be sent to Santa Clara Airfield with the 32nd Fighter Aviation Regiment. It eventually was deployed to the airfield at Holguin. *Source*: R. Malinovsky, *Memorandum from R. Malinovsky to N. S. Khrushchev, September 6, 1962*.

18. FKR—*Frontoviye Krilatiye Raketi* (Frontal Rocket).

19. For reasons of operational security during Operation Anadyr, the FKR-1 Regiments were reflagged as "Independent Aviation Engineering Regiments," or OAIPs. Thus, the 561st FKR Regiment became the 231st OAIP, while the 584th became the 222nd OAIP. For purposes of clarity, their true designations will be used. *Source*: R. Malinovsky, *Memorandum from R. Malinovsky to N. S. Khrushchev, September 6, 1962*.

20. The Royal Navy initiated development of a nuclear mine to be carried by X-craft midget submarines into Soviet ports (Operation Cudgel); however, that project was halted before the mines were produced.

21. U.S. Navy records of the Cuban Missile Crisis list five Foxtrot-class submarines detected in the Western Atlantic/Caribbean area. However, Soviet sources list four submarines being dispatched to the area: *B-4*, *B-36*, *B-59*, and *B-130*. *Sources*: I. Kasatonov, *The Fleet Goes Out to the Ocean: The Story of Fleet Admiral V. A. Kasatonov* (St. Petersburg: Astra-Luxe, 1995), p. 269; and Aleksey Dubivko interview with William Howard, Moscow, June 18, 2002. Then Captain 2nd Rank Dubivko commanded the *B-36*.

22. Stephen J. Zaloga, *The Kremlin's Nuclear Sword: The Rise and Fall of Russia's Strategic Nuclear Forces, 1945–2000* (Washington, D.C.: Smithsonian Institution Press, 2002), pp. 82–89.

23. Sergei N. Khrushchev, *Nikita Khrushchev*, p. 490 (see chap. 2, n. 12).

24. Deadweight tonnage.

25. Peter A. Huchthausen, *October Fury* (Hoboken, N.J.: John Wiley & Sons, 2002), p. 8.

26. Sergei N. Khrushchev, *Nikita Khrushchev*, p. 511.

27. Ibid., p. 512.

28. Mikhail Burnov interview with William Howard, Moscow, June 19, 2002.

29. Karl K. Werder, "Continuing Lessons of the Cuban Missile Crisis, October 1962" (USAF Air War College paper, Maxwell AFB, Ala., 1995), pp. 27–28.

30. Gribkov and Smith, *Operation Anadyr*, p. 39.

31. Ibid.

32. Later, in mid-October, CIA analysts called attention to the *Poltava*, noting, "A new Soviet ship, the *Poltava*, possibly designed as a ballistic missile transport, has been noted making frequent trips between the USSR and Cuba." *Source*: *Joint Evaluation of Soviet Missile Threat in Cuba, 2000 hours, October 19, 1962*, in McAuliffe, *CIA Documents on the Cuban Missile Crisis 1962*, p. 206 (see chap. 3, n. 22).

33. Gribkov and Smith, *Operation Anadyr*, p. 45.

34. Murmansk, with a population of about half a million people, is the largest city north of the Arctic Circle. The port is ice-free throughout the year.

35. The story of the CIA's attempts to track the warheads is laid out in a previously classified (SECRET) study. *Source*: Dwayne Anderson, *On the Trail of the Alexandrovsk*. Available on the CIA's Center for the Study of Intelligence Web site at www.cia.gov/csi/kent _csi/docs/v10i1a03p_0001.htm (declassified and released on September 18, 1995).

Chapter 6. Surveillance and Discovery

1. Dino A. Brugioni, *Eyeball to Eyeball: The Inside Story of the Cuban Missile Crisis* (New York: Random House, 1991), p. 201.

2. *Maskirovka* is a concept dating back decades in Soviet and Russian military doctrine. Technically a merging of strategic, political, operational, and tactical deception,

maskirovka also embraces elements of camouflage, propaganda, and disinformation to create a total mask of concealment for operations ranging from covert deployments to major military offensives.

3. Christopher Andrew and Vasili Mitrokhin, *The Sword and the Shield* (Cambridge, Mass.: Basic Books, 1999), pp. 180–84.

4. Jeffrey T. Richelson, *The Wizards of Langley* (Boulder, Co.: Westview Press, 2001), pp. 50–62.

5. William E. Burrows, *Deep Black* (New York: Berkley Books, 1988), pp. 66–74.

6. Victor K. McElheny, *Insisting on the Impossible* (Reading, Mass.: Perseus Books, 2001), pp. 278–305.

7. Technically known as the Lockheed Advanced Projects Division, the "Skunk Works" nickname came from the "Kickapoo Joy Juice" factory in Al Capp's comic strip "Li'l Abner" and referred to the informal and sometimes unconventional methods employed by Kelly Johnson and his successors. *Source*: Gregory W. Pedlow and Donald E. Welzenbach, *The CIA and the U-2 Program, 1954–1974* (Washington, D.C.: CIA Center for the Study of Intelligence, 1998), p. 45.

8. Polmar, *Spyplane*, pp. 27–46 (see chap. 2, n. 8).

9. Edwin H. Land, *Memo to Allen W. Dulles, November 5, 1954*, in Dwight D. Eisenhower Presidential Library.

10. Curtis Peebles, *Shadow Flights: America's Secret Air War against the Soviet Union* (Novato, Calif.: Presidio Press, 2000), pp. 130–63; and Polmar, *Spyplane*, pp. 149–68.

11. Peebles, *Shadow Flights*, pp. 236–41.

12. At various times during the Cold War, the United States managed to tap phone lines directly under the noses of the USSR and its allies. Among the more successful operations, U.S. nuclear submarines crept into the territorial waters of the USSR and other nations, to lay so-called tap pods filled with tape recorders (Operation Ivy Bells). *Source*: Sherry Sontag and Christopher Drew, *Blind Man's Bluff: The Untold Story of American Submarine Espionage* (New York: Public Affairs, 1998), pp. 158–327.

13. The top secret or "Black" Corona program was covered inside of an open Air Force research program known as Discoverer. During the early days of the Discoverer program, a biomedical or other payload would occasionally be substituted for a camera system to help maintain the cover. *Source*: Curtis Peebles, *The Corona Project: America's First Spy Satellite* (Annapolis, Md.: Naval Institute Press, 1997), pp. 39–62 and 278–82.

14. In addition to Corona, the CIA was also developing the Mach 3+, high altitude (over 80,000 feet) A-12 spyplane. The A-12 evolved into the Air Force SR-71 Blackbird. *Source*: Richard M. Bissell Jr., *Project Corona Memo, April 15, 1958*, CIA FOIA Online Archive.

15. F. Dow Smith, *Corona between the Sun and the Earth: The Design and Engineering of Corona's Optics* (Bethesda, Md.: American Society of Photogrammetry and Remote Sensing, 1997), pp. 111–20.

16. Robert M. Powell, *Corona between the Sun and the Earth: Evolution of Standard Agenda: Corona's Spacecraft* (Bethesda, Md.: American Society of Photogrammetry and Remote Sensing, 1997), pp. 121–32.

17. Dwayne A. Day, John M. Logsdon, and Brian Latell, eds., *Eye in the Sky: The Story of the Corona Spy Satellites* (Washington, D.C.: Smithsonian Institution Press, 1998), pp. 119–42.

18. The first successful Corona mission, Number 1003/9009, flown in August 1960, photographed more territory in the USSR than did all twenty-three of the completed U-2 overflights combined. *Source*: Kevin Ruffner, *Corona: America's First Satellite Program* (Washington, D.C.: CIA Center for the Study of Intelligence, 1995), pp. 1–39.

19. Peebles, *Corona Project*, pp. 271–315.

20. Chief, Design and Analysis Division, *Memo on Briefing General Maxwell Taylor on Photographic Satellite Support—Middle East Crisis, August 31, 1967* (memo written on September 8, 1967), CIA FOIA Online Archive.

21. This became particularly evident in the late 1960s, when the Corona and other film-based reconnaissance satellites were unable to provide useful predictive photography during the Six-Day Arab/Israeli War in 1967 and the Soviet invasion of Czechoslovakia in 1968. This inability to obtain so-called real time imagery led to the development of new reconnaissance requirements and the creation in the 1970s of the KH-11 camera system. *Source*: Peebles, *Corona Project*, pp. 232–82.

22. The four Corona missions flown during June and July 1962 were Missions 9037 (code-named Tight Skirt), 9038 (Trial Track), 9039 (Adobe Home), and 9040 (Anchor Rope). *Source*: Peebles, *Corona Project*, pp. 284–85.

23. *Source*: Dwayne Anderson, *On the Trail of the Alexandrovsk*. Available on the CIA's Center for the Study of Intelligence Web site at www.cia.gov/csi/kent_csi/docs/ v10i1a03p_0001.htm (declassified and released on September 18, 1995).

24. Polmar and Allen, *Spy Book*, pp. 402–5 (see chap. 4, n. 32).

25. National Security Agency, *NSA and the Cuban Missile Crisis*, pp. 1–4.

26. SOSUS dates back to the 1950s and today consists of a large worldwide network of fixed and ship-based acoustic sensors. *Source*: Polmar and Allen, *Spy Book*, pp. 524–25.

27. Brugioni, *Eyeball to Eyeball*, pp. 72–74.

28. Werder, "Continuing Lessons of the Cuban Missile Crisis," pp. 27–28 (see chap. 5, n. 29).

29. Pedlow and Welzenbach, *The CIA and the U-2 Program, 1954–1974*, pp. 197–99.

30. Interview with Dino A. Brugioni, *Secret Satellite*, documentary film for Discovery Communications.

31. The USS *Oxford* was an electronic eavesdropping ship, extensively converted from a merchant ship for that role. Officially designated as a technical research ship (AGTR), the *Oxford*'s role was similar to that of the ill-fated U.S. spy ships *Liberty* and *Pueblo*. Although Navy manned, the operation of these ships was controlled by the NSA. National Security Agency, *Teletype Message of 16 July 1962 from Director NSA—Chief of Naval Operations* and *Memorandum for the Secretary of the Navy (July 19, 1962)*, Online NSA Archive.

32. National Security Agency, *First Elint Evidence of Scan Odd Radar in Cuba Area (June 6, 1962)* and *Electronic Intercepts in Cuban Area (June 22, 1962)*, Online NSA Archive.

33. National Security Agency, *Unusual Number of Soviet Passenger Ships en Route Cuba (June 24, 1962)*, Online NSA Archive.

34. Each Cuban U-2 reconnaissance mission had a number, beginning with 3086 and listed hereafter as (Mission and number).

35. At the time, the Sopka anti-ship cruise missile system was unknown outside of the Soviet Union, and the U-2 photos from Mission 3088 created something of a stir

while photo analysts tried to assess exactly what the missile was capable of, and armed with. Brugioni, *Eyeball to Eyeball*, pp. 120–25.

36. Pedlow and Welzenbach, *The CIA and the U-2 Program, 1954–1974*, pp. 200–201.

37. The photos from Mission 3089 showed eleven confirmed SA-2 SAM sites, with several more possibly under construction. The photos also showed a MiG-21 Fishbed interceptor on the Cuban airfield at Santa Clara, along with crates for nineteen more nearby. What made this particular mix of systems unique was that while the SA-2 had been exported to several nonaligned countries, such as Egypt and Indonesia, this was the first time that the MiG-21 had been seen outside of the Warsaw Pact countries.

38. During the four decades since the Cuban Missile Crisis, DCI McCone has rarely been given credit for having logically reasoned that Cuba would become a base for Soviet ballistic missiles or even for being the first senior Kennedy administration official to do so. The fact that McCone lacked prior experience in the OSS or other intelligence agencies meant that he suffered from discrimination within the CIA. Also, that he had replaced the immensely popular Allan Dulles did not help his image within the agency. However, what most of McCone's critics fail to take into account is that he may have been one of the most qualified individuals within the CIA to actually make an accurate assessment of the USSR potentially sending ballistic missiles to Cuba.

39. While Keating died in 1975 without revealing the source of his information, the possibilities range from Cuban refugees released from Opa-Locka to journalists or leaks from senior Kennedy administration officials.

40. Senator Keating's reference to "six rocket bases" likely referred to the SA-2 SAM sites detected on Mission 3088 on August 29. While classified, this was information that might have come to him from a variety of sources, including some of the regularly circulated intelligence documents that were (and still are) part of government life in Washington, D.C.

41. Fursenko and Naftali, *One Hell of a Gamble*, pp. 205 and 220 (see chap. 3, n. 26).

42. Walt W. Rostow, *Memorandum to the President Assessing Soviet Military Aid to Cuba (September 3, 1962)*, National Security Archive.

43. Thomas, *Robert Kennedy*, pp. 203–6 (see chap. 4, n. 1).

44. Pierre Salinger for President John F. Kennedy, *Statement by President John F. Kennedy on Cuba, September 4, 1962*, Department of State Archives.

45. The Director of Central Intelligence (DCI) was the head of the Central Intelligence Agency (CIA) and the leader of the intelligence community, the grouping of U.S. government organizations that carried out intelligence activities. The term *DCI* was first used in 1946, when President Harry S. Truman created the National Intelligence Authority (NIA) to coordinate U.S. foreign intelligence activities. The NIA was dissolved when the CIA was founded on September 20, 1947. There is no position known as the director of the CIA.

46. Pedlow and Welzenbach, *The CIA and the U-2 Program, 1954–1974*, pp. 201–6.

47. Polmar, *Spyplane*, p. 162 and 199–203.

48. In fact, the September 9 U-2 shoot down over China was the fourth aircraft downed by the SA-2 SAM system. The first was an RB-57D Canberra high-altitude reconnaissance aircraft, also flown by a Taiwanese pilot, shot down over China on October 2, 1959. The other two were the Mission 4154 U-2 flown by Francis Gary Powers, along with a Soviet MiG-19 trying to intercept the American spyplane, on May 1, 1960, over Sverdlovsk. *Source*: Peebles, *Shadow Flights*, pp. 249–50 and 259–68.

49. The A-12 was an internal Lockheed project name and not a military designation. It was also *not* related to the failed Navy stealth A-12 Avenger aircraft program.

50. The SR-71's predecessor, the A-12 Oxcart, had become operational in November 1965. The CIA proposed to use the A-12 for overflights of Cuba, but those missions were not undertaken; rather, the only operational flights of the A-12 were made in 1967–1968 over North Vietnam (code name Black Shield) and North Korea. A-12s flew twenty-six photo missions over North Vietnam between May 31, 1967, and early 1968. Although some A-12 flights were detected, and SA-2 surface-to-air missiles were launched against the aircraft, no planes were shot down or damaged. On January 26, 1968, an A-12 flew a photo mission over North Korea to take photos of the captured U.S. spy ship *Pueblo*. A second mission over North Korea was flown on May 8, 1968—the last A-12 operational mission. The SR-71 Blackbird's first operational mission was over North Vietnam in 1968; the aircraft was retired from the operational role in 1990 because of funding issues.

51. National Security Agency, *Cuban MiGs Scramble on Two U.S. Navy Patrol Planes (September 11, 1962)*, Online NSA Archive.

52. *Statement by Soviet Union That a U.S. Attack on Cuba Would Mean Nuclear War (September 11, 1962)*, National Security Archive.

53. Fursenko and Naftali, *One Hell of a Gamble*, p. 210.

54. Like DCI McCone, General Blake was convinced early that the Anadyr deployment had an offensive component. Awarded a Silver Star for gallantry under fire at Pearl Harbor on December 7, 1941, Blake was as obsessed as any U.S. leader with never allowing another preemptive attack on the United States. *Source*: James Bamford, *Body of Secrets*, pp. 97–104 (see chap. 4, n. 22).

55. Lieutenant General Gordon A. Blake, USAF (DIRNSA), *Memo on "Funnel" Handling Codeword (September 11, 1962)* and *Memo on Funnel Project (September 12, 1962)*, Online NSA Archive.

56. National Security Agency, *New Radar Deployment in Cuba (September 19, 1962)*, Online NSA Archive.

57. McAuliffe, *CIA Documents on the Cuban Missile Crisis, 1962*, pp. 91–93 (see chap. 3, n. 22).

58. Gil Merom, "The 1962 Cuban Intelligence Estimate: A Methodological Perspective," *Intelligence and National Security Review* 14, no. 3 (Autumn 1999).

59. Colonel John R. Wright, USA, *Cuba Intelligence—Top Secret (September 28, 1962)*, Personal Papers of General Maxwell Taylor via National Defense University and the Avalon Project.

60. Pedlow and Welzenbach, *The CIA and the U-2 Program, 1954–1974*, p. 206.

61. Polmar, *Spyplane*, pp. 199–203.

62. Power had flown B-24 and B-29 bombers during World War II. On the night of March 9–10, 1945, he led the first B-29 firebombing raid on Tokyo. This raid was the most destructive of World War II, burning out sixteen square miles of downtown Tokyo and killing almost eighty-four thousand Japanese. These immediate fatalities were greater than those at the atomic attacks on Hiroshima or Nagasaki.

63. General Carter had been given temporary authority over day-to-day CIA operations because DCI McCone needed to attend to a family emergency. His son-in-law had died as a result of injuries suffered in an auto race.

64. Mr. "Bonn" and Colonel "Coleman" (USAF historians), *Interview with General Power, Conducted by Mr. Bonn, November 15, 1962*, U.S. Air Force Historical Research Agency, Maxwell AFB, Ala.

65. Polmar, *Spyplane*, pp. 53–58.

66. Gary P. Myers, ed., *Executive Summary of the Missiles in Cuba, 1962: The Role of SAC Intelligence* (Omaha, Neb.: Strategic Joint Intelligence Center [n.d.]), pp. 2–7.

67. Robert Kipp (USAF historian), *Interview of Major Richard S. Heyser, U-2 Reconnaissance Pilot, conducted by Robert Kipp, November 27, 1962*, U.S. Air Force Historical Research Agency, Maxwell AFB, Ala.

68. Thomas R. Johnson and David A. Hatch, *NSA and the Cuban Missile Crisis* (Fort George G. Meade, Md.: NSA Center for Cryptologic History, May 1998), p. 6.

69. For this new series of U-2 overflights, the numbering sequence was restarted at 3101. The so-called 3100-series is normally associated with the "hot" period of the Cuban Missile Crisis and the monitoring period that followed.

70. From this point forward in the narrative, all times will be presented as local.

71. Brugioni, *Eyeball to Eyeball*, pp. 186–87.

72. Meyers, *Executive Summary of the Missiles in Cuba, 1962*, pp. 6–7.

73. Michael Davis interview with Norman Polmar, Alexandria, Va., July 24, 2002. Davis left the Air Force in August 1963 and joined the CIA's NPIC as a photo interpreter.

74. Tighe, a career Air Force intelligence officer, rose to the rank of lieutenant general and was director, Defense Intelligence Agency, when he retired in 1981.

75. Carrying out General Power's order, Davis did not talk about his role in the missile crisis until he spoke at the SAC Museum–sponsored conference "Cuban Missile Crisis: A Look Back 30 Years," at Offutt AFB on October 16, 1992. Later, Davis came to believe that General Power was "upset" that a U-2 had discovered the missiles, that aircraft having been developed by the CIA with the Air Force initially opposing the project. The U-2's success in overflights of the USSR (1956–1960) led to the CIA—and not the Air Force—being given responsibility for developing the subsequent A-12 Oxcart and SR-71 Blackbird spyplanes, as well as reconnaissance satellites. *Source*: Davis telephone conversation with Norman Polmar, August 1, 2002.

76. Brugioni, *Eyeball to Eyeball*, pp. 3–27.

77. Ibid., pp. 187–97.

78. Ibid., pp. 281–82.

79. Ibid., p. 201.

80. Ibid., pp. 200–10.

Chapter 7. ExComm

1. Robert F. Kennedy, *Thirteen Days: A Memoir of the Cuban Missile Crisis* (New York: W. W. Norton, 1969), p. 9.

2. Despite being flagged as a "textbook mission" and nearly doubling the total number of space flight hours for the United States, *Sigma-7*—the name derived from the math symbol for summation, and the number of astronauts in the first group assigned to Project Mercury—was a far cry from the manned space achievements of the Soviet Union. In August, the USSR had launched a pair of manned spacecraft (*Vostok 3* and *Vostok 4*) within a day of each other, the first time that two manned craft flew in space simultaneously.

3. Beschloss, *Mayday*, p. 140 (see chap. 2, n. 11).

4. Peebles, *Corona Project*, pp. 94–96 (see chap. 6, n. 13).

5. *Probable Soviet MRBM Sites in Cuba* is reproduced in McAuliffe, *CIA Documents on the Cuban Missile Crisis*, pp. 140–44.

6. Khrushchev openly threatened to make a separate peace treaty with East Germany, outside the scope of the four-power agreement signed at Potsdam in 1945. He also refused to discuss with Kennedy any of the young president's ideas for a nuclear test ban treaty, one of the key goals of the new administration. *Source*: Fursenko and Naftali, *One Hell of a Gamble*, pp. 124–31 (see chap. 3, n. 26).

7. Interestingly, the U.S. Air Force took strong issue with NIE 11-8/1-61; in his comments on the report, the Air Force Assistant Chief of Staff, Intelligence, wrote that he "believes that the Soviets will continue to deploy first generation missiles [SS-6], as an interim measure until the second generation missiles become available." And he predicted that the Soviet ICBM deployment would be "more accelerated than indicated in the [NIE] text." In fact, only one operational SS-6 launch facility with just four launchpads was ever constructed.

8. Just as the Cuban Missile Crisis was developing, the CIA was beginning to move to its present-day headquarters in Langley, Virginia. Previously, the CIA had been scattered throughout Washington and the adjoining suburbs of Maryland and Virginia, including in a number of so-called temporary buildings on the Mall.

9. Brugioni, *Eyeball to Eyeball*, p. 190.

10. There have been a number of spellings for the term, which actually did not come into general use until later in the crisis. The authors have chosen to standardize on ExComm for reader ease and consistency.

11. Nitze would later serve as Secretary of the Navy, Under Secretary of Defense, and ambassador to the major U.S.-Soviet strategic arms negotiations.

12. Robert Dallek, *An Unfinished Life* (New York: Little, Brown, 2003), pp. 397–99.

13. Ibid., p. 576.

14. Ibid., pp. 580–81.

15. Nigel Hamilton, *JFK: Reckless Youth* (New York: Random House, 1995).

16. Timothy Naftali, ed., *The Presidential Recordings: John F. Kennedy*, vol. 1 (New York: W. W. Norton, 2001), pp. xvii–xxix.

17. Ernest R. May and Philip D. Zelikow, *The Kennedy Tapes: Inside the White House during the Cuban Missile Crisis* (Cambridge, Mass.: Harvard University Press, 1997), pp. 45–76.

18. Timothy Naftali and Philip D. Zelikow, *The Presidential Recordings: John F. Kennedy*, vol. 2 (New York: W. W. Norton, 2001), pp. 391–427.

19. The commander-in-chief (CinC) Atlantic Command was responsible for all U.S. military forces in the Atlantic area; he simultaneously served as Supreme Allied Commander, Atlantic, in the NATO chain of command.

20. Despite having earlier dueled with McCone over whether the Soviets were installing offensive weapons into Cuba, Bundy was extremely conciliatory about having been wrong, openly stating the fact. *Source*: May and Zelikow, *The Kennedy Tapes*, p. 89.

21. Ibid., pp. 118–21.

22. Ibid., p. 119.

23. Fursenko and Naftali, *One Hell of a Gamble*, pp. 230–31.

24. May and Zelikow, *The Kennedy Tapes*, pp. 121–67.

25. Fursenko and Naftali, *One Hell of a Gamble*, pp. 231–32.

26. Naftali and Zelikow, *The Presidential Recordings: John F. Kennedy*, vol. 2, pp. 572–77.

Chapter 8. Consensus and Notification

1. John McCone, *Memorandum for File Regarding October 18, 1962, ExComm Meeting*, in McAuliffe, *CIA Documents on the Cuban Missile Crisis*, pp. 193–194.

2. Guided Missile and Aeronautics Intelligence Committee, Joint Atomic Energy Intelligence Committee, and National Photographic Intelligence Center, *Joint Evaluation of the Soviet Missile Threat in Cuba, 2000 Hours, 19 October 1962*, in McAuliffe, *CIA Documents on the Cuban Missile Crisis*, pp. 203–8.

3. Central Intelligence Agency, *SNIE 11-18-62: Soviet Reactions to Certain U.S. Courses of Action on Cuba: October 19, 1962*, in McAuliffe, *CIA Documents on the Cuban Missile Crisis*, pp. 197–202.

4. The Soviet-Cuban defense pact was negotiated and signed in great secrecy on July 8, 1962, during a visit by Raúl Castro to Defense Minister Malinovsky in Moscow. The plan was to conduct the Anadyr deployment covertly, then announce the treaty when the existence of the ballistic missile complex in Cuba was made public in November 1962. *Source*: James H. Hansen, "Learning from the Past: Soviet Deception in the Cuban Missile Crisis," *Studies in Intelligence* (vol. 46, no. 1, 2002). It can be accessed online at www.cia.gov/csi/studies/vol46no1/article06.html.

5. Brugioni, *Eyeball to Eyeball*, pp. 524–25.

6. While the SS-4 missiles and supporting equipment were road mobile, the SS-5 was a larger system, requiring an established launch base, with concrete launch stands, along fixed support and control facilities. *Source*: Pavel Podvig, ed., *Russian Strategic Nuclear Forces* (Cambridge, Mass.: MIT Press, 2001), pp. 182–88.

7. Arthur Lundahl, Memorandum for Director of Central Intelligence and Director, Defense Intelligence Agency, Additional Information—Mission 3107, October 19, 1962.

8. In fact, the SS-5 actually had a range of 2,745 statute miles, allowing it to strike all of the continental United States, much of Canada, and northern South America. *Source*: Podvig, *Russian Strategic Nuclear Forces*, p. 188.

9. Hamilton, *JFK: Reckless Youth*, pp. 406–8 (see chap. 7, n. 15).

10. Then Lieutenant Kennedy's first PT squadron commander was removed from command for having mistakenly ordered his boats to sink the amphibious force flagship *McCawley* during the invasion of Rendova. That officer's replacement is alleged to have been a physical coward, who commanded his squadron by radio from a log bunker on Rendova, thirty to fifty miles from where the PT boats were fighting. *Source*: Ibid., pp. 548–58.

11. Naftali and Zelikow, *The Presidential Recordings: John F. Kennedy*, vol. 2, pp. 578–79 (see chap. 7, n. 18).

12. Only three of the principal ExComm members wrote in-depth accounts of their service during the Kennedy and Johnson years, and all are suspect. The presidential speechwriter and senior advisor Theodore Sorenson (*Kennedy* [New York: Harper Collins, 1965]) was a conscientious objector in World War II and never a supporter of military leaders or action. The senior advisor Arthur Schlesinger (*A Thousand Days* [Boston, Mass.: Houghton Mifflin, 1965]) was even more vehement in his dislike of the military, openly criticizing the military forces inherited from Dwight Eisenhower as unready for combat and later accusing senior military leaders of being warmongers. Least credible of all are the writings, appearances, and interviews of secretary of defense Robert McNamara (with Brian VandeMark, *In Retrospect* [New York: Times Books/Random House, 1995]) and the documentary film *The Fog of War* ([Julie Bilson-Ahlberg/Columbia Tri-Star],

2004), who has spent four decades *not* talking about the Cuban Missile Crisis. McNamara has endured being the senior surviving national security official from both the Kennedy and Johnson administrations, having been subjected to vicious attacks from all sides for his handling of everything from military procurement to strategy in Vietnam. His comments on the missile crisis have been short and limited, with little of insight or worth.

13. Several times during the crisis, General Power upset President Kennedy and his inner circle by aggressively commanding the Strategic Air Command to elevated alert levels and sending messages in the clear to his forces that were threatening the Soviet Union. However, despite taking SAC to DEFCON-2 on his own authority and announcing SAC's readiness over open radio channels, he was completely within his authority as laid down in the U.S. Code.

14. Dwight D. Eisenhower, *Crusade in Europe: A Personal Account of World War II* (Garden City, N.Y.: Doubleday, 1948), pp. 183–84.

15. The Joint Chiefs of Staff minutes of the crisis period have been destroyed; Dr. Walter S. Poole had access to those minutes and has produced several documents that address the period, among them, "How Well Did the JCS Work?" *Naval History Magazine* (Winter 1992), pp. 19–21, and "The Cuban Missile Crisis: How Well Did the Joint Chiefs of Staff Work?" paper presented at the Naval Historical Center colloquium, Washington, D.C., June 18, 1992.

16. One of the great naval officers in American history, Arliegh Burke served in the position of Chief of Naval Operations for six years (1955–1961), longer than any other officer.

17. The most flamboyant and controversial general officer of his day, LeMay practically defined the U.S. Air Force while he served. A pre–World War II navigator on B-17s, LeMay commanded bombers in Europe, China, and the Pacific, eventually leading the XXI Air Force, which firebombed Japan into ashes in 1945. One story, from his days as a B-17 bomber division commander in Europe, told of his crew chief asking him to put out his signature cigar, as the battle-damaged bomber was leaking fuel and might explode. In response, LeMay is reported to have taken a long drag from the stogie, tapped the ash, and replied, "It wouldn't dare."

18. The National Security Act of 1947 provided the legislation basis for the Joint Chiefs of Staff to include a chairman and three service chiefs—the Chief of Staff of the Army, the chief of Naval Operations, and the Chief of Staff of the Air Force. The Marine Corps was a separate service within the Navy Department and was not accorded membership within the JCS. In 1952, President Truman signed Public Law 416, which enabled the commandant of the Marine Corps to sit with the JCS and vote on issues of direct interest to the Marine Corps. Not until the 1979 Defense Authorization Act, signed into law by President Carter in 1978, was the commandant made a full member of the JCS.

19. Naftali and Zelikow, *The Presidential Recordings: John F. Kennedy*, vol. 2, pp. 580–99.

20. Robert F. Kennedy, *Thirteen Days*, pp. 21–24 (see chap. 7, n. 1).

21. The first of the SS-4 regiments, either the 539th or the 546th, became operational on October 20. Late equipment deliveries caused the second regiment's combat readiness to be delayed until October 25. The initial readiness call probably came from the analysis of photos from U-2 Mission 3011, flown on October 18, which was confirmed on October 21 by electronic emissions from a supporting radar system detected by the NSA-manned spy ship *Oxford*. The *Oxford* was standing just offshore the northern coast of

Cuba, "bouncing" intercept data "real time" off the moon, or summary data via encrypted radio. *Sources*: Bamford, *Body of Secrets*, pp. 111–12 (see chap. 4, n. 22); Guided Missile and Aeronautics Intelligence Committee, Joint Atomic Energy Intelligence Committee, and National Photographic Intelligence Center, *Supplement 1 to Joint Evaluation of the Soviet Missile Threat in Cuba, 2200 Hours, October 20, 1962,* in McAuliffe, *CIA Documents on the Cuban Missile Crisis*, pp. 227–34; and the authors' interviews with Anatoli Glinkin, February 16, 1994, and November 15, 1995, in Moscow, Russia.

22. Naftali and Zelikow, *The Presidential Recordings: John F. Kennedy*, vol. 2, pp. 601–14.

23. Joint Chiefs of Staff, *Transcripts of the Joint Chiefs of Staff, October–November 1962*, p. 13.

24. Sorenson, *Kennedy*, pp. 678–97.

25. Dino A. Brugioni interview with John D. Gresham, Hartwood, Va., July 25, 2002.

26. John McCone, *Memorandum of Meeting with the President, Attorney General, Secretary McNamara, General Taylor, and Mr. McCone, 10 AM–10/21/62.*

27. May and Zelikow, *The Kennedy Tapes*, pp. 468–69 (see chap. 7, n. 17).

28. The word *quarantine* is derived from the Latin *quadraginta*, meaning "forty." In the Roman era, officials kept a ship outside of a port for forty days if they suspected that crewmen or passengers were infected.

29. May and Zelikow, *The Kennedy Tapes*, p. 209.

30. Michael R. Beschloss, *The Crisis Years* (New York: HarperCollins, 1991), pp. 678–97.

31. Thomas, *Robert Kennedy*, pp. 220–21 (see chap. 4, n. 1).

32. Schlesinger, *A Thousand Days*, pp. 808–13.

33. Philip Zelikow and Ernest May, *The Presidential Recordings: John F. Kennedy*, vol. 3 (New York: W. W. Norton, 2001), pp. 16–32.

34. Ibid., pp. 33–39.

35. The full text of NASM 196 can be found, along with a number of other significant documents, on the Web site of the John F. Kennedy Presidential Library at www.jfklibrary.org/cmc_misc_transcripts.html.

36. Beschloss, *The Crisis Years*, p. 477.

37. Zelikow and May, *The Presidential Recordings: John F. Kennedy*, vol. 3, pp. 478–81.

38. Beschloss, *The Crisis Years*, p. 482.

39. The full text of the October 22 speech can be obtained from the University of San Diego Web site at www.acusd.edu/~trook/page1.html.

40. Beschloss, *The Crisis Years*, pp. 482–85.

41. In addition to the combat troops, there were about 130,000 Cubans mobilized as medical workers, fire fighters, and in other support roles, many of whom were women (as were a significant percentage of the combat troops). Numbers provided by Jorge Risquet in an interview with Norman Polmar and Brian Kelly in Havana, September 3, 2002.

Chapter 9. Taking Action

1. John McCone, *Memorandum for Discussion Today, October 17, 1962, "Subject: The Cuban Situation,"* in McAuliffe, *CIA Documents on the Cuban Missile Crisis*, p. 163.

2. May and Zelikow, *The Kennedy Tapes*, p. 202 (see chap. 7, n. 17).

3. Admiral Dennison simultaneously held three positions: he was the NATO supreme allied commander Atlantic, commanding all alliance naval forces in the Atlantic area; the commander in chief U.S. Atlantic Command, directing all U.S. military operations in the Atlantic area; and the commander in chief Atlantic Fleet, directing U.S. naval forces in the Atlantic (the naval component commander for the U.S. Atlantic Command).

4. Rear Admiral Thomas A. Brooks, USN (Ret.), interview with Norman Polmar, Fairfax Station, Va., June 18, 2002.

5. Naval Air Station Jacksonville, Fla.: seventy-six fighters, ten maritime patrol; Naval Air Station Key West, Fla: twenty-six fighters, five anti-submarine aircraft; at Naval Base Guantánamo: seven fighters, twelve attack, five maritime patrol; Naval Air Station Roosevelt Roads, Puerto Rico: fifteen maritime patrol; Homestead Air Force Base, Fla.: eighteen fighter-interceptors; and at McCoy Air Force Base, Fla.: twelve radar-surveillance aircraft (EC-121).

6. The A4D was also suitable for close air support of ground troops, and Marine pilots were especially skilled in that role.

7. The aircraft used to transfer nonflying personnel and equipment to and from the *Enterprise* were C-1A Trader cargo aircraft; the process was known as COD for Carrier On-board Delivery.

8. A "sortie" is one attack mission by one aircraft.

9. May and Zelikow, *The Kennedy Tapes*, pp. 205–6.

10. Walter S. Poole, "The Cuban Missile Crisis: How Well Did the Joint Chiefs of Staff Work?" (see chap. 8, n. 15).

11. The twenty-four reserve troop carrier squadrons had three hundred C-123 and C-119 aircraft, manned and supported by fourteen thousand personnel.

12. Minutes of the 506th Meeting of the National Security Council, White House, Washington, D.C., October 21, 1962, 2:30–4:50 P.M. *Source*: Kennedy Library, National Security Files, Meetings and Memoranda Series, NSC Meetings.

13. The RB-47H aircraft were from the 55th Strategic Reconnaissance Wing, based at Offutt AFB, Neb.

14. May and Zelikow, *The Kennedy Tapes*, p. 240.

15. Ibid., p. 213.

16. Ibid., p. 212.

17. The NATO Supreme Allied Commander, Europe (SACEUR), General Lauris Norstad, USAF, had been ordered to try to persuade NATO forces to assume a comparable alert posture, but he was authorized to "exercise his discretion in complying this directive." Norstad conferred with British prime minister Macmillan, who strongly argued against "mobilizing" European forces. Aware that a U.S. alert might weaken European support for the United States, Norstad decided not to put U.S. forces in Europe at DEFCON-3. *Sources*: Cable from Joint Chiefs of Staff Announcing DEFCON 3 Military Alert, October 22, 1962; text of message to Lauris Norstad on the impact of the Cuban Crisis on NATO, October 22, 1962.

18. May and Zelikow, *The Kennedy Tapes*, p. 296.

19. Ibid., p. 336.

20. The pilots of VFP-62 were among the most skilled in the U.S. Navy, having exceptional low-level flying and navigation skills. Among the pilots whom Commander Ecker led during the missile crisis was a young naval aviator, Lieutenant Roger Chaffee, who became part of the third group of NASA astronauts selected in 1963. Tragically, Chaffee was killed, along with the astronauts Virgil "Gus" Grissom and Ed White, during

a launchpad fire on January 27, 1967, in the first Apollo spacecraft due to fly the following month. *Source*: NASA Online Biographical Index. The record can be accessed at www.jsc.nasa.gov/Bios/htmlbios/chaffee-rb.html.

21. These land-based reconnaissance flights by Navy aircraft are detailed in Brugioni, *Eyeball to Eyeball* (see chap. 6, n. 1), and in his "Chalk up Another Chicken!" *U.S. Naval Institute Proceedings* (October 1992), pp. 96–101. Ecker commanded Navy Light Photographic Squadron 62.

22. The early models of the SA-2 SAM system had a very limited capability to engage high-speed, low-level targets like the F-8U-P1. *Source*: Zaloga, *Soviet Air Defense Missiles*, pp. 42–52 (see chap. 5, n. 4).

23. Mikhail Burnov interview with William Howard, Moscow, June 19, 2002.

24. Captain William Ecker discussion with Norman Polmar, Offutt AFB, Neb., October 16, 1992; Ecker interview with Norman Polmar, Alexandria, Va., August 2, 2002; and Ecker, "Photo Reconnaissance over Cuba," *Naval History Magazine* (Winter 1992), pp. 54–56.

25. *Thirteen Days* (Kevin Costner/New Line Cinema), 2000.

26. Captain William Ecker discussion with Norman Polmar, Offutt AFB, Neb., October 16, 1992; Ecker interview with Norman Polmar, Alexandria, Va., August 2, 2002; and Ecker, "Photo Reconnaissance over Cuba," *Naval History Magazine* (Winter 1992), pp. 54–56.

27. Robert F. Kennedy, *Thirteen Days*, p. 67 (see chap. 7, n. 1).

28. Some sources misidentified the *Komiles* as the *Kimovsk*.

29. Ambrose Greenway, *Soviet Merchant Ships* (Emsworth, Hampshire, U.K.: Kenneth Mason, 1985), p. 63.

30. May and Zelikow, *The Kennedy Tapes*, p. 353.

31. Fursenko and Naftali, *One Hell of a Gamble*, p. 247 (see chap. 3, n. 26).

32. Walter S. Poole, "The Cuban Missile Crisis: How Well Did the Joint Chiefs of Staff Work?"

33. Oral history of Admiral George W. Anderson Jr., USN (Ret.), January 27, 1981.

34. Ironically, Secretary McNamara publicly revealed the existence of SOSUS during 1967 congressional hearings, much to the chagrin of some senior naval officers. The Soviet Union knew of SOSUS years earlier, in part because the seafloor acoustic sensors were laid from surface ships.

35. May and Zelikow, *The Kennedy Tapes*, p. 417.

36. Ibid., p. 430.

37. Lieutenant Joseph P. Kennedy Jr., USN, was killed on August 12, 1944, when a premature explosion destroyed his four-engine bomber over England. The plane, loaded with explosives and a radio remote control guidance system, crashed into a German missile site in Europe. Kennedy and his copilot were about to turn the bomber over to radio control by another aircraft and bail out when their PB4Y-1 (B-24) Liberator exploded. *Source*: Jack Olsen, *Aphrodite Desperate Mission* (New York: ibooks, 2004), pp. 234–40 and p. 316.

38. Oral history of Admiral Robert L. Dennison, USN (Ret.), July 17, 1973.

39. During this search, an RB-47H Stratojet crashed on takeoff from Kindley AFB in Bermuda, killing its four-man crew. Other operational losses occurred on October 26 when a U-2 crashed into the Gulf of Mexico on a routine surveillance mission near Cuba, killing the pilot, Joe Nayd. Three days earlier, on October 23, an Air Force KC-135 tanker/transport crashed while landing at Guantánamo, killing seven crewmembers. *Source*: Sergei N. Khrushchev, *Nikita Khrushchev*, p. 589 (see chap. 2, n. 12).

40. Technically, the Moscow response to General Pliyev, drafted by Defense Minister Malinovsky, authorized the use of weapons against American aircraft in the event of a "massive" air attack involving preinvasion strikes. There was no guidance on the use of the SA-2 SAMs against reconnaissance aircraft, as these systems were not fully operational at the time. *Source*: Ibid., pp. 599–600.

41. David Isby, *Weapons and Tactics of the Soviet Army* (London: Jane's, 1981), pp. 220–24.

42. There is also an account that indicates that the authorization came from Gen. Igor Statsenko, the commander of the air defense division the Banes SAM site was assigned to. *Source*: Zaloga, *Soviet Air Defense Missiles*, p. 51.

43. Aleksandr Fursenko and Timothy Naftali, *One Hell of a Gamble*, pp. 277–79; and Sergei N. Khrushchev, *Nikita Khrushchev*, pp. 606–8.

44. For his dedication, courage, and professionalism in flying U-2 missions during the Cuban Missile Crisis, Major Anderson was awarded the first Air Force Cross, a decoration second only to the Medal of Honor. *Source*: John L. Frisbee, "The First Air Force Cross," *Air Force Magazine Online* (December 1995). The online version of this article can be accessed at www.afa.org/magazine/valor/1295valor.asp.

45. Jorge Risquet interview with Brian Kelly and Norman Polmar, Havana, September 3, 2002.

46. Chris Pocock, *Dragon Lady: The History of the U-2 Spyplane* (Osceola, Wisc., Motorbooks International, 1989), pp. 59–74.

47. The GAR-11 Falcon was a radar-homing air-to-air missile, designed to attack incoming waves of Soviet bombers. Launched from F-102 Delta Dagger interceptors, the GAR-11 had a range of five to ten miles and had a W54 .25 kiloton warhead. Pocock, *Dragon Lady: The History of the U-2 Spyplane*, pp. 59–74.

48. Only one or two nuclear-tipped GAR-11 air-to-air missiles were carried by each of the F-102s launched to support Major Maultsby. This was due to the GAR-11 being in relatively short supply in late 1962, and the F-102's weapons bay being limited to carriage of only two of the nuclear Falcons. While the F-102 could carry up to six Falcons—but only two of the nuclear GAR-11s—conventionally armed GAR-1/3 (radar guided) or GAR-3/4 (infrared guided) versions would have also been carried on the remaining launch points.

49. Chairman Khrushchev to President Kennedy, October 28, 1962, reproduced in Robert F. Kennedy, *Thirteen Days*, p. 210.

50. Ibid., p. 214.

51. Sergei N. Khrushchev, *Nikita Khrushchev*, p. 609.

Chapter 10. Crisis beneath the Waves

1. Robert F. Kennedy, *Thirteen Days*, pp. 69–70 (see chap. 7, n. 1).

2. The other major naval powers at the time were Great Britain with 69 submarines, France with 77, Italy with 115, Japan with 62, and the United States with 99.

3. The travails of the *K-19* are portrayed in the film *K-19—The Widowmaker*, starring Harrison Ford and Liam Neeson. *K-19—The Widowmaker* (Kathryn Bigelow/ Paramount), 2002.

4. The revised deployment order for Operation Anadyr, dated May 24, 1962, calls for a squadron of diesel-electric submarines to be deployed, consisting of the 18th Division

of seven Project 629 (NATO Golf) boats, a brigade of four Project 641 (NATO Foxtrot) torpedo attack submarines, and a pair of submarine tenders. *Source*: R. Malinovsky and M. Zakharov, *Memorandum on Deployment of Soviet Forces to Cuba, May 24, 1962.*

5. William E. Knox, "Close-up of Khrushchev during a Crisis," *New York Times Magazine* (November 18, 1962), p. 32.

6. May and Zelikow, *The Kennedy Tapes,* p. 353 (see chap. 7, n. 17).

7. Robert F. Kennedy, *Thirteen Days*, p. 69.

8. Huchthausen, *October Fury*, p. 56 (see chap. 5, n. 25).

9. Sergei N. Khrushchev, *Nikita Khrushchev*, p. 566 (see chap. 2, n. 12).

10. The West's only nuclear torpedo was the U.S. Navy's Mark 45 ASTOR (antisubmarine torpedo), operational from 1958 to 1977. It carried a W34 nuclear warhead rated at 11 kilotons. Soviet nuclear torpedoes are described in V. P. Kuzin and V. I. Nikol'skiy, *Voyenno-morskoy Flot SSSR, 1945–1991* (*The Navy of the USSR, 1945–1991*) (St. Petersburg: Historical Oceanic Society, 1996); and in A. B. Shirokorad, *Sovetskiye Podvodnyye Lodki Poslevoyennoy Postroyki* (*Soviet Submarines of Postwar Construction*) (Moscow: Arsenal Press, 1997). Also see Polmar and Moore, *Cold War Submarines,* pp. 28–29 (see chap. 2, n. 21).

11. Georgi Kostev interview with William Howard, Moscow, June 18, 2002.

12. Aleksey Dubivko interview with William Howard, Moscow, June 18, 2002.

13. Sergei N. Khrushchev, *Nikita Khrushchev*, p. 566.

14. May and Zelikow, *The Kennedy Tapes*, p. 356.

15. Pennant numbers are generally painted on ships; they are not "true" designations of the ships or the submarines. The *Pamir* was subsequently converted to an intelligence-collection ship and was renamed *Peleng*.

16. Huchthausen, *October Fury*, p. 63.

17. Recollections of Vadim Orlov (USSR Submarine *B-59*), "We Will Sink Them All, but We Will Not Disgrace Our Navy," extracted from the article by Alexander Mozgovoi, "The Cuban Samba of the Quartet of Foxtrots: Soviet Submarines in the Caribbean Crisis of 1962" (Moscow, *Military Parade*, 2002). Translated by Svetlana Savranskaya of the National Security Archive.

18. Aleksey F. Dubivko, "In the Depths of the Sargasso Sea," extracted from *On the Edge of the Nuclear Precipice* (Moscow: Gregory Page, 1998). Translated by Svetlana Savranskaya of the National Security Archive.

19. Orlov, "We Will Sink Them All, but We Will Not Disgrace Our Navy."

20. CUBEX = Cuban Exercise.

21. Commander, Anti-Submarine Warfare Force, U.S. Atlantic Fleet, to Chief of Naval Operations, Subj.: "Summary, Analysis and Evaluation of CUBEX," Ser 008187/43, November 5, 1963, p. I-3-1.

22. Deputy Chief of Naval Operations (Fleet Operations and Readiness), *Compilation of Lessons Learned/Deficiencies Noted as a Result of Cuban Operations,* Ser 00230P30, February 20, 1963, p. 19.

23. Huchthausen, *October Fury*, pp. 240–60.

24. In Mark Rascovich's book *The Bedford Incident* (1963) and the subsequent film of the same name starring Richard Widmark and Sidney Poitier, an exhausted U.S. sailor misunderstands a command and fires an ASROC rocket-assisted torpedo at a Soviet submarine; before it is destroyed, the submarine fires several nuclear torpedoes at the USS *Bedford*. *The Bedford Incident* (James B. Harris and Richard Widmark/Columbia Tri-Star, 1965).

Chapter 11. The View from the Kremlin

1. Robert K. Massie, *Nicholas and Alexandra* (New York: Atheneum, 1967), p. 5.

2. Karl Marx and Friedrich Engels, *The Communist Manifesto* (New York: Signet Classics, original edition 1845, reprint edition 1998).

3. Zubok and Pleshakov, *Inside the Kremlin's Cold War*, pp. 210–35 (see chap. 2, n. 5).

4. In 1966, the Presidium was renamed the Politburo. *Source*: Thomas Parish, *The Cold War Encyclopedia* (New York: Henry Holt, 1996), p. 254.

5. Ibid., pp. 57–58.

6. Sergei Khrushchev, *Nikita Khrushchev*, pp. 92–101 and 163–73 (see chap. 2, n. 12).

7. Parish, *The Cold War Encyclopedia*, p. 352.

8. In the Soviet system, the minister of defense was a multifaceted position, possessing the roles and responsibilities of the American secretary of defense, the chairman of the Joint Chiefs of Staff, and the national security advisor. In addition, the defense minister had authority over the Soviet General Staff and the Soviet Military Intelligence (GRU) and was in the chain of command for nuclear release authority.

9. Parish, *The Cold War Encyclopedia*, pp. 201–2.

10. Ibid., pp. 123–25.

11. Polmar and Allen, *Spy Book*, pp. 501–2 (see chap. 4, n. 32).

12. Semichastny would be a key participant in the October 1964 ouster of Khrushchev; however, he reportedly prevented the assassination of Khrushchev, which was favored by some coup leaders.

13. Polmar and Allen, *Spy Book*, pp. 428–31.

14. There is an excellent discussion on the history, structure, and membership of the Politburo/Presidium online at Answers.com (www.answers.com/topic/politburo-of-the-cpsu-central-committee).

15. Parish, *The Cold War Encyclopedia*, pp. 40–42.

16. Ibid., pp. 178–79.

17. Ibid., pp. 216–17.

18. *Perestroika* (Restructuring) and *Glasnost* (Openness) were initiatives put forth by Mikhail Gorbachev in the mid-1990s in an attempt to gently wean the Soviet Union away from the Stalinist-style repressions of the Brezhnev era and begin to build the kind of Western-style infrastructure that would allow a movement toward a market-driven, consumer-based economy. While there were some well-publicized successes, such as the freeing of Andrei Sakharov and the founding of opposition newspapers, these initiatives came too late to save the Soviet Union, which broke up in 1991. *Source*: Parish, *The Cold War Encyclopedia*, pp. 116 and 250.

19. Sergei N. Khrushchev, *Nikita Khrushchev*, p. 446.

20. In July 1961, in response to Soviet-U.S. tensions, President Kennedy announced an increase in the size of the active Army by 133,000 personnel; a call-up of 250,000 reservists for one year (mostly from the Army Reserve); retention of several B-47 bomber units that were to have been discarded; and an addition to the active fleet of an aircraft carrier, an anti-submarine carrier, twenty-six amphibious ships, eleven fleet support ships, forty-one destroyer escorts, and five radar picket destroyers. The majority of the ships came from the reserve fleet.

21. White House, *President Kennedy's Statement on Soviet Military Shipments to Cuba*, September 4, 1962.

22. TASS Statement on U.S. Provocations, September 11, 1962.

23. May and Zelikow, *The Kennedy Tapes*, p. 168 (see chap. 7, n. 17).

24. Sergei N. Khrushchev, *Nikita Khrushchev*, pp. 548–49.

25. R. Malinovsky and M. Zakharov, *Memorandum on Deployment of Soviet Forces to Cuba, May 24, 1962.*

26. Anatoli Burnov interview with William Howard, Moscow, June 19, 2002.

27. Sergei N. Khrushchev, *Nikita Khrushchev*, p. 554.

28. Polmar and Allen, *Spy Book*, pp. 428–31.

29. Sergei N. Khrushchev, *Nikita Khrushchev*, p. 558.

30. Jerold L. Schecter and Peter S. Deriabin, *The Spy Who Saved the World: How a Soviet Colonel Changed the Course of the Cold War* (New York: Charles Scribner's Sons, 1992), p. 262. Schecter was the Time-Life bureau chief in Moscow from 1968 to 1970 and was instrumental in bringing Nikita Khrushchev's memoirs to the West; Deriabin was a KGB officer from 1947 until he defected to the United States in 1954.

31. Ibid., p. 263.

32. Some Western and Russian sources have incorrectly cited October 22—during the height of the crisis—as the date of the Distant telephone call. After the Distant call (actually, on November 2), McCone promptly informed President Kennedy of the call and of the CIA's evaluation of it.

33. Penkovsky's execution was announced on May 17, 1963.

34. One reason for concern by the Soviet leaders over the security of their nuclear and thermonuclear warheads had to do with more than just protecting the design secrets. The array of atomic ordnance deployed to Cuba for Operation Anadyr represented a large percentage of the total nuclear and thermonuclear inventory of the USSR. The 1-megaton warheads for the SS-4s and the SS-5s alone probably constituted between 15 and 20 percent of the total Soviet inventory for strategic missiles. While committing these warheads to Operation Anadyr theoretically got them within range of targets in the American homeland, replacing them might take a year or more if they were lost.

35. Sergei N. Khrushchev, *Nikita Khrushchev*, p. 559.

36. In preparation for a briefing to President Eisenhower in 1957, CIA photographic specialists examined all available maps of the area to see if they could find a place name for the missile facility. Only one map, made by the Germans in World War II, showed a community in the vicinity of the facility. The settlement's name was Tyuratam, which means "arrow burial ground" in the Kazakh language, and this was the name the CIA gave to the missile facility. Subsequent Soviet statements concerning the facility have always referred to it as Baikonur, but the community of Baikonur is more than 200 miles north of Tyuratam.

37. There were two SS-6 launch complexes at Tyuratam in 1962. Site 2, Pad 1, with its huge flame pit, was the famous launch facility where *Sputnik I*, Yuri Gagarin, and the first lunar probes had been launched into space. A second launch facility, Pad 31, was constructed to provide additional capacity and redundancy. Both could support the full range of space operations, from manned *Vostok*, *Voshkod*, and *Soyuz* launches, to combat firings of SS-6 ICBMs. *Source*: Rex Hall and David J. Shayler, *Rocket Men: Vostok and Voskhod, the First Soviet Manned Spaceflights* (Chichester, U.K.: Springer in association with Praxis Publishing, 2001), pp. 40–47.

38. Zaloga, *The Kremlin's Nuclear Sword*, pp. 82–87 (see chap. 5, n. 22).

39. At the time of the Cuban Missile Crisis, the USSR had a total of six launchers for SS-6 ICBMs, four at a northern launch site known as Pletesk (which later became a major spaceport), and two at Tyuratam. Also at Tyuratam were a pair of test launch stands

for the new R-9 (SS-8 Sasin), which could be used for combat launches. In addition, there were a few SS-7 regiments at locations like Yurya; each regiment was equipped with eight above-ground "coffin" launchers. None of these operational Soviet ICBM launch facilities were hardened against nuclear (counterforce) attack, and the ICBMs could not be fueled and held at launch readiness for any great length of time. *Source*: Central Intelligence Agency, *SNIE 11-8/1-61: Strength and Deployment of Soviet Long-Range Ballistic Missile Forces*, in Kevin Ruffner, ed., *Corona: America's First Satellite Program*, pp. 127–55 (see chap. 6, n. 18).

40. Nikita Khrushchev, *Khrushchev Remembers,* p. 497 (see chap. 2, n. 1).

41. Sergei N. Khrushchev, *Nikita Khrushchev,* p. 565.

42. Ormsby-Gore was a longtime friend of John Kennedy, and there was total trust between the two men.

43. This "atomic spy network" had compromised much of the design information of America's atomic bomb program, as well as of other military programs, and had greatly accelerated the development of Soviet nuclear weapons in the late 1940s. *Source*: Alexander Feklisov, *The Man behind the Rosenbergs* (New York: Enigma Books, 2001).

44. Brugioni, *Eyeball to Eyeball*, pp. 444–46 (see chap. 6, n. 1).

45. Alexander Feklisov interview with William Howard, Moscow, June 20, 2002.

46. Sergei N. Khrushchev, *Nikita Khrushchev*, p. 613.

47. Jorge Risquet in an interview with Brian Kelly and Norman Polmar in Havana, September 3, 2002.

48. Sergei N. Khrushchev, *Nikita Khrushchev*, p. 599.

49. Robert F. Kennedy, *Thirteen Days*, p. 98 (see chap. 7, n. 1). The Cuban government returned Anderson's body to the United States on May 4, 1963.

50. Following the downing of Anderson's U-2, there was a moratorium on further high-altitude reconnaissance flights over Cuba. In the interim, low-level missions by the F8U-1Ps and the RF-101s would keep track of developments on the ground, as they had proven to be too fast and agile to be hit by Cuban anti-aircraft gunners.

51. Sergei N. Khrushchev, *Nikita Khrushchev*, p. 608.

52. Chairman Khrushchev to President Kennedy, October 28, 1962, reproduced in Robert F. Kennedy, *Thirteen Days*, pp. 205–10.

53. There have been reports that a 37-mm anti-aircraft round struck one of these F8U-1P aircraft. However, according to Captain William Ecker, who commanded the Navy photo planes of Light Photographic Squadron 62, no aircraft were hit during the entire Blue Moon operation. *Sources*: Ecker interview with Norman Polmar, Alexandria, Va., August 2, 2002; and Ecker, "Photo Reconnaissance Over Cuba," *Naval History Magazine* (Winter 1992), p. 56.

54. Those meeting in the Oval Office with the president were Rusk, McNamara, Robert F. Kennedy, Bundy, Thompson, and Sorenson.

55. Robert F. Kennedy, *Thirteen Days*, p. 108.

56. R. Malinovsky, "Copy of Outgoing Ciphered Telegram No. 20076," October 27, 1962. *Source*: Archive of the President of the Russian Federation, Special Declassification, April 2002. Translated by Svetlana Savranskaya of the National Security Archive.

57. The message is reproduced in Gribkov and Smith, *Operation Anadyr*, p. 182 (see chap. 3, n. 14).

58. Sergei N. Khrushchev, *Nikita Khrushchev*, p. 626.

59. State Department cable on UN Secretary General U Thant's meetings with Castro, November 1, 1962.

Chapter 12. "Until Hell Freezes Over!"

1. Brugioni, *Eyeball to Eyeball*, pp. 330–32 (see chap. 6, n. 1).

2. Hamilton, *JFK: Reckless Youth*, pp. 79–199 (see chap. 7, n. 15).

3. Llewellyn Thompson probably knew Nikita Khrushchev and the Soviet leadership better than any other American diplomat did in 1962, having recently finished a tour as the American ambassador to the USSR. During that tour, Thompson attended numerous meetings and social gatherings with the Soviet leadership, becoming one of a handful of Americans who had personal relationships with Khrushchev and his inner circle. See Kevin Mahoney, *American Decision Making During the Cuban Missile Crisis*, www.authortrek.com.

4. This special relationship was not new for presidents and the press. Perhaps the ultimate example of press discretion came during the administration of Franklin Roosevelt (1933–1945), when it was understood that the president was *never* to be photographed in his wheelchair and that his health problems with polio and heart disease would never be written about. For a description of Kennedy's myriad health problems, see Seymour M. Hersh, *The Dark Side of Camelot* (New York: Little, Brown, 1997), pp. 14–15, 123, and 230–37.

5. Interviews with Pierre Salinger and Art Buchwald in the History Channel program *Time Machine: Missiles in Cuba* (1992).

6. In this way, Khrushchev also used his son-in-law Aleksei Adzhubei, married to his daughter Rada; Adzhubei was the editor in chief of the government newspaper *Izvestia* at the time.

7. Sherman Kent, "The Cuban Missile Crisis of 1962: Presenting the Photographic Evidence Abroad," *Studies in Intelligence* (Spring 1972). That publication has not been completely declassified; however, the Kent article is available online at www.cia.gov/csi/books/shermankent/10cuban.html.

8. James Q. Reber, Memorandum for Brigadier General Andrew J. Goodpaster, "Categories of Billets Planned for T-KH Certification," August 26, 1960, in Ruffner, *Corona*, pp. 63–74 (see chap. 6, n. 18). The British government shared U-2 photography because of its active participation in the program; see Polmar, *Spyplane*, pp. 83–84, 198 (see chap. 2, n. 8).

9. Brugioni, *Eyeball to Eyeball*, pp. 393–94.

10. The new ambassador to France, David "Chip" Bohlen, was aboard a passenger liner in transit to his new post in Paris during the crisis. The American ambassador to Germany, Walter Dowling, was on compassionate leave in the United States; he was flown back to his post. See Kent, "The Cuban Missile Crisis of 1962," pp. 2–3.

11. Brugioni, *Eyeball to Eyeball*, pp. 323–30.

12. Prime Minister Macmillan's suggestion was accepted, and at 5 P.M. on October 22, a "deep background" briefing was conducted for British newspapers, the BBC, and ITV. While the media representatives were shown the briefing boards, no reproductions were initially made available, and all information was on a "not-for-attribution" basis. Later that day, though, at the request of Ambassador Bruce, copies of the photos with the target locations and other data were supplied to the British media. *Source*: Kent, "The Cuban Missile Crisis of 1962," pp. 3–4.

13. President de Gaulle had survived two assassination attempts in the previous year, including an ambush by dissident French Army officers in August 1962. He would

eventually survive at least a dozen known attempts on his life prior to his death of natural causes in 1970 at age seventy-nine.

14. Kent, "The Cuban Missile Crisis of 1962," pp. 6–7.

15. Sherman Kent, telegram from the Embassy in Paris to the Department of State, October 22, 1962. *Source*: The Avalon Project of the Yale Law School.

16. Kent, "The Cuban Missile Crisis of 1962," p. 8.

17. Ibid., p. 5.

18. Ibid., pp. 9–14.

19. May and Zelikow, *The Kennedy Tapes,* pp. 39–41 (see chap. 7, n. 17).

20. Brugioni, *Eyeball to Eyeball,* pp. 365–68. Also, Brugioni interview with John Gresham and William Howard, Hartwood, Va., July 25, 2002.

21. Brugioni, *Eyeball to Eyeball,* pp. 378–80.

22. Ibid., pp. 421–29.

23. Adlai Stevenson, *Statement by Ambassador Stevenson to UN Security Council* (UN press release 4074), October 25, 1962. See Department of State, Bulletin, vol. 47, no. 1220, November 12, 1962, pp. 737–40.

24. Stevenson, *Statement by Ambassador Stevenson to UN Security Council.*

25. Brugioni, *Eyeball to Eyeball,* pp. 421–29.

26. Stevenson, *Statement by Ambassador Stevenson to UN Security Council.*

27. Fursenko and Naftali, *One Hell of a Gamble,* pp. 257–58 (see chap. 3, n. 26).

Chapter 13. Back Channels and Telegrams

1. Thomas Fensch, ed., *The Kennedy-Khrushchev Letters* (The Woodlands, Tex.: New Century Books, 2001), pp. 310–21.

2. Parish, *The Cold War Encyclopedia,* pp. 163–66 and 168–71 (see chap. 11, n. 4).

3. Sergei N. Khrushchev, *Nikita Khrushchev,* pp. 274–79 (see chap. 2, n. 12).

4. Beschloss, *Mayday,* pp. 216–326 and 353–82 (see chap. 2, n. 11).

5. Sorenson, *Kennedy,* pp. 240–48 (see chap. 8, n. 12).

6. Fursenko and Naftali, *One Hell of a Gamble,* pp. 124–31 (see chap. 3, n. 26).

7. Beschloss, *The Crisis Years,* pp. 72–77 (see chap. 8, n. 30).

8. Letter from Chairman Khrushchev to President Kennedy, February 21, 1962; and telegram from the Department of State to the Embassy of the Soviet Union, February 21, 1962. See Fensch, *The Kennedy-Khrushchev Letters,* pp. 174–77.

9. Message from Chairman Khrushchev to President Kennedy, September 28, 1961. See ibid., pp. 275–308.

10. Beschloss, *The Crisis Years,* pp. 152–57.

11. The Soviet military attachés and their staff in Washington at that time were housed in a large building on Belmont Road, Northwest, just off Massachusetts Avenue.

12. Polmar and Allen, *Spy Book,* pp. 79–80 (see chap. 4, n. 32).

13. Vladislav M. Zubok, *Spy vs. Spy: The KGB vs. the CIA: Cold War History Project Bulletin 4* (Fall 1994), pp. 22–23.

14. Dino Brugioni interview with John D. Gresham and William Howard, Hartwood, Va., July 25, 2002.

15. Sergei N. Khrushchev, *Nikita Khrushchev,* pp. 554–55.

16. Ibid., pp. 556–57.

17. Telegram from the Department of State to the Embassy of the Soviet Union, October 23, 1962. See Fensch, *The Kennedy-Khrushchev Letters*, pp. 301–3.

18. Sergei N. Khrushchev, *Nikita Khrushchev*, pp. 558–61.

19. Part of the Strategic Rocket Forces alert involved ordering the team under "Chief Designer" Sergi Korolev to get ready to remove a modified SS-6 ICBM carrying the world's first unmanned probe to Mars and replace it with an armed missile. Though the probe was eventually launched from the Tyuratam/Baikonur Cosmodrome on October 24 (it failed after launch into earth orbit), the space team stood ready to launch SS-6s from their two launchpads in Kazakhstan. *Source*: James Harford, *Korolev* (New York: John Wiley & Sons, 1997), pp. 151–52.

20. Robert F. Kennedy, *Memorandum from Attorney General Kennedy to President Kennedy about His Meeting with Soviet Ambassador Dobrynin, October 24, 1962*, in U.S. Department of State, *Foreign Relations of the United States, 1961–1963*, vol. 11, *Cuban Missile Crisis and Aftermath*, item no. 53.

21. Sergei N. Khrushchev, *Nikita Khrushchev*, p. 567.

22. Beschloss, *The Crisis Years*, pp. 496–97.

23. When the Allies required a secure voice connection between Washington and overseas headquarters during World War II, the equipment (known as SIGSALY) required at each phone terminal was the size of a small house. Each of these terminals required a staff to operate and maintain the complex equipment, which was very expensive and difficult to manufacture. *Source*: J. V. Boone and R. R. Peterson, *The Start of the Digital Revolution: SIGSALY Secure Digital Voice Communications in World War II* (Fort Meade, Md.: National Security Agency, 2000).

24. Just in case, the Soviet Embassy would usually send a KGB officer to follow the Western Union courier to the Union Station office, to make sure the messages were not stolen or diverted. *Source*: Sergei N. Khrushchev, *Nikita Khrushchev*, pp. 567–68.

25. John D. Gresham, *Cycle Times in Simulations and Games: The Practical Uses of ODA Loops*, presentation for the USAF Air Command and Staff College Connections Conference, Maxwell AFB, Ala., and Air National Guard/Air Force Reserve Intelligence Officers Annual Conference, Warner-Robbins AFB, Ga., October 20, 2000.

26. Holeman was temporarily unemployed due to a strike at the *New York Daily News* and was freelancing for Robert F. Kennedy's Justice Department spokesman Ed Guthman. *Source*: Thomas, *Robert Kennedy*, pp. 221–23.

27. Fursenko and Naftali, *One Hell of a Gamble*, pp. 248–250.

28. Zelikow and May, *The Presidential Recordings: John F. Kennedy*, vol. 3, pp. 178–83.

29. Polmar and Allen, *Spy Book*, pp. 310–14.

30. The American spy ring run by Feklisov had been dismantled in the early 1950s. Many of the leads to U.S. counterintelligence agencies were based upon Soviet World War II communications traffic, broken and analyzed under the so-called Venona program, run initially by the U.S. Army Intelligence and, subsequently, by the NSA. *Source*: Polmar and Allen, *Spy Book*, pp. 202–7, 223–24, 474–75, and 575–78.

31. For almost four decades, American historians have mistakenly used Feklisov's cover name of Alexander Fomin when describing his role in the Cuban Missile Crisis. For purposes of consistency, he is referred to in this volume by his real name.

32. Fursenko and Naftali, *One Hell of a Gamble*, pp. 257–58.

33. The GRU ran a small radio intercept station at the Soviet military attaché offices on Belmont Road in northwest Washington. This listening post had detected the mes-

sages that upgraded SAC's readiness to DEFCON-2. Such messages were transmitted "in the clear," that is, they were not coded or encrypted in any way. Fursenko and Naftali, in *One Hell of a Gamble*, p. 258, state that the listening post was in the Soviet Embassy on 16th Street, but it is highly unlikely that any GRU activities were there and collocated with the competitive KGB activities.

34. Foreign Minister Gromyko was aware of the errand that would be assigned to Feklisov, although the instructions were transmitted confidentially through the KGB communications network. *Source*: Sergei N. Khrushchev, *Nikita Khrushchev*, pp. 582–85.

35. While Feklisov's account of the meeting generally agrees with Scali's account, the KGB officer left out of his autobiography the fact that he was ordered to make the contact by a higher authority. Ever the professional intelligence officer, even in retirement and in his memoirs, Feklisov took responsibility for initiating the meeting, protecting his superiors and tradecraft. *Source*: Feklisov, *The Man behind the Rosenbergs*, pp. 377–83 (see chap. 11, n. 43). Also see chapter 9.

36. Dino Brugioni interview with John D. Gresham and William Howard, Hartwood, Va., July 25, 2002.

37. There has long been a disdain of the Scali-Feklisov discussions among some Cold War scholars. In particular, Fursenko and Naftali cite the apparent lack of Kremlin guidance in the offer and the fact that the final responses between Kennedy and Khrushchev did not arrive prior to the final Scali-Feklisov settlement offers on October 27. However, the fact that a dialogue was active through the two men clearly affected the attitudes of leaders on *both* sides to negotiate and may well have provided the narrow margin of trust needed to reach a final settlement that weekend. Sergei Khrushchev's biography of his father clearly details the covert offer made through Feklisov, and it appears to be more reliable, as well as more recent, than earlier sources. See Aleksandr Fursenko and Timothy Naftali, "Using KGB Documents: The Scali-Feklisov Channel in the Cuban Missile Crisis," *Cold War International History Project Bulletin* 5 (Spring 1995), p. 58.

38. Feklisov, *The Man behind the Rosenbergs*, pp. 380–81.

39. Ibid., pp. 381–83.

40. Sergei N. Khrushchev, *Nikita Khrushchev*, pp. 582–85.

41. Letter from Chairman Khrushchev to President Kennedy, October 27, 1962, in Fensch, *The Kennedy-Khrushchev Letters*, 322–28.

42. Zelikow and May, *The Presidential Recordings: John F. Kennedy*, vol. 3, pp. 349–55.

43. The Jupiter missiles in Italy and Turkey were operated under a dual-key system and thus were technically owned by the host nations as well as the United States. Though obsolete due to the rapid march of technology during the previous few years, the weapons were important symbols of NATO solidarity.

44. Zelikow and May, *The Presidential Recordings: John F. Kennedy*, vol. 3, pp. 356–87.

Chapter 14. OPLAN 316: Invasion!

1. *OPLAN 314, JTF-126, Air Force Annex*, Seymore Johnson AFB, N.C., pp. 6–7 (document located at the Air Force Historical Research Agency, Maxwell AFB, Ala.).

2. Nikita Khrushchev, *Khrushchev Remembers: The Glasnost Tapes* (Boston: Little, Brown, 1990), pp. 167–75.

3. Fursenko and Naftali, *One Hell of a Gamble*, pp. 149–51 (see chap. 3, n. 26).

4. Oral history of Admiral Alfred G. Ward, USN (Ret.), interview no. 7, p. 176.

5. The available details and comments related to those "lessons" are described in Kornbluh, *Bay of Pigs Declassified* (see chap. 4, n. 28), and Wyden, *Bay of Pigs* (see chap. 4, n. 21).

6. Fursenko and Naftali, *One Hell of a Gamble*, pp. 149–51.

7. Wyden, *Bay of Pigs*, pp. 289–312.

8. Headquarters, Nineteenth Air Force, USAF, *OPLAN 314, JTF-126, Air Force Annex*, pp. 11–40.

9. Oral history of Admiral Robert L. Dennison, USN (Ret.), interview no. 10, p. 416.

10. Ibid., pp. 416–19.

11. Ibid., pp. 414–21.

12. Oral history of Admiral Alfred G. Ward, USN (Ret.), interview no. 10, p. 187.

13. Admiral Ward relieved Vice Admiral Jack Taylor, whom some senior officers did not consider suitable for the command; see the oral history of Admiral Horacio Rivero Jr., USN (Ret.), interview no. 4, pp. 351–52.

14. The USAF RF-101 aircraft at the time of the Cuban Missile Crisis were fitted with KA-1 and KA-2 cameras, which were unsuitable for high-speed, low-level photography. Only after KA-45 cameras produced by Chicago Aero Industries for the Navy were installed could the RF-101s undertake the Cuban photo missions. However, the RF-101s were more stable camera platforms than the Navy-Marine Corps F8U-1P aircraft. *Source*: Michael Davis interview with Norman Polmar, Alexandria, Va., July 24, 2002.

15. *Joint Evaluation of the Soviet Missile Threat in Cuba, 0200 Hours, October 27, 1962*, in McAuliffe, *CIA Documents on the Cuban Missile Crisis*, pp. 323–25.

16. Joint Chiefs of Staff, *Memorandum for the Special Assistant to the Secretary of Defense, Subject: Secretary of Defense's Report for the Congress, December 29, 1962*, in Laurence Chang and Peter Kornbluh, eds., *The Cuban Missile Crisis, 1962*, 2nd ed. (New York: New Press, 1998), pp. 285–86.

17. General William Y. Smith, USAF (Ret.), interview with Norman Polmar, Alexandria, Va., July 17, 2002.

18. What made American air losses over North Vietnam so heavy was the Soviet development of the Integrated Air Defense System (IADS), consisting of manned interceptors (MiGs), SAMs (SA-2s), and AAA guns in a networked system controlled by ground control radar. The Cuban IADS was the first such system deployed outside the Soviet sphere of influence, and it became a model for future systems in North Vietnam, Egypt, and Syria. *Sources*: Lon O. Nordeen, *Air Warfare in the Missile Age*, 2nd ed. (Washington, D.C.: Smithsonian Institution Press, 2002), pp. 1–38; and Chris Hobson, *Vietnam Air Losses* (Hinckley, England: Midland, 2001).

19. Tactical Air Command, *OPLAN 314, JTF-126, Air Force Annex*, pp. 16–40.

20. *Memorandum from Malinovsky and Zakharov Informing of Decision to Provide Il-28s and Luna Missiles and of the Pre-Delegation of Launch Authority to Pliyev, September 8, 1962. Source*: Gribkov and Smith, *Operation Anadyr*, p. 183 (see chap. 3, n. 14).

21. While Khrushchev had rescinded Pliyev's local nuclear release authority on the evening of October 26 when a negotiated solution looked probable, it would not have been difficult to reinstate such authority, if required. It should be noted that Soviet attitudes toward the use of tactical nuclear weapons were much different from U.S. attitudes

during that period. *Sources*: Fursenko and Naftali, *One Hell of a Gamble*, pp. 149–51; and Chuck Hansen, *U.S. Nuclear Weapons* (Arlington, Tex.: Orion Books/Aerofax, 1988), pp. 106–22.

22. Rear Admiral Thomas A. Brooks, USN (Ret.), interview with Norman Polmar, Fairfax Station, Va., June 18, 2002. Brooks was the director of U.S. Naval Intelligence from July 1988 to August 1991.

23. Cornelius Ryan, *The Longest Day* (New York: Simon & Schuster, 1959), p. 8.

24. Samuel Glasstone, ed., *The Effects of Nuclear Weapons*, rev. ed., February 1964 (Washington, D.C.: Atomic Energy Commission, 1964), pp. 547–97.

25. Ibid.

26. Hansen, *U.S. Nuclear Weapons*, pp. 149–54.

27. Rear Admiral E. L. Feightner, USN (Ret.), interview with Norman Polmar, Arlington, Va., May 17, 2002. The Navy's ammunition ships in the Caribbean carried additional nuclear bombs, to replenish the stocks of the aircraft carriers if required. *Source*: Vice Admiral Gerald E. Miller, USN (Ret.), e-mail to Norman Polmar, May 11, 2002.

28. American tactical nuclear weapons in 1962 had almost none of the controls we know today, such as Permissive Action Locks (PALs). Prior to the Cuban Missile Crisis, security for tactical nuclear warheads and bombs were the simple expedients of detailed background checks and lifestyle monitoring (the Personnel Reliability Profile or "PRP") of key personnel and keeping the nuclear bomb cores stored separately from the actual devices. *Source*: *Personnel Reliability Program Factsheet* (Albuquerque, N.M.: Defense Threat Reduction Agency Corporate Communications, July 6, 2001).

29. Lieutenant General Keith Compton, USAF (Ret.), interview with Norman Polmar and John D. Gresham, Washington, D.C., July 15, 2002.

Chapter 15. From SIOP to Dr. Strangelove

1. General Curtis E. LeMay, USAF (Ret.), *Mission with LeMay* (Garden City, N.Y.: Doubleday, 1966), p. 481.

2. Lewis L. Strauss, *Men and Decisions* (London: Macmillan, 1963), p. 202.

3. The first American attempt to launch an earth-orbiting satellite, *Vanguard-1*, failed on December 6, 1957, when the booster exploded on the pad during launch. The first successful American satellite launch occurred on January 31, 1958, with *Explorer-1*.

4. In 1962, other than the United States and the USSR, the nations with nuclear weapons were Great Britain and France. China did not detonate its first atomic bomb until 1964.

5. The first commanding general of SAC was General George C. Kenney, from March 1946 to October 1948. Kenney had served during much of World War II as the commander of General Douglas MacArthur's air forces in the Southwest Pacific.

6. LeMay served as commanding general and, from June 1953, as commander-in-chief of SAC. He had the longest tenure of any U.S. military force commander in the twentieth century.

7. Walter Millis, ed., *The Forrestal Diaries* (New York: Viking Press, 1951), p. 458.

8. Ibid., pp. 460–61.

9. David E. Lilienthal, *The Journals of David E. Lilienthal*, vol. 2 (New York: Harper & Row, 1964), p. 391.

10. Captain William B. Moore, USN, memorandum, "Briefing Given to the Representatives of All Services at SAC Headquarters," March 18, 1954, p. 2; this memo of the March 15, 1954, briefing is analyzed and published in Dr. David Alan Rosenberg, "A Smoking Radiating Ruin at the End of Two Hours," *International Security* (Winter 1981/1982), pp. 3–38.

11. Richard Rhodes, *Dark Sun* (New York: Simon & Schuster, 1995), pp. 574–75.

12. Ibid., p. 566.

13. Walter D. Moody, *Building a Strategic Air Force* (Washington, D.C.: Air Force History and Museum Program, 1995), pp. 187–462.

14. The Mk 39 was rated at 3 to 4 megatons of explosive power. *Source*: Hansen, *U.S. Nuclear Weapons*, pp. 146–47 (see chap. 14, n. 21).

15. There was fear in the 1950s of Soviet submarine-launched air attacks against SAC bomber bases. A secret Project Rand study in 1953—sponsored by the U.S. Air Force—concluded that "Using the submarine-launched or low-altitude Tu-4 surprise attack, *the enemy can destroy a major part of SAC potential at relatively small cost in A-bombs and aircraft.* With no more than 50 aircraft and [nuclear] bombs, two-thirds or more of SAC bomber and reconnaissance aircraft could be destroyed" (emphasis in original). *Source*: Project Rand, *Vulnerability of U.S. Strategic Air Power to a Surprise Enemy Attack in 1956*, Special Memorandum SM-15 (Santa Monica, Calif.: Rand Corp., April 15, 1953), p. ii.

16. Office of the Historian, Headquarters, SAC, *The Development of Strategic Air Command* (Offutt AFB, Neb.: September 1, 1986), p. 83.

17. Rhodes, *Dark Sun*, p. 571.

18. Norman Polmar and Timothy Laur, *Strategic Air Command: People, Aircraft and Missiles*, 2nd ed. (Baltimore, Md.: Nautical and Aviation, 1990), pp. 79–84.

19. The Soviet ICBM force was deployed on either open-air launchpads or enclosed "coffin" launchers, none of which were yet "hardened" to survive a nearby nuclear blast.

20. A number of tactical nuclear weapons did require the simultaneous turning of a pair of keys by physically separated personnel to complete the firing circuit.

21. *Personnel Reliability Program Factsheet.*

22. Joint Strategic Target Planning Staff, U.S. Air Force Fact Sheet (Offutt AFB, Neb., April 1, 1978), p. 1; and Secretary Thomas S. Gates interview with Norman Polmar, New York City, May 22, 1975.

23. Ibid.

24. A decade after its establishment, in 1970 the JSTPS staff numbered more than three hundred men and women—65 percent from the Air Force, 25 percent from the Navy and the Marine Corps, and about 10 percent from the Army, plus British representatives.

25. During the course of the Cold War, U.S. missile submarine tenders were forward based at Holy Loch, Scotland; Rota, Spain; and Apra Harbor, Guam.

26. Each ICBM at the time carried a single warhead; the B-52 could carry up to four nuclear bombs, the B-47 two, and the B-58 one. In addition, some B-52s could carry two Hound Dog stand-off cruise missiles with a range of up to 750 miles, each armed with a 1-MT Mk 28 nuclear warhead.

27. While SIOP-62 did have sixteen options for the actual execution of the plan, these referred only to the total number of nuclear weapons delivered. Under SIOP-62, there was no ability to select alternative target sets or to limit the strikes to particular

types of facilities like ICBM launchpads or bomber bases. *Source*: General Maxwell D. Taylor, U.S.A., *Memorandum to General Leminteer, September 19, 1961.*

28. Major General William Y. Smith, USAF, *Memorandum for General Taylor; Subject: Strategic Air Planning and Berlin*, September 7, 1961.

29. General Taylor, *Memorandum to Gen. Leminteer*, September 19, 1961.

30. Nikita Khrushchev, *Khrushchev Remembers*, pp. 268–332 (see chap. 2, n. 1).

31. Major General Smith, *Memorandum for Gen. Taylor*, September 7, 1961.

32. For example, the later Minuteman III missile carried three multiple independently targeted reentry vehicles (MIRVs), while the Poseidon C-4 missile, the successor to the Polaris series, could carry up to fourteen MIRVs.

33. Fred Kaplan and Martin J. Sherwin, *The Wizards of Armageddon* (Stanford, Calif.: Stanford University Press, 1991), p. 246.

34. Robert R. Bowie and Gerard C. Smith, *Memorandum for the Secretary; Subject: Policy Regarding Use of Atomic Weapons*, May 15, 1957.

35. *Dr. Strangelove or How I Learned to Stop Worrying and Love the Bomb* (Stanley Kubrick/Columbia Pictures, 1963).

36. General William Y. Smith, USAF, researched the issue of General Power sending SAC to DEFCON-2 status and discusses it in his oral history, for which he was interviewed from April 1990 to April 1996; see pp. 282–83. The oral history is held by the Air Force Historical Research Agency, Maxwell Air Force Base, Ala.

37. The SAC Worldwide Broadcast System used a powerful single-sideband radio system, which had the virtue of excellent range, clarity, and bandwidth. While capable of transmitting encrypted signals, major changes in SAC alert status and U.S. Defense Condition (DEFCON) were transmitted by voice in the clear. Although this protocol guaranteed that people receiving commands would clearly understand the instructions emanating from SAC headquarters at Offutt AFB in Omaha, it also meant that anyone with a single-sideband receiver could easily intercept and listen to the signals.

38. Fursenko and Naftali, *One Hell of a Gamble*, p. 258 (see chap. 3, n. 26).

39. Robert K. Dyar, *History of the 4347th Combat Crew Training Wing (M), McConnell Air Force Base, Kansas, 1–26 November 1962* (official unit history).

40. Airman 1st class John F. Cody, *History of the 100th Bombardment Wing (M), Pease Air Force Base, New Hampshire, 1–31 October 1962* (official unit history).

41. *306th Bomb Wing—McCoy AFB History*, Web site hosted by the 306th Bomb Wing Association at www.306thbw.org/306thhistory/history_306BW.htm.

42. *The Cuban Missile Crisis: A Chronology of Events, October 1, 1962—October 25, 1962.* Web site hosted by George Washington University at www.gwu.edu/~nsarchiv/nsa/cuba_mis_cri/cmcchron2.html.

43. Sergei N. Khrushchev, *Nikita Khrushchev*, pp. 579–82 (see chap. 2, n. 12).

44. *Doomsday Mission* (Hoggard Films/The Discovery Channel, 1997).

45. Only once has the Continuity of Government program been activated. This occurred on the morning of September 11, 2001, following the Al-Qaeda terrorist attacks on the World Trade Center and the Pentagon. Helicopters and large armored sport-utility vehicles moved administration figures in the line of succession, congressional leaders, and other key government personnel out to what became publicly known as "undisclosed locations." While most of the more senior and public figures were returned to Washington, D.C., by nightfall on September 11, elements of the COG program have been continuously in effect since that date.

46. During the Cold War, the USSR, along with many nations within NATO, had its own COG-type program. Allegedly, the Soviet Union had a Mount Weather–style bunker built into a huge rock mountain near Kuybyshev (present-day Samara) that could hold and sustain the Kremlin leadership in the event of war. Great Britain, Canada, and other NATO nations had their own COG programs and facilities, many of which have been declassified and now are open to the public as museums and tourist attractions.

47. N. J. McCamley, *Cold War Secret Nuclear Bunkers* (Barnsley, South Yorkshire, U.K.: Leo Cooper, 2003), pp. 5–23.

48. Gup, "The Ultimate Congressional Hideaway," p. W11 (see chap. 1, n. 6).

49. Department of Defense, *Appendix 1 to Annex F: Joint Air Transportation Plan (Short Title: JATS PLAN)*, C-3020.26 (Incl 1) June 10, 1960 (Washington, D.C.: June 10, 1960), pp. F–1 to F–9.

50. Department of Defense, *Appendix 1 to Annex E: Joint Emergency Evacuation Plan (Short Title: JEEP PLAN)*, C-3020.26 (Incl 1) December 23, 1961 (Washington, D.C.: June 10, 1960), pp. E-2 to E-9.

51. Gup, "The Ultimate Congressional Hideaway," p. W11.

52. Dino A. Brugioni interview with John D. Gresham and Bill Howard, Hartwood, Va., July 25, 2002.

53. Fursenko and Naftali, *One Hell of a Gamble*, pp. 266–79.

54. Paul H. Nitze interview with Norman Polmar, Washington, D.C., June 26, 2002.

55. Paul H. Nitze, *From Hiroshima to Glasnost: At the Center of Decision—a Memoir* (New York: Grove Weidenfeld, 1989), p. 237.

56. The Canadian nuclear munitions were controlled by U.S. teams in Canada.

57. Lieutenant General Keith Compton, USAF (Ret.), interview with Norman Polmar and John D. Gresham, Washington, D.C., July 15, 2002.

58. Jerry Miller, *Nuclear Weapons and Aircraft Carriers* (Washington, D.C.: Smithsonian Institution Press, 2001), p. 132.

59. There were 515 KC-135 jet-propelled tankers and 500 KC-97 piston-powered tankers in service with SAC in 1962.

60. Fursenko and Naftali, *One Hell of a Gamble*, pp. 266–79.

61. Interview with Fidel Castro, March 1998. Web site for *Cold War*, Episode 10, online at www.cnn.com/SPECIALS/cold.war/episodes/10/interviews/castro/.

Chapter 16. The Deal: The Turkish Card

1. Nikita Khrushchev, *Khrushchev Remembers: The Last Testament* (Boston: Little, Brown, 1974), p. 512.

2. The Polaris was considered for surface ships, both warships and dedicated strategic missile ships; in the event, Polaris and its successor missiles—Poseidon and Trident—were carried only by submarines.

3. Following withdrawal from the Jupiter-S program in 1956 and using state-of-the-art management planning, the Navy was able to fire its first Polaris A1 missile from the USS *George Washington* on July 20, 1960. By November 1960, the *George Washington*—loaded with sixteen Polaris A1 SLBMs—was on its first deterrence patrol. By comparison, the first Italian-based Jupiters did not become operational until June 1961.

4. The Thor missiles were installed at Feltwell, Hemswell, North Luffenham, and Waddington.

5. The W49 also armed the Atlas-D, the first operational U.S. ICBM.

6. At one point during the Cold War, Turkey ranked behind West Germany, Britain, and South Korea as the fourth largest repository of nuclear weapons in allied countries. Reportedly, there were ten storage sites in Turkey with some five hundred nuclear warheads. *Source*: Natural Resources Defense Council, *Worldwide Nuclear Deployments 1998* (Washington, D.C.: March 1998), p. 78.

7. Kohler subsequently was appointed U.S. ambassador to the Soviet Union, serving in Moscow from September 1962 to November 1966, that is, during the missile crisis of 1962.

8. The U.S. intelligence community consisted of the Central Intelligence Agency and the intelligence offices of the Department of State, the Department of Defense, the military services, the Atomic Energy Commission, and the Federal Bureau of Investigation.

9. Director of Central Intelligence, *Probable Sino-Soviet Reaction to US Deployment of IRBMs on the Soviet Bloc Periphery*, SNIE 100-4-58 (Washington, D.C.: April 28, 1958), p. 1; reprinted in Scott A. Koch, ed., *Selected Estimates on the Soviet Union, 1950–1959* (Washington, D.C.: CIA Center for the Study of Intelligence, 1993), pp. 271–79.

10. Director of Central Intelligence, *Probable Sino-Soviet Reaction to US Deployment of IRBMs on the Soviet Bloc Periphery*, pp. 2–3.

11. Nikita Khrushchev, *Khrushchev Remembers*, p. 493 (see chap. 2, n. 1).

12. Message to Commander in Chief U.S. Forces Europe, JCS 6866, October 22, 1962.

13. Fursenko and Naftali, *One Hell of a Gamble*, p. 274 (see chap. 3, n. 26).

14. Telegram from the Department of State to the Embassy in Turkey, October 24, 1962, 11:24 P.M., Department of State Central Files, 611.3722/10-2462. Drafted by George Ball and approved by Dean Rusk.

15. Telegram from the U.S. Embassy in France to the Department of State, October 25, 1962, 9 P.M., Department of State, S/S Files: Lot 65 D 438, Jupiter—Cuba. Received at 6:41 P.M. on October 25.

16. A total of forty-one nuclear-propelled Polaris submarines were completed from 1960 to 1967.

17. Fursenko and Naftali, *One Hell of a Gamble*, p. 275.

18. The closest that the U.S. government came to giving foreign navies access to submarine nuclear propulsion was the transfer of an S5W reactor plant for British use in the Royal Navy's first nuclear-propelled submarine, HMS *Dreadnought*, completed in 1963.

19. The U.S. destroyer *Claude V. Ricketts* was employed as the MLF test ship with a multinational crew in 1964–1965.

20. May and Zelikow, *The Kennedy Tapes*, p. 482 (see chap. 7, n. 17).

21. Ibid.

22. Humphrey Wynn, *RAF Nuclear Deterrent Forces* (London: Her Majesty's Stationery Office, 1994), p. 358.

23. This was the first Polaris submarine visit to a foreign port other than Holy Loch, Scotland, which had served as a forward base for Polaris submarines since March 1961.

24. Ambassador Raymond Hare's cable to secretary of state, October 26, 1962, at 6 P.M.; received October 27, 1962, at 1:18 P.M.; Department of State control no. 19238.

Chapter 17. Withdrawal

1. Nitze, *From Hiroshima to Glasnost*, p. 237 (see chap. 15, n. 55).

2. ExComm on October 28 also proposed the use of U.S. Air Force RB-66 Destroyer camera planes for the inspection role, with United Nations observers on board.

3. See, for example, the memorandum *Deployment and Withdrawal of Soviet Missiles and Other Significant Weapons in Cuba, November 29, 1962*, in McAuliffe, *CIA Documents on the Cuban Missile Crisis 1962*, p. 357 (see chap. 3, n. 22). The CIA report states that the sources for most of those reports "are untested and some of their reports are manifestly erroneous."

4. The Komars were missile-armed craft but were often referred to as motor *torpedo* boats.

5. Mikoyan had been dispatched to New York and Havana by Khrushchev, who knew that Mikoyan's wife was gravely ill. Khrushchev reportedly stated that Mikoyan's wife "was beyond help and that, without him, the situation in Cuba was very grave." *Source*: Sergei N. Khrushchev, *Nikita Khrushchev*, p. 643 (see chap. 2, n. 12).

6. Various U.S. and Soviet sources differ on how many Il-28s were assembled; the numbers vary from seven to twenty.

7. Summary Record of National Security Council Executive Committee Meeting No. 19, November 3, 1962.

8. U.S. subversive operations against Cuba—Operation Mongoose—were continuing even as the negotiations were under way. As late as November 8, a six-man CIA sabotage team would carry out a long-planned attack on an industrial facility in Cuba.

9. Two Komar-class missile boats, moored in Port Said, Egypt, on October 21, 1967, launched three Styx missiles that sank the Israeli destroyer *Eilat* steaming offshore. It was history's first sinking of a warship by surface-to-surface missiles. (In World War II, several ships, including the Italian battleship *Roma*, had been sunk by air-to-surface missiles.)

10. Oral history of Admiral Robert L. Dennison, USN (Ret.), July 17, 1973.

11. In fact, at least one SS-4 training missile, not capable of carrying a nuclear warhead, was left behind. It is now on display in Havana, along with (unarmed) FKR-1, FROG-3, and P-15 Styx missiles.

12. Memorandum *Soviet Offensive Weapons in Cuba, October 29, 1962*, in McAuliffe, *CIA Documents on the Cuban Missile Crisis 1962*, p. 351.

13. The Il-28 remained in service in large numbers with Soviet *tactical* air forces in 1962. The Il-28, which flew for the first time on July 8, 1948, was mass-produced in the USSR (about three thousand aircraft) and China (more than five hundred as the Hong-5); it was also flown by about twenty other air forces.

14. Joint Chiefs of Staff, *Chairman's Talking Paper for Meeting with the President*, November 16, 1962.

15. United Nations Press Services, "Text of Communication Dated 19 November 1962 from Prime Minister Fidel Castro of Cuba to Acting Secretary-General U Thant," press release SG/1379, November 20, 1962.

16. Memorandum *Deployment and Withdrawal of Soviet Missiles and Other Significant Weapons in Cuba, November 29, 1962*, in McAuliffe, *CIA Documents on the Cuban Missile Crisis 1962*, p. 360. The CIA estimated that it would require four months and on the order of a hundred voyages to remove those forces from Cuba.

17. The U.S. Corona photographic satellite had become operational in 1960, shortly after Francis Gary Powers's U-2 was shot down. However, providing rapid, repeat coverage of a specific area was difficult, and the U-2 and the SR-71 continued in service.

Chapter 18. Legacy: The Anadyr Effect

1. Paul H. Nitze, *Hiroshima to Glasnost*, p. 219 (see chap. 15, n. 55).

2. Admiral Anderson died in early 1992, just months before the first public revelations about the Soviets having deployed battlefield nuclear weapons to Cuba as part of Operation Anadyr. *Source*: Oral history of Admiral George W. Anderson Jr., USN (Ret.), January 27, 1981.

3. Robert F. Kennedy, *Thirteen Days*, pp. 69–70 (see chap. 7, n. 1).

4. The U.S. destroyers were fitted with the ASROC (Anti-Submarine Rocket), a short-range weapon that could launch a conventional homing torpedo or a nuclear depth bomb with a W44 warhead (1-KT yield). The ASW aircraft could carry the Lulu nuclear depth bomb with the W34 warhead (11-KT yield).

5. Nikita Khrushchev, *Khrushchev Remembers*, p. 497 (see chap. 2, n. 1).

6. Paul H. Nitze interview with Norman Polmar, Washington, D.C., June 26, 2002.

7. Nikita Khrushchev, *Khrushchev Remembers*, p. 497.

8. Interview with former Secretary of Defense Robert S. McNamara, in *The Fog of War* (Julie Bilson Ahlberg/Columbia Tri-Star, 2004).

9. Some historians have credited Khrushchev's life being preserved to his own charity with the plotters of the 1957 coup against him. Instead of having them killed or imprisoned, Khrushchev allowed them to be transferred to minor posts, their pensions paid, and the men honorably retired. Stalin unquestionably would have had all involved in such an action immediately executed and continuing retribution delivered against their families and friends. Leonid Brezhnev and his confederates had little choice but to offer Khrushchev and his family similar charity, perhaps the most positive and lasting of the contributions made during his tenure.

10. Sergei Khrushchev, *Nikita Khrushchev*, p. 704 (see chap. 2, n. 12).

11. The next U.S. mass-produced strategic bomber to be delivered was a B-1B Lancer in 1985; only a hundred were produced. The subsequent U.S. strategic bomber was the B-2 "stealth" bomber, the first of twenty-one aircraft being delivered in 1997.

12. Missiles with MIRV warhead capabilities often traded out warheads for decoys and other so-called penetration aids to counter possible enemy defenses such as antiballistic missile systems. To do this, the mount for the MIRV warheads (called a "bus") would download one or more nuclear warheads and then replace them with the decoys.

13. An engineer by training, Brezhnev had overseen the Soviet space and missile programs for Khrushchev. Source: Sergei Khrushchev, *Nikita Khrushchev*, pp. 417–25 and 449.

14. The massive Soviet national air-defense system (PVO *Strany*) would undoubtedly have blunted or even destroyed much of the U.S. attacking bomber force. When the United States began deploying large numbers of missiles with MIRV warheads, a large portion of the U.S. strategic missile force was targeted against Soviet air defenses. Thus, U.S. land- and submarine-based missiles would help the vulnerable manned bombers penetrate to their targets.

15. If the Tu-22M (NATO Backfire) aircraft is included, the Soviet Union overtook the United States in the number of strategic bombers in about 1981. The Soviets had stated that the Backfire was a medium bomber intended for theater strike; however, the U.S. Department of Defense's technical assessments of the Backfire's performance indicated that the aircraft could carry out intercontinental strikes with in-flight refueling.

16. The numbers do not include twenty-nine Soviet diesel-electric Project 629 (NATO Golf) submarines, which carried two short-range ballistic missiles. These later deployed as far away as the Caribbean.

17. The first Soviet nuclear-propelled aircraft carrier, the *Admiral Kuznetsov*, was under construction when the Cold War ended in 1991.

18. Lyle J. Goldstein and Yuri M. Zhukov, "A Tale of Two Fleets," *Naval War College Review* (Spring 2004), pp. 27–63.

19. This executive-level post-traumatic stress syndrome of ExComm members is shown with great accuracy and effect in the 2003 Home Box Office film *Path to War. Path to War* (John Frankenheimer/HBO Home Video, 2003).

20. President Johnson refused on a number of occasions to use military force to react to attacks on American ships and interests during the late 1960s. These included the Israeli attack on the USS *Liberty* in June 1967, the North Korean seizing of the USS *Pueblo* in January 1968, and the Soviet invasion and occupation of Czechoslovakia in August 1968.

21. Throughout the Vietnam War, President Johnson and Secretary of Defense McNamara continually established rules of engagement and bombing restrictions designed to reduce the chances that Soviet or Chinese "advisors" and other personnel who might be manning air defenses, merchant ships, and transportation facilities might become casualties.

22. The economic assistance to North Vietnam was sent by ship.

23. Under Khrushchev's regime, the Soviet Union was providing nuclear weapons technology to China in the 1950s. However, the shipment of a nuclear bomb for the Chinese to use as a prototype was halted at the last minute. *Source*: Nikita Khrushchev, *Khrushchev Remembers: The Last Testament*, pp. 268–69 (see chap. 16, n. 1).

24. The Soviets began to establish the Lourdes intelligence complex in August 1962, taking over a boys' reformatory at Torrens and several adjacent farms. The facility was reported to eventually cover an area of twenty-eight square miles. See Bill Gertz, "Soviets Said to Operate Spy Base in Cuba Able to Monitor U.S. Phones," *New York Tribune* (March 25, 1985), p. 1; and Federation of American Scientists, "Lourdes [Cuba] Signals Intelligence (SIGINT) facility, 23° 00′ 01″ N 82° 28′ 56″ W," on FAS Web site at www.fas.org/irp/imint/c80_04.htm.

25. Gertz, "Soviets Said to Operate Spy Base in Cuba Able to Monitor U.S. Phones."

26. As the last of the Russian personnel were being withdrawn from Lourdes in 2002, the Cubans were planning to turn the facility into a center for computer technology and learning.

27. Che Guevara was hunted down and executed by a special unit of the Bolivian Army while he was conducting guerrilla operations in Bolivia in 1967. The unit apparently had CIA advisors.

28. The United States launched an airborne-amphibious invasion of Grenada in October 1983, which ousted the Marxist government.

29. The vehicle, a Soviet-made SU-100 self-propelled gun, is preserved in front of the Museum of the Revolution in Havana. Built on a modified T-34 tank chassis, it is commonly referred to as "Castro's tank."

30. José Fernández interview with Brian Kelly and Norman Polmar, Havana, September 2, 2002. Fernández had been an officer in Batista's army and had attended the U.S. Army's artillery school at Fort Sill, Okla., before joining Castro's forces.

31. Jorge Risquet interview with Brian Kelly and Norman Polmar, Havana, September 3, 2002.

32. Carlos Lechuga, *Cuba and the Missile Crisis* (Melbourne: Ocean Press, 2001), p. 4.

33. Ibid., p. 109.

34. Jorge Risquet interview with Brian Kelly and Norman Polmar, Havana, September 3, 2002.

35. Ibid.

36. Lyle J. Goldstein and Yuri M. Zhukov, "A Tale of Two Fleets: A Russian Perspective on the 1973 Naval Standoff in the Mediterranean," *Naval War College Review* (Spring 2004), pp. 27–63.

37. Quoted in Admiral Elmo R. Zumwalt Jr., *On Watch* (New York: New York Times Book Co., 1976), p. 447. Admiral Zumwalt, the Chief of Naval Operations at the time, provided a detailed description of that naval confrontation.

38. The Navy was also testing the hypothesis held by some senior admirals that Soviet intelligence was intercepting and reading U.S. military communications. The officers who held that hypothesis were vindicated in 1985 when the FBI arrested the retired Navy communications specialist John A. Walker Jr., and members of his spy ring. Walker had been selling the cipher material to the KGB since at least 1967.

39. "Replies of Yu. V. Andropov to Questions from a Pravda Correspondent," *Pravda*, March 27, 1983.

40. Christopher Andrew and Oleg Gordievsky, *Instructions from the Centre: Top Secret Files on KGB Foreign Operations, 1975–1985* (London: Hodder & Stoughton, 1991), p. 67.

41. Andrew and Gordievsky, *Instructions from the Centre*, p. 70.

42. William Fuller Jr., *Strategy and Power in Russia, 1600–1914* (New York: Free Press, 1992), p. 12.

43. Quoted in Don Oberdorfer, *The Turn: From the Cold War to a New Era: The United States and the Soviet Union 1983–1990* (New York: Poseidon Press, 1991), p. 67.

44. Christopher Andrew and Oleg Gordievsky, *KGB: The Inside Story of Its Foreign Operations from Lenin to Gorbachev* (London: Hodder and Stoughton, 1990), p. 605. Andrew and Gordievsky provide a detailed discussion of RYAN on pp. 584–605. Also see Ben B. Fisher, *A Cold War Conundrum: The 1983 Soviet War Scare*, CSI 97-10002 (Washington, D.C.: Central Intelligence Agency, September 1997).

45. Gil Merom, "The 1962 Cuban Intelligence Estimate: A Methodological Perspective," *Intelligence and National Security* (Autumn 1999), pp. 48–80.

46. Brugioni, *Eyeball to Eyeball*, pp. 190–217 (see chap. 6, n. 1).

47. Bamford, *Body of Secrets*, pp. 110–12 (see chap. 4, n. 22).

48. Lieutenant General Keith Compton, USAF (Ret.), interview with Norman Polmar and John D. Gresham, Washington, D.C., July 15, 2002.

49. Zelikow and May, eds., *The Presidential Recordings: John F. Kennedy*, vol. 3, pp. 173–83 (see chap. 8, n. 33).

50. McGeorge Bundy, *Forecast Weather over Cuba and Missions Status, September 5–October 14, 1962*, JFK Presidential Library, Boston, Mass., February 27, 1963.

51. Between October 23 and 27, a total of twenty-seven two-aircraft missions were flown by F8U-1Ps. Peter Mersky, *RF-8 Crusader Units over Cuba and Vietnam* (Botley, Oxford, U.K.: Osprey, 1999), pp. 9–15.

52. *Supplement 7 to Joint Evaluation of the Soviet Missile Threat in Cuba, October 27, 1962*, in McAuliffe, *CIA Documents on the Cuban Missile Crisis 1962*, pp. 323–24 (see chap. 3, n. 22).

53. Memorandum *Soviet Offensive Weapons in Cuba, October 29, 1962*, in McAuliffe, *CIA Documents on the Cuban Missile Crisis 1962*, p. 351.

54. National Commission on the Terrorist Attacks upon the United States, *The 9/11 Commission Report* (New York: W. W. Norton, 2004), pp. 1–14.

55. The INF accord allowed for ballistic missiles to be retained in museums on both sides. Today, the National Air and Space Museum in Washington, D.C., and a similar facility in Russia each have an American Pershing II and a Soviet-era SS-20 on display.

56. The full text of President Kennedy's June 10, 1963, commencement speech (as delivered) at American University can be found online at www.american.edu/media/speeches/Kennedy.htm.

BIBLIOGRAPHY

Books

Abel, Elie. *The Missile Crisis*. New York: J. B. Lippincott, 1966.

Allison, Graham, and Philip Zelikow. *Essence of Decision: Explaining the Cuban Missile Crisis*, 2nd ed. New York: Addison Wesley Longman, 1999.

Andrew, Christopher, and Oleg Gordievsky. *Instructions from the Centre: Top Secret Files on KGB Foreign Operations 1975–1985*. London: Hodder & Stoughton, 1991.

————. *KGB: The Inside Story of Its Foreign Operations from Lenin to Gorbachev*. London: Hodder & Stoughton, 1990.

Andrew, Christopher, and Vasili Mitrokhin. *The Sword and the Shield*. Cambridge, Mass.: Basic Books, 1999.

Bamford, James. *Body of Secrets: Anatomy of the Ultra-Secret National Security Agency*. New York: Anchor Books, 2002.

Beach, Captain Edward L., USN (Ret.). *The United States Navy: 200 Years*. New York: Henry Holt, 1986.

Beschloss, Michael R. *The Crisis Years*. New York: HarperCollins, 1991.

————. *Mayday: Eisenhower, Khrushchev and the U-2 Affair*. New York: Harper & Row, 1986.

Bissell, Richard M., Jr. *Reflections of a Cold Warrior: From Yalta to the Bay of Pigs*. New Haven, Conn.: Yale University Press, 1996.

Blight, James G., and David A. Welch. *On the Brink: Americans and Soviets Reexamine the Cuban Missile Crisis*. New York: Hill and Wang, 1989.

Brown, Anthony Cave. *Bodyguard of Lies*. New York: Harper and Row, 1975.

Brugioni, Dino A. *Eyeball to Eyeball: The Inside Story of the Cuban Missile Crisis*. New York: Random House, 1991.

Bundy, McGeorge. *Danger and Survival: Choices about the Bomb in the First Fifty Years*. New York: Random House, 1988.

Burrows, William E. *Deep Black*. New York: Berkley Books, 1988.

Butowski, Piotr, with Jay Miller. *OKB MiG: A History of the Design Bureau and Its Aircraft*. Stillwater, Minn.: Aerofax, Inc., for Specialty Press, 1991.

Chang, Laurence, and Peter Kornbluh, eds. *The Cuban Missile Crisis, 1962*, 2nd ed. New York: New Press, 1998.

Crickmore, Paul F. *Lockheed SR-71: The Secret Missions Exposed*. London: Osprey Aerospace, 1993.

Dallek, Robert. *An Unfinished Life*. New York: Little Brown, 2003.

Day, Dwayne A., John M. Logsdon, and Brian Latell, eds. *Eye in the Sky: The Story of the Corona Spy Satellites.* Washington, D.C.: Smithsonian Institution Press, 1998.

Dubivko, Aleksei F. "In the Depths of the Sargasso Sea," extracted from *On the Edge of the Nuclear Precipice.* Translated by Svetlana Savranskaya of the National Security Archive. Moscow: Gregory Page, 1998.

Eisenhower, Gen. of the Army Dwight D., USA. *Crusade in Europe: A Personal Account of World War II.* Garden City, N.Y.: Doubleday, 1948.

Feklisov, Alexander. *The Man behind the Rosenbergs.* New York: Enigma Books, 2001.

Fensch, Thomas, ed. *The Kennedy-Khrushchev Letters.* The Woodlands, Tex.: New Century Books, 2001.

Freedman, Lawrence. *Kennedy's Wars: Berlin, Cuba, Laos, and Vietnam.* New York: Oxford University Press, 2000.

Friedman, Norman. *The Fifty Year War: Conflict and Strategy in the Cold War.* Annapolis, Md.: Naval Institute Press, 2000.

Fuller, William, Jr. *Strategy and Power in Russia, 1600–1914.* New York: Free Press, 1992.

Fursenko, Aleksandr, and Timothy Naftali. *One Hell of a Gamble: Khrushchev, Castro, and Kennedy, 1958–1964.* New York: W. W. Norton, 1997.

Garthoff, Raymond L. *Détente and Confrontation.* Washington, D.C.: Brookings Institution, 1994.

————. *Reflections on the Cuban Missile Crisis.* Washington, D.C.: Brookings Institution, 1989.

Gibbons, Tony. *The Complete Encyclopedia of Battleships: A Technical Directory of Capital Ships from 1860 to the Present Day.* New York: Crescent Books, 1983.

Glasstone, Samuel, ed. *The Effects of Nuclear Weapons*, rev. ed., reprinted February 1964. Washington, D.C.: Government Printing Office for the Department of Defense of the Atomic Energy Commission, 1964.

Green, William. *The World Guide to Combat Planes*, vol. 1. Garden City, N.Y.: Doubleday, 1967.

Greenway, Ambrose. *Soviet Merchant Ships.* Emsworth, Hampshire, U.K.: Kenneth Mason, 1985.

Gribkov, Lieutenant General Anatoli I., and General William Y. Smith, USAF (Ret.). *Operation Anadyr: U.S. and Soviet Generals Recount the Cuban Missile Crisis.* Chicago: Edition q., 1994.

Grose, Peter. *Gentleman Spy: The Life of Allen Dulles.* New York: Houghton Mifflin, 1994.

Gunston, Bill, with Peter Gilchrist. *Jet Bombers from the Messerschmitt Me 262 to the Stealth B-2.* Over Wallop, Hampshire, U.K.: Osprey, 1993.

————. *Mikoyan MiG-21.* London: Osprey-Motorbooks; Washington, D.C.: Brookings Institution, 1989.

Halberstam, David. *The Best and the Brightest.* New York: Random House, 1972.

Hall, Rex, and David J. Shayler. *Rocket Men: Vostok and Voskhod, the First Soviet Manned Spaceflights.* Chichester, U.K.: Springer in association with Praxis Publishing, 2001.

Hamilton, Nigel. *JFK: Reckless Youth.* New York: Random House, 1992.

Hansen, Chuck. *U.S. Nuclear Weapons.* Arlington, Tex.: Orion Books/Aerofax, 1988.

Harford, James. *Korolev: How One Man Masterminded the Soviet Drive to Beat America to the Moon.* New York: John Wiley & Sons, 1997.

Hauchthausen, Peter. *K-19: The Widowmaker*. Washington, D.C.: National Geographic, 2002.

—————. *October Fury*. Hoboken, N.J.: John Wiley & Sons, 2002.

Heinl, Col. Robert Debs, Jr., USMC. *Soldiers of the Sea: The United States Marine Corps, 1775–1962*, 2nd ed. Charleston, S.C.: Nautical & Aviation Publishing, 1991.

Herrick, Robert Waring. *Soviet Naval Strategy: Fifty Years of Theory and Practice*. Annapolis, Md.: U.S. Naval Institute, 1968.

—————. *Soviet Naval Theory and Policy: Gorshkov's Inheritance*. Annapolis, Md.: Naval Institute Press, 1968.

Hersh, Seymour M. *The Dark Side of Camelot*. Boston: Little, Brown, 1997.

Hobson, Chris. *Vietnam Air Losses*. Hinckley, U.K.: Midland, 2001.

Holloway, David. *Stalin and the Bomb*. New Haven, Conn.: Yale University Press, 1994.

Institute for Strategic Studies. *The Military Balance 1964–65*. London: ISS, 1964.

Isaacs, Jeremy, and Taylor Downing. *Cold War: An Illustrated History, 1945–1991*. New York: Little, Brown, 1998.

Kaplan, Fred, and Martin J. Sherwin. *The Wizards of Armageddon*. Stanford, Calif.: Stanford University Press, 1991.

Kasatonov, I. *The Fleet Goes Out to the Ocean: The Story of Fleet Admiral V. A. Kasatonov*. St. Petersburg: Astra-Luxe, 1995.

Kennedy, Robert F. *Thirteen Days: A Memoir of the Cuban Missile Crisis*. New York: W. W. Norton, 1969.

Khrushchev, Nikita. *Khrushchev Remembers*. Boston: Little, Brown, 1970.

—————. *Khrushchev Remembers: The Glasnost Tapes*. Boston: Little, Brown, 1990.

—————. *Khrushchev Remembers: The Last Testament*. Boston: Little, Brown, 1974.

Khrushchev, Sergei N. *Nikita Khrushchev and the Creation of a Superpower*. University Park: Pennsylvania State University, 2000.

Kornbluh, Peter, ed. *Bay of Pigs Declassified: The Secret CIA Report on the Invasion of Cuba*. New York: New Press/National Security Archive, 1998.

Kuzin, V. P., and V. I. Nikolskiy. *Voyennomorskoy Flot SSSR, 1945–1991 (The Navy of the USSR, 1945–1991)*. St. Petersburg: Historical Oceanic Society, 1996.

Lashmar, Paul. *Spy Flights of the Cold War*. Annapolis, Md.: Naval Institute Press, 1996.

Lechuga, Carlos. *En el Ojo de la Tormenta: F. Castro, N. Khrushchev, J. F. Kennedy y la Crisis do los Missiles*. [In the Eye of the Storm: F. Castro, N. Khrushchev, J. F. Kennedy and the Crisis of the Missiles]. Havana, Cuba: SI-Mar S.A., 1995. A revised, English-language edition was published as *Cuba and the Missile Crisis* (Melbourne: Ocean Press, 2001).

LeMay, General Curtis E., USAF (Ret.). *Mission with LeMay: My Story*. Garden City, N.Y.: Doubleday, 1965.

Lewin, Ronald. *The American Magic*. New York: Farrar, Straus & Giroux, 1982.

Lilienthal, David E. *The Journals of David E. Lilienthal*, vol. 2. New York: Harper & Row, 1964.

Marx, Karl, and Friedrich Engels. *The Communist Manifesto*. New York: Signet Classics, original edition 1845, reprint edition, 1998.

Massie, Robert K. *Nicholas and Alexandra*. New York: Atheneum, 1967.

May, Ernest R., and Philip D. Zelikow, ed. *The Kennedy Tapes: Inside the White House during the Cuban Missile Crisis*. Cambridge, Mass.: Harvard University Press, 1997.

McCamley, N. J. *Cold War Secret Nuclear Bunkers*. Barnsley, South Yorkshire, U.K.: Leo Cooper, 2003.

McCullough, David. *The Path between the Seas: The Creation of the Panama Canal 1870–1914*. New York: Simon & Schuster, 1977.

McDonald, Robert A. *Corona between the Sun and the Earth: The First NRO Reconnaissance Eye in Space*. Bethesda, Md.: American Society of Photogrammetry and Remote Sensing, 1997.

McElheny, Victor K. *Insisting on the Impossible: The Life of Edwin Land*. Reading, Mass.: Perseus Books, 1998.

McPherson, James M. *Battle Cry of Freedom*. New York: Oxford University Press, 1988.

Mersky, Peter. *RF-8 Crusader Units over Cuba and Vietnam*. Botley, Oxford, U.K.: Osprey, 1999.

Miller, David. *The Cold War: A Military History*. New York: St. Martin's Press, 1998.

Miller, Edward S. *War Plan ORANGE: The U.S. Strategy to Defeat Japan, 1897–1945*. Annapolis, Md.: Naval Institute Press, 1991.

Miller, Jerry. *Nuclear Weapons and Aircraft Carriers: How the Bomb Saved Naval Aviation*. Washington, D.C.: Smithsonian Institution Press, 2001.

Millis, Walter, ed. *The Forrestal Diaries*. New York: Viking Press, 1951.

Moody, Walter D. *Building a Strategic Air Force*. Washington, D.C.: Air Force History and Museum Program, 1995.

Murphy, David E., and Sergi A. Kondrashev. *Battleground Berlin: CIA vs. KGB in the Cold War*. New Haven, Conn.: Yale University Press, 1997.

Naftali, Timothy, ed. *The Presidential Recordings: John F. Kennedy*, vol. 1. New York: W. W. Norton, 2001.

Naftali, Timothy, and Philip Zelikow, eds. *The Presidential Recordings: John F. Kennedy*, vol. 2. New York: W. W. Norton, 2001.

National Commission on the Terrorist Attacks upon the United States. *The 9/11 Commission Report*. New York: W. W. Norton, 2004.

Neufeld, Jacob. *Ballistic Missiles in the United States Air Force, 1945–1960*. Washington, D.C.: Office of Air Force History, 1989.

Newhouse, John. *War and Peace in the Nuclear Age*. New York: Alfred A. Knopf, 1989.

Newkirk, Dennis. *Almanac of Soviet Manned Spaceflight*. Houston, Tex.: Gulf, 1990.

Nichols, John, and Barrett Tillman. *On Yankee Station*. Annapolis, Md.: Naval Institute Press, 1989.

Nitze, Paul H. *From Hiroshima to Glasnost: At the Center of Decision—a Memoir*. New York: Grove Weidenfeld, 1989.

Nordeen, Lon O. *Air Warfare in the Missile Age*, 2nd ed. Washington, D.C.: Smithsonian Institution Press, 2002.

Oberdorfer, Don. *The Turn: From the Cold War to a New Era: The United States and the Soviet Union 1983–1990*. New York: Poseidon Press, 1991.

Olsen, Jack. *Aphrodite Desperate Mission*. New York: ibooks, 2004.

Overy, Richard. *Russia's War: Blood upon the Snow*. New York: TV Books, 1997.

Peebles, Curtis. *The Corona Project: America's First Spy Satellites*. Annapolis, Md.: Naval Institute Press, 1997.

———. *Dark Eagles: A History of Top Secret U.S. Aircraft Programs*. Novato, Calif.: Presidio Press, 1995.

———. *Shadow Flights: America's Secret Air War against the Soviet Union*. Novato, Calif.: Presidio Press, 2000.

Pedlow, Gregory W., and Donald E. Welzenbach. *The CIA and the U-2 Program, 1954– 1974*. Washington, D.C.: CIA Center for the Study of Intelligence, 1998.

Podig, Pavel, ed. *Russian Strategic Nuclear Forces*. Cambridge, Mass.: MIT Press, 2001.

Polmar, Norman. *Guide to the Ships and Aircraft of the U.S. Fleet*, 17th ed. Annapolis, Md.: Naval Institute Press, 2001.

————. *Spyplane: The U-2 History Declassified*. St. Paul, Minn.: MBI Publishing, 2001.

Polmar, Norman, and Thomas B. Allen. *Spy Book: The Encyclopedia of Espionage*. New York: Random House, 1996.

Polmar, Norman, and Timothy Laur. *Strategic Air Command: People, Aircraft, and Missiles*, 2nd ed. Baltimore, Md.: Nautical & Aviation, 1990.

Polmar, Norman, and K. J. Moore. *Cold War Submarines: The Design and Construction of U.S. and Soviet Submarines*. Washington, D.C.: Brassey's, 2004.

Polmar, Norman, Eric Wertheim, Andrew Bahjat, and Bruce Watson. *Chronology of the Cold War at Sea 1945–1991*. Annapolis, Md.: Naval Institute Press, 1998.

Powell, Robert. *Corona between the Sun and the Earth: Evolution of Standard Agenda: Corona's Spacecraft*. Bethesda, Md.: American Society of Photogrammetry and Remote Sensing, 1997.

Pringle, Peter, and William Arkin. *S.I.O.P.: The Secret U.S. Plan for Nuclear War*. New York: W. W. Norton, 1983.

Rhodes, Richard. *Dark Sun: The Making of the Hydrogen Bomb*. New York: Simon & Schuster, 1995.

Richelson, Jeffrey T. *The Wizards of Langley*. Cambridge, Mass.: Westview Press, 2001.

Schecter, Jerold L., and Peter S. Deriabin. *The Spy Who Saved the World: How a Soviet Colonel Changed the Course of the Cold War*. New York: Charles Scribner's Sons, 1992.

Schlesinger, Arthur M., Jr. *A Thousand Days: John F. Kennedy in the White House*. Boston: Houghton Mifflin, 1965.

Schwartz, Stephen I., ed. *Atomic Audit: The Costs and Consequences of U.S. Nuclear Weapons since 1940*. Washington, D.C.: Brookings Institution Press, 1998.

Shirokorad, A. B. *Sovetskiye Podvodnyye Lodki Poslevoyennoy Postroyki* [Soviet Submarines of Postwar Construction]. Moscow: Arsenal Press, 1997.

Smith, F. Dow. *Corona between the Sun and the Earth: The Design and Engineering of Corona's Optics*. Bethesda, Md.: American Society of Photogrammetry and Remote Sensing, 1997.

Sontag, Sherry, and Christopher Drew. *Blind Man's Bluff: The Untold Story of American Submarine Espionage*. New York: Public Affairs, 1998.

Sorensen, Theodore C. *Kennedy*. New York: Konecky & Konecky, 1965.

Steury, Donald P., ed. *Intentions and Capabilities: Estimates on Soviet Strategic Forces, 1950–1983*. Washington, D.C.: Central Intelligence Agency, 1996.

Strauss, Lewis L. *Men and Decisions*. London: Macmillan, 1963.

Stumpf, David K. *Titan II: A History of a Cold War Missile Program*. Fayetteville: University of Arkansas Press, 2000.

Szulc, Tad. *Fidel: A Critical Portrait*. New York: William Morrow, 1986.

Thomas, Evan. *Robert Kennedy: His Life*. New York: Simon & Schuster, 2000.

————. *The Very Best Men: The Early Years of the CIA*. New York: Simon & Schuster, 1995.

Vandemark, Brian. *In Retrospect*. New York: Random House, 1995.

Wagner, William. *Lightning Bugs and Other Reconnaissance Drones*. Fallbrook, Calif.: Armed Forces Journal International, in cooperation with Aero Publishers, 1982.

Warncock, A. Timothy, ed. *Short of War: Major USAF Contingency Operations*. Maxwell AFB, Ala.: Air Force History Museums Program, in association with Air University Press, 2000.

Wyden, Peter. *Bay of Pigs: The Untold Story*. New York: Simon & Schuster, 1979.

Yergin, Daniel. *The Prize: The Epic Quest for Oil, Money and Power*. New York: Simon & Schuster, 1991.

Yesin, V. *Strategicheskaya Operaciya "Anadyr": Kak eto bylo?* [Strategic Operation Anadyr: How Did It Happen?] Moscow: MOOVVIK [Interregional Social Organization of Veterans Who Served in Cuba], 2000.

Zaloga, Steven J. *The Kremlin's Nuclear Sword: The Rise and Fall of Russia's Strategic Nuclear Forces, 1945–2000*. Washington, D.C.: Smithsonian Institution Press, 2002.

————. *The Scud and Other Russian Ballistic Missile Vehicles*. Hong Kong: Concord Publications, 2000.

————. *Soviet Air Defense Missiles: Design, Development and Tactics*. Coulsdon, Surrey, U.K.: Jane's Information Group, 1989.

————. *Target America*. Novato, Calif.: Presidio Press, 1993.

Zelikow, Philip, and Ernest May, eds. *The Presidential Recordings: John F. Kennedy*, vol. 3. New York: W. W. Norton, 2001.

Zubok, Vladislav and Constantine Pleshakov. *Inside the Kremlin's Cold War: From Stalin to Khrushchev*. Cambridge, Mass.: Harvard University Press, 1996.

Zumwalt, Admiral Elmo R., Jr., USN (Ret.). *On Watch*. New York: New York Times Book Co., 1976.

Articles

Cline, Ray S., Jr. "Nuclear War Seemed Remote . . ." *Washington Post*, February 5, 1989, p. D7.

Ecker, Captain William, USN (Ret.). "Photo Reconnaissance over Cuba." *Naval History* (Winter 1992), pp. 54–56.

Fursenko, Aleksandr, and Timothy Naftali. "Using KGB Documents: The Scali-Feklisov Channel in the Cuban Missile Crisis." *Cold War International History Project Bulletin* 5 (Spring 1995).

Gertz, Bill. "Soviets Said to Operate Spy Base in Cuba Able to Monitor U.S. Phones." *New York City Tribune*, March 25, 1985, p. 1.

Goldstein, Lyle J., and Yuri M. Zhukov. "A Tale of Two Fleets: A Russian Perspective on the 1973 Naval Standoff in the Mediterranean." *Naval War College Review* (Spring 2004), pp. 27–63.

Gresham, John D. "NIE 11-8/1-61: The Most Dangerous Document of the Cold War." *Military History* (June 2000), pp. 22–27.

Gup, Ted. "The Ultimate Congressional Hideaway." *Washington Post Magazine*, May 31, 1992, p. W11. (Online at www.washingtonpost.com/wp-srv/local/dailyjuly/25/brierl.htm.)

Haney, Patrick J. "Soccer Fields and Submarines in Cuba: The Politics of Problem Definition." *Naval War College Review* (Autumn 1997), pp. 67–84.

Hansen, James H. "Learning from the Past: Soviet Deception in the Cuban Missile Crisis." *Studies in Intelligence* 46, no. 1 (2002). (Online at www.cia.gov/csi/studies/vol46no1/article06.html.)

Hardesty, Von. "Made in the USSR." *Air and Space/Smithsonian* (February/March 2001), pp. 68–79. (Online at www.airandspacemagazine.com/ASM/Mag/Index/2001/FM/TU-4.html.)

Hughes, John T., and A. Dennis Clift. "The San Cristobal Trapezoid." *Studies in Intelligence* (Winter 1992; reprinted in Fall 2002 issue). (Online at www.cia.gov/csi/studies/fall00.)

Kent, Sherman. "The Cuban Missile Crisis of 1962: Presenting the Photographic Evidence Abroad." *Studies in Intelligence* (Spring 1972). (Online at www.cia.gov/csi/books/shermankent/10cuban.html.)

Knox, William E. "Close-up of Khrushchev during a Crisis." *New York Times Magazine*, November 18, 1962, p. 32.

Merom, Gil. "The 1962 Cuban Intelligence Estimate: A Methodological Perspective." *Intelligence and National Security Review* (Autumn 1999), pp. 48–80.

Orlov, Vadim. "We Will Sink Them All, but We Will Not Disgrace Our Navy," extracted from the article by Alexander Mosgovi, "The Cuban Samba of the Quartet of Foxtrots: Soviet Submarines in the Caribbean Crisis of 1962." Translated by Svetlana Savranskaya of the National Security Archive. Moscow, *Military Parade*, 2002.

Poole, Walter S. "How Well Did the JCS Work?" *Naval History Magazine* (Winter 1991), pp. 19–21.

Rosenberg, David Alan. "A Smoking Radiating Ruin at the End of Two Hours." *International Security* (Winter 1981/1982): 3–38.

Rosenfeld, Stephen S. "October 1962: A Close Call That Isn't Over Yet." *Washington Post*, September 26, 1997, p. A25.

Smith, Charles L. "Soviet *Maskirovka.*" *Airpower Journal* (Spring 1988).

Uhl, Matthias, and Vladimir I. Ivkin. "'Operation Atom': The Soviet Union's Stationing of Nuclear Missiles in the German Democratic Republic, 1959." *Cold War International History Project Bulletin* (Fall/Winter 2001), pp. 299–307.

Zubok, Vladislav M. "Spy vs. Spy: The KGB vs. the CIA." *Cold War History International Project Bulletin* 4 (Fall 1994).

Government Documents

Benson, Robert Louis, and Michael Warner, eds. *Venona: Soviet Espionage and the American Response 1939–1957.* Washington, D.C.: National Security Agency and Central Intelligence Agency, 1996.

Bissell, Richard M., Jr. *Project Corona Memo, April 15, 1958.* (Online at www.cia.gov/documents/.)

Blake, Lieutenant General Gordon A., USAF. *Memo on "Funnel" Handling Code Word, September 11, 1962,* and *Memo on Funnel Project, September 12, 1962.* (Online at National Security Agency Archive.)

Mr. "Bonn" and Colonel "Coleman" (USAF historians). *Interview with General Power, conducted by Mr. Bonn, November 15, 1962.* Maxwell AFB, Ala.: U.S. Air Force Historical Research Agency.

Boone, J. V., and R. R. Peterson. *The Start of the Digital Revolution: SIGSALY Secure Digital Voice Communications in World War II.* Fort Meade, Md.: National Security Agency, 2000.

Bowie, Robert R., and Gerard C. Smith. *Memorandum for the Secretary; Subject: Policy Regarding Use of Atomic Weapons.* May 15, 1957.

Brugioni, Dino A. *The Cuban Missile Crisis—Phase 1, 29 August–16 October 1962.* DDS&T Historical Series, NPIC-1. CIA: NPIC, 1971.

Bundy, McGeorge. *Forecast Weather over Cuba and Mission Status, September 5–October 14, 1962.* February 27, 1963.

Chief, Design and Analysis Division. *Memo on Briefing to General Maxwell Taylor on Photographic Satellite Support to Middle East Crisis, August 31, 1967,* memo written on September 8, 1967. (CIA Online Archive.)

Cody, A1C (Airman 1st class) John F. *History of the 100th Bombardment Wing (M),* Pease Air Force Base, New Hampshire, October 1–31, 1962.

Commander, Anti-Submarine Warfare Force, U.S. Atlantic Fleet, to Chief of Naval Operations, Subj.: "Summary, Analysis and Evaluation of CUBEX," Ser 008187/43, November 5, 1963.

Defense Intelligence Agency. *Handbook on the Soviet Armed Forces,* July 1969.

Defense Threat Reduction Agency Corporate Communications. *Personnel Reliability Program Factsheet,* Albuquerque, N.M., July 6, 2001.

Department of Defense. *Appendix 1 to Annex F: Joint Air Transportation Plan (Short title: JATS PLAN),* C-3020.26 (Incl 1). Washington, D.C., June 10, 1960.

——— . *Appendix 1 to Annex F: Joint Emergency Evacuation Plan (Short Title: JEEP PLAN),* C-3020.26 (Incl 1). Washington, D.C.: June 10, 1960.

Deputy Chief of Naval Operations (Fleet Operations and Readiness). *Compilation of Lessons Learned/Deficiencies Noted as a Result of Cuban Operations,* Ser 00230P30, February 20, 1963.

Dyar, Robert K. *History of the 4347th Combat Crew Training Wing (M),* McConnell Air Force Base, Kan., November 1–26, 1962.

Fisher, Ben B. *A Cold War Conundrum: The 1983 Soviet War Scare,* CSI 97-10002. Washington, D.C.: CIA Center, September 1997.

Headquarters, Nineteenth Air Force, U.S. Air Force. *OPLAN 314, JTF-127 Air Force Annex.* Seymore Johnson AFB, N.C. (Document located at the Air Force Historical Research Agency, Maxwell AFB, Ala.)

Hoppe, Herbert, Norman Polmar, and A. C. Trapold. *Measures and Trends US and USSR Strategic Force Effectiveness.* Alexandria, Va.: Santa Fe Corp., March 1978. Prepared for director, Defense Nuclear Agency.

Johnson, Thomas R., and David A. Hatch. *NSA and the Cuban Missile Crisis.* Fort Meade, Md.: Center for Cryptological History/National Security Agency, 1998.

Joint Chiefs of Staff. *Transcripts of the Joint Chiefs of Staff, October–November 1962,* p. 13. In Records of the U.S. Joint Chiefs of Staff (JCS), Record Group 218, 1941–1947. College Park, Md.: National Archive and Research Administration.

Joint Chiefs of Staff. *Chairman's Talking Paper for Meeting with the President, November 16, 1962.*

Kennedy, Robert. *Memorandum from Attorney General Kennedy to President Kennedy about His Meeting with Soviet Ambassador Dobrynin, October 24, 1962. Source:* U.S. Department of State, *Foreign Relations of the United States, 1961–1963,* vol. 11, *Cuban Missile Crisis and Aftermath.*

Kent, Sherman. Telegram from the Embassy in Paris to the Department of State, October 22, 1962. The Avalon Project of the Yale Law School.

Kipp, Robert. *Interview of Major Richard S. Heyser, U-2 Reconnaissance Pilot, conducted by Robert Kipp, November 27, 1962.* Maxwell AFB, Ala.: U.S. Air Force Historical Research Agency.

Koch, Scott A., ed. *Selected Estimates on the Soviet Union 1950–1959.* Washington, D.C.: CIA Center for the Study of Intelligence, 1993.

Kuhns, Woodrow J., ed. *Assessing the Soviet Threat: The Early Cold War Years.* Washington, D.C.: CIA Center for the Study of Intelligence, 1997.

Land, Edwin H. *Memo to Allen W. Dulles, November 5, 1954.* Dwight D. Eisenhower Presidential Library.

Malinovsky, Marshal Rodion, and Marshal M. V. Zakharov. *Memorandum to the Commander of the Group of Soviet Forces in Cuba, September 8, 1962.* The full text is available on the Web site of the Cold War International History Project at http://cwihp.si.edu/CWIHPlib.nsf.

————. *Memorandum on Deployment of Soviet Forces to Cuba, May 24, 1962.*

McAuliffe, Mary S., ed. *CIA Documents on the Cuban Missile Crisis, 1962.* Washington, D.C.: Central Intelligence Agency, October 1992.

McCone, John. *Memorandum of Meeting with the President, Attorney General, Secretary McNamara, General Taylor, and Mr. McCone, 10:00 a.m.—10/21/62,* in McAuliffe, *CIA Documents on the Cuban Missile Crisis, 1962.*

————. *Memorandum for the File, October 19, 1962,* in McAuliffe, *CIA Documents on the Cuban Missile Crisis, 1962.*

————. *Memorandum for File Regarding October 18, 1962, ExComm Meeting,* in McAuliffe, *CIA Documents on the Cuban Missile Crisis, 1962.*

Moore, Captain William B., USN. *Memorandum on Briefing Given to the Representatives of All Services at SAC Headquarters, March 18, 1954.* In David Alan Rosenberg, "A Smoking Radiating Ruin at the End of Two Hours." *International Security* (Winter 1981/1982).

Myers, Gary P., ed. *Executive Summary of the Missiles in Cuba, 1962: The Role of SAC Intelligence.* Omaha, Neb.: Strategic Joint Intelligence Center [n.d.].

National Security Agency Files. Available online from National Security Agency archive at www.nsa.gov/docs/cuba/archive.htm.

Office of the Historian, Headquarters, SAC. *The Development of Strategic Air Command.* Offutt AFB, Neb.: September 1, 1986.

Project Rand. *Vulnerability of U.S. Strategic Air Power to a Surprise Enemy Attack in 1956.* Special Memorandum SM-15. Rand Corp., April 15, 1953.

Rostow, Walt W. *Memorandum to the President Assessing Soviet Military Aid to Cuba, September 3, 1962,* National Security Archive.

————. Memorandums *Notes on Cuba Policy, Steps to Isolate and Weaken Castro Regime, Draft Plan for Cuba,* and *Plan for Cuba,* all dated April 24, 1961, JFK Presidential Library.

Ruffner, Kevin C., ed. *Corona: America's First Satellite Program.* Washington, D.C.: CIA Center for the Study of Intelligence, 1995.

Salinger, Pierre, for President John F. Kennedy. *Statement by President John F. Kennedy on Cuba, September 4, 1962,* Department of State Archive.

Science Advisory Committee, Technological Capabilities Panel. *Meeting the Threat of Surprise Attack,* February 14, 1955.

Smith, Louis J., ed. *Foreign Relations of the United States.* Vol. 10, *Cuba 1961–1962.* Washington, D.C.: Department of State, 1997.

Smith, Major William Y., USAF. *Memorandum for General Taylor: Subject: Strategic Air Planning and Berlin,* September 7, 1961.

Steury, Donald P., ed. *Intentions and Capabilities: Estimates on Soviet Strategic Forces, 1950–1983.* Washington, D.C.: CIA Center for the Study of Intelligence, 1996.

Stevenson, Adlai. *Statement by Ambassador Stevenson to UN Security Council* (UN press release 4074), October 25, 1962. *Department of State Bulletin* 47, no. 1220 (November 12, 1962).

Strategic Air Command. *The Development of Strategic Air Command.* Offutt AFB, Neb.: Headquarters, SAC, September 1, 1986.

Taylor, General Maxwell D., USA. *Memorandum to General Leminteer,* September 19, 1961.

Union of the Soviet Socialist Republics. *Statement by Soviet Union That a U.S. Attack on Cuba Would Mean Nuclear War.* September 11, 1962. National Security Archive.

United Nations Press Services. "Text of Communication Dated 19 November 1962 from Prime Minister Fidel Castro of Cuba to Acting Secretary-General U Thant." Press Release SG/1379, November 20, 1962.

U.S. Air Force. *The Air Force Response to the Cuban Crisis,* October 14–November 24, 1962. National Security Archive.

————. *Joint Strategic Target Planning Staff,* U.S. Air Force Fact Sheet, April 1, 1978.

White House. *President Kennedy's Statement on Soviet Military Shipments to Cuba.* September 4, 1962.

Wright, Colonel John R., USA. *Cuba Intelligence—Top Secret, September 28, 1962.* Personal papers of Gen. Maxwell Taylor via National Defense University and the Avalon Project.

Wynn, Humphrey. *RAF Nuclear Deterrent Forces: Their Origins, Roles and Deployment 1946–1969.* London: Her Majesty's Stationery Office, 1994.

Papers

Bushnell, Major W. D., USMC. *American Military Intervention: A Useful Tool or Curse?* Quantico, Va.: Marine Corps Command and Staff College, 1984.

Defense Threat Reduction Agency Corporate Communications. *Personnel Reliability Program Factsheet.* Albuquerque, N.M., July 6, 2001.

Fursenko, Aleksandr, and Timothy Naftali. "The Pitsunda Decision: Khrushchev and Nuclear Weapons." Washington, D.C.: Cold War International History Project, Woodrow Wilson International Center for Scholars [n.d.].

Johns, Forrest R. "The Naval Quarantine of Cuba, 1962." Thesis submitted for the master's program at the University of California, San Diego, 1984.

Mahoney, Kevin Patrick. *American Decision Making During the Cuban Missile Crisis,* 1991. Available online at www.geocities.com/SoHo/Nook/1082/president_john_fitzgerald _kennedy_and_the_cuban_missile_crisis_essay_page.html.

Natural Resources Defense Council. *Worldwide Nuclear Deployments 1998.* Washington, D.C.: March 1998.

Poole, Walter S. "The Cuban Missile Crisis: How Well Did the Joint Chiefs of Staff Work?" Paper presented at the Naval Historical Center colloquium, Washington, D.C., June 18, 1992.

Weakley, Charles E., executive officer for ASW readiness at the Sea Power Symposium sponsored by the Navy League, Washington, D.C., March 3, 1959.

Werder, Karl K. "Continuing Lessons of the Cuban Missile Crisis, October 1962." USAF Air War College paper, Maxwell AFB, Ala.

Briefings

Gresham, John D. *Cycle Times in Simulations and Games: The Practical Uses of OODA Loops*, for the U.S. Air Force Air Command and Staff College (Maxwell AFB, Ala.), and the Air National Guard/Air Force Reserve (Warner-Robbins AFB, Ga.), October 15–16, 2000.

Films

The Bedford Incident (Richard Widmark/Columbia Pictures), 1965.

DEFCON-2 (Henninger Films/The Discovery Channel), 2002.

Doomsday Mission (Hoggard Films/The Discovery Channel), 1997.

Dr. Strangelove or: How I Learned to Stop Worrying and Love the Bomb (Stanley Kubrick/ Columbia Pictures), 1963.

Fail Safe (Max E. Youngsten and Sidney Lumet/Columbia Pictures), 1992.

The Fog of War (Julie Bilson Ahlberg/Columbia Tri-Star), 2004.

K-19: The Widowmaker (Walter Murch/Paramount), 2002.

Missiles in Cuba (Time Machine/Arts & Entertainment), 1992.

The Missiles of October (MPI Home Video), 2001.

Path to War (John Frankenheimer/HBO Home Video), 2003.

Secret Satellite (documentary for Discovery Communications), 1995.

Thirteen Days (Kevin Costner/New Line Cinema), 2000.

Oral Histories

All held by the U.S. Naval Institute, Annapolis, Md., except for General Smith's oral history, which is held by the Air Force Historical Research Agency, Maxwell AFB, Ala.

Anderson, Admiral George W., USN (Ret.). January 27, 1981; extracts published as "This Joint Chief Took a Bolder Stance." *Naval History* (Winter 1992), pp. 46–48.

Dennison, Admiral Robert Lee, USN (Ret.). July 17, 1973; extracts published as "Waiting in the Wings: The USS *Enterprise*." *Naval History* (Winter 1992), pp. 51–53.

Rivero, Admiral Horacio, Jr., USN (Ret.). May–November 1975 (multiple interviews); extracts published as "Amphibious Commander at the Ready." *Naval History* (Winter 1992), pp. 49–51.

Smith, General William Y., USAF (Ret.). April 1990–April 1996 (multiple interviews).

Ward, Admiral Alfred G., USN (Ret.). April 22, 1971.

PHOTO CREDITS

CIA, 15, 18, 78, 79, 81, 91, 92, 140 (top), 197, 220

DIA, 26, 55–58, 115 (bottom)

Alexander Feklisov, 213

JFK Presidential Library, 7, 23, 47, 101, 103, 111, 124, 128, 286, 302

Sergei Khrushchev, 11, 25, 56, 97, 171, 265

National Archives, 150, 202, 215

Laura Newsome, 30, 40, 52, 65, 176–177, 250

Official U.S. Air Force Photo, 13, 237, 256, 266

Official U.S. Air Force Photo via Bob Dorr, 229

Official U.S. Navy Photo, 67, 68, 75, 84, 115 (top), 116, 140 (bottom), 141–144, 148, 162–164, 268, 271, 276, 299, 303

Norman Polmar, 29, 45, 63, 93, 224, 225

INDEX